Python:
The Complete Reference

About the Author

Martin "MC" Brown is the author of many programming titles, including *Python Annotated Archives*, *Perl Annotated Archives*, *Perl: The Complete Reference*, and *Debugging Perl*. He has been programming for over 15 years and playing around with computers for more than 20. He now writes full time on subjects as diverse as programming, CD writing, and cross-platform integration.

Python:
The Complete Reference

Martin C. Brown

Osborne/**McGraw-Hill**
New York   Chicago   San Francisco
Lisbon   London   Madrid   Mexico City
Milan   New Delhi   San Juan
Seoul   Singapore   Sydney   Toronto

Osborne/**McGraw-Hill**
2600 Tenth Street
Berkeley, California 94710
U.S.A.

To arrange bulk purchase discounts for sales promotions, premiums, or fund-raisers, please contact Osborne/**McGraw-Hill** at the above address. For information on translations or book distributors outside the U.S.A., please see the International Contact Information page immediately following the index of this book.

Python: The Complete Reference

1234567890 DOC DOC 01987654321

ISBN 0-07-212718-X

Publisher
   Brandon A. Nordin

Vice President & Associate Publisher
   Scott Rogers

Acquisitions Editor
   Ann Sellers

Project Editor
   Barbara Brodnitz

Acquisitions Coordinator
   Paulina Pobocha

Technical Editor
   Chris Herborth

Copy Editor
   Sarah Lemaire

Proofreader
   Carol Burbo

Indexer
   Valerie Robbins

Computer Designers
   Jean Butterfield
   Roberta Steele
   Mickey Galicia

Illustrators
   Lyssa Wald
   Michael Mueller

Series Design
   Peter F. Hancik

This book was composed with Corel VENTURA™ Publisher.

To Darcy and Leon, two now-bigger kittens
who find outside far more interesting
than inside—unless food is involved.

Contents at a Glance

Part III   Application Development

Part IV   Web Development

Part V   Cross-platform Development

Part VI   Inside Python

Contents

Part I

Fundamentals of the Language

Part II

Applying the Python Libraries

Part III

Application Development

Acknowledgments

First of all, I'd like to thank my wife Sharon. After two and a half years, she still lets me sit down and basically play on computers all day. I have to do the cooking in exchange, but that's almost as much fun as the computing. She continues to listen to my rants and occasionally joins me for a slap-up meal when things go right. Without her support I wouldn't be in my third year of doing this, nor would I be in a position to already be working on the titles for my fourth year.

Next, I'd like to thank all the people at Osborne who made this book possible. They include Wendy Rinaldi, for offering me the opportunity; Rebekah Young, for keeping me in check; Paulina Pobocha, for taking in chapters and making sure I stayed on course; and Timothy Madrid, who took over from Paulina in the final stages. I hope, Paulina, that the course is going well!

Thanks also go to Barbara Brodnitz, Madhu Prasher, and everybody else at Osborne whose names I never know that turn what I've written into the final printed product. You all do a sterling job with someone who, from my point of view, can be a bit of a pain.

For technical input I need to thank the ever-present Chris Herborth. Not only does Chris tell me where I've gone wrong technically, he also provides input on content and is one of the best sounding boards for new ideas that I've come across. Thanks as well to the wealth of information and commentary that is Cix. Without the ideas and input that come from the members of the various Cix conferences, I'm sure I'd be writing even less interesting books. For those Cix readers looking for something from the Python conference that's featured in the book, check Chapters 9 and 10, especially the regular expression section. You know who you are!

Finally, I need to thank all those people behind the scenes who give me support and help me write, even thought they may not be aware of it.

If there's anybody I've forgotten to acknowledge, I apologize unreservedly in advance now. I have done my best to check and verify all sources and contact all parties involved, but it's perfectly possible I made a mistake.

Introduction

The primary aim of this book is to provide a comprehensive guide to almost everything your want to know about Python. That's not actually as easy it sounds. Writing a *Complete Reference* is a bit like asking, "How long is a piece of string?" Although we can cover a lot of information, there's always something that we can't fit into the book or that we don't get to cover as thoroughly as we'd like.

That doesn't mean we're lacking in information. Between the covers of this title you'll find all of the reference information you need on how to use the basic Python interpreter, including its built-in data types, loops, and control statements and the Python error handling system, otherwise known as exceptions.

I've also gone into detail about how to use the modules in the Python standard library, how to work with and develop user interfaces using Tk, and web programming. Along the way, we'll also look at how and why to use Python as a rapid application development tool, how to read and write good documentation, and information on how to extend and embed Python using C.

Who This Is Book For

This book is a reference, and so while I've tried to make it as easy to use and follow as possible, it won't teach you how to use Python if you've never used it before. If you know Python at a basic level and want to learn more, you should be able to use the reference material and programming/style guides to go to the next level of Python experience.

If you don't know Python but do know another a scripting language, particularly Perl, you should be able to pick up a lot of the Python language. Although this book isn't a Perl-to-Python migration title, I have included basic information on some of the differences between the two languages. (If you want a guide to programming Perl, check out one of my Perl titles.)

How to Use This Book

If you have a specific feature that you want to learn about, look it up in the index. The table of contents will point you to broader topics. The scripts and script fragments included in the book should all work without modification on your machine. Python is about 95% cross-platform compatible, so you shouldn't have any trouble running these scripts on any machine that supports Python. (If you want to get a copy of Python, visit the Python website at www.python.org.)

Part I covers the fundamentals of the language, from a general discussions of what makes Python Python, to what makes Python different from other languages like Perl, to the meat of the language. You get detailed coverage on the basic Python components, and how to create functions and modules and handle exceptions, along with details on making use of Python's object orientation.

Part II looks at the Python standard library—that is, all of the modules that come as standard with the Python distribution and provide the bulk of the functionality, from the built-in functions to the extensions that allow you to store information, work with files, and manipulate the file system and basic networking features.

Part III talks about using Python for developing applications, starting with a look at using Python for rapid application development and going on to the tools and resources available that will make the process easier. The last chapter in this section talks about the process behind distributing applications.

Part IV covers web development from Python. We look at the basic process of creating a Python web script, the CGI interface, and then some specific libraries that help in the process. We also look at how to use Python to process different *ML technologies, such as HTML and XML, before going over some of the web tools and applications written in Python that might help in the process.

Part V is a quick guide to using Python for cross-platform development. Although Python hides most of the complexity of the process, there are still traps that can trip up the unwary programmer.

Part VI looks inside the Python language, from a basic look at the internals of the Python interpreter to the methods for extending the Python library with modules written in C and how to embed the Python interpreter into your existing C applications. Along the way we look at how to debug Python scripts and optimize them for the best execution speed and how to document and comment your code to make it more readable by you and other people.

Conventions Used in This Book

Keywords (functions, modules, and variable names) that appear in text are highlighted in **bold**.

```
Examples and code are displayed using a fixed-width font.
```

Note *Notes are formatted like this and include additional information about a particular topic. You'll also find similarly formatted Warnings, which highlight possible dangerous tools or tricks to watch out for when programming.*

Contacting the Author

I always welcome comments and suggestions on my work. I particularly appreciate guides and recommendations on better ways of achieving different goals, especially with Python. I've done my best to cover as much as I can, but there are always new things coming online. The best way to contact me is via email. You can use either **books@mcwords.com**. Alternatively, visit my website, **http://www.mcwords.com**, which contains resources and updated information about the scripts and contents of this book, as well follow-up articles and corrections to the content in this tome. You can find the homepage for this book at **http://www.mcwords.com/projects/books/pytcr/**.

The
Complete
Reference

Part I

Fundamentals of the Language

The
Complete
Reference

Chapter 1

Introducing Python

Before getting into the specifics of the Python language, let's take a little time to understand the principles behind the Python language and what it can and can't be used for. Let's also look at who uses Python and how Python differs from other programming languages.

What Is Python?

Python is an interpreted language that employs an object-oriented approach. It's a high-level programming language, which means that it separates the user from the underlying operating system as much as possible. However, unlike other languages, Python provides you with the ability to access the operating system at a lower level if you desire. Because of this ability, Python is often classified somewhere between such languages as Visual Basic or Perl and the system-level C language.

Although Python is considered an interpreted language like Perl, Tcl, and some others, it employs a compilation stage that translates the raw-text Python script into a series of *bytecodes*, which are then executed by the Python Virtual Machine. The use of the compilation and bytecode stages helps to improve performance and makes Python much faster than pure interpreters such as BASIC, but slower than the truly compiled languages such as C and Pascal. However, unlike many other languages, the bytecode versions of modules can be saved and executed without having to recompile them each time they are required, thereby improving performance by eliminating the compilation stage. Note that the bytecode that is created is completely platform and operating system independent, much like the bytecode produced by Java.

Python also has the added benefit of providing rapid application development on the MacOS, Windows (95/98/NT), and Unix platforms. Python is supplied with a module to the Tk interface libraries, and it's possible to write an application on one platform and use it on all three platforms without making any modifications. In addition to the core platforms, Python also runs on MS-DOS, Amiga, BeOS, OS/2, VMS, QNX, and many other operating systems. You can even run Python on your Psion organizer!

Before going any further I should probably explain the name. The name Python is taken from the comedy group Monty Python, which is best known for the talents of Eric Idle, John Cleese, Terry Jones, Terry Gilliam, Michael Palin, and Graham Chapman.

Python Is Free

Although this is not that unique—many of the most popular programming languages are available free—it does mean that you can write and deploy Python programs without having to purchase any software and without having to worry about licensing issues. You can even download the source code to the software if you want to take a closer look at how the Python language works.

Being free often means that there is little or no support. With Python this is not the case. There is a huge following of Python programmers, and the people involved in developing Python are always welcome to help new users get to know the language. There are also a number of commercial companies and individuals who provide custom programming and more in-depth support if you need it and are willing to pay for it.

Python Is Portable

Python is supported on a huge range of operating system platforms. It comes in ready-compiled format for Windows and MacOS and includes the Tk extensions so you can develop user interfaces. On Unix and all other platforms, Python is available as source code which you compile yourself. You can also visit one of the web sites offering precompiled binaries (see Appendix A). In all cases, the compatibility is invisible. You can write a script on a Unix platform, and 95% of the time you can execute it without modification on a Mac or a PC. Because of the Tk support, you can even run the same GUI-based application on all three platforms without any major modifications and have a consistent user interface in each case.

In addition to the native cross-platform capability, Python also supports some platform-native extensions to help ease the porting process or bridge gaps with other languages and environments. For example, the SunOS/Solaris implementation includes a driver for Sun audio devices, and the SGI version comes with tools for interfacing to the audio and video capabilities (including OpenGL) built into SGI workstations. The Windows Python interpreter comes with toolkits to interface to the Visual C++ libraries and the Windows audio drivers. You can even communicate with COM (Component Object Model) objects.

Python Is Powerful

There is very little you cannot do with Python. The core of the language is very small, but it provides enough of the basic building blocks to allow you to design most applications. Furthermore, because the language can be extended using C, C++, and even Java in certain circumstances, you should be able to develop any type of program. The Python interpreter actually comes with a huge library of additional modules that extend the capabilities of the language to allow network communication, text processing (including extensive XML support in Python 2.0), and regular expression matching.

Although Python's main objective is to hide much of the low-level complexity from the programmer, it also supports the necessary hooks, extensions, and functions to allow low-level access to certain areas of the operating system. By supporting both the high-level and low-level functionality, Python can be used at the same level as C or at the same level as Visual Basic, as well as at all the other levels in between. You can even use Python as a macro or application extension language by embedding it into your applications, much like Visual Basic is the macro language used in Microsoft Office products.

Python Is Extensible

Because Python is written in C (some extensions are written in C++) and because you have access to the source code, you can also write extensions to the language. Many of the standard modules supplied with the language are supported by a C or C++ interface. This includes basic facilities such as networking and DBM database access, along with more advanced toolkits such as Tk.

In addition, Python can be embedded into C or C++ applications so you can provide a scripting interface to your application using the Python language. Because of the support for cross-language development, you can use Python to design and conceptualize an application and then port it, over time, to C. There is no need to rewrite the application in C before using it; Python and C can work together in tandem.

Finally, Jython is a complete Python interpreter written entirely in Java. This means that you can write a Python program that interfaces to Java objects, or you can write a Java application that uses Python objects. Better still, because the interpreter is written entirely in Java, you can deploy a Python application on any platform that supports Java—even a web browser can directly execute a Python script.

Python Is Easy

Once you understand the basic principles of the Python language, learning the rest is easy. The core of the language is very small, and its semantics and style are very simple. Since all the other components and extensions use exactly the same syntax and structure, you should be up to speed programming in Python like an expert in no time at all.

That's not to say that there aren't complexities in the Python language that you'll need to learn. Many of the extensions and libraries require some careful thought to make effective use of the language. This is especially true when you start to integrate and interface to other languages such as Tk and SQL.

What Is Python Good For?

Not surprisingly, with such wide support and extensive features, Python is very effective for a large number of tasks. Here's a quick list of the more common uses of the Python language.

Mathematics

Python supports an extension called NumPy, which provides interfaces to many standard mathematics libraries. The Python language also supports unlimited precision. If you want to add two 100-digit numbers together, you can do so with Python without requiring a third-party extension. If you need real speed in mathematical applications, the NumPy extension is written in C and as a result, operates faster than the native math supported by Python.

Text Processing

Python can split, separate, summarize, and report on any data. It comes with modules that separate out the elements of a log file line. You can then use the built-in data types to record and summarize the information before writing it all out again. In addition, Python comes with expression libraries that allow you to use the same expressions as Emacs, Perl, and many other utilities. This means that Python can do all of the things that other languages can do. For example, a number of programmers have produced a complex SGML-processing tool using Python.

Python actually comes with SGML-, HTML-, and XML-parsing modules for reading, writing, and translating the different formats. With Python's support for other text-processing engines (regular expressions and the natural splitting/combining of information) and flexible variable and object handling, Python becomes a very useful tool for the text-processing programmer.

Rapid Application Development

Because Python is so straightforward to develop applications with, you can use Python to develop applications very quickly. The extensive module library that comes with Python provides direct interfaces to many of the protocols, tools, and libraries that you would otherwise have to develop yourself.

Furthermore, because scripts are interpreted and don't have to go through the normal compilation and linking stages, you can make modifications very quickly. If there's something that you need to test quickly, you can easily check it with the interpreter shell before actually making changes to your program, and you can even interactively debug your script using the same shell and environment that you use for programming.

Also, because Python supports Tk, you can have not just an interface example, but a complete application in hours instead of days. I've written a cross-platform, Tk-based database query tool in less than day, something that would have taken me two or three days with Perl, and a week or more in C.

Cross-Platform Development

You now know that Python supports a wide range of platforms in a completely neutral format. If you are deploying an application across a network that uses a variety of different platforms, you can use Python to develop the application. You can also use Python where you want to be sure that future implementations of your system are going to work. Many companies start with a specific platform and then move to a different platform as the performance starts to suffer. Using Python, you will never need to rewrite your software as you move between platforms.

Of course, you can also look at Python as an alternative when supplying software to end users. Instead of developing three separate applications, with operating system-specific compilation processes, testing systems, and interfaces, you only have to develop it once, saving significant time and money.

System Utilities

Although much of the ethos with Python is to hide from you the low-level parts of the operating system, the tools and extensions are there if you want to access the lowest levels. Because Python has access to the same set of functions as the operating system, you can use it to duplicate and extend the functionality of the operating system, while still retaining all of the compatibility and interface issues that you already know Python supports.

Internet Programming

Python comes with a standard set of modules that allow you to communicate over the network sockets, both at a basic level and at a protocol level. If you want to read e-mail from a POP server, for example, Python already comes with the library module that enables you to do that. In addition, Python also supports XML, HTML, and CGI libraries so you can parse user input and produce top-quality formatted output via a web server.

In fact, the combination of Python's high-level module support and RAD powers gives you an enormous, but speedy, development toolkit. Most Internet modules allow you to communicate directly with an Internet server using a simple object class and a number of different methods. One programmer even managed to write a newsreader entirely in Python within a couple of afternoons. On my home network, I have a Web-based e-mail interface to my IMAP server that took me about an hour to write in Python.

You can even compile a module for Apache, the Unix and Windows web server that embeds the Python interpreter. This means that when you want to execute a Python script, the interpreter does not need to be loaded separately each time, thus providing the maximum possible performance from your CGI scripts.

Database Programming

There are a myriad of extension modules that interface to all of the common database systems, from Oracle to Informix and free systems such as mSQL and mySQL. There is even a toolkit called Gadfly that provides a complete SQL environment within Python—no external modules or extensions are required. Because Python has strong text- and data-handling abilities, you can use Python to interface between databases and to act as a better summary and report tool than many of the interfaces that come with the database systems themselves. Furthermore, because Python supports a number of different operating systems, instead of only one, you can use the same interface with any database. You can even use Tk to build the front end and then put it on any of the supported platforms—you'll get an instant cross-platform, database independent query tool!

Everything Else

Python can be used for anything—there are literally no limits to what this language can do. By supporting a small core set of functions, data types, and capabilities, Python provides an excellent base on which to build. Because you can extend the functionality with C and C++, you get the best of both worlds—unlimited and unfettered expansion to do whatever you want, but in a structured and manageable format.

What Isn't Python Good For?

It's very difficult to give a precise list of the problems that Python is unable to solve. Python provides most of its functionality in the extension modules that are supplied with the language, and this just demonstrates how easy it is to add functionality to the language. If you can't do what you want to within Python, then it's just as easy to write a C or C++ extension to do the job for you.

Some people criticize Python not because it's not capable of doing a particular task, but because they don't understand *how* to do a particular task. One of the most common complaints relates to Python's apparent lack of regular expression support, when in fact there are two modules (**re** and the older **regex**) that enable you to handle regular expressions; regex even supports the same syntax that is used in Perl. Regular expression handling may not be built into Python, and it probably isn't as fast as Perl's expression handling, which has been highly optimized over the years, but it's still possible.

The advantage of Python over a language such as Perl, Rebol, or Java is that the core of the language is very small. This improves the execution time—there's less code to be loaded each time the script is run—and helps make the rest of the language easier to learn and more flexible.

Once you are familiar with the minimalist style of programming that Python supports, you'll find that you still have all the power, but without the extra baggage. And you can read your code the next day, week, or year you look at it.

Who Uses Python?

Python is used by a large number of people for solving all sorts of tasks. Most of these are not well known, or at least not publicized, purely because the companies concerned do not normally divulge this sort of information. However, there are some larger companies that use Python within a commercial environment and that are proud to announce and even celebrate the fact.

- Red Hat (**www.redhat.com**), who makes the popular Red Hat Linux distribution, uses Python in combination with Tk to provide a visual interface for configuring and managing the Linux operating system. The configuration system gives you complete control over all aspects of the Linux operating system and automatically updates the configuration files according to your selections.

- Infoseek (**www.infoseek.com**) uses Python within certain parts of its public search engines. Python is also used for customizing the Infoseek software that can be downloaded from this site for use on end users' machines.

- NASA (**www.nasa.gov**) uses Python in a number of different areas. The most significant use of Python is in the Mission Control Center, where Python is used in certain parts of the system for planning missions. Other uses take advantage of the strong numerical abilities of Python, which make it ideal for calculating the location of celestial objects and for plotting the paths taken by satellites.

- Industrial Light and Magic (**www.ilm.com**), famous for doing the special effects on films such as *Star Wars, The Abyss, Star Trek,* and *Indiana Jones,* uses Python to produce commercial-grade animation. In fact, if you visit their web site, you'll see they have a number of vacancies for Python programmers!

Python History

Python has a long history—noticeably longer than most people probably realize. In the year 2000, the Python development efforts underwent a great deal of reorganization as Guido van Rossum, the designer and primary developer of Python, and the rest of the Python team (including Tim Peters, Barry Warsaw, Jeremy Hylton, and Fred Drake) moved the development efforts first from CNRI (Centre for National Research Initiatives) to BeOpen, and ultimately, to Digital Creations.

Python Up to 1.5.2

Up until September 5, 2000, Python was developed and released through a public license supported by CNRI. Python 1.5.2 contained most of the functionality of Python that we are familiar with today. The final 1.5.2 release was released on April 13, 1999.

Python 1.6 (September 2000)

In September 2000, after Guido left CNRI, two versions of Python 1.6 were released. The first version came from CNRI and was their last official release of the Python language. Python 1.6b1, the beta version of the language, had been in development and testing for some time, so it was not a complete surprise to see Python 1.6b1 released by Guido van Rossum and the BeOpen development team.

Version 1.6 included some minor improvements, including a change in the way list objects worked and some improvements in the socket and string-to-number conversion tools.

Python 2.0 (September 5, 2000)

Within 24 hours of CNRI's announcement, Guido and the rest of the development team released version 2.0b1 (a beta release) of Python to steal a coup from CNRI's 1.6 release. The entire Python team had moved from CNRI to the BeOpen initiative (**www.beopen.com**) on May 5, 2000 to continue the development of Python outside of CNRI and under an open-source agreement.

Version 2.0 included some important updates to Version 1.6, including new operators, new list syntax, and better module importing methods. Version 2.0 also included one of the most significant updates to the standard Python library for more than a year, fixing numerous bugs and adding several new features and an entirely rewritten suite of XML tools. The final version of Python 2.0 was released on October 16, 2000.

Aside from the obvious language improvements, the move to BeOpen also enabled the development team to make other improvements for Python behind the scenes, such as moving the Python sources to SourceForge (**www.sourceforge.net**), and executing the final stages for moving JPython, the old Java-based Python interpreter, to the new Jython hybrid.

Python 2.0 (October 28, 2000)

On October 28, 2000, Guido announced on the newsgroups and the main Python web site that the Python team had moved again, this time to Digital Creations. Digital Creations are the people behind Zope (Z-Objects Publishing Environment), one of the best-known Python projects.

Python 3000

No further releases have come out since the Python 2.0 release from BeOpen, but work is planned for the new Python 3000 product, due to be released sometime in 2002. Hopefully, given Digital Creations' existing Python evangelism, there shouldn't be any further moves for the Python team.

Python 3000 itself is expected to be a major update of the language, in much the same way that Perl 6.0 is expected to be a major update to Perl 5.6. Python 3000 is unlikely to be the final name of the new version of Python; it's just a code name for the new version.

Similar Languages

The range of scripting languages that are available today is growing at a rapid rate. Although most people have heard of Perl, VBScript, and almost certainly BASIC, there are other useful scripting languages that can be used to solve a number of problems. But where does Python fit in, and how does it compare to these other languages?

The question is even more complex if you try to enforce usage environments onto the programming languages. Perl is great at text processing, so is Python, and so is Awk, but which should you choose? I tend to use Perl when it's simple text processing from a file, Python when I'm converting, translating, or otherwise encapsulating data into a new data-storage format, and Awk when I need to filter text from within a shell.

Perl

Perl and Python are the two most similar languages available at the moment. They are the two top interpreted scripting languages available, even though they have different syntax and were designed with different goals in mind.

Perl was developed by Larry Wall, originally as a tool for processing text suitable for summarizing and reporting; the word Perl stands for Practical Extraction and Report Language. Unlike Python, Perl was built using many of the principles and semantics from other languages and from the Unix environment. You can integrate the commands you use within the Unix shell with other advanced features such as regular expressions, and then bond it all together with some very flexible, but powerful variables.

However, Perl also has some difficulties. The object-orientation (OO) feature is easy to use, but it was bolted on after the language was originally developed. This doesn't cause any problems, but it makes object orientation an added rather than an integrated feature. The lack of a cohesive OO element gives you the flexibility to choose whether to write OO code or not. Unfortunately, this has the effect of making programming more difficult because you have a combination of object and nonobject entities to deal with, even during the development of a simple program.

When comparing most features, the features offered by Python and Perl are difficult to differentiate. The main difference is that the ethos is different. Perl was designed and is still largely used as a system for processing text and binary data. These tasks encompass most of the tasks for which Perl is most famous, including its use within the Internet for handling CGI (Common Gateway Interface) scripts. There are other strengths: Perl has very good system-level support, which makes it ideal for replicating and improving on many of the core system functions under Unix. But Perl's roots lie within the realm of text processing.

Python, on the other hand, was developed as an application programming language. With Python, you can develop full-blown, cross-platform applications for everything from utilities to complete integrated environments for application development.

When it comes to performance, there is probably little to choose between them. Both languages use the same system of compiling raw source into a bytecode, which is then executed by a virtual machine. However, if you try to compare semantics and other language features, there are undoubtedly some differences. Python has incredibly flexible data handling, and because all data-storage containers are objects, the same methods are used to process most pieces of information, which improves performance.

Perl is somewhat limited when it comes to built-in data types, and objects are handled using references that can take time to access and process and are difficult to learn. However, Perl's text processing and regular expression parsing capabilities are the fastest available, surpassed only by Gawk.

Python has a smaller built-in function set than Perl, but it has a much larger library of supplied extensions that resolve most of the so-called "missing" elements (see the section "What Isn't Python Good For" earlier in this chapter). The object orientation is Python's biggest feature, and because it applies everywhere, including the extension modules, it allows for a greater level of flexibility and extensibility. This is particularly true if you want to use Python within a fully object-oriented environment and take advantage of the OO features, especially inheritance and polymorphism.

The final part of the comparison is less obvious immediately; Python is clean and easy to read. Perl can be confusing, with many elements of the language using a complex set of punctuation rather than textual characters. Although you can make certain aspects of Perl easier to read, you still have to contend with elements like variable prefixes and references that make heavy use of braces. As if that weren't enough, you have a number of magic variables, assumed and implied treatments of that information, and various standard and nonstandard shortcuts that can make debugging Perl a little more challenging. In short, a lot of Perl can look like line noise.

Java

Unlike Python and Perl, which are quasi-interpreted languages, Java is a true compiler-based language: Java source code must be compiled into bytecode before it is executed by a Java Virtual Machine (JVM) on a host computer. Although Python compiles programs into bytecode, the compilation stage is handled by the interpreter, so you can still execute a Python program directly from the raw-text source code.

Because the compiled Java scripts have a much tighter bytecode format, Java scripts generally run slightly faster than Python scripts. However, they take longer to develop because of the increased time required to compile the Java application into its bytecode format before it can be executed. With Python, you execute the script directly, but with Java, you need to compile the script before executing it.

Better still, you can use Python directly. You can enter Python statements interactively to the Python interpreter. You can test statements and sequences to ensure that they work correctly, and you can verify these as you go. Often, this means that Python programs work the first time because you checked each statement in the interpreter as you added it to the source file.

The true difference, though, is in the philosophy of the language. Java is very much a low-level language, at the same practical level as C and C++, from which it inherits much of its design and methodologies. Python, on the other hand, is a high-level language. This helps hide the complexity of the underlying operating system from the programmer, while still providing all of the tools and features a programmer needs to complete the task at hand. Python is therefore far more suited to rapid development of an application within a structured framework.

Python is an excellent prototyping language for any object-oriented task, so it can be used for rough development before the design and implementation is properly developed in Java. Furthermore, Python and Java can be used together; there is even a Python interpreter (Jython) that has been written entirely in Java. Jython allows Java programs to use Python objects and Python programs to use Java objects. You can even use Python bytecode modules that were compiled with the C-based interpreter in Jython without conversion.

The issue of whether Python and a web or Tk interface is better than Java is a matter of personal opinion. I prefer Tk to Java because it's cleaner, clearer, and frequently easier to program, especially for small jobs. Tk's OO style fits well into the Python language. Tk is, in my opinion, easier to customize when you want to develop a new interface widget. Python has this advantage because it has true cross-platform compatibility, something that Java is still lacking at a production level. On the other hand, Java is currently supported on more platforms than Tk, which currently only works with Unix, Windows, and MacOS. In those situations, Java is obviously a better solution.

JavaScript

JavaScript and Python are similar in their design, but they have very different goals. Both are object-based but both also allow you to use the functions and capabilities of each language without requiring you to use the object features. However, JavaScript is not really a true scripting language, and by its very design, it isn't a competitor to Python.

The JavaScript language is an embedded language for controlling the interaction between the user and a web page. Because JavaScript is stored as part of the HTML text that is transferred when a page is accessed, there is no communication required between the user's browser and the web server as there is with CGI-based interfaces. However, JavaScript is not a stand-alone language, and outside of a web page, JavaScript is unusable. Furthermore, despite assurances to the contrary, JavaScript is not really cross-platform compliant or secure.

Programmers who already know how to program in JavaScript will feel comfortable with the Python environment because the terminology and many of the constructs are identical. The program layout and semantics are also very similar, and once you have learned the principles of JavaScript, Python is easy to migrate to. Python also provides JavaScript programmers with a much more open environment since it's possible to expand on the capabilities of the Python language—something not possible at all with JavaScript.

Tcl

Tcl was developed as a macro language to be used for extending existing applications, although it has also matured over the years into a stand-alone programming language. Most people are exposed to Tcl when they want to develop applications using the Tk interface builder. Tk is a system that provides a consistent and powerful interface for creating window-based applications. Tk is cross-platform, supporting the X Windows System on Unix and other operating systems that support X Windows, such as QNX, and the native environments under Windows 95/98/NT and MacOS. However, the Tk system is limited to those three main platforms, so while Tk is a cross-platform solution, you can't use it under lesser-used operating systems such as BeOS.

Tcl's disadvantage is that it is very weak on data structures. Languages like Perl provide much better features, and Python's strength over all the other languages discussed in this chapter is its data structuring and manipulation. Recent advances in Tcl, particularly with the version 8.1.1 release, have improved the support for data structures and provided a byte compiler to help improve the performance of Tcl applications. But in comparison to Python, Tcl still feels clumsy and slow. Since it has a good interface to Tk, Python provides an easier to use and faster solution for developing applications.

Rebol

Rebol is a very new language. Like Python, Rebol was developed with object orientation in mind. Rebol was designed as a message-style language, focusing on supporting the use of messages to transfer and communicate information. This makes Rebol ideal for Internet-based services, since Rebol can natively talk to e-mail, Usenet, web, and FTP servers, among many others. Because it instinctively knows how to access and handle many of these services, Rebol can be used to develop highly complex network-aware applications without much of the baggage normally required by languages such as Perl and Python.

Because Rebol is so highly focused, it's not entirely suited to the more general programming tasks normally applied with Perl or Python, but that functionality may come in time as the language matures.

Visual Basic

Visual Basic (VB) is the development environment offered by Microsoft as an extension to the original BASIC language that shipped with the early versions of DOS. Like JavaScript, VB has a specific target market and as such, is limited in a number of areas compared to proper programming languages such as Python.

Although it is often pitched as a general-purpose programming language, in fact, Visual Basic is targeted squarely at the development of interfaces to databases.

Although you can program complex environments for your databases within applications such as Microsoft Access or Visual FoxPro, VB is limited when it comes to developing a complete customizable interface to a database.

What VB provides is a completely customizable language that provides direct hooks into accessing data from ODBC (Open Database Connectivity) compliant databases. With VB, you have access to some of the same constructs so you can make decisions about what to display or what has been entered, but at the end of the day, you are still working with just a user-interface language.

Python has a number of extensions that provide you with access to a number of different database systems, including Oracle, Informix, mSQL/mySQL, and of course, ODBC. Because you can also program other elements with Python, you can do much more than just display the information to the user or get the information back—you can also communicate that data over the network or embed it in a web page. Perhaps more usefully, because Python supports so many different database systems, you can use Python to translate and transfer data from one system to another.

Awk/Gawk

Awk is a very old programming language; it was supplied with the early versions of the Unix operating system. Although it has its proponents (myself included), Awk and its GNU cousin Gawk are highly specialized languages for processing text. The features built into Awk and Gawk go far beyond those supported even by Perl. For summarizing and reporting on large volumes of data, Gawk far exceeds the performance of Python or Perl, and even in some instances, C.

The limitations of Gawk, however, are not restricted to text processing. Recent versions of Gawk include limited communication facilities, although it still doesn't have proper network socket facilities, and Gawk still lacks any serious file-management capabilities.

Gawk's main advantage over Python or Perl is that it is easy to write a quick script to process the output from a command within a Unix shell. In a line or two of Gawk code, you can achieve the same effect as a few lines of Python script or a large number of pipes through **cut**, **paste**, and **expr** within a Unix shell.

Awk still comes standard with most Unix distributions. Although many modern Linux distributions also tend to include Perl and Python, most of the commercial distributions do not. Python is compatible on all of them, but it still needs to be sourced, compiled, and installed.

Finally, Awk's regular expression syntax is much more advanced than either Perl's or Python's. You can use the regular expression syntax in both the search and replacement sections of substitution expressions. You can even do nested searches directly within a regular expression, something that would require a loop in most other languages.

C/C++

C is the source language for most operating systems, and it's also the language used to develop many new languages, including most of the other scripting languages mentioned in this chapter. The reason is very simple: C is a good low-level programming language that provides such fundamental access to most parts of the operating system that it can easily be designed to emulate and provide the functions and facilities required to develop other languages. Python itself is written in C, and this is one of the features that makes Python so cross-platform compatible—C is the system-level language for most operating systems.

However, Python offers much more than the facilities offered by C or C's object-oriented cousin, C++. First of all, Python is a much higher level language, hiding some of the low-level complexity of C within its own range of functions and structures. That doesn't mean you can't use Python for low-level programming; the facilities are there if you want them, but they are not required to write programs in Python.

Both C and C++ are complex languages that use a range of different terminology and constructs to support the functions and capabilities of the language. In particular, the object-oriented features of C++ are particularly complex, and they enforce a programming style that is very regimented. It's not possible in most instances to easily mix and match C++ and C functions into the same program; if you develop a C++ application, it needs to be completely C++ compliant. With Python, you can choose to use object orientation where you want to and ignore what you don't require. Furthermore, you can't take a C++ program from one platform and move it entirely to a new one; both platforms have to be using compatible compilers and run-time libraries that are simply not standard across platforms.

However, with all that in mind, it's worth remembering that Python is still written in C, and all of the functionality of the Python language relies on C source code somewhere. This reliance on C is not a limitation; in fact, you can develop extensions to the Python language using C or C++. You can also use the Python language within C programs, which enables you to embed Python statements. The embedding feature is particularly useful for programs where you want to support scripting abilities, but don't want to develop a new language for the purpose.

Unix/DOS Shells

Although they can't really be classified as programming languages, the Unix shells and the DOS command line do provide some basic scripting capabilities. Under Unix, the primary choices are the Bourne, Korn, and C shells, and variants such as the **bash** and **tcsh** shells. Many of the more advanced shells provide some data-handling and storage capabilities, but they are very limited. In all cases, when it comes to processing or collating information within a shell, you need to use an external utility such as **sort** or **cut**; many programs actually use Awk or Gawk to achieve some of the more complex options.

Advanced programming within the shell requires heavy use of pipes, and it's often the case that you will have 10 or 15 processes, all joined together by pipes to perform a simple operation that would take just one or two lines within Python. Therefore, although shell-script programming is possible for most solutions, it's just not practical.

Under DOS, and therefore Windows, the only scripting ability you have is through the batch file. Like shells, batch files are only suitable for executing a simple series of commands; they're not really suitable for real programming. Data storage is limited to environment variables only, and you can only pipe or redirect with certain commands. Also, despite attempts with products for DOS, the limitation is still with the available commands, rather than with the environment itself. DOS does not come with even 1% of the tools that are supplied standard with Unix.

The
Complete
Reference

Chapter 2

Python Fundamentals

Before we start explaining the semantics of the language, you need to know how to execute Python programs. Python is slightly different from many other scripting languages in that there are a number of different ways in which you can execute Python statements, including interactively directly to the Python interpreter.

Many programming languages rely on the following sequence of events for executing an application:

1. Write the application in one or more source files.

2. Compile the source files into object files.

3. Link the object files into an application.

4. Execute the application.

With scripting languages, the steps are simpler because the interpreter works directly with the source file. So the sequence is more likely to be as follows:

1. Write the application in one or more source files.

2. Execute the interpreter, supplying the main source file.

With Perl, Python, and some other scripting languages, steps 2 and 3 from the first list are actually built into the interpreter. When you execute an application, the interpreter compiles the source into an internal bytecode format and then executes the compiled program using a "virtual machine." The virtual machine executes the bytecode in the same way that a compiled application executes native machine code.

Executing Python Programs

Python follows the same basic process for writing applications as other programming languages do; the Python interpreter takes raw-text source code and executes each statement. The difference in Python is that you can also execute statements directly within the interpreter—you don't have to place Python statements into a file before you execute them.

In addition, Python also allows you to record the compiled bytecode instructions in a file and then execute the bytecode directly, without going through the (relatively) lengthy process of compiling the source code first. Although this technique is not normally used for applications, it is used for modules and extensions to the Python language.

There are also other ways in which you can execute Python applications. Let's take a look at each one individually.

Interactively

The Python interpreter works slightly differently from other interpreters in that you can enter Python statements directly into the interpreter, rather than having to create a file and then execute that file. This is very useful when you want to quickly try a particular statement or for very short applications.

Unix

Under Unix (details on Windows and MacOS follow), you can just execute the Python interpreter at the command line and start typing in Python statements, as in the following example:

```
$ python
Python 2.0 (#4, Dec 16 2000, 07:30:29)
[GCC 2.95.2 19991024 (release)] on sunos5
Type "copyright", "credits" or "license" for more information.
>>>
```

When you enter a Python statement, the interpreter automatically compiles and then executes the statement—you don't have to go through the compilation stage first. The interactive approach means you can try different statements all within the same session. You can modify the statements at the command line before they are executed. Once you press ENTER, the statement is executed—you can't go back and modify it.

If you want to try it, enter the following statement at the Python command line:

```
>>> print 63*56
3528
>>>
```

As you can see, you get the response and the correct result immediately—the statement has been compiled and executed for you on the fly.

The interactive interface is not one shot—you can execute multiline statements just as if you were entering the individual statements into a single file to be executed. This means you can enter very small programs straight into the interpreter to see what happens. Consider the following example:

```
Python 2.0 (#4, Dec 16 2000, 07:30:29)
[GCC 2.95.2 19991024 (release)] on sunos5
Type "copyright", "credits" or "license" for more information.
>>> pi = 3.141592654
>>> radius = 4
>>> area = pi*(radius**2)
>>> print 'Area of circle is:',area
Area of circle is: 18.849555924
>>>
```

Don't worry too much about the syntax for the moment—we'll be using the interactive interface a lot in this book to quickly show the effects and operation of statements and functions within Python. This is precisely what it is there for—to try out statements.

To exit Python's interactive interpreter, press the end-of-file key combination. For most Unix terminals this is CTRL-D.

Windows

Once you have installed the Python interpreter, you should be able to execute Python statements interactively in exactly the same fashion as you would under Unix:

```
C:\> python
Python 2.0 (#8, Oct 16 2000, 17:27:58) [MSC 32 bit (Intel)] on win32
Type "copyright", "credits" or "license" for more information.
>>>
```

You may need to add the directory that contains the Python interpreter to your **%PATH%**. Under Windows 95/98, you need to add this directory to your **AUTOEXEC.BAT** file. Under Windows NT, you need to modify the PATH setting in the System Control Panel. If you prefer, you can find the command-line Python interpreter in the Start Menu.

Once you are in the interactive interpreter, it works exactly like the Unix version. However, to exit the interpreter you need to use CTRL-Z.

MacOS

Under MacOS, you need to start the Python application. This opens a simple, terminal-style window, which is the interactive interface to the Python interpreter. Figure 2-1 shows the Python application in action under MacOS.

From a File

The difficulty with entering statements interactively is that you can never store the statements you have entered—they are executed and essentially deleted immediately. Just like other scripting languages, you can also put Python statements into a file and execute the file as a whole application. Under other scripting languages, this is called a *script file*, a *batch file*, or even an *application*.

With Python, script files are called *modules.* There is nothing special about the format of a Python module; it's a simple text file so you can edit it with your favorite text editor—Emacs, Notepad, BBEdit, whatever you like. The major benefit of using a module is that you don't have to reenter the statements; you can use them in the module again and again.

By tradition, you should give your Python modules the extension **.py** to indicate that they are Python scripts. Under Unix and MacOS, the significance of the extension given to the file is ignored, but under Windows, the extension enables the module to

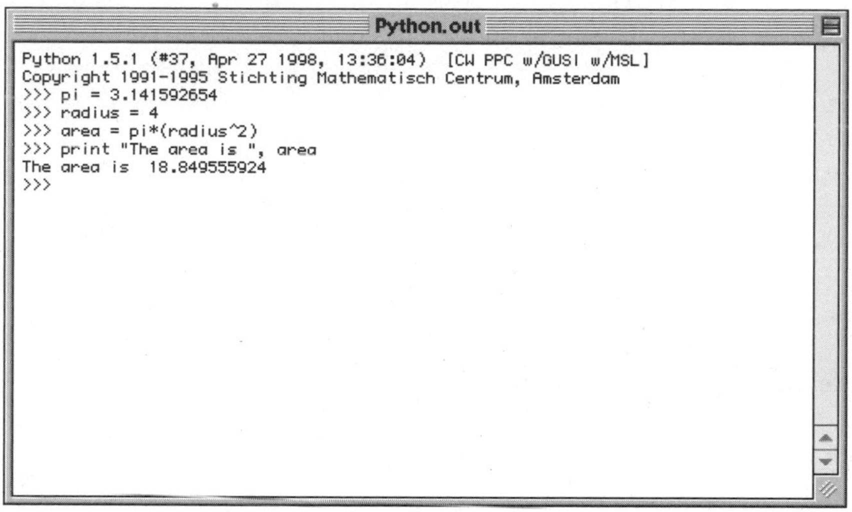

```
Python.out

Python 1.5.1 (#37, Apr 27 1998, 13:36:04)  [CW PPC w/GUSI w/MSL]
Copyright 1991-1995 Stichting Mathematisch Centrum, Amsterdam
>>> pi = 3.141592654
>>> radius = 4
>>> area = pi*(radius^2)
>>> print "The area is ", area
The area is  18.849555924
>>>
```

Figure 2-1.   *Using the Python interpreter under MacOS*

be executed just by double-clicking on the file. We'll explain the different platform-specific options shortly.

There is one advantage with Python modules that is not available in other languages: With Python, any module can be imported by another module without requiring modification—there is no need to modify the original module or change its name. You don't even need to write the module in a special way; just save it as a file with the **.py** extension. This makes the process of sharing previous functions and objects much easier and promotes much better reuse of the objects you have created before.

As a Unix Script

When you create a Python module under Unix, to execute the statements in the module you need to supply the name of the module to the Python interpreter. Let's try it with a simple script:

```
import sys
print 'Hello ', sys.argv[1]
```

Save these commands in a file called **test.py**. Then supply the filename as the first argument to the Python interpreter:

```
$ python test.py Martin
Hello Martin
```

Alternatively, insert the following line as the first line of the file. This is known as the *shebang line:*

```
#!/usr/local/bin/python
```

You also need to change the mode of the file so that it is executable; this makes the Unix shell examine the shebang line to determine what application to use to execute the text script:

```
$ chmod 755 test.py
```

You can now run the script directly:

```
$ test.py Martin
Hello Martin
```

The shebang line tells Unix what application to use to execute the file. The shebang line in the preceding example specifies the location of the Python interpreter directly. A more compatible method, which causes the script to search the value of the **PATH** environment variable, is to use the following shebang line instead:

```
#!/usr/bin/env python
```

Make sure you check where the **env** utility is located; otherwise the shell will signal an error. You might find **env** in **/bin**, **/usr/bin**, **/usr/local/bin**, or **/usr/sbin**.

Configuring the Python Interpreter   Whichever method you decide to use when executing a Python script, there may be times when you want to supply additional command-line switches to the Python interpreter. For scripts to be manually executed by the Python interpreter, you must supply those options before you supply the script name. For example, to cause the interpreter to go into interactive mode after the script has been executed, you need to specify the following:

```
$ python -i sample.py
```

Or, use the following shebang line:

```
#!/usr/local/bin/python -i
```

Table 2-1 contains the full list of command-line options and environment variables.

Option	Environment Variable	Description
-d	PYTHONDEBUG	Generates debug information from the interpreter after the script has been compiled.
-i	PYTHONINSPECT	Causes the interpreter to go into interactive mode after the script has been executed.
-O	PYTHONOPTIMIZE	Optimizes the bytecode generated by the interpreter before it is executed.
-OO		Optimizes the bytecode and removes the embedded document strings from the optimized code before it is executed.
-S		Does not automatically import the **site.py** module, which contains site-specific Python statements, when the interpreter starts.
-t		Generates warnings when tab-based indentation of the script is inconsistent. See Chapter 3 for details on Python blocks.
-ll		Generates errors (and stops parsing) when the indentation of the script using tabs is inconsistent.
-u	PYTHONUNBUFFERED	Forces the standard output and error filehandles to operate unbuffered. If not specified, then buffered output is used.
-v	PYTHONVERBOSE	Generates information about modules imported by the script when executed.
-x		Skips the first line of the source file. Useful when executing a script on a different platform than the source when you want to skip the shebang line.
-X		Disables the class-based exceptions that are built into the interpreter. (See Chapter 6 for more information.)
-c *cmd*		Uses *cmd* as the script source instead of a source file.
-		Reads the source file from the standard input.

Table 2-1.   *Python Command-Line Options and Environment Variables*

Where a variable is available for configuring an option, its existence and value are used to determine whether the option is set. For example, merely creating the variable is not enough, as in the following example:

```
$ export set PYTHONINSPECT
$ sample.py
Hello World!
```

You must give the variable a value:

```
$ export set PYTHONINSPECT=1
$ sample.py
Hello World!
>>>
```

In addition, Python supports the environment variables described in Table 2-2.

On a Windows Host

Under Windows, you have two options. If you want to execute a Python script from the DOS prompt, just supply the name of the file to the application:

```
C:\> python test.py
```

The other alternative is to define the **.py** extension as a file type within Windows Explorer (the File Types tab under Folder Options). The Python installer does this for you when the interpreter is installed. When you double-click on the file within a

Variable	Description
PYTHONSTARTUP	The name of a file to be executed when starting the interpreter in interactive mode.
PYTHONPATH	A list of directories (separated by colons under Unix or semicolons under Windows) to be searched when importing modules. The resulting list is available internally as **sys.path**.
PYTHONHOME	The directory in which the core Python libraries can be found. Defaults to **$PYTHONHOME/python2.0**.

Table 2-2.   *Python Environment Variables*

Windows Explorer window, the Python interpreter opens with that file displayed, just as if you'd typed the instruction on the command line.

The only problem with this double-click method is that you cannot supply any arguments on the command line to the script; the script is only interactive if you add the necessary code to request information from the user when the script is executed. The solution is to create a batch file that executes the Python interpreter, your script, and any arguments you want to supply to the script.

One final option eliminates the need to open the command-line prompt at all. If you name the file with a **.pyw** extension, then a DOS command prompt is not opened when the script is run, allowing the script to appear just like a normal Windows application. However, in this mode there is no form of interaction unless it's been defined within the script—you'll need to open a console window or more likely, develop a Tk-based interface within the script to allow interaction from the user. Chapter 14 describes how to use Tk to develop interfaces within Python.

Python under Windows does not support the shebang line that is used under Unix to define which options to be used when running the interpreter. This means that if you want to supply specific options to the interpreter when you run a script, you need to embed the call within a batch file. This is actually a limitation of the operating system, rather than a limitation of Python. All of the command-line options available under Windows are identical to those under Unix. See Table 2-1 for details.

On a MacOS Host

Under MacOS there is no way to identify the type of file by its name. The MacOS does not use extensions to identify file types; instead, it employs a special system using special four-character type and creator codes. For example, a Python applet under MacOS has a type TEXT and a creator Pyth. Without special tools such as FileTyper or Snitch, there is no way to modify this information.

To execute a Python script on a MacOS machine, you need to create a normal text file. You can do this with the SimpleText application, or you can use an editor such as BBEdit or Emacs to create the file. You can even use Microsoft Word or AppleWorks—just make sure that when you save the file, you save it as a normal text file, not as a Word or AppleWorks document.

Once you create the script file, you need to drag and drop the file onto the Python application in order for the application to execute the script. Double-clicking on the file at this stage only opens the file again within the editor. Note that when the file is executed, the Python application is opened, the script is run, and then the application exits. If you want to display some information to the user, you need to either pause the output by waiting for some input or delay the normal exit procedure of the program. See the next section, "Configuring Python under MacOS," for details on how to handle other execution options.

If you want to create a Python application that can just be double-clicked to be executed, you need to use the **BuildApplet** application. Drag and drop your Python script onto this application and a new application will be created. When you double-click on the new application, the Python library is loaded by the application and then the script is executed, just as if you had dropped the script onto the Python interpreter.

Note, however, that the application is not completely self-contained—you cannot supply the application to end users without also asking them to install the Python interpreter. The application that is created is really only a placeholder to allow for easier execution of a Python script.

Also, if you modify the source script, you will need to rebuild the applet to incorporate the changes—the modifications are not automatically applied to the applet as well.

Configuring Python under MacOS   MacOS does not support environment variables or command-line options. To modify the operation of the interpreter or a Python applet, you must use the **EditPythonPrefs** application. If you want to modify the main Python application, and therefore any scripts dragged and dropped onto the interpreter, just double-click on the Python application. The first window, as seen in Figure 2-2, enables you to specify the library search path for the interpreter. You can also specify the HOME location for the execution of the interpreter; this information is used when looking for modules to be imported. Modifying this information is analogous to modifying the **PYTHONPATH** and **PYTHONHOME** environment variables under Windows and Unix.

If you click on Default Startup Options, you can configure many of the options available to Unix and Windows users, as well as some of the options that are specific to the MacOS platform. Figure 2-3 contains this option window.

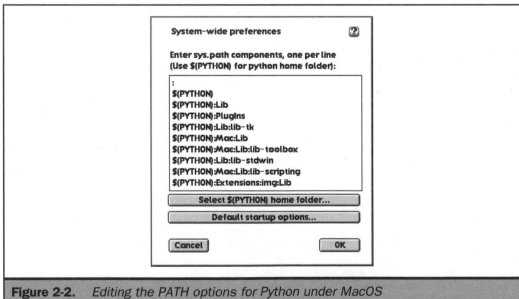

Figure 2-2.   *Editing the PATH options for Python under MacOS*

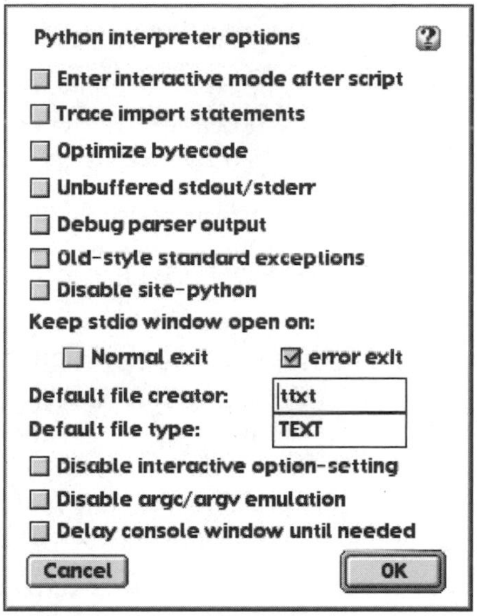

Figure 2-3. *Editing other MacOS options for the Python interpreter*

Table 2-3 lists the options in the window in Figure 2-3 that match the command-line versions.

Table 2-4 describes the other options under the MacOS version of the Python interpreter.

MacOS Option	Command-Line Equivalent
Enter Interactive Mode After Script	**-I**
Trace Import Statements	**-v**
Optimize Bytecode	**-O**
Unbuffered stdout/stderr	**-u**
Debug Parser Output	**-d**
Old-Style Standard Exceptions	**-X**

Table 2-3. *MacOS/Command-Line Equivalent Options for the Python Interpreter*

MacOS Option	Description
Keep stdio Window Open on Normal Exit	Keeps the console window created by the Python application open after the script exits, even if the execution was successful.
Keep stdio Window Open on Error Exit (default)	Keeps the console window created by the Python application open after the script exits only if there was an error or an exception.
Default File Creator	Specifies the four-letter code used as the file creator type when files are generated by a Python script. The creator code is used to define which application opens the file when it is double-clicked. Use the code **ttxt** for TeachText/SimpleText, **MSWD** for Microsoft Word, and **R*ch** for BBEdit.
Default File Type	Specifies the four-letter code to be used as the file type code for files created by Python scripts. **TEXT** is a normal text file, and **bina** is a binary file. Others are application/operating system-specific. Note that if you want to use your own code, you need to register the code with Apple before supplying a public application.
Disable Interactive Option-Setting	If you hold down the OPTION key when starting the interpreter, you are allowed to specify some of these options on the fly. Setting this option disables this feature.
Disable argc/argv Emulation	Disables the ability to supply command-line options by holding down the OPTION key while starting.
Delay Console Window Until Needed	If the application does not require a console window or does not use one until later in the application, you can avoid displaying an empty window by setting this option.

Table 2-4.   *MacOS-Specific Options for the Python Interpreter*

Note that you can also specify these options on individual Python applets (but not scripts) by dragging and dropping the applet onto the **EditPythonPrefs** application.

Other Methods

There are, of course, methods for executing Python statements. The Python language was written as much more than just a simple interpreter. You can embed the Python interpreter into a C or C++ application, and therefore execute Python statements and even entire modules within the confines of another application. This topic is too advanced for this book so we won't go into any detail, but it is another practical and very useful way of executing Python applications.

If you want to embed Python into an application, see Chapter 28 for more information. Alternatively, check the documentation that comes with Python. The standard documentation set includes the manual *Extending and Embedding the Python Interpreter*, which should contain all the information you need. See Appendix B for information on how to obtain and use the Python documentation.

Script, Program, or Module?

New users to the Python language sometimes get confused about the difference between the different names for Python applications. Is a Python application a script, program, module, or is it something else?

Strictly speaking, a text file that contains Python statements should be referred to as a *module*. Modules within Python have special significance; they can be executed and they can also be imported by other modules. For some users this is doubly confusing because they are used to separate terms for different types of files—importable scripts in Perl are generally called modules rather than scripts. Python doesn't distinguish between the two, and there are no special tricks for creating Python modules that can be imported.

However, Python is a scripting language, so it's also perfectly legal to call a Python module a script. In addition, a Python module that performs a particular task could also be called a program or application, since both terms apply to a file that instructs a computer to do a number of specific tasks.

At the end of the day, there is really nothing special about any of the terms, but module is the generally accepted and recognized term for files that contain any Python statements.

The
Complete
Reference

Chapter 3

Components of a
Python Program

Now that you know how to write simple Python programs and how to execute them on the different implementations, it's time to take a closer look at the Python language. This chapter begins with a description of the basic components that make up a Python program. Since you have probably already done some form of programming, it's safe to describe programming as manipulating variables, since this is what all programs do regardless of their host language.

It's worth remembering throughout this chapter, and indeed during any Python programming exercise, that Python deals with *objects*. Although objects in Python may appear to be similar to the variables used in other languages (and we'll be making those comparisons in this chapter), all Python variables are, in truth, objects.

The Python language follows the same basic principles as many others:

- An individual application is made up of a number of files, which Python calls *modules*.

- Each module is composed of a number of statements.

- The statements create, use, and modify variables; Python creates object variables.

This chapter describes the two main areas make up a Python program; *Built-in Object Types* and the *Statement*. Since the logical flow is from the lowest common denominator, the object, to the highest, a module, we'll look at objects first and then look at statements. Chapter 6 looks at modules in depth, after you've mastered the basic components of the Python language.

Built-in Object Types

All languages support a number of built-in variable types. These are the building blocks used for all the other variable types available within the language. By combining or extending the basic variables, you can create some quite complex variables. For example, in C there is a basic type called **char**, which is a single character. By defining a **char** array, you create a text string, and by defining a two-dimensional array, you create an array or a string of strings.

Python supports a number of built-in object types. Unlike C, which approaches the problem of variables by supporting the lowest common denominator, Python supports a number of high-level variables that are more practical for most program solutions. Unlike other languages, Python variables are actually objects. By using objects at the basic storage level, the overall language is object-based. This has a number of advantages. You can use the same methods and functions to operate on different types of objects. Furthermore, because new objects inherit object methods, you can continue to use the same methods in the more complex objects that you create. You'll see some examples of this later in this chapter.

Just like other scripting languages, Python handles the creation, memory allocation, and the access routines that enable you to use the objects. This is the same model as offered by Visual Basic (VB) and Perl, but it's different from C, where you are responsible for allocating memory for the variables and information you need to store.

Python actually supports a wide variety of built-in object types that help to make your programs easier to write. Many of the basic types offered by Python would actually require a separate library or development process to be implemented before the object could be used. By providing these built-in, optimized versions, you can start programming right away with Python without worrying about the complexities of the objects you are using.

The use of built-in object types also has another advantage. The code for using built-in object types is highly optimized (and debugged) and has been developed over a number of years to be as efficient as possible. Although it is possible to write your own routines for implementing the same objects within your own applications, it is difficult to improve upon the versions supplied as built-in objects with the Python interpreter.

Python Objects and Other Languages

Python supports five main built-in object types and an external data type that is accessible just like the built-in objects. The built-in objects are Numbers, Strings, Lists, Dictionaries, and Tuples.

The primary external data type supported by Python is the file. Although it may seem odd to include files as a data type, Python supports access to files in much the same way that it supports access to the built-in object types. You'll see how this works and how the file and object types compare later in this chapter.

Some of the built-in object types will be familiar to you, such as numbers and strings and possibly lists, although Python supports a few different options on some of these objects. The other object types are probably unfamiliar to you with their current names. Table 3-1 offers a comparison of Python's built-in object types with data types offered by other languages.

Python	C/C++	Perl	Visual Basic
Number	int, long, float, double	scalar	double, integer, long, single, currency
String	char[] or char *	scalar	string
List	int[] or char[]	array	Any array type
Dictionary	N/A	hash or associative array	N/A
Tuple	*See Text*	*See Text*	*See Text*
File	FILE * or fd	FILE	No built-in type

Table 3-1. *Python and Other Language Data Types*

The *tuple* is a special type of list that cannot be modified. Since it's similar to a list, there is no reason why you can't use a normal array in C/C++, Perl, or VB. See the section "Tuples" later in this chapter for details on how tuples differ from normal lists.

Unlike other languages, it is the way in which the information is assigned to the object that defines the object type used to store the information. In C, you must explicitly define the type of the variable you are creating. In some languages, including Perl, the leading character in the variable name tells the language's interpreter what the object type is. With Python, the interpreter examines the information being placed into the object, and then creates or modifies the object to match the new type.

To see this in action, the following code shows different ways in which you can create objects. The operation is called an *assignment*, since you assign a value to a variable:

```
integer = 12345
float = 123.45
string = 'Hello'
list = [1, 'Two', 3]
dictionary = {'one':1, 'two':2, 'three':3}
tuple = (1, 'Two', 3)
```

In each case, Python identifies the information you are assigning to the variable and uses the correct object type for the data that needs to be stored. You'll learn more about the semantics of the assignment process when we describe each individual object type.

Operator Basics

It's impossible to talk about objects without also talking about the operators that can be used to operate on the objects. Because Python uses objects rather than variables to store information, you can actually use the same operators on a variety of different objects; Python automatically calls the corresponding method required to perform the operation on each object in question (see "Operator Overloading" later in this chapter).

Like other languages, Python follows the same basic mathematical notation and format when using operators on individual objects. Table 3-2 lists the operators and their precedence—operators at the bottom of the table have the highest precedence.

Many of these operators will be familiar to C/C++, Perl, and VB programmers, among others. For example, the expression **a+b** does exactly what you expect—it adds the value of variable **a** to variable **b**. Other operators, such as **lambda** and **in**, are specific to the Python language, and will be discussed when you learn about the individual semantics of each object type.

Parentheses

Despite the intonation in Table 3-2, the use of the parentheses, **()**, does not automatically imply the creation of a tuple. You can still use parentheses to modify the precedence

Operators	Description
x or y **lambda args: expression**	Logical or (**y** is evaluated only if **x** is false) Anonymous function
x and y	Logical and (**y** is evaluated only if **x** is true)
not x	Logical negation
<, <=, >, >=, ==, <>, != **is, is not** **in, not in**	Comparison tests Identity tests Membership tests
x | y	Bitwise or
x^y	Bitwise exclusive or
x&y	Bitwise and
x<<y, x>>y	Shift **x** left or right by **y** bits
x+y, x-y	Addition/concatenation, subtraction
x*y, x/y, x%y	Multiplication/repetition, division, remainder/format
-x, +x, ~x	Unary negation, identity, bitwise complement
x[i], x[i:j], x.y, x(...)	Indexing, slicing, qualification, function call
(...), [...], {...}, `...`	Tuple, list, dictionary, conversion to string

Table 3-2.   *Python Operators and Expression Precedence*

of an expression. As with other languages, any expression contained within parentheses is evaluated first—before the precedence shown in Table 3-2 goes into effect.

For example, the expression

```
result = 3*4+5
```

yields the value 17—correct according the precedence in Table 3-2. But note that the expression

```
result = 3*(4+5)
```

returns a value of 27.

Mixed Types in Expressions

Where applicable, Python follows the same basic rule as C/C++. If an expression contains mixed variable types, then the return value is of the most complex type contained within the expression. For example, the calculation

```
result = 3*2.5
```

sets the value of **result** to 7.5, a floating-point number, even though you started off with an integer and a floating-point value. Although this applies primarily to numerical calculations, there are some special cases with other object types. We'll discuss them separately.

Operator Overloading

The term *operator overloading* refers to the ability of a language to perform different operations on different object types when using the same operator. From a programming perspective, the ability of a language to support operator overloading allows for a simplified programming process. The + operator, for example, adds two numbers together when given two number objects. However, if given two strings, the strings are "added" together; in other words; the two strings are concatenated into a single string. Operator overloading also applies to other operators; the [] operators, for example, extract slices from strings, lists, and tuples.

It's important to understand the principle being used here—the operator performs the same *operation* on each object, even though the objects store and use their information in different ways.

Numbers

Python uses a simple object to hold a number. There are no restrictions on what type of number can be stored within a number object, unlike C, where you need to use a different data type to store integer and floating-point numbers. In addition to these basic types, Python also supports complex numbers and arbitrarily large integers.

As you already know, Python creates an object using the object type as determined from information that is assigned to the object when it is created. With number objects, the format of the number determines the method in which the information is stored. Therefore, you need to know how to introduce numerical constants into your Python programs.

Integer Constants

You can create integer number objects by supplying a sequence of numbers, as in the following example:

```
number = 1234
number = -1234
```

The objects created are integers, and they are actually stored internally as a C **long** data type, which is at least 32 bits long, and may be longer depending on the C compiler and processor being used. Also note that 0 is considered to be a number:

```
zero = 0
```

Again, this is as you would expect. It also follows that Python uses integer values when determining the logical value of an expression. As with other languages, 0 equates to a value of **false**, and any other number equates to **true**. This allows you to use integers for simple Boolean values without the need for an additional data type.

The use of only integer constants (or object values) in your expressions causes Python to use integers, instead of floating-point math routines. For highly repetitive calculations, the use of integers can increase performance. However, as described earlier, introducing a floating-point value into the expression causes the returned value to also be a floating-point number. See the "Floating-Point Constants" section later in this chapter for some examples.

Hexadecimal and Octal Constants

You can specify hexadecimal (base 16) and octal (base 8) constants using the same notation available in Perl and C/C++. That is, **0x** or **0X** prefixed to a number forces Python to interpret it as a hexadecimal number, while a single leading **0** (zero) indicates an octal number. For example, to set the value of an integer to decimal 255, you can use any one of the following statements:

```
decimal = 255
hexadecimal = 0xff
octal = 0377
```

Since these are simply integers, Python stores them in the same way as decimal integers. If you actually want to print an integer in octal or hexadecimal format, there is an interpolation method shown for formatting string objects that is described later in this chapter.

Long Integers

The built-in basic integer type is limited to a storage width of at least 32 bits. This means that the maximum number that you can represent is 2^{31}-1, since you must use one bit to allow for negative numbers. Although for many situations this is more than enough, there are times when you need to work with long integers. Python supports arbitrarily long integers—you can literally create an integer one thousand digits long and use it within Python as you would any other number.

To create a long integer, you must append an **l** or **L** to the end of the number constant, as in the following example:

```
long = 123456789123456789123456789123456789123456789123456789L
```

Once you have created a long integer, you can execute expressions as if they were normal numbers—the Python interpreter handles the complexities of dealing with the super-sized number. For example, the statements

```
long = 123456789123456789123456789123456789123456789123456789L
print long+1
```

produce the following output:

```
123456789123456789123456789123456789123456789123456790L
```

Or you can continue to do long integer math:

```
long = 123456789123456789123456789123456789123456789123456789L
print long+876543219876543219876543219876543219876543219876543219L
```

which generates

```
211111111111111111111111111111111111111111111111111110L
```

Although Python uses these long integers as if they were normal integer values, the interpreter has to do a significant amount of extra work to support this option, even though support for such large numbers is written in C. If you can, use the built-in integer or floating-point types in preference to using long integer math.

Floating-Point Constants

Python supports the normal decimal point and scientific notation formats for representing floating-point numbers. For example, the following constants are all valid:

```
number = 1234.5678
number = 12.34E10
number = -12.34E-56
```

Internally, Python stores floating-point values as C doubles, giving the objects as much precision as possible. Note that there is no "long" floating-point variable.

Remember that floating-point or mixed floating-point and integer expressions return floating-point values. The easiest way to demonstrate this is to show the output from the same simple calculation—one using integer constants and the other floating-point constants:

```
>>> print 5/12
0
>>> print 5.0/12
0.416666666667
```

You can see from the preceding example that the first expression returns 0—the rounded-down version of 5/12. The second expression prints the expected decimal fraction.

For those situations where you are not using constants and therefore don't have overall control of the object types you are using for your calculations, you can force an integer value to be returned by using the built-in **int** function. This forces Python to imply integer status to the expression supplied to the function. See the section "Type Conversion" at the end of this section.

Complex Number Constants

Python employs the normal notation for supporting complex numbers—the real and imaginary parts are separated by a plus sign, and the imaginary number uses a single **j** or **J** suffix. For example, the following are examples of complex number constants:

```
cplx = 1+2j
cplx = 1.2+3.4j
```

Python uses two floating-point numbers to store the complex number, irrespective of the precision of the original. Because complex numbers are a separate entity within Python, the interpreter automatically performs complex math on expressions that include complex numbers.

Numeric Operators

Most of the operators in Table 3-2 apply to numbers. Table 3-3 contains a more explicit list of numeric operators used for calculations—these are all the familiar mathematical operations.

Operation	Description
x+y	Add x to y
x-y	Subtract y from x
x*y	Multiply x by y
x/y	Divide x by y
x**y	Raise x to the power of y
x%y	Modulo (returns the remainder of x/y)
-x	Unary minus
+x	Unary plus

Table 3-3.   *Numeric Operators for all Number Types*

There are also a series of shift and bitwise operators that can be used for binary and bit math; these are listed in Table 3-4. Note that these operators can only be applied to integers; trying the operations on a floating-point number raises an exception.

In addition to these base operators, a series of augmented assignment operators was introduced with Python 2.0. For example, you can rewrite the fragment

```
a = a + 5
```

using an augmented assignment operator, as

```
a += 5
```

More clearly, the expression

```
x = x + y
```

can be rewritten as

```
x += y
```

The following is the full list of augmented assignment operators; the effects of these operators are the same as for the base operators listed in Table 3-4:

```
+=  -=  *=  /=  %=  **=  <<=  >>=  &=  ^=  |=
```

Operation	Description
x << y	Left shift (moves the binary form of **x**, **y** digits to the left), for example, **1 << 2 = 4**
x >> y	Right shift (moves the binary form of x, y digits to the right), for example, **16 >> 2 = 4**
x & y	Bitwise and
x | y	Bitwise or
x ^ y	Bitwise exclusive or (xor)
~x	Bitwise negation

Table 3-4.   *Bitwise/Shift Operators for Integer Numbers.*

Numeric Functions

In addition to the operators mentioned in Table 3-2 earlier in this chapter, Python also has a small set of built-in functions that operate directly on numerical objects. See Table 3-5 for a list of these functions. Note that this list does not cover those functions that convert objects between different types; the section "Type Conversion" later in this chapter explains those functions.

There are more numeric functions and some common constants defined in the **math** module; they are described in Chapter 10.

Function	Description
abs(x)	Returns the absolute (numerical) value of a number, ignoring any signage. If the **x** is a complex number, the magnitude is returned.
coerce(x,y)	Translate the two numbers **x** and **y** into a common type, using the normal expression rules, returning the two numbers as a tuple. For example, the statement **coerce(2,3.5)** returns **(2.0,3.5)**.
divmod(x, y)	Divides **x** by **y** returning a tuple containing the quotient and remainder as derived by long division. This function is effectively equivalent to **(a/b, a%b)**.
pow(x, y [, z])	Raises **x** to the power of **y**. Note that the return value type is the same as the type of **x**. This means that you can't raise an integer to the negative power or raise any number to a power beyond the range of the object type. For example, the statements **pow(2,-1)** and **pow(2,250)** both raise exceptions. Similarly, the expression **pow(256,(1/2))** returns 1 because the **1/2** calculation rounds down to 0. If the argument **z** is added, the return value is **pow(x,y)%z**, but it's calculated more efficiently.
round(x [, y])	Round the floating-point number **x** to 0 digits, or to **y** digits after the decimal point if **y** is specified. Note that the number returned is still a floating-point number. Use **int** to convert a floating-point number to an integer, but note that no rounding takes place.

Table 3-5. *Numeric Functions*

Strings

Strings in Python work differently from those in other scripting languages. Python strings operate in the same basic fashion as C character arrays—a string is a sequence of single characters.

The term *sequence* is important here because Python gives special capabilities to objects that are based on sequences. Other sequence objects include lists, which are sequences of objects, and tuples, which are immutable sequences of objects. Strings are also immutable; that is, they cannot be changed in place. You'll see what that really means shortly. Python strings are also your first introduction to the complex objects that Python supports, and they form the basis of many of the other object types that Python supports.

String constants are defined using single or double quotes:

```
string = 'Hello World!'
string = "Hi there! You're looking great today!"
```

Note the two formats here—there is no difference within Python between using single or double quotes in string constants. By allowing both formats, you can include single quotes in double-quoted constants and double quotes in single-quoted constants without the need to escape individual characters.

Python also supports triple-quoted blocks:

```
helptext = """This is the helptext for an application
that I haven't written yet. It's highly likely that the
help text will incorporate some form of instruction as
to how to use the application which I haven't yet
written. Still, it's good to be prepared!"""
```

Python continues to add the text to the string until it sees three triple quotes. You can use three single or three double quotes—just make sure you use the same number of quotes to start and terminate the constant! Also, you don't have to follow the normal rules regarding multiline statements; Python incorporates the end-of-line characters in the text unless you use the backslash to join the lines. The preceding example, when printed, is split onto the same five original lines. To create a single, unbroken paragraph of text, you need to append a backslash to the end of each line, as follows:

```
helptext = """This is the helptext for an application \
that I haven't written yet. It's highly likely that the \
help text will incorporate some form of instruction as \
to how to use the application which I haven't yet \
written. Still, it's good to be prepared!"""
```

Putting more than one quoted constant on a line results in the constants being concatenated, such that

```
string = 'I' "am" 'the' "walrus"
print string
```

creates the output "Iamthewalrus". Note the lack of spaces.

You can also concatenate string objects and/or constants using the + operator, just as you would with numbers:

```
greeting = 'Hello '
name = 'Martin'
print greeting + name
```

Note, however, that you cannot concatenate strings with other objects. The expression

```
print 'Johnny ' + 5
```

raises an exception because the number object is not automatically translated to a string. There are ways around this—you'll see some examples shortly.

Strings can also be multiplied (repeated) using the * operator. For example, the expression

```
'Coo coo ca choo' * 5
```

produces the string

```
'Coo coo ca chooCoo coo ca chooCoo coo ca chooCoo coo ca chooCoo
coo ca choo'
```

Finally, Python provides the built-in **len** function which returns the number of characters in a string. The expression

```
len('I am the walrus')
```

returns the value 15.

The **len** function actually calculates the length of any object that has a size (lists, dictionaries, etc.).

Strings Are Just Arrays

Strings are, as you've already seen, sequences. This means that you can access the individual characters in a string using array notation, and you can access strings as if they were lists.

The array notation for a string follows the same basic format as for other languages; you append square brackets to the variable name, such that:

```
string = 'I returned a bag of groceries'
print string[0]
```

displays the first character of the string.

Like C, the offset starts at 0 as the first character or element of the string. But unlike C, the indexing also allows you to specify a range, called *slicing*, and Python is able to determine the position in the string from the end, rather than from the beginning of the string. For example, the script

```
string = 'I returned a bag of groceries'
print string[0]
print string[2:10]
print string[-1]
print string[13:]
print string[-9:]
print string[:-9]
```

creates the following output:

```
I
returned
s
bag of groceries
groceries
I returned a bag of
```

The format of a slice is:

```
string[start:end]
```

The processes of indexing and slicing use the following rules:

- The returned string contains all of the characters starting from **start** up until but not including **end**.
- If **start** is specified but **end** is not, the slice continues until the end of the string.

- If **end** is specified but **start** is not, the slice starts from 0 up to but not including **end**.
- If either **start** or **end** are specified as a negative number, the index specification is taken from the end, rather than from the start of the string where -1 is the last character.

These rules make more sense when used in combination with the diagram shown in Figure 3-1.

You should now be able to determine that the statement

```
print string[0]
```

prints the first character,

```
print string[2:10]
```

prints characters 3 through 9,

```
print string[-1]
```

prints the last character,

```
print string[13:]
```

prints all of the characters after the fourteenth character,

```
print string[-9:]
```

prints the last nine characters, and

```
print string[:-9]
```

prints everything except for the last nine characters.

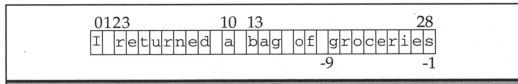

Figure 3-1.   *Indexes and slices with strings*

Although Python allows you to perform slices and other operations on strings, you must remember that strings are immutable sequences—they cannot be changed in place. Therefore, the statement

```
string[:-9] = 'toffees'
```

raises an exception. The only way to change the contents of a string is to actually make a new one. This means that for apparently simple operations such as the one just attempted, you'd have to use the following sequence:

```
newstring = string[:-9] + 'toffees'
string = newstring
```

There are, of course, easier ways to change the contents of a string. One way is to use a function supplied in an external module (**string**) to do the work for us. The other way is to use string formatting, which is discussed in the next section.

Formatting

The % operator in Python allows you to format strings and other objects using the same basic notation as supported by the **sprintf** function in C. Because you're using an operator and not a function, the usage is slightly different. You put the format string on the left of the % operator, and the object (or tuple of objects) that you want interpolated into the returned expression on the right. For example, the statement

```
'And the sum was $%d, %s' % (1, 'which wasn't nice')
```

returns

```
And the sum was $1, which wasn't nice
```

The return value is always a string. The % operator accepts the same list of options as the C **sprintf** function; see Table 3-6 for a complete list of conversion formats.

Python also supports flags that optionally adjust the output format. These are specified between the % and conversion letter, as shown in Table 3-7.

The % operator also works with dictionaries by quoting the name of the dictionary element to be extracted using the format **%(NAME)** followed by the formatting codes listed in Tables 3-6 and 3-7. For example, the statements

```
album = {'title':'Flood', 'id':56}
print "Catalog Number %(id)05d is %(title)s" % album
```

produce the string "Catalog Number 00056 is Flood".

Format	Result
%%	A percent sign.
%c	A character with the given ASCII code.
%s	A string. Python in fact converts the corresponding object to a string before printing, so **%s** can be used for any object. (See the section "Type Conversion" for more details.)
%d	A signed integer (decimal).
%u	An unsigned integer (decimal).
%o	An unsigned integer (octal).
%x	An unsigned integer (hexadecimal).
%X	An unsigned integer (hexadecimal using uppercase characters).
%e	A floating-point number (scientific notation).
%E	A floating-point number (scientific notation using **E** in place of **e**).
%f	A floating-point number (fixed decimal notation).
%g	A floating-point number (**%e** of **%f** notation according to value size).
%G	A floating-point number (as **%g**, but using **E** in place of **e** when appropriate).
%p	A pointer (prints the memory address of the value in hexadecimal).
%n	Stores the number of characters output so far into the next variable in the parameter list.

Table 3-6.   *Conversion Formats for the % Operator*

Flag	Result
space	Prefix positive number with a space.
+	Prefix positive number with a plus sign.
-	Left justify within field.
0	Use 0s, not spaces, to right justify.
#	Prefix non-zero octal with **0** and hexadecimal with **0x**.
number	Minimum field width.
.number	Specify precision (number of digits after decimal point) for floating-point numbers.

Table 3-7.   *Optional Formatting Flags*

Escape Characters

In string constants, you already know that you can embed a single or double quote, provided that you use double or single quotes respectively to define the entire string. With a triple-quoted block of text, you can use either single or double quotes directly. For those situations where you need to insert a quote or other special character into a string, Python supports the backslash (\) escape character. Table 3-8 lists Python's supported escape sequences.

Escape Character	Description
\ (at end of line)	Continuation (appends next line before parsing).
\\	Backslash.
\'	Single quote.
\"	Double quote.
\a	Bell.
\b	Backspace.
\e	Escape.
\000	Null. Python strings are not null terminated.
\n	Newline or linefeed.
\v	Vertical tab.
\t	Horizontal tab.
\r	Carriage return.
\f	Formfeed.
\0yy	Character represented by the octal number **yy**. (For example, \012 is equivalent to a newline.)
\xyy	Character represented by the hexadecimal number **yy**. (For example, \x0a is equivalent to a newline).
\y	Any other character **y** not listed above is output as normal.

Table 3-8. *Python's Supported Escape Character Sequences*

Raw Strings

For raw strings—those situations where you do not want any escape character processing—you can use the **r"** and **R"** raw strings. For example, the statement

```
print r'\a\n\x99'
```

actually outputs the string "\a\n\x99".

Raw strings are used primarily for regular expressions, where the backslash character is required for escaping regular expression operations. Chapter 10 discusses raw strings and regular expressions in more detail.

Other String Operations

Python has some facilities for sequences that are not included here. These are the iteration, membership, and **min** and **max** functions. Although these functions can be readily used on any type of sequence, including strings, they often make more sense when applied to lists or tuples. See the section on "Working with Sequences" later in this chapter for more details.

Lists

Lists are another form of sequence object and therefore they inherit many of the operational parameters of strings; after all, a string is just list of characters. However, unlike strings, Python lists can contain a list of any objects. You can store numbers, strings, other lists, dictionaries, and indeed any other object type that you create within a list, and even within the same list. Because it is a list of objects—and because all Python data is stored as an object—the list can be made up of any combination of information you choose.

Python stores a list of objects (or rather names that refer to objects), rather than a list of strings or numbers. This allows the Python list to be used in any situation where you want a list of information but don't want to be restricted to the type of information that you can store. See the section "What are Objects?" later in this chapter for more information how Python stores objects. .

Using Lists

Python creates a list when you enclose a series of objects or constants within a pair of square brackets, as in the following statements:

```
list = [1, 2, 3, 4]
songs = ['I should be allowed to think', 'Birdhouse in your Soul']
```

The use of the square brackets automatically implies a list of objects. Perl users take note; using parentheses instead of square brackets results in a tuple, described later in this chapter. You can also nest lists like the following one, which is actually a list containing two lists:

```
hex = [[0,1,2,3,4,5,6,7,8,9], ['A', 'B', 'C', 'D', 'E', 'F' ]]
```

Like strings, lists are referenced according to the index of the item you are looking for—indexes start at 0. Using the preceding examples, the first song name could be extracted by the following statement:

```
print songs[0]
```

To access an entire nested list, specify the index for the list object:

```
print 'Numbers:', hex[0]
```

To access a specific object within a nested list, use the following technique:

```
print 'D:', hex[1][3]
```

Also, note that the same slice operations work:

```
print 'A-C', hex[1][0:3]
```

To get the length of a list, use the **len** function:

```
print len( hex )
```

You can concatenate lists by using the + operator, which works in the same fashion as with string and numeric objects:

```
>>>hex[1] + list
['A', 'B', 'C', 'D', 'E', 'F', 0, 1, 2 ,3]
```

In addition, you can use the augmented addition assignment to add items to the list, but you must specify a list as the object to be added, as in the following example:

```
>>> songs += ['AKA Driver']
```

Finally, you can multiply lists by a numeric object to repeat the elements within a list:

```
>>>list * 2
[0, 1, 2, 3, 0, 1, 2, 3]
```

Note though that you cannot multiple a list by a list—not that it would make much sense if you could!

However, you can create a new list based on a simple expression. For example, given the list

```
>>> list = [1,2,3,4]
```

If you want a list of the cubes of each element, you could use the **map** function (described in Chapter 9) in combination with an anonymous **lambda** function (described in Chapter 4):

```
>>> cubes = map(lambda(x): x**3, list)
```

With Python 2.0 onwards, you can simply rewrite the preceding statement as follows:

```
>>> cubes = [x**3 for x in list]
```

Lists are Mutable

Remember how we said strings were immutable objects but lists were mutable? Well, the significance is that you can modify a list in place. With a string, the following operations raise an exception:

```
string = 'Narrow your Eyes'
string[7:11] = 'her'
```

However, with a list, the following operations work:

```
list = [0, 1, 2, 4, 16]
list[3:4] = [4, 8]
```

and the result is a list with six elements, **[0, 1, 2, 4, 8, 16]**. Note that you have to specify a slice; if you tried using **list[3]** in the second line in the preceding example, you'd replace the fourth element with an embedded two-element list. Also, the number of elements you're replacing doesn't have to match the number of elements you're inserting.

To delete items from the list, you need to use the **del** function, which accepts an element or slice from a list to be deleted, such that:

```
del list[3]
```

deletes the fourth element and

```
del list[1:4]
```

deletes the middle three elements from the list.

List Methods

Programmers familiar with objects know that many objects come with their own set of methods. Methods are special functions that are part of the object type definition. Methods are in fact just functions that happen to be specific to a particular type of object. Lists support a number of default methods that control the list contents. To use a method, you must qualify the method with an object name, for example, to call the **sort** method:

```
numbers = [3, 5, 2, 0, 4]
numbers.sort()
```

Note that with most methods, the new list is not returned; the list is modified in place. In the following example, the **numbers** object is now sorted. This complicates operations when you want to output a sorted list because the following statement will not print what you expect:

```
print numbers.sort()
```

Instead, you must do it in two lines:

```
numbers.sort()
print numbers
```

On the other hand, performing operations on the list makes it clear that we are modify a list, and that subsequent accesses will be on a sorted version of the list.

Table 3-9 lists the methods supported for lists.

Method	Description
append(x)	Appends the single object **x** to the end of the list. Supplying multiple arguments raises an exception. To append a tuple, explicitly supply a tuple, for example, **list.append((1,2,3))**. Returns **None**.
count(x)	Returns a count of the number of times the object **x** appears in the list.
extend(L)	Adds the items in the list **L** to the list. Returns **None**.
index(x)	Returns the index for the first item in the list matching the object **x**. Raises an exception if there is no matching element.
insert(i, x)	Inserts the object **x** before the element pointed to be **i**. Thus, **list.insert(0,x)** inserts the object before the first item. Returns **None**.
pop(x)	Removes the item at point **x** within the list and returns its value. If no index is specified, **pop** returns the last item in the list.
remove(x)	Deletes the first element from the list that matches the object **x**. Raises an exception if there is no matching element. Returns **None**.
reverse()	Reverses the order of the elements in the list, in place. Returns **None**.
sort()	Sorts the list in place. Returns **None**.

Table 3-9. *Methods Supported by List Objects*

Here are some examples using the methods described in Table 3-9:

```
list = [1,2,3]
more = [11,12,13]
list.append(4)            # [1,2,3,4]
list.append(('5a','5b'))# [1,2,3,4,(5a,5b)]
list.extend(more)         # [1,2,3,4,(5a,5b),11,12,13]
list.index(11)            # Returns 5
list.insert(5,'Six')      # [1,2,3,('5a','5b'),'Six',11,12,13]
list.pop()                # Returns (and removes) 13
list.pop(4)               # Returns the tuple ('5a','5b')
list.remove('Six')        # [1,2,3,11,12]
list.reverse()            # [12,11,3,2,1]
list.sort()               # [1,2,3,11,12]
```

You haven't come across the **None** value before, although it can apply to any object. The value **None** really means nothing—it does not imply an empty list or a zero-length string; instead, it implies an object that has no value. The **None** value is important because it can be used to identify an unpopulated object, similar in a sense to the C **NULL** value and identical in essence to the Perl **undef**.

Other List Operations

Because lists are another type of sequence, there are some additional features of list objects that have not been covered in this section. Please see the section "Working with Sequences" later in this chapter for details.

Tuples

Tuples are, to all intents and purposes, identical to lists except for one detail: tuples are immutable. Unlike lists, which you can chop and change and modify as you like, a tuple is a nonmodifiable list. Once you have created a new tuple, it cannot be modified without making a new tuple.

To create a tuple instead of a list, use parentheses instead of square brackets when defining the tuple contents, as in the following example:

```
months = ('Jan', 'Feb', 'Mar', 'Apr', 'May', 'Jun',
          'Jul', 'Aug', 'Sep', 'Oct', 'Nov', 'Dec')
```

The preceding statement is actually a very good example of why Python has tuples. Because they cannot be modified, you can use them to store information that you do not want to be altered. In the case of the preceding statement, you are interested in the order of the elements. If you had created this object as a list instead of as a tuple and then accidentally sorted it, the list of months would be largely useless. Without the ordered sequence, the information has no value.

Note that if you try to modify a tuple, an exception is raised to notify you of the error. This can be useful during development and debugging because it helps spot instances where you are misusing an object type.

The following are all examples of tuple use:

```
one = (1,)
four = (1, 2, 3, 4)
five = 1, 2, 3, 4, 5
nest = ('Hex', (0,1,2,3,4,5,6,7,8,9), ('A', 'B', 'C', 'D', 'E', 'F'))
```

The first and third lines in the preceding statements are important to understand. In the case of the first line, to create a one-element tuple you must use the redundant-looking comma; otherwise, the Python interpreter parses **(1)** as a constant expression—the inclusion of the comma forces Python to interpret the statement as a tuple.

The third line shows tuple creation without the use of parentheses. Python allows you to create a tuple without using parentheses in those situations where the lack of parentheses is not ambiguous. In this instance, it's obvious you are creating a tuple. As a general rule, you should use parentheses to highlight to you and any other programmers looking at your code that you are introducing a tuple.

Using Tuples

Tuples support the same basic operations as lists. You can index, slice, concatenate, and repeat tuples just as you can lists. The **len** function also works since a tuple is a sequence. The only actions you can't perform with a tuple are to modify them or to perform any of the methods available to lists since these methods make modifications.

It's also worth noting again that tuple operations return tuples. The statement

```
three = five[:3]
```

makes **three** a tuple, not a list.

Some functions also return tuples rather than lists, and some functions even require tuples as arguments. See "Type Conversions" for information on translating between Python object types.

Working with Sequences

The object types of strings, lists, and tuples belong to a generic Python object class called *sequences*. A sequence object is any object whose elements can be accessed using a numbered index. In the case of a string, each character is available via the index; for lists, it's each object. Because sequences have an order and are made up of one or more elements, there are occasions when you want to use the list as either a sequence or a traditional list of values to use as a reference point.

Python provides a single operator, **in**, that allows you to access the contents of a list in a more logical fashion.

Membership

If you are working with a list of possible values for a particular structure and want to verify the existence of a single element within the list, there are normally two choices available to you. Either you write a function to work through the contents of the list looking for the object, or you use a superior data structure such as a dictionary to store the item and then use the object's built-in methods to determine whether the object is a member of your pseudo-list.

Within Python, you can use the **in** operator to determine whether a single object is a member of the list, returning 1 if the element is found, as in the following example:

```
>>> list = [1, 2, 3]
>>> 1 in list
1
>>> 4 in list
0
```

This process also works with strings:

```
>>> word = 'supercalifragilisticexpialidocious'
>>> 'x' in word
1
```

and tuples:

```
>>> days = ('Mon', 'Tue', 'Wed', 'Thu', 'Fri', 'Sat', 'Sun')
>>> 'Mon' in days
1
```

Iteration

You haven't yet learned about the loop operators supported by Python. Most of the usual operations of **while** and **for** are supported, and we can also iterate through the individual elements of a sequence. Again, Python uses the **in** operator, which this time returns each element of the sequence to each iteration of the loop:

```
for day in days:
    print day
```

You'll see more examples of this later in this chapter and throughout the rest of the book.

Dictionaries

A dictionary is an associative array; instead of using numbers to refer to individual elements of the list, you use other objects—generally strings. A dictionary element is split into two parts, the *key* and the *value*. You access the values from the dictionary by specifying the key.

Like other objects and constants, Python uses a strict format when creating dictionaries:

```
monthdays = {'Jan' : 31, 'Feb' : 28, 'Mar' : 31,
             'Apr' : 30, 'May' : 31, 'Jun' : 30,
             'Jul' : 31, 'Aug' : 31, 'Sep' : 30,
             'Oct' : 31, 'Nov' : 30, 'Dec' : 31}
```

You can also nest dictionaries, as in the following example:

```
albums = {'Flood' : {1:'Birdhouse in your Soul'}}
```

To access an entry you use the square brackets to define the index entry of the element you want to be returned, just as you do with strings or lists:

```
print 'January has',monthdays['Jan'],'days'
print 'First track is',albums['Flood'][1]
```

However, the interpreter raises an exception if the specified key cannot be found. See the section "Dictionary Methods" later in this chapter for details on the **get** and **has_key** methods. Again, just like lists, you can modify an existing key/value pair by redefining the entry in place:

```
monthdays['Feb'] = 29
```

If you had specified a different key, you would have added, rather than updated the entry. The following example

```
monthdays['feb'] = 29
```

introduces a thirteenth element to the dictionary.

You can delete entries in a dictionary using the **del** function:

```
del monthdays['Feb']
```

Dictionaries are not sequences, so concatenation and multiplication will not work—if you try them, both operations will raise an exception.

Using Dictionaries

Although dictionaries appear to work just like lists, the two are in fact very different. Dictionaries have no order—like lists, the indexes (keys) must be unique—but there is no logical order to the keys in the dictionary. This means that a dictionary is not a sequence; you cannot access the entries in a dictionary sequentially in the same way you can access entries in a string, list, or tuple. This also has the unpleasant side effect that when accessing the same dictionary at two separate times, the order in which the information is returned by the dictionary does not remain constant.

However, the dictionary object provides two methods, **keys** and **values**, that return a list of all the keys and values defined within the dictionary. For example, to get a list of months from the dictionary of months in the earlier example, use the following statement:

```
months = monthdays.keys()
```

The **months** object is now a list of the month strings that formed the keys of the **monthdays** dictionary.

The **len** function returns the number of elements, the key/value pairs, stored in a dictionary, such that the statement

```
len (monthdays)
```

returns the correct value of 12.

Dictionary Methods

Table 3-10 lists the full list of the methods supported by the dictionary object type.

Method	Description
has_key(x)	Returns true if the dictionary has the key **x**.
keys()	Returns a list of keys.
values()	Returns a list of values.
dict.items()	Returns a list of tuples; each tuple consists of a key and its corresponding value from the dictionary **dict**.
clear()	Removes all the items from the dictionary.
copy()	Returns a copy of the top level of the dictionary, but does not copy nested structures; only copies the references to those structures. See the section "Nesting Objects."
update(x)	Updates the contents of the dictionary with the key/value pairs from the dictionary **x**. Note that the dictionaries are merged, not concatenated, since you can't have duplicate keys in a dictionary.
get(x [, y])	Returns the key **x** or **None** if the key cannot be found, and can therefore be used in place of **dict[x]**. If **y** is supplied, this method returns that value if **x** is not found.

Table 3-10.   *Methods for Dictionaries*

Sorting Dictionaries

The **keys()** and **values()** methods to a dictionary object return a list of all the keys or values within the dictionary. This is useful when iterating over a dictionary or when using a dictionary for de-duplicating values. However, we cannot nest the **keys()** or **values()** and the corresponding list or tuple **sort()** methods into one call. To get a sorted list, it's a two-stage process:

```
months = monthdays.keys()
months.sort()
```

Many users try the following:

```
months = monthdays.keys().sort()
```

But that won't work. The reason is quite simple—the **sort** method modifies a list in place; it doesn't return the new list. Although the object generated by the **keys** method is sorted, the information is never returned and when the statement ends, the temporary sorted list object is destroyed, while **months** contains the special value **None**.

The problem with this method is not really apparent until you try to list the contents of a dictionary in an ordered fashion. You have to use the two-stage method shown in the first example of sorting a dictionary:

```
keys = monthdays.keys()
keys.sort()
for key in keys:
    ...
```

If you want to sort the list based on the values rather than on the keys, the process gets even more complicated. You can't access the information in a dictionary using values, only using the keys. What you need to do is sort a list of tuple pairs by supplying a custom comparison function to the **sort** method of a list.

You can get a list of tuple pairs using the **items** method. The process looks something like this:

```
monthdays = {'Jan' : 31, 'Feb' : 28, 'Mar' : 31,
             'Apr' : 30, 'May' : 31, 'Jun' : 30,
             'Jul' : 31, 'Aug' : 31, 'Sep' : 30,
             'Oct' : 31, 'Nov' : 30, 'Dec' : 31}
months = monthdays.items()
months.sort(lambda f, s: cmp(f[1], s[1]))
for month, days in months:
    print 'There are',days,'days in',month
```

We haven't covered many of the techniques used in the above example, but here's how it works. Line 5 in the preceding example gets a list of the key/value pairs as tuples. Line 6 sorts the list by comparing the value component of each tuple; the **lambda** is an anonymous function. (See Chapter 4 for more information on the **lambda** function and see Chapter 7 for an explanation of the custom element to the **sort** method.) Then the **for** loop extracts the month and number of days in each individual tuple from the list of tuples before printing each one.

When executed, the script output looks like this:

```
There are 28 days in Feb
There are 30 days in Jun
There are 30 days in Nov
There are 30 days in Apr
There are 30 days in Sep
There are 31 days in Aug
There are 31 days in May
There are 31 days in Oct
There are 31 days in Jul
There are 31 days in Jan
There are 31 days in Dec
There are 31 days in Mar
```

Dictionaries are one of the most useful storage elements because they enable you to access information using anything as a key—Python allows you to use any object as a key to the key/value pair. Chapter 10 takes a closer look at dictionaries in Python.

Files

Python's access to files is built into Python in the same way as the other object types you've already seen. You create a file object by using the built-in **open** function, and then you use methods on the new object to read and write information to and from the file. This eliminates a lot of the complexity of the file handle model used by C, Perl, and VB; instead, you get a consistent interface to what is essentially just another form of storage available on your machine.

We won't look at the specifics of using files for the moment; we'll leave that to Chapter 11 when you'll learn how to use Python for processing and managing files. However, to get a taste, look at the following script that opens and reads each line from the file **myfile.txt** before displaying the lines to the screen:

```
input = open('myfile.txt')
for line in input.readlines():
    print line
input.close()
```

Object Storage

Although Python always creates objects when you create a variable, it's important to understand the association between the name, the object, and the variable. At the risk of sounding like a stuck record, we'll reiterate again the statement we made at the beginning of this chapter: Python stores information as objects. In truth, Python actually stores references or pointers to the internal structures used to store the information for a specific object type. This is the equivalent of the C pointer or the Perl reference—a Python object is merely the address of a structure stored in memory.

With C, to introduce a special variable into your application you have to use either a pointer to a structure or predefine a structure before you use the data type. Using pointers, while practical at a system level, is difficult and adds extra layers of complexity that you don't need. In addition, the programmer needs to be aware that the variable they're dealing with is a pointer and therefore requires special treatment.

With Perl, the programmer has to make a conscious effort to use a reference as a specific data type. You must dereference a Perl reference before you can access the information. If you don't dereference or you dereference to the wrong type (i.e., try to access a hash as a scalar), you get either the physical address of the variable or an error during compilation. This problem is easy to spot, but it adds extra complication to the programming process that frankly you could do without.

Unlike Perl and C however, the Python programmer never needs to be aware of the fact that the pointers exist. When you access an object, you are accessing the information stored in it, irrespective of how the object is defined or where or how the object information is actually stored.

Objects, Names, and Variables

The Python *name* is the alphanumeric name given to the pointer that points to the object. Note the following example:

```
greeting = 'Hello World'
```

In the preceding statement, the name is **greeting**. The object has no identifiable name; it's just an allocated patch of memory which is pointed to by **greeting**. But the object's type is a string. The combination of the two can be thought of as a typical *variable*.

The significance of the pointer is important. Consider what happens when you reassign the "value" of the variable:

```
greeting = ['Hello', 'World']
```

The name has remained the same, but the object to which it points is in a different physical location within memory, and is of a completely different type.

Variable Name Rules

Python follows some very basic rules for naming variables:

- Variables must begin with an underscore or a letter, and they may contain any combination of letters, digits, or underscores. You cannot use any other punctuation characters.

- Variables are case sensitive—**string** and **String** are two different variable names.

- Reserved words cannot be superceded by variables. The full list of reserved words is as follows:

and	assert	break	class	continue
def	del	elif	else	except
exec	finally	for	from	global
if	import	in	is	lambda
not	or	pass	print	raise
return	try	while		

Because Python is case sensitive, there is no reason why you cannot have variables called **Return** and **RETURN**, although it's probably a bad idea.

Python Copies References, Not Data

When you refer to a Python object by name when assigning information to an object, Python stores the reference, not the data. For example, the following code appears to create two objects:

```
objecta = [1,2,3]
objectb = objecta
```

In fact, you have only created one object but you have created two names (pointers) to that object, as demonstrated by trying the statements interactively:

```
>>> objecta = [1,2,3]
>>> objectb = objecta
>>> objecta[1] = 4
>>> print objectb
[1, 4, 3]
```

To create a copy of an object, you must force Python to explicitly assign either the value of the object or you can use one of the type converters described shortly. The former method is often the easiest with lists and tuples:

```
objectb = objecta[:]
```

The effects of copying the pointer to the object rather than copying the contents of the object pose some interesting possibilities. Most useful of all is the fact that because this is Python's normal behavior, building complex structures becomes a natural rather than a forced process. For example, you can use objects to specify the keys used for dictionaries. You can build a list of tables for your **contacts** database like this:

```
tables = {contacts : 'A list of contacts',
          addresses : 'The address list'}
```

It doesn't matter if the contents of **contacts** change because the key specified in the **tables** dictionary is just a pointer to the **contacts** object; it's not a copy of the **contacts** dictionary.

Nesting

Because Python copies object pointers, you can use objects anywhere; you are not limited to the normal boundaries and restrictions placed on variables in other languages. For example, you have already seen that a list can contain a mixture of strings and numbers and even other lists. For example, the following structure describes a list of contacts using a combination of lists and dictionaries to describe the information:

```
contacts = [{'Name' : 'Martin',
             'Email' : 'mc@mcwords.com'},
            {'Name' : 'Bob',
             'Email' : 'bob@bob.com'}]
```

Part 3 of this book contains more examples of nesting as you start to learn in more detail how you can use Python to solve specific problems.

Type Conversion

Beyond the methods and operators already discussed for the individual object types, there are a number of built-in functions that can convert data from one type to another. Table 3-11 contains the full list of such functions.

There is also a special operator supported by Python that works in the same way as the **str()** built-in function. The ` (back ticks) operator evaluates the enclosed statement and then returns a string representation, as in the following example:

```
>>> print `(34*56.0)`
1904
>>> album = ('TMBG', 'Flood', 'Theme from Flood', 'Birdhouse in your Soul')
>>> album
('TMBG', 'Flood', 'Theme from Flood', 'Birdhouse in your Soul')
>>> `album[:2]`
```

```
"('TMBG', 'Flood')"
>>> str(album[:2])
"('TMBG', 'Flood')"
>>> `list(album)`
"['TMBG', 'Flood', 'Theme from Flood', 'Birdhouse in your Soul']"
```

Note that the format used by both **str** and `` ` `` when returning the information is the same as would be required to build the object. Therefore, to display the Python statements required to build the earlier album list, use the following statements:

```
contacts = [{'Name' : 'Martin',
            'Email' : 'mc@mcwords.com'},
           {'Name' : 'Bob',
            'Email' : 'bob@bob.com'}]
>>> >>> `contacts`
"[{'Email': 'mc@mcwords.com', 'Name': 'Martin'}, {'Email': 'bob@bob.com',
'Name': 'Bob'}]"
```

Function	Description
str(x)	Translates the object **x** into a string.
list(x)	Returns the sequence object **x** as a list. For example, the string "hello" is returned as **['h', 'e', 'l', 'l', 'o']**. Converts tuples and lists to lists.
tuple(x)	Returns the sequence object **x** as a tuple.
int(x)	Converts a string or number to an integer. Note that floating-point numbers are truncated, not rounded; **int(3.6)** becomes 3.
long(x)	Converts a string or number to a long integer. Conversion as for **int**.
float(x)	Converts a string or number to a floating-point object.
complex(x,y)	Creates a complex number with real part of **x** and imaginary part of **y**.
hex(x)	Converts an integer or long to a hexadecimal string.
oct(x)	Converts an integer or long to an octal string.
ord(x)	Returns the ASCII value for the character **x**.
chr(x)	Returns the character (as a string) for the ASCII code **x**.
min(x [, ...])	Returns the smallest element of a sequence.
max(x [, ...])	Returns the largest element of a sequence.

Table 3-11. *Built-in Type Conversions*

Type Comparisons

When you compare two objects within Python, the interpreter compares the values of
both objects before returning the result of the comparison. This means that when you
compare two lists, the contents of both lists are examined to determine whether they
are identical. The same is true of all other object tests—the interpreter checks the
contents of each data structure when making the comparison.

Table 3-12 lists the supported operators for type comparisons.

There are some special cases shown in Table 3-12. If you create two identical lists
and compare their values, you should get a return value of 1, to indicate that the two
lists are of equal value:

```
>>> lista = [1, 2, 3]
>>> listb = [1, 2, 3]
>>> lista == list
1
```

Note as well that the order as well as the values is important:

```
>>> listb = [2, 3, 1]
>>> lista == listb
0
```

Operator	Description
x < y	Less than.
x <= y	Less than or equal to.
x > y	Greater than.
x >= y	Greater than or equal to.
x == y	Have equal value.
x != y, x <> y	Do not have equal value.
x is y	Pointers to same object.
x is not y	Different objects.
not y	Inverse—returns true if x is false/false if x is true.
x or y	Returns x if x is true, or y if x is false.
x and y	Returns x if x is false, or y if x is true.
x < y < z	Chained comparisons; returns true only if all operators return true.

Table 3-12.   *Comparison Operators*

To compare whether the two objects are identical, e.g., that they both point to the same physical object, you need to compare the two objects using the **is** operator:

```
>>> lista is listb
0
```

You need to use the **is** operator because there are two separate objects. Copying the object reference from **lista** to **listb** however

```
>>> listb = lista
>>> lista is listb
1
```

gives us the result you expect.

The **is** operator is useful when you want to check the source and validity of a object against a source or control object.

Python makes its comparisons using the following rules:

- Numbers are compared by magnitude.

- Strings are compared character by character.

- Lists and tuples are compared by element, from the lowest to highest index.

- Dictionaries are compared by comparing sorted key/value pairs.

All comparisons within Python return 1 if the result is true, or 0 if the comparison fails. In addition, Python treats any non-zero value as true, including a string. The only exceptions to this rule are **None**, which is false, and any empty object (list, tuple, or sequence). Table 3-13 contains a summary of the different true/false values.

Object/Constant	Value
''	False
'string'	True
0	False
>1	True
<-1	True
() (empty tuple)	False
[] (empty list)	False
{} (empty dictionary)	False
None	False

Table 3-13.   *True/False Values of Objects and Constants*

Statements

The statement is the most basic form of executable element within a Python program. A variable on its own does nothing—it must be part of a statement in order to be created, modified, and manipulated. There are a number of generic statement types that you'll learn about in this section, including basic statements, assignments, function calls, and the control and loop statements.

Statement Format

Python uses a very simple method for parsing the individual statements that make up a typical program. Within Python, each line is identified as a single statement; the normal line termination of a carriage-return or linefeed acts as the statement terminator. For example, the following two-line program is valid:

```
print "Hello World!"
print "I am a test program"
```

For extra long lines, such as the following line, you have a number of options, depending on the line contents:

```
print "Hello, I am a test program and I am printing an extra long
line so I can demonstrate how to split me up"
```

For most lines, the easier method is to append a backslash to the end of the line where you want to split it, as in the following example:

```
print "Hello, I am a test program and I am printing an extra \
long line so I can demonstrate how to split me up"
```

When the Python interpreter sees the backslash as the last character in a line it automatically appends the next line before the entire line is parsed. This process is cyclic, so a line can span as many lines as you like, providing that each line ends in a backslash:

```
print "Hello, I am a test program \
and I am printing an extra \
long line so I can demonstrate \
how to split me up"
```

For statements that incorporate a pair of matching parentheses, you do not have to use the backslash technique. Python automatically searches the next line looking for the terminating parenthesis. You can modify your **print** statement in the preceding example to print a tuple of the message, which requires parentheses and therefore implies a termination character:

```
print ("Hello, I am a test program ",
"and I am printing an extra ",
"long line so I can demonstrate ",
"how to split me up")
```

Finally, there are situations where without either the backslash or parentheses, Python automatically expects further information and therefore examines the next line.

For C and Perl programmers, Python also accepts the semicolon as a line terminator if it makes you feel more comfortable. However, the use of a semicolon is completely optional and using one has no effect on how Python parses lines—you must continue to use one of the tricks described earlier whether you use semicolons or not.

Comments

Python allows you to incorporate comments by inserting the hash symbol (#) into code as in the following example:

```
version = 1.0 # This is the current version number
```

Everything after the hash sign is taken to be a comment and is ignored by the Python interpreter. Note that this does affect hash signs embedded within quotes, as you might expect.

Assignments

The assignment is the most basic statement in Python, assigning data and an object type to a variable name. You have already seen a number of different examples of this when you learned about the different Python object types. Unlike C, but like Perl (in non-strict mode), you do not need to predeclare Python variables before you assign them a value. However, variables must exist when used within an expression or other form of statement.

There are four basic methods of assignments: basic assignments, tuple assignment, list assignment, and multiple-target assignment.

Basic Assignments

The basic assignment is the one you have seen most examples of in this chapter. A basic assignment creates a new object using the correct type according to the value assigned to the object, and then points the specified name to the new object, as in the following examples:

```
number = 45
message = 'Hello World'
mylist = ['I Palindrome I', 'Mammal']
mytuple = ('Mon', 'Tue', 'Wed', 'Thu', 'Fri')
mydict = {'Twisting':Flood, 'Mammal':'Apollo 18'}
```

Tuple and List Assignments

You can extract the individual elements from a tuple or list using a different operator of assignment. For tuples, you can just specify the list of variables to assign to, each separated by a comma:

```
title, name = 'Mr', 'Martin'
album = ('TMBG', 'Flood', 'Theme from Flood', 'Birdhouse in your Soul')
artist, title = album[0:2]
track1, track2 = album[-2:]
```

What you're in fact doing in the preceding statements is creating a new tuple on the left-hand side of the assignment operator. However, the tuple with the variable names is anonymous and the information about the entire tuple is not recorded. Because you don't have to use parentheses to indicate a tuple, the assignment looks more natural, although you could have written them as:

```
album = ('TMBG', 'Flood', 'Theme from Flood', 'Birdhouse in your
Soul')
(artist, title) = album[0:2]
(track1, track2) = album[-2:]
```

What you end up with in each case is a new variable pointing to the information on the right-hand side. Note as well that you can also use slices and indexes to extract multiple elements from a tuple.

For lists, you must create a new, anonymous list in the same way that you create an anonymous tuple:

```
album = ['TMBG', 'Lincoln', 'Ana Ng', 'Cowtown']
[artist, title] = album[0:2]
```

The tuple and list assignments have another trick up their sleeve. Because names are merely pointers, you can "swap" two object/name combinations by performing a tuple or list assignment as follows:

```
artist, title = title, artist
```

You can see this better in the following interactive session:

```
>>> title = 'Flood'
>>> artist = 'TMBG'
>>> artist, title = title, artist
>>> artist, title
('Flood', 'TMBG')
```

Multiple-Target Assignments

You can create a single object with multiple pointers using the multiple-target assignment statement:

```
group = title = 'They Might Be Giants'
```

In the preceding statement, you created a single string object with two different pointers called **group** and **title**. Remember that because the two pointers point at the same object, modifying the object contents using one name also modifies the information available via the other name. This is effectively the same as:

```
group = 'They Might Be Giants'
title = group
```

Print

Unlike other languages, the default method for communicating with the user is via a statement rather than via a function. The statement has the same basic name, **print**, but is embedded into the interpreter. Unlike similar **print** functions however, the Python **print** statement actually outputs string representations of the supplied objects to the standard output of the interpreter. The destination is the same as the C **stdout** or Perl **STDOUT** file handles, and cannot normally be pointed elsewhere.

Actually, you can redirect the standard output by modifying the object used to point to the standard output device. It should be no surprise that Python uses objects to communicate with the outside world. The following code demonstrates this point:

```
import sys
fp = open( 'somefile.txt', 'w' )
sys.stdout = fp
print 'this goes in the file, not on your stdout'
```

*This works because instead of pointing the standard output to its originial location, you copy the object data for the new **fp** object instead. The **stdout** object, which is used by the **print** function, now sends all of its output to the file **somefile.txt**.*

When printing, the statement follows these basic rules:

- Objects and constants separated by commas are separated by spaces when printed. Use string concatenation or the % formatting operator to avoid this.

- A linefeed is appended to every output line. To avoid this, append a comma to the end of the line.

For example, the following script, when executed, displays the different forms supported:

```
print 'Hello','World'
print 'This is a' + ' concatenated', string
print 'The first line',
print 'Plus some continuation'
print 'I ordered %d dozen %s today' % (6, 'eggs')
contacts = [{'Name' : 'Martin',
             'Email' : 'mc@mcwords.com'},
            {'Name' : 'Bob',
             'Email' : 'bob@bob.com'}]
print contacts
```

The preceding script produces the following output:

```
Hello World
This is a concatenated string
The first line Plus some continuation
I ordered 6 dozen eggs today
[{'Email': 'mc@mcwords.com', 'Name': 'Martin'}, {'Email': 'bob@bob.com',
'Name': 'Bob'}]
```

Note how in the last line, **print** displays the complex object in the same format as **str** and the `` operator.

The ability to print out the contents of an object in this way is extremely useful, both as a programming tool and for debugging. For example, you can store the configuration parameters for an application in one or more variables. When you want to save the information, just use **print** or the **str** function to write out the statements. To get the information back, all you need do is import the file contents in the same way that you would with any other module.

Control Statements

Python processes program statements in sequence until the program states otherwise through the use of a control statement or a function call. Python supports three different control statements, **if**, **for**, and **while**. The **if** statement is the most basic control statement; it selects a statement block to execute based on the result of one or more expressions. Both **for** and **while** are loop statements.

if

The **if** statement accepts an expression and then executes the specified statements if the statement returned true. The general format for the **if** statement is:

```
if EXPRESSION:
    BLOCK
elif EXPRESSION2:
    BLOCK2
else:
    BLOCK3
```

The **EXPRESSION** is the test you want to perform (see Table 3-12); a result of true means that the statements in **BLOCK** are being executed. The optional **elif** statement performs further tests when **EXPRESSION** fails, executing **BLOCK2** if **EXPRESSION2** returns true or executing **BLOCK3** otherwise. You can have multiple **elif** statements within a single **if** statement. If no expressions match, then the optional block to the **else** statement is executed.

Note that in each case, the preceding line to the statement block ends with a colon. This indicates to Python that a new statement block should be expected. Unlike many other languages, Python is a little more relaxed about its definitions of the code block. Both C and Perl use curly brackets (or braces) to define the start and end of a block. Python uses indentation—any lines after the colon must be indented (to the same level) if you want them to be in the same logical code block.

You can see how the indentation and blocks work by looking at Figure 3-2. Notice in this figure that Block 1 continues after the indentations for Block 2 and Block 3 no longer exist. See the rest of the script for details on the block definitions and indentation.

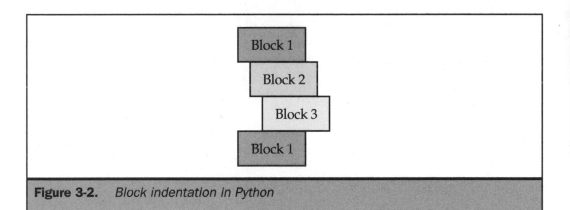

Figure 3-2.   *Block indentation in Python*

Consider the following example combining **if** and **elif** statements:

```
if (result == 1):
    print 'Got a one'
elsif (result >1):
    print 'Got more than one'
else:
    print 'Got something else'
```

For simple tests, you can combine the statement and block onto a single line:

```
if (1): print 'Hello World'
```

This really only works for single-line blocks.

Note   *If you want to perform a **switch** or **case** statement in Python, you must use an **if** statement with multiple **elif** expressions.*

while

The **while** loop accepts a single expression and the loop continues to iterate as long as the test continues to return true. The expression is reevaluated before each iteration. The basic format is therefore:

```
while EXPRESSION:
    BLOCK
else:
    BLOCK
```

For example, to work through the characters in a string, you might use

```
string = 'I Palindrome I'
while(len(string)):
    char = string[0]
    string = string[1:]
    print 'Give me a',char
```

which outputs

```
Give me a I
Give me a

...

Give me a
Give me a I
```

Note that in this particular example, it's probably easier to use a **for** loop.

The optional **else** block is only executed if the loop exits when **EXPRESSION** returns false, rather than the execution being broken by the **break** statement. See the example of a **for** loop in the next subsection.

for

The **for** loop is identical to the list form of the **for** loop in Perl. The basic format for the **for** loop is:

```
for TARGET in OBJECT:
    BLOCK
else:
    BLOCK
```

You specify the object to be used as the iterator within the loop and then supply any form of sequence object to iterate through. For example:

```
for number in [1,2,3,4,5,6,7,8,9]:
    print 'I can count to',number
```

For each iteration of the loop, **number** is set to the next value within the array producing the output

```
I can count to 1
I can count to 2
...
I can count to 8
I can count to 9
```

Because it works with any sequence, you can also work through strings as in

```
for letter in 'Martin':
    print 'Give me a', letter
```

which generates

```
Give me a M
Give me a a
Give me a r
Give me a t
Give me a i
Give me a n
```

In addition, just like the **while** loop, the **else** statement block is executed when the loop exits normally as in

```
for number in [1,3,5,7]:
    if number > 8:
        print "I Can't work with numbers that are higher than 8!"
        break
    print '%d squared is %d' % (number, pow(number,2))
else:
    print 'Made it!'
```

which outputs

```
1 squared is 1
3 squared is 9
5 squared is 25
7 squared is 49
Made it!
```

Ranges

Because the **for** loop does not support the loop counter format offered by Perl and C, you need to use a different method to iterate through a numerical range. There are two possible methods. Either use the **while** loop:

```
while(x <10):
    print x
    x = x+1
```

Alternatively, you can use the **range** function to generate a list of values:

```
for x in range(10):
...
```

The **range** function returns a list. The basic format of the **range** function is

```
range([start, ] stop [, step])
```

In its single-argument form, **range** returns a list consisting of each number up to, but not including, the number supplied:

```
>>> range(10)
[0, 1, 2, 3, 4, 5, 6, 7, 8, 9]
```

If the **range** function is supplied two arguments, it returns a list of numbers starting at the first argument, up to but not including the last argument:

```
>>> range(4,9)
[4, 5, 6, 7, 8]
```

The final form, with three arguments, allows you to define the intervening step:

```
>>> range(0,10,2)
[0, 2, 4, 6, 8]
```

Because the **range** function returns a list, it can create, for very large ranges, very large lists that require vast amounts of memory to store. To get around this, use the **xrange** function. The **xrange** function has the exactly format and indeed, performs exactly the same function as **range**, but it does not create an intervening list and therefore requires less memory for very large ranges. On the other hand, it produces a very large list that results in a processing overhead as new objects are created and added to the list structure.

Loop Control Statements

Python supports three loop control statements that modify the normal execution of a loop. They are **break**, **continue** and **pass**.

The **break** statement exits the current loop, ignoring any **else** statement, continuing execution after the last line in the loop's statement block.

The **continue** statement immediately forces the loop to proceed to the next iteration, ignoring any remaining statements in the current block. The loop statement expression is reevaluated. The example

```
x=20
while (x):
    x = x-1
    if not x % 3: continue
    print x,'is not a multiple of 3'
```

generates the following output:

```
19 is not a multiple of 3
17 is not a multiple of 3
16 is not a multiple of 3
...
4 is not a multiple of 3
2 is not a multiple of 3
1 is not a multiple of 3
```

The **pass** statement is effectively a no-op—it does nothing. The statement

```
if (1): pass
```

does nothing at all.

Although it may seem pointless, there are times when you want to be able to identify a specific event, but ignore it. This is especially true of exceptions, the Python error-handling system. You'll see **pass** and exceptions in action in Chapter 5.

Common Traps

For the programmer migrating to Python, there are a number of common traps that trick the unwary. Most relate to the very minor differences between Python and other languages, particularly if you have been used to Perl or Shellscript.

Variable Names

Variables within Python follow these basic rules and differences from other languages:

- You do not need to predeclare variables before they are used; Python sets the object type based on the value it is assigned.
- Variables are given simple alphanumeric names.
- Variables do not require qualification using special characters.
- Some variables have embedded methods that operate on the object's contents.

Blocks and Indentation

Blocks start after a colon on the preceding line. For example:

```
if (1):
    print 'I am a new block'
```

The block continues until a new block is created, or until the indentation for the block ends.

When indenting, use either tabs or spaces—do not mix the two because this is likely to confuse the Python interpreter and people maintaining the code.

Method Calls

The most common error with a method call to an object is to assume that the call returns information. The statement

```
sorted = list.sort()
```

sorts the object **list**, but sets the value of **sorted** to the special **None**.

The
Complete
Reference

Python

Chapter 4

Functions

One of the fundamentals of any programming language is that there are often repeated elements in your programs. You can cut and paste code from one section to another, but this is messy. What happens when you need to update that particular part of the program? You'd have to modify each duplicated section individually. For very small programs this is unlikely to generate any significant overhead, but as the size and complexity of the program increases, so does the time required to modify and update essentially the same piece of code over and over.

Duplication also runs the risk of introducing additional syntactic, logical, and typographical errors. Imagine duplicating a sequence that contained a simple typing mistake—you would have to trace every single instance to isolate the problem! This is where *functions* solve all your problems. By placing the repeated code into a function, you isolate that code sequence and provide easier access to improve the code or isolate bugs.

This method of taking repeated pieces of code and placing them into a function is called *abstraction*. In general, a certain level of abstraction is always useful—it speeds up the programming process, reduces the risk of introducing errors, and makes a complex program easier to maintain. For the space-conscious programmer, using functions also reduces the number of lines in your code and the overall memory footprint of the program during execution.

You already know that Python has three basic levels of abstraction:

1. A program can be split into multiple modules.

2. Each module contains multiple statements.

3. Each statement operates on objects.

Functions sit around stage 2—they provide a way of collating repeated sequences of statements into one place.

Python also provides one of the best systems for code reuse. Once you have written a Python function, it is immediately available to any other program just by importing the function from the source file. There is no need to create a special library and header file, as you need to in C/C++, nor do you need to create a special "module" as you do in Perl. With Python, code reuse is as simple as knowing which file the function is stored in.

Beyond the normal features offered by other languages for implementing functions, Python allows a greater level of control and integration over the arguments that you supply to the function and how they are treated. You also have complete flexibility over the values you return to the caller—you are not restricted as you are with C or C++ to a specific data type.

With Python, functions form the basis of *methods*, the functions that operate and perform specific actions on objects and object classes. The creation of object classes and the use of modules for code reuse are covered in Chapters 5 and 6. For the moment, we'll concentrate on the basic mechanics of functions and how they can be employed within a single Python module file.

Function Definition and Execution

The general format for creating a new function is as follows:

```
def NAME(ARG1 [, ...]):
    STATEMENT BLOCK
    [return VALUE]
```

The **NAME** should follow the same rules as object names:

- Functions must begin with an underscore or letter and may contain any combination of letters, digits, or underscores. You cannot use any other punctuation characters.

- Functions are case sensitive—**combine** and **Combine** are two different function names. However, you should avoid creating functions of the same name but different case.

- You cannot use a reserved word for a function name, but remember the case-sensitive rule above.

When you define the function, you must include the parentheses, even if you are not accepting any arguments to the function. If you are accepting arguments to the function, the arguments must be named within the parentheses, although the way they are named is slightly different from other languages. We'll look at the specifics of argument passing shortly.

As with control statements, the statement block for the function must be preceded by a colon. The closing **return** statement is optional; if you don't use it, the function returns to the caller without returning a value. A Python function without a **return** statement always returns the special value **None**.

The following example is a simple function that calculates the area of a circle based on the radius supplied:

```
def area(radius):
    area = 3.141*(pow(radius,2))
    return area
```

Note   *The value of π given in the preceding example is an approximation. A better value can be found in the Python **math** library as **pi**.*

To use the **area** function, just call it with an argument:

```
print area(2)
```

which returns 12.564. Note the precision in the result is identical to the precision you use for the value of π. If you supply a value with a higher decimal precision, the return value is also of a higher precision. The statement

```
print area(3.141592654)
```

which returns 31.0004274319.

When calling a function, make sure that you include the parentheses; Python does not allow function calls of the form

```
area 2
```

This is a common error of Perl programmers who often leave out the parentheses to make a program more readable. This is further complicated by the fact that **print** is a statement rather than a function, so you can call **print** without using parentheses. If you do use parentheses, **print** outputs a tuple!

Finally, unlike other languages, functions within Python can be defined on the fly—you can create a function anywhere within the normal execution of a program. The following code is perfectly valid:

```
if (message):
    def function():
        print "Hello!\n";
else:
    def function():
        print "Goodbye!\n";
```

and opens up all sorts of possibilities, especially when it comes to the development of objects and methods.

The scoping, argument definition, return values, and the methods for calling functions all have extended feature sets within the Python language so let's look at each feature individually.

Scoping

Python uses the concept of *namespaces* in order to store information about objects and their location within an application. Namespaces are specific to a particular level of abstraction—there are individual namespaces for functions and modules, and there's a special namespace for the built-in functions, statements, and objects. At each level, when you access an object or function, Python searches the namespace tables looking for the specified name so it can look up the reference and decide what to do with the information stored at that location. Scoping within Python follows these basic rules:

1. Each module has its own scope. This means that multiple modules have their own scope, and therefore their own namespaces. Chapter 5 discusses this in more detail.

2. The enclosing module for a function is called the *global scope*. This is the location of objects created at the top level of a module file.

3. New function definitions create new scopes; the scopes are unique to the function.

4. New objects are assigned to the local scope unless declared otherwise. Any variable or function that is defined will be a member of the local scope unless you declare it global with the **global** keyword.

5. Arguments to a function are defined within the local function scope.

The scoping rules mean that objects created within a function do not interfere with identically named objects in the module (global) or built-in namespaces. Our **area** function is a good example:

```
def area(radius):
    area = 3.141*(pow(radius,2))
    return area
```

The **area** *function* is global, because it's defined within the top-level of the module. The **area** *variable* is defined within the local scope of the **area** *function*. This means that although they have the same name, they do not interfere with each other. If you want to create a recursive function, you obviously have to use a different name for the variable, since Python would see the **area** variable before it identified the function and would therefore raise an exception. (See Chapter 7 for a detail discussion of exceptions.)

Making Objects Global

There are occasions when you want to assign the value of a variable within a function, but you have it modify the global variable instead of creating a new one. The traditional method for this is to predeclare the variable before the function is called:

```
name = 'Unknown'
def set_defaults():
    name = 'Martin'
set_defaults()
print name
```

However, in Python this doesn't work because the moment you assign the **name** variable within the function, Python creates a new variable within the local scope. To get around this, you need to use the **global** keyword to define which variables you want to use in this way. The **global** keyword tells Python to create a local alias to the global variable. For example, if you modify the preceding script:

```
name = 'Unknown'
def set_defaults():
    global name
    name = 'Martin'
set_defaults()
print name
```

This function does what you expect; it prints the name "Martin."

The **global** keyword also creates objects within the global namespace if they don't already exist, as in the following example:

```
def set_defaults():
    global name,address
    name = 'Martin'
    address = 'mc@mcwords.com'
set_defaults()
print "Name:",name,"Address:",address
```

The preceding fragment, when executed, produces

```
Name: Martin Address: mc@mcwords.com
```

The LGB Rule

The LGB rule is a simple way for remembering how Python looks up names within the scope of

- Name references search the three scopes in order: local, then global, then built-in (LGB).

- Name assignments create new objects or update objects in the local scope. Thus if you want to assign to global objects within a local scope, you must use the **global** keyword.

- Global declarations map assigned names to the scope of the enclosing module. This means you must either explicitly import objects from imported modules or use the fully qualified module/object name.

The last entry in this list will not make sense until you learn about the mechanics of modules in Chapter 5, but be aware that so-called global definitions are only global to the current module.

Consider the following code fragment:

```
radius = 2
pi = 3.141592654
def area(radius):
    area = pi *(pow(radius,2))
    return area

print area(4)
```

In this example, you've defined two global variables, **radius** and **pi**. The **area** function looks for the name **radius** when it is executed and finds it locally, ignoring the global variable. The **pi** variable cannot be found locally, so Python looks globally and finds the variable there.

You can see a layout more clearly in Figure 4-1.

Caution *The more observant reader will have noticed that the LGB rule also means that local variables can override global variables and that both local and global variables can override the built-in variables. For example, a local variable can be called* **open***, but using this would make it impossible to call the function* **open** *within the same scope unless it was explicitly identified. It's therefore a bad idea to use locals with the same name as globals or built-ins.*

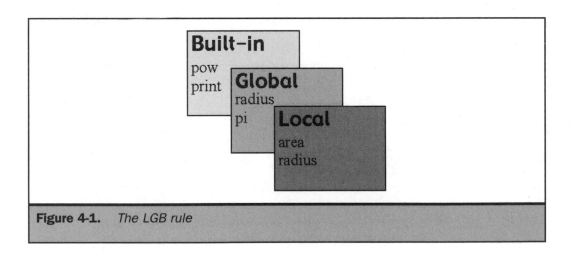

Figure 4-1.   *The LGB rule*

Scope Traps

There is one significant trap that catches many people off guard. The name-resolving process only searches the three abstraction layers—local, global and built-in (see the earlier section "The LGB Rule"). It's possible in Python to define functions within other functions. This can often be useful when you want to create a group of functions that are not publicly available to the outside world. The problem is that the scoping rules still apply. Consider the following example:

```
def funca():
    value = 59
    funcb()
    def funcb():
        print (value*2)
```

The preceding code will fail because **funcb** is trying to access the variable **value**. However, **value** does not exist within either the local, global, or built-in scope—and it fails the LGB rule. Functions do not automatically inherit the scope of the parent, nor does the Python namespace manager search the parent scope of a function.

The way to get around this is to make **value** an argument to the embedded function:

```
def funca():
    value = 59
    funcb()
    def funcb(value):
        print (value*2)
```

You can use the same name because **value** will still be local to the **funcb** scope and so it still works with the LBG rule.

Arguments

The arguments specified in a function definition are taken in the order in which they are defined, for example:

```
def message(to, text):
    print "This is a message for",to,":\n",text
message('Martin','Your dinner is ready!')
```

Arguments are passed to the function by assignment; the normal rules of assignment apply to the arguments contained in a function definition. The argument-passing process therefore follows these rules:

1. Arguments are copied by reference into locally scoped objects. This means that the variables used to access function arguments are not related to the objects supplied to the function. This also means that changing a local object does not modify the original argument.
2. Mutable objects can be changed in place. When you copy a list or dictionary, you copy a list of object references. If you change the value of a reference, you modify the original argument.

The first rule means that you can safely use the local versions of an object without worrying about modifying the original. For example, the code

```
def modifier(number, string, list):
    number = 5
    string = 'Goodbye'
    list = [4,5,6]
    print "Inside:", number, string, list

number = 1
string = 'Hello'
list = [1,2,3]

print "Before:", number, string, list
modifier(number,string,list)
print "After:", number, string, list
```

generates the following output:

```
Before: 1 Hello [1, 2, 3]
Inside: 5 Goodbye [4, 5, 6]
After: 1 Hello [1, 2, 3]
```

The local versions of **number, string**, and **list** have been modified, but the original versions still retain their original values.

The second rule says that any mutable object can be modified in place. This allows us to change the information pointed to by a specific element of a mutable list or dictionary. Consider the following example:

```
def modifier(list):
    list[0:3] = [4,5,6]
    print "Inside:", list
```

```
list = [1,2,3]

print "Before:", list
modifier(list)
print "After:", list
```

This code generates the following output when executed:

```
Before: [1, 2, 3]
Inside: [4, 5, 6]
After: [4, 5, 6]
```

To copy the list or dictionary object instead of copying its reference, you must explicitly do a copy. The next example inserts the following line as the first line in the **modifier** function:

```
list = list[:]
```

Executing the script, you get

```
Before: [1, 2, 3]
Inside: [4, 5, 6]
After: [1, 2, 3]
```

Arguments Are Objects

Although this may seem obvious now, arguments are just names for objects—the underlying type of the object in question remains the same. Also, because an argument is just a pointer, the type of the object passed does not need to be defined. The example

```
def multiply(x,y):
    return x * y
```

when run on numerical objects, returns a number:

```
>>> multiply(2,3)
6
```

Or it could return a string:

```
>>> multiply('Ha',5)
'HaHaHaHaHa'
```

Or it could return a list:

```
>>> multiply([1,2,3],5)
[1, 2, 3, 1, 2, 3, 1, 2, 3, 1, 2, 3, 1, 2, 3]
```

However, be aware that object types that are not number sequences will raise an exception, because the types are incompatible (see Chapter 7 on exceptions). By using objects rather than strict variable types, you can create individual functions that appear to do a number of different things just by accepting different types of objects as arguments.

Argument Calling by Keywords

Beyond the normal sequence of argument calling, where each argument is assigned in order to the function's argument definition, Python also supports a number of other function/argument-calling formats. The problem with the traditional sequence assignment is that it is limited to accepting a specific number of arguments in a specific sequence. For readability, this technique is not always practical, and it's useful to have some flexibility when supplying information to a function if it can be made to do a number of different things other than the traditional single-purpose function supported by C, C++, or Visual Basic.

The most basic extension beyond sequence assignment is the ability to specify arguments by keyword assignment. For example, you could have called the **multiply** function like this:

```
multiply(x=5,y=10)
```

In this case, the order of the arguments is not important so you can also do this:

```
multiply(y=10,x=5)
```

Default Arguments

Within the function definition, Python allows you to specify the default values for each argument. Normally, you must supply the same number of arguments as defined by the function definition. Using defaults, you can call a function and omit arguments and the function will still execute. The format for defining default values is

```
def function(ARG=VALUE)
```

where **VALUE** is the default to be applied to the argument if it is not supplied.

For example, let's create a function that calculates the volume of a cone. The function definition looks like this:

```
def cone_volume(height,radius=1,pi=3.141592654):
    cone = (1.0)/(3.0)*height*pi*pow(radius,2)
    return cone
```

Now you can call this function in any of the following ways:

```
cone_volume(4,3,(22.0/7.0))
cone_volume(4,3)
cone_volume(4)
cone_volume(radius=3, height=4)
cone_volume(pi = (22.0/7.0),
            radius=4,
            height=4)
```

Note that you cannot omit the **height** value—that argument does not have a default value and consequently, Python treats it as a required value.

Also note that default values should ideally be the last arguments in the definition, although the following definition will work:

```
def cone_volume(radius=1,pi=3.141592654,height):
```

If you call the function with only one argument, the compiler will raise an exception because Python cannot decide to which argument the supplied value should be applied:

```
>>> cone_volume(4)
Traceback (innermost last):
  File "<stdin>", line 1, in ?
  File "<stdin>", line 2, in cone_volume
TypeError: number coercion failed
```

Note *You get a **TypeError** exception here because the **height** argument is passed a value of **None**. This is implied because you haven't supplied enough values. When Python attempts the calculation, it tries to convert the value supplied to a number, but of course **None** is not a value that can be converted, so have you have a type mismatch.*

Argument Tuples

For accepting a variable length of arguments when you don't want to use default values, you can use the argument tuple:

```
def function(*ARG)
```

All the arguments are placed into the tuple specified by **ARG**. For example, the following function accepts a variable list of arguments that are appended to the list defined in the first argument:

```
def multi_insert(list, *items):
    for item in list:
        list.append(item)
```

Argument tuples pick up all the remaining nonpositional arguments in a function call. As such, they should be specified last. It should also be obvious that you can only have one argument tuple in a function definition.

Argument Dictionaries

Argument dictionaries work in a similar way to keyword argument passing, except that instead of assigning values to individual variables, each keyword/value pair creates an entry in the specified dictionary:

```
def function(**ARG):
```

For example, the function

```
def message(text, **header):
    for field in data.keys():
        print field+":",data[field]
    print
    print text
```

can be called to create a standard email message:

```
message('I pulled the chain but nothing happened!',
        From='mc@mcwords.com',
        To='mc@mcwords.com',
        Subject='Hello')
```

When called, this function generates the following output:

```
Subject: Hello
To: mc@mcwords.com
From: mc@mcwords.com

I pulled the chain but nothing happened!
```

Like tuple arguments, a dictionary argument must be last, following any sequential or default arguments. You can also combine a tuple and dictionary arguments, as in the modified version of the **message** function:

```
def message(text, *lines, **header):
    for field in header.keys():
        print field+":",header[field]
    print
    print text
    for line in lines:
        print line

message('I pulled the chain but nothing happened!',
        'Another line',
        'Second line',
        From='mc@mcwords.com',
        To='mc@mcwords.com',
        Subject='Hello')
```

When called, this function creates a multiline e-mail message:

```
Subject: Hello
To: mc@mcwords.com
From: mc@mcwords.com

I pulled the chain but nothing happened!
Another line
Second line
```

Function Rules

Python has strict rules about how it parses function calls and definitions. Python follows these rules when you are defining the function:

■ Defaults must follow nondefault arguments.

■ You can only have one tuple argument (***arg**) and one dictionary argument (****arg**) within a single definition.

■ The tuple argument (***arg**) must appear after sequential arguments and defaults.

■ The dictionary argument must appear last.

When calling a function, Python follows these rules:

- Function calls must include parentheses; **func** and **func()** are not the same. The first accesses the function reference, and the second executes the function.
- Keyword arguments must appear after all the nonkeyword arguments.

In addition, Python tries the following steps, in order, when determining the arguments to be assigned within the function:

- Assign nonkeyword arguments by sequence.
- Assign keyword arguments by argument name.
- Assign extra nonkeyword arguments to the argument tuple.
- Assign extra keyword arguments to the argument dictionary.
- Assign default values to any unassigned arguments.

Return Values

The **return** statement returns the objects specified to the calling program. The basic format is:

```
return OBJECT [, OBJECT, ...]
```

The **return** statement is not limited to returning single objects; it can return tuples, lists, or dictionaries. The tuple is probably the most useful, because it allows you to assign multiple objects to the returned value.

For example, here's a transform function that accepts two arguments and returns the first argument squared and the second argument cubed:

```
def sqsq(first,second):
    first = first*first
    second = second**3
```

You can now call the **sqsq** function and immediately get the results:

```
squared, cubed = sqsq(2,3)
```

See the discussion on "Tuple and List Assignments" in Chapter 3 for more information.

Advanced Function Calling

Beyond the basics of functions that you've already seen, Python also supports some advanced function handling. The **apply** statement is a required feature if you want to be able to dynamically call a function without knowing beforehand its name or the arguments you need to supply it. The **map** statement provides the same functionality as the Perl **map** function; it allows you to apply the same function to an arbitrary list.

The last two features are connected. It should come as no surprise that functions are just Python objects. As such, you can assign functions to names and then call them dynamically and therefore indirectly. As an extension of this, you can also create a name that points to a function that has no real name—an anonymous function that is created within Python using the **lambda** statement.

The *apply* Statement

There are times when you want to be able to call a function within an application, but you don't know the name of the function or the number of arguments that you need to supply to the function. The **apply** function allows you to apply a number of arguments to a function, executing the function as if you were calling it explicitly. The format of an **apply** statement is:

```
apply(FUNCTION, TUPLE)
```

Here's an example of calling the **apply** function:

```
apply(multiple,(2,4))
```

The big benefit here is that because the arguments are supplied as a tuple and therefore as a data structure, the function call can be computed at run time, instead of at development time. You'll see examples of the **apply** statement throughout this book.

The *map* Statement

Imagine that you have a list of numbers and you want to turn it into a list of cubes. The normal process might be:

```
for index in range(len(list)):
    list[index] = pow(list[index],3)
```

For this simple function it makes sense, but for complex functions, having to manually embed the function call on each item in a list within a loop creates unnecessary overhead.

A simpler method is to use the **map** statement. The **map** statement accepts the name of a function and a list or tuple on which to act. You can therefore rewrite the preceding code fragment as

```
def cube(x):
    return pow(x,3)
map(cube,list)
```

Although it doesn't look any shorter, it is much more practical. The **map** function does the loop operation and reassignment for you, and you can supply any function as the first argument to the **map** statement. More often, the **map** statement is used in combination with the **lambda** statement, which creates anonymous functions, allowing you to rewrite the preceding statements as

```
map(lambda x:pow(x,3), list)
```

You'll learn about the creation of anonymous functions later in this chapter, see "Anonymous Functions" for more details.

These two formats, calling a named function and using an anonymous function, are syntactically similar to the expression and block formats used by Perl. The Perl statement

```
map EXPR, LIST
```

is roughly equivalent to the Python statement

```
map (FUNC, LIST)
```

while the Perl statement

```
map BLOCK LIST
```

is roughly equivalent to the Python statement

```
map(lambda ARG: EXPRESSION, LIST)
```

Indirect Function Calls

Functions are just Python objects, which means they can be assigned to names and passed to other functions just like any other object. For example, you can create an alias to a function as in the following example:

```
def hello():
    print "Hello World"
x = hello
x()
```

Note the notation used in the preceding example. You assign the **hello** object to the **x** name. By specifying the function by its object reference, **hello**, instead of calling it as a function, **hello()**, you copy the reference to the function instead of executing it and assigning the result.

This use of function references also means you can supply a function object as an argument to a function:

```
def call(function, *args):
    function(args)

call(multiply,2,2)
```

Finally, using the same methods, you can also place function objects inside other data structures:

```
obj_dict = { 'function' : multiply, 'args' : (2,2) }
apply(obj_dict['function'],obj_dict['args'])
```

Note in the preceding example the use of **apply**, which accepts the first argument as a function reference and accepts the tuple as the arguments to be supplied to the function.

Anonymous Functions

Anonymous functions are a vital component of the flexibility offered by languages such as Perl and Python. You've already seen a few examples of anonymous functions within Python. In C/C++, the closest approximation to an anonymous function is the inline function feature; you can define a block or expression to be executed just as if it was a real function call, but without the overhead associated with predeclaring a typical function.

The format for creating an anonymous function in Python is to use the **lambda** expression. Because **lambda** is an expression, not a statement, you can call **lambda** in places where a typical **def** statement could not be used. In addition, the **lambda** expression returns a function object without giving it a name. The returned object can then be used just like an indirect function call.

The general format for the **lambda** expression is

```
lambda ARG [, ARG, ...]: EXPR
```

The **ARG** is an argument, just like a typical **def** statement. The arguments work just like sequential arguments in a normal function. You can also use defaults within a **lambda** definition, but you cannot use any other argument feature.

The **EXPR** is a single-line expression that is executed when the function is called. When creating and using **lambda** functions, you need to remember the following important differences from ordinary functions:

1. Functions created by **lambda** only accept a single expression—you cannot have multiline anonymous functions.

2. The result of the expression in a **lambda** function is always returned to the caller.

For example, you can use **lambda** to create an anonymous function that cubes a number and then assigns the result to a name:

```
f = lambda x: x*x*x
f(2)
```

The preceding statement is actually how a typical **def** statement works; the difference is that the assignment to a name is automatic.

Compared to Perl, the use of the **lambda** expression is identical to the **sub {}** anonymous function statement; Python has just given the process a separate name instead of combining the operation into a single statement. In essence, the **lambda** expression is no different than the **def** statement.

The **lambda** function is used in a large number of areas such as sorting and as inline functions when creating user interfaces. You'll see more examples of this as you work through the book.

The
Complete
Reference

Chapter 5

Modules

As programs get larger and larger, it makes more and more sense to split one large file into a number of smaller files. This keeps the code nice and tight and it also makes modification of the code easier, especially if the project is being developed simultaneously by a number of different people.

In Python you have the ability to split up a program into a number of individual files called *modules*. Modules can then be imported into your existing scripts, providing you with access to the functions, objects, and classes you have defined within each module. This concept is similar to the modules used in Perl and to the libraries and class definitions used in Visual Basic, C/C++, and many other languages.

This chapter looks at how to import modules from the standard library and those libraries you create yourself. It also explains how to create module packages, which are nested groups of modules that can be loaded either on an individual basis or as one complete package, depending on how they are configured.

Importing a Module

In Python you *import* the module into a script—you are importing information about how to use the functions, objects, and classes within the module, rather than importing the different entities themselves into the script. This will become clearer when you understand the different methods for importing modules and what happens when you use the **import** statement.

Importing an Entire Module

To import, that is, to give yourself access to the functions, objects, and classes within a given module, you use the **import** statement:

```
import ftplib
```

The **import** statement in Python does three things:

- It creates a new namespace to hold all the objects defined within the given module.
- It executes the code in the module within the confines of the given namespace.
- It creates a name within the caller that refers to the module's namespace.

In the preceding example, a new namespace **ftplib** was created, the **ftplib.py** file in the Python library directory was found and executed within the **ftplib** namespace, and then an object called **ftplib** was created within the namespace of the current module—

in this case the main script. See "Module Loading and Compilation" later in this chapter for information on how Python searches for modules.

You can also import multiple modules simultaneously by separating each module name by a comma in the **import** statement:

```
import os, sys, getopt, ftplib
```

Each module name is interpreted individually so the preceding example is equivalent to the following statements:

```
import os
import sys
import getopt
import ftplib
```

If you are going purely for clarity, then writing an **import** statement for each module being imported is preferred. In most situations, importing several modules in one **import** statement works just as well, and most programmers can probably spot which modules have been imported just by reading the rest of the code.

Importing a Module Under an Alias

An extension of the basic **import** method made available in Python 2.0 is the ability to import a module within a namespace different than the default namespace selected by the module's apparent name. For example, you can import the **ftplib** module as simple **ftp** using

```
import ftplib as ftp
```

Now all calls to the **ftplib** module must be identified within the **ftp** namespace.

Using aliases can be a great way to test a new version of a module without upsetting the original. For example, imagine you've got two modules where the stable version is **mylib** and the development version is **newmylib**. You could change references in your test scripts to

```
import newmylib as mylib
```

No changes need to be made to the rest of the script for it to work—provided that your new module doesn't break any of the APIs.

Importing Specific Module Entities

To import specific functions and objects from a given module, use the **from ... import ...** statement. For example, to import the objects **foo** and **bar** from the module **foobar**, use the following statement:

```
from foobar import foo, bar
```

The major difference between the preceding statement and the **import ...** statement is that the objects that you import become available within the current namespaces, so you no longer have to specify them as explicitly. For example, the following script is now valid:

```
from Foobar import foo, bar
foo()
bar()
```

To import everything from a given module into the current namespace, use *:

```
from Foobar import *
```

Reloading a Module

You can reload a module that has previously been loaded by calling the built-in function **reload()**. This forces Python to reinterpret and import the module again, as in the following example:

```
import foo
...
reload(foo)
```

However, the **reload** function only reloads Python modules; those modules that rely on a C/C++ dynamic library will not work. Also, reloading does not modify any existing objects that use the methods defined in the module—they will continue to use the old methods until they are destroyed. See Chapter 8 for more information.

Module Search Path

When you load a module, the Python interpreter searches a standard set of directories to find the module that you specify. The path is system and installation specific, but you can find the current list of directories using **sys.path**. The following is the list of directories under a Solaris 8/x86 installation of Python 2.0:

```
['', '/usr/local/lib/python2.0',
 '/usr/local/lib/python2.0/plat-sunos5',
 '/usr/local/lib/python2.0/lib-tk',
 '/usr/local/lib/python2.0/lib-dynload',
 '/usr/local/lib/python2.0/site-packages']
```

And here are the equivalent directories under MacOS 9.1:

```
['', 'development:applications:python 2.0',
'development:applications:python 2.0:mac:plugins',
'development:applications:python 2.0:mac:lib',
'development:applications:python 2.0:mac:lib:lib-toolbox',
'development:applications:python 2.0:mac:lib:lib-scriptpackages',
'development:applications:python 2.0:lib',
'development:applications:python 2.0:extensions:img:mac',
'development:applications:python 2.0:extensions:img:lib',
'development:applications:python 2.0:extensions:numerical:lib',
'development:applications:python 2.0:extensions:numerical:lib:packages',
'development:applications:python 2.0:extensions:imaging:pil',
'development:applications:python 2.0:lib:lib-tk',
'development:applications:python 2.0:lib:site-packages']
```

The ' ' in both directory lists refers to the current directory.

To add directories to the module search path, you can add them to **sys.path**, for example to add **./lib/python** to the search list:

```
import sys
sys.path.append('./lib/python')
```

Now all future **import** statements will not only search the standard libraries, but also the directory you've just added.

To insert new directories before the standard search path, use the **insert()** method to add the directory to the start, rather than to the end of the list:

```
sys.path.insert(0,'./lib/perl')
```

Alternatively, on platforms that support environment variables (Windows, Unix, BeOS, etc.), you can add directories to the **PYTHONPATH** variable before execution.

Module Loading and Compilation

When you request to load a particular module, the Python interpreter looks in the following places for the module you want to load:

- Programs/modules written in Python
- C or C++ extensions that have been compiled into shared libraries or DLLs
- Packages containing a collection of modules (see "Packages" later in this chapter)
- Built-in modules written in C that have been linked into the Python interpreter

What Python is actually seeking is files within the Python library search path (in the following order, assuming a module called **foo**):

1. A directory defining a package called **foo**.
2. A compiled extension or library named **foo.so**, **foomodule.so**, **foomodule.sl**, or **foomodule.dll**. The exact interpretation, of course, depends on the host operating system. Not all operating systems support dynamically loadable modules.
3. A file called **foo.pyo** (assuming that the **-O** option has been used).
4. A file called **foo.pyc** (the precompiled bytecode version of **foo.py**).
5. A file called **foo.py**.
6. A built-in module called **foo**.

When Python finds the file **foo.pyc**, the timestamp is checked against **foo.py**. If **foo.py** is newer, then the file is compiled and the compiled bytecode for the module is written into **foo.pyc**. Python therefore always attempts to load a precompiled bytecode for modules loaded through **import**. Modules execute as a script are not precompiled and stored in any way.

If the **-O** command-line option is in effect, Python loads an optimized form of the precompiled bytecode, as stored in **.pyo** files. These are identical in content to the **.pyc** file except that the line numbers, assertions, and other debugging information that can be used to trace the execution of the module are removed.

If, after trying to load all these different components, one still cannot be found, then the **ImportError** exception is raised.

Tricks for Importing Modules

Beyond the basic mechanics described here, Python also supports a number of different techniques and tricks that you can use to import modules within a Python script. Most of these techniques should only be used by expert programmers. Other techniques allow you to be more flexible in your approach to using modules.

Using import **in a Script**

The normal mode of operation is to import the modules you want to use at the top of the script, for example:

```
import os,sys,getopt

# Start processing
def start():
...
```

The Python interpreter only executes the **import** statement at the point at which it sees the statement within the code during the execution process. This allows you to execute **import** statements just as you would any other piece of Python code, including within the confines of an **if** or other control statement:

```
if (module == 'os'):
    import os
else:
    import sys
```

This technique is actually used by modules like **os** that load a platform-specific module such as **posix** or **mac**, depending upon the host on which the Python interpreter is running.

It's also perfectly legal to load modules only when a function is actually called, as in the following example:

```
def sendmymail():
    import smtplib
```

For all this flexibility, however, you cannot import a module using a variable or string as the module name without using the **exec** statement, as in the following example:

```
module = 'os'
exec 'import '+module
```

See Chapter 8 for more information on the **exec** statement.

Trapping import Statements

The **import** statement raises an **ImportError** exception if a module fails to load correctly. You can safely trap a failed module load directly within the script, allowing you to exit graciously, as in the following example:

```
try:
    import mymodule
except ImportError:
    print "Whoa! We seem to be missing a module we require here"
    import sys
    sys.exit()
```

Identifying a Module or a Script

Each module defines a variable, **__name__**, that contains the name of the module. You can use this variable as a way to determine which module a particular piece of code is executing within. However, it also becomes a handy way to determine whether a given module is running as a script or whether it has been imported. Modules running as scripts set **__name__** to **__main__**, and you can test for this:

```
if __name__ == '__main__':
    # Work as a script
else:
    # Work as a module
```

Note that **__name__** returns the original name of the module rather than the alias name specified when using the **import ... as** import technique. If you use the preceding trick, this won't make any difference, but be careful using the module name internally as a key to its name when imported.

Although this particular trick shouldn't be used to affect the functions or classes defined within the module, it can and often is used as a handy testing mechanism for a module. When you run the module as a script, it tests itself, but when the module is imported, it just defines the functions. This saves you from having a separate test script and aids Python's code reuse because each module can be used as both script and library addition.

If you check any of the standard modules that come with Python you'll probably find such a block. For example, running the **smtplib** module as a script allows you to send an e-mail message:

```
$ python smtplib.py
From: mc@mcslp.com
```

```
To: mc@mcwords.com
Enter message, end with ^D:
Hello Doppleganger!
Message length is 20
send: 'ehlo twinsol\015\012'
reply: '250-twinsol.mchome.com Hello localhost [127.0.0.1], pleased
to meet you\015\012'
reply: '250-ENHANCEDSTATUSCODES\015\012'
reply: '250-EXPN\015\012'
...
```

The output in the preceding example has been trimmed for clarity, but you can see
the effect. Importing **smtplib** as a module has no effect—you import the module and
it functions as normal.

Packages

Packages in Python allow a set of modules to be grouped under a common package
name. Programmers from a Perl background might expect the statement

```
import package.module
```

to search the various directories for the file **package/module.py** automatically, but it
doesn't. For the **import** statement to work in this way you must have previously set
up a package and its corresponding directory structure.

A package is defined by creating a directory with the same name as the package
and then creating the file **__init__.py** within that directory. This file contains the
necessary instructions to the Python interpreter to allow the importing of modules and
module groups within the package. For example, the following directory structure
shows the layout of a project called MediaWeb which, as a network management tool,
has been placed in the **Net** directory:

```
Net/
    __init__.py
    MediaWeb/
        __init__.py
        Weather.py
        Weblog.py
        Systemlog.py
```

Now, from within Python, you can import modules from this structure in a number of ways. The statement

```
import Net.MediaWeb.Weather
```

imports the submodule **Weather** from the **Net/MediaWeb** directory. As with other **import** statements, you must refer to functions in this module explicitly, i.e., **Net.MediaWeb.Weather.report()**.

The statement

```
from Net.MediaWeb import Weather
```

imports the same module, **Weather**, but without the package prefix, allowing you to use **Weather.report()**.

The statement

```
from Net.MediaWeb.Weather import report
```

imports **report** into the local namespace, enabling you to call it using **report()**.

In each case, the code in **__init__.py** is executed in order to perform any package-specific initialization. All the **__init__.py** files are processed as they are seen within the import process. For example, importing **Net.MediaWeb.Weather** would execute **Net/__init__.py** and **Net/MediaWeb/__init__.py**.

The contents of each **__init__.py** file are entirely up to you—they may be empty, in which case nothing happens except to import the module you've selected. But they *must* exist for the directory nesting to work as you would expect it within Perl.

On the other hand, you may want to enforce certain options. For example, the statement

```
import Net.MediaWeb
```

does not automatically force Python to import the contents of the **Net/MediaWeb** directory and neither does the statement

```
from Net.MediaWeb import *
```

In these examples you can do one of two things. In the first example you may want to put the following statements into the **Net/MediaWeb/__init__.py** file:

```
# Net/MediaWeb/__init__.py
import Weather,Weblog
```

In the second example, you can use the __all__ attribute within the __init__.py file. This should be initialized with a list of modules that you want to import:

```
# Net/MediaWeb/__init__.py
__all__ = ['Weather', 'Weblog']
```

Creating a Module

Creating a new module in Python is as easy as writing the original script. Any file or script that you have created in Python is immediately available as a module without making any modifications to the code. In fact, apart from copying the file into a standard location to make it readily available, there's nothing else you need to do.

For example, imagine you've create a small script called **mymath.py** that defines a single function, **add()**:

```
def add(a,b):
    return a+b

print add(1,1)
```

You can import the **mymath.py** file and make use of the **add()** function within another script just by importing the **mymath** file and calling the function:

```
import mymath
print mymath.add(2,2)
```

The **import** statement automatically looks for the file **mymath.py** and then creates a new namespace and imports the **add()** function into that namespace.

Furthermore, you can also explicitly import **add()** into the current namespace using the statement

```
from mymath import add
```

It really is that simple!!

Because of this flexibility, all of the code and functions that you write and create in Python are available to all the other scripts and modules that you create without any modifications. All of your code is immediately reusable, and you don't have to worry about deliberately creating a module or doing anything special to make your code reusable.

In comparison, to create a flexible module **MyModule** in Perl, you'd have to add the following preamble to a file called **MyModule.pm**:

```
package MyModule;

require Exporter;
use vars qw/@ISA @EXPORT/;
@ISA = qw/Exporter/;
@EXPORT = qw/add/;
```

You'd also have to update **@EXPORT** for each entity that you want to explicitly export, and append a "true" value to be returned by the file when it is imported. In comparison to Python, Perl is quite fussy and it's possible to stop a module from working entirely by getting this preamble wrong.

Chapter 6

Object Orientation

Object-oriented programming is a mechanism that allows you to create intelligent variables—called *objects*—that can be used to store complex structures that not only hold data but also know what functions and operations can be performed on them. The system works through the creation of a *class*. A class defines the format and structure of individual objects—called *instances*—and defines the functions that operate on those objects.

Classes can also be organized into a tree structure so that there are generic classes and within the generic classes, there are specific classes for modeling other structures. Classes can also inherit methods from their parent classes, which promotes code reuse by allowing you to define a method only once, no matter how many different classes rely on its abilities.

For example, imagine that you are creating a system to manage your bank and credit card accounts. You create a base class called **Account** that holds two pieces of information: the account name and its current balance. The class definition also includes two methods, one to deposit funds into the account, which automatically updates the balance, and a similar method for withdrawing money from the account.

This base **Account** class on its own is not enough to hold specific information about an account. You're also going to create a subclass called **BankAccount** that inherits the attributes and methods of **Account**, but includes new attributes to hold the bank account number, sort code, and bank name. You can still deposit and withdraw funds using the methods defined in the **Account** class, but you don't have to recreate them for the **BankAccount** class.

In addition, you can create a **CreditCard** class that also inherits from the **Account** class. The **CreditCard** class includes attributes for the account number, expiration date, credit limit, and interest rate. The **add_interest**() method updates the account's balance by calculating the interest on the account for the previous period.

Let's look at the specifics of creating these classes as you learn how to create classes, objects, and methods using Python.

Python uses objects for all of its internal data types so you should already be familiar with how to create different objects and use the information and methods that apply to them. In this chapter you'll see how to create new classes so that you can model your own classes and objects, and you'll learn about the ways in which you can extend the classes you create to operate with the built-in functions and operators used by Python.

Creating a Class

Creating a new class in Python requires the **class** statement, which works like any other block definition in Python; everything contained within the **class** block becomes a part of the class you're defining.

The format for creating a new class looks like this:

```
class CLASSNAME([CLASS_PARENT, ...]):
    [ STD_ATTRIBUTES]
```

```
...
    def METHOD(self, [METHODARGS]):
...
```

CLASSNAME is the name of the class that you want to create. Python uses the same basic rules for classes as for any other object. However, as a general rule, user-defined class names are often in title case to distinguish them from the standard library classes supplied with Python. The parentheses following the class are optional and are used only for specifying any classes from which you inherit attributes. See the section "Class Inheritance" later in this chapter for more information.

The **STD_ATTRIBUTES** are the default attributes that you want applied to all instances of this class. These are given static values at this point, unlike the attributes that you might set during the initialization. We'll look in more detail at the class methods shortly.

For example, you can create the **Account** class as follows:

```
class Account:
    account_type = 'Basic'
    def __init__(self, name, balance):
        self.name = name
        self.balance = balance
    def deposit(self, value):
        self.balance += value
    def withdraw(self, value):
        self.balance -= value
```

To create a new object based on our new class, you call the class as if it is a function:

```
bank = Account('HSBC', 2000)
```

Class Methods

Class methods are in fact just functions that have been defined within the scope of a given class. The only difference between a class method and an ordinary function is that the first argument to *any* class method is the object on which it is operating. For example, when you call the **deposit()** method on an instance,

```
bank.deposit(1000)
```

Python actually calls the **deposit()** function within the **Account** class, supplying the object as the first argument (typically **self**) and the argument you supplied to the **deposit** function as the second argument:

```
Account.deposit(bank, 1000)
```

This enables you to access the object attributes and update their values from within the function. Without the **self** argument, you'd never be able to modify the object. You can see this more clearly in the following simplified class and method definition of the **Account** class:

```
class Account:
    account_type = 'Basic'
    def __init__(self, name, balance):
        self.name = name
        self.balance = balance
    def deposit(self, value):
        self.balance += value
```

Object Constructors

The **__init__()** function is the special name you should use within a class for the constructor—this function is called when you create a new object based on this class. The method can accept arguments using any of the forms described in Chapter 4. In our example

```
def __init__(self, name, balance):
        self.name = name
        self.balance = balance
```

The method accepts two arguments: the name of the account you're creating and the balance of the account. These are used to initialize the values of the object's attributes.
What this actually does is call:

```
bank = Account.__init__('HSBC', 2000)
```

The new variable, **bank**, is an object or an instance of the **Account** class. You can get the balance of the account by accessing the **balance** attribute.

Object Destructors

All class instances have a reference count for the number of times they have been referenced; this count can include, for example, each name that refers to that instance, each time the instance is included as part of a list, tuple, or dictionary, and so on. When the reference count reaches 0, the instance is automatically destroyed, freeing up the memory used to hold the object data.

If you want to define a custom sequence for destroying an object (a *destructor* function) (perhaps also to dereference other objects or log the instance deletion), you need to define the __del__() method. Python automatically calls the __del__() method when an object needs to be destroyed—all objects inherit a built-in __del__() method if the class does not define its own. Because of this, most basic objects, such as the example created here, don't require the __del__() method.

However, be aware that the call to __del__() cannot be relied on in situations where destroying the object requires the closing of files, network connections, or releasing of other system resources.

Special Methods

Python also supports a number of special methods that provide the necessary hooks for interfacing to the built-in functions and operators employed within the Python interpreter. These methods all follow the same basic model as __init__() and __del__(), using the leading and trailing double underscore characters. For example, you can add support for adding two accounts together using the standard + operator by defining a __add__() method within your class.

The full list of the special methods that Python supports is shown in Table 6-1. This table lists the basic methods that you can define within a given class for the most basic operations. Nearly all of these methods should be defined in an object class, especially if you plan to release the class to the public and they're appropriate for the class you are creating.

Method	Description
__init__(self [,args])	Called when creating a new instance of a class.
__del__(self)	Called when an instance is destroyed.
__repr__(self)	Called when the **repr()** function or backtick operator is employed—should return a string representation of the object that is compatible with **eval()** to recreate the object.
__str__(self)	Called when the **str()** function is called—should return an informal representation of the string.

Table 6-1. *Special Class Methods*

Method	Description
__cmp__(self, other)	Called when comparing two objects, should return a negative value when **self** is logically smaller than **other**, zero when the two objects are logically equivalent and a positive number when **self** is logically greater than **other**.
__hash__(self)	Called when computing a hash value—should return a 32-bit hash index.
__nonzero__(self)	Should return 0 when **self** if logically false or 1 when **self** is logically true.
__getattr__(self, name)	Called when **self.name** is used, should return the value of the attribute **name**.
__setattr__(self, name, value)	Called when **self.name = value** is used, should set the value of the attribute **name** to **value**.
__delattr__(self, name)	Called when **del self.name** is called, should delete the attribute **name**.

Table 6-1.   *Special Class Methods* (continued)

The __str__() and __repr__() methods should be set up to return suitable string representations of the given object. In the case of __str__() this can be a basic string:

```
def __str__(self):
    return "%s: %g" % (self.name, self.balance)
```

The __repr__() method should return a value that will recreate the object when parsed by **eval()**. This means returning a string that represents the call necessary to recreate the object; for example, with the **Account** class you'd have to return a string that generated

```
Account(name, balance)
```

The real method definition would look something like this:

```
def __repr__(self):
    return "Account('%s',%g)" % (self.name, self.balance)
```

Emulating Sequence or Dictionary Objects

If you have created an object type that provides access to information through a
sequence or dictionary interface, you must define the methods listed in Table 6-2.
These are the methods called when you used the **len()** function or access slices or
elements directly from the objects.

Overloading Mathematical Operators

All user-defined objects can be made to work with all of Python's built-in operators
by adding implementations of the special methods that Python actually calls when an
operator is used on any object, even the built-in types. This process is called *operator
overloading* because you are effectively overloading an operator's abilities to enable
them to operate on a different object type.

Be aware however that overloading operators should be done where it makes sense
to support the operator in context. For example, overloading with the **__add__()** method
to create a new type of bank account based on two older accounts makes sense. Creating
an **HTTP** class and overloading with the **__add__()** method probably doesn't make
sense, no matter how "cool" it might be to use the + operator to perform the operation.

Overloading an operator to handle your own classes and objects is straightforward;
all you need to do is define a specific method to handle the operation. For example,
the **__add__()** method defines what happens when two objects of the same type are
added together using the + operator. For example, you can merge two of the bank
accounts defined in the **Account** class:

```
def __add__(self, other):
    return Account(self.name + ' and ' + other.name,
                   self.balance + other.balance)
```

Method	Description
__len__(self)	Should return the length of **self**, called by the built-in **len()** function.
__getitem__(self, key)	Should return **self[key]**.
__setitem__(self, key, value)	Should set the value of **self[key]** to **value**.
__delitem__(self, key)	Should delete **self[key]**.
__getslice__(self, i, j)	Should return **self[i:j]**.
__getslice__(self, i, j, value)	Should set **self[i:j]** to **value**.
__delslice__(self, i, j)	Should delete **self[i:j]**.

Table 6-2. *Methods for Emulating Sequences and Mapping Objects*

In this case, **__add__**() returns the balance of the two accounts, as in this example:

```
bank = Account('HSBC', 2000)
creditcard = Account('MBNA', -1000)
assets = bank + creditcard
```

Now **assets** contains a new object whose **name** attribute is "HSBC and MBNA" and whose **balance** is 1000.

Although these are technically listed as mathematical operators, they apply to all objects where you would expect to use operators to manipulate them. For example, strings and other sequences define the **__add__**() and **__mul__**() methods. Table 6-3 lists all the methods that you need to define when emulating numeric objects.

Method	Result
__add__(self, other)	self + other
__sub__(self, other)	self – other
__mul__(self, other)	self * other
__div__(self, other)	self / other
__mod__(self, other)	self % other
__divmod__(self, other)	divmod(self, other)
__pow__(self, other [, modulo])	self ** other, pow(self, other, modulo)
__lshift__(self, other)	self << other
__rshift__(self, other)	self >> other
__and__(self, other)	self & other
__or__(self, other)	self | other
__xor__(self, other)	self ^ other
__radd__(self, other)	other + self
__rsub__(self, other)	other – self
__rmul__(self, other)	other * self
__rdiv__(self, other)	other / self
__rmod__(self, other)	other % self

Table 6-3. *Methods for Overloading Standard Python Operators*

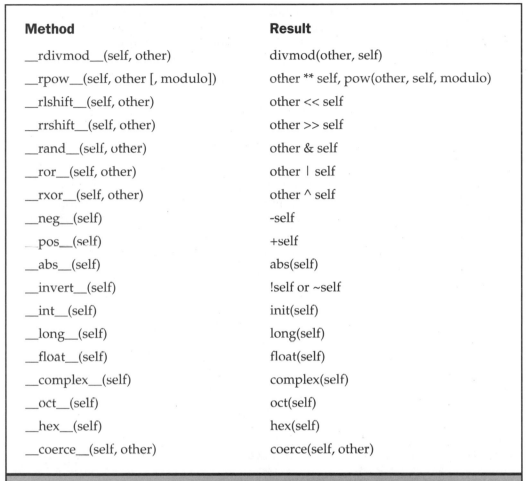

Method	Result
__rdivmod__(self, other)	divmod(other, self)
__rpow__(self, other [, modulo])	other ** self, pow(other, self, modulo)
__rlshift__(self, other)	other << self
__rrshift__(self, other)	other >> self
__rand__(self, other)	other & self
__ror__(self, other)	other | self
__rxor__(self, other)	other ^ self
__neg__(self)	-self
__pos__(self)	+self
__abs__(self)	abs(self)
__invert__(self)	!self or ~self
__int__(self)	init(self)
__long__(self)	long(self)
__float__(self)	float(self)
__complex__(self)	complex(self)
__oct__(self)	oct(self)
__hex__(self)	hex(self)
__coerce__(self, other)	coerce(self, other)

Table 6-3.   *Methods for Overloading Standard Python Operators* (continued)

Additional Methods

Any other functions that you define within a given class become the additional methods for your class. The format for each method is:

```
def METHOD(self [, args])
```

As mentioned earlier, the **self** argument is passed to every class method as it provides the connection to the object itself so that you can use and/or modify the attributes of a given object. In the earlier example, the **deposit()** and **withdraw()** methods are the other methods to the **Account** class.

There is no limit to the number of methods that you can create within a class or to what they can do. Methods are invoked by calling the method by name. For example, you can create a new instance of the **Account** variable in Python using

```
bank = Account('HSBC', 2000)
```

You can deposit money to the account using

```
bank.deposit(1000)
```

Note that in the preceding case, the **deposit()** method doesn't return any value because it's modifying the **balance** attribute of the object directly. If you want to return a value, for example, to get the balance of the account, use the **return** statement as you would in other functions to return a value to the caller:

```
def accbalance(self):
    return self.balance
```

However, be aware that using a method for this operation is just duplicating the process of accessing the attribute directly. Given the **accbalance()** method above, the following two statements have identical results:

```
print "Balance:",bank.accbalance()
print "Balance:",bank.balance
```

Unless you are reformatting the output (as you do with the **__str__()** and **__repr__()** methods), duplicating the effects of accessing an object's attributes is largely pointless.

Making Objects Callable

You can make an object callable as if it operates just like a function. To do this, you need to define the **__call__()** method. This means that the statement

```
object(arg1, arg2, ...)
```

actually calls

```
object.__call__(self, arg1, arg2, ...)
```

This can be useful if you want a quick way to perform a specific operation on an object; the **Account** class, for example, might specify that calling an instance of the class automatically returns its balance.

Other uses of callable objects include instances where there is only one method defined within the class. For example, you may create a recipe object that when called, regurgitates a formatted version of itself suitable for display on the Web.

Class Inheritance

The parentheses following a class name are used by Python to identify the classes from which you inherit attributes and methods. As an extension to the example in the introduction to this chapter, you could define the two classes **CreditCard** and **BankAccount**, each of which inherits artifacts from the base class **Account**, like this:

```
class BankAccount(Account):
    account_type = 'Bank Account'
    def __init__(self, name, balance):
        self.name = name
        self.balance = balance
    def __init__(self, name, balance, accno, sortcode, bankname):
        Account.__init__(self, name, balance)
        self.accno = accno
        self.sortcode = sortcode
        self.bankname = bankname
class CreditCard(Account):
    account_type = 'Credit Card'
    def __init__(self, name, balance, accno, expiry, limit, rate):
        Account.__init__(self, name, balance)
        self.accno = accno
        self.expiry = expiry
        self.limit = limit
        self.rate = rate
    def withdraw( self, amount ):
        if abs( self.balance - amount ) < self.limit:
            self.balance -= amount
        else:
            raise ValueError, "You're past your limit!"
    def add_interest(self):
        self.balance -= ((abs(self.balance)*(self.rate/100))/12)
```

Note that the **withdraw()** method within the **CreditCard** class overrides the default method defined in the **Account** class. Note also that an exception was added that is raised when you try to withdraw money beyond your limit.

If you now create a **CreditCard** instance, notice that you can use the **withdraw()** and **deposit()** methods:

```
>>> visa = CreditCard('HSBC', -1000, '12345678', '02/99', 8000, 18)
>>> visa.deposit(500)
>>> visa.balance
-500
>>> visa.withdraw(2000)
>>> visa.balance
-2500
```

One thing to note is that when you create an instance of a class that inherits from another class, the constructor for the new class does not automatically call the constructor method for the base class, hence the need for the following line in the constructor for both the **BankAccount** and **CreditCard** classes:

```
Account.__init__(self, name, balance)
```

This directly calls the constructor for the base class using the **name** and **balance** supplied to the class constructors to initialize an instance within the current class. Note that you don't have to call the base class constructor immediately if you don't want to, but it's probably a good idea.

Chapter 7

Exceptions and
Error Trapping

U p until now this book has carefully avoided the problems of trapping errors. This is because we've concentrated on the fundamentals of the language such as variable types and classes. Most other languages use a standard method for trapping an error. This chapter will use Perl as an example language because most people have probably been exposed to Perl as a scripting language. Consider, for example, the following Perl code for opening a file:

```
open(FILE,"file.txt") || die "Couldn't open file.txt: $!";
```

The way the error is trapped is that the interpreter looks for a return value from the function; the return value will be a positive integer, representing a true value, if the function call works. If the **open** function call fails, the **die** function kills the Perl interpreter (or the enclosing **eval** block) and reports the error, using the string obtained from the **$!** special variable.

There are a few problems with this method of error trapping:

- You can only detect success or failure—there's no in between.
- If you want to detect the reason for the failure, you have to examine the **$!** variable.
- You can only really handle the failure—not the reason for the failure—unless you embed every call into an **eval** block.

This is a limitation not only of Perl, but also of C/C++, which uses a similar method of error checking, although the C headers normally include the specific error numbers which you can trap, but only within multiple **if** or **switch** statements. C++ supports an exception system, but it is underused because of historical problems with the compilers that support exceptions. Pascal, Visual Basic (VB), and most other languages also follow the same basic methodology—they check for a true/false return status.

Now let's look at a different, but also common situation when you might want to trap an error:

```
$den = 25;
$num = 0;
print $den/$num,"\n";
```

In Perl, this code causes a fatal error (the interpreter terminates) at run time because division by zero is undefined. It's impossible to trap this error within the normal execution of Perl unless you either check the values to make sure you aren't dividing by zero or you embed the statement into an **eval** block, which is essentially the same as embedding a Perl interpreter into the Perl interpreter. The problem here is that you can't always embed everything into an **eval** block, and checking every value before you do a calculation is excellent programming practice, but excessive if you want an optimized script.

There are no other ways to trap the execution of individual statements at execution time either in Perl, C, or C++. Python, however, provides a different method. When an error occurs within Python, an exception is raised and you can use built-in statements to raise your own exceptions and to trap the exceptions and handle them safely.

What Is an Exception?

An *exception* is a special type of Python object that can be used to pass information about a failure from the called module to the caller. When an exception is raised, it can be trapped, and the exception information is passed to an exception handler. Unlike Perl and C, you can get a precise description of the problem and even additional information about the error that occurred.

The best way to think about an exception is as a configurable and expandable signal handler (see "Exceptions and goto"). You create an exception handler using the **try** statement and then execute the statements that you want to monitor. As soon as an exception occurs, control returns to the **try** statement. You don't have to monitor each function call, and you don't have to rely on simple return values to determine whether a block of code executed successfully; you just need to be able to handle the exception if it occurs.

Exceptions and goto

You might think that Python's exceptions sound a bit like the C, VB, and Perl **goto** functions in their various guises. Or you might think that exceptions provide a similar functionality to the C **setjmp()**/**longjmp()**. However, in all these cases there are some limitations. Any system based on the premise of a **goto** statement is open to abuse, even with the advanced status recording offered by the **setjmp()** functions.

The problem with a **goto** statement is that you jump from the current location to the new location without clearing up loose ends—what happens with files and variables that had been opened within the context of the code block you were in? It's also not possible, without global variables, to pass any useful information during the jump. Any form of **goto** is considered bad programming practice because it breaks the normal flow and the safe execution of a program.

The Python exception-handling system is much more advanced. Exceptions are just like **return** statements used in functions, except that an exception can be raised anywhere in the caller and handled by a caller further up the chain, irrespective of where the exception handler is located or where the exception was raised.

Because exceptions are a built-in feature of the language, the process is much cleaner than other methods—you don't have to rely on signals or other features. Exceptions are also objects and because they are objects, they can have values and methods assigned to them. When you raise an exception, you are returning an object, and that means you can actually use exceptions for more than just error checking. Other uses for exceptions include:

- Multiple error handling: You don't need to check individual return values and compare them against a known list. When you call a function or execute a block, you only need to know how to handle specific exceptions; any other errors can either be ignored or trapped using a generic exception handler.

- Special control flow: By using exception handlers, you can alter the flow of an application based on the capability to perform a specific action. Imagine, for example, a program that either opens a network connection or uses a local file instead. Using an exception handler, you can switch to the default file if the network connection fails.

- Event monitoring: You can use the exception system to return the results from an event without having to use separate global variables and without having to check the return value explicitly. The normal way within Perl or C to handle an event is to check the return value; to verify whether any information has been returned, you check the number of items returned in a list or hash. With C, you have to use an integer return value and a global value, or supply a pointer argument to the function for the information to be written to.

Exceptions are based on objects or object classes, and there is a certain level of inheritance between individual exceptions. All exceptions are members of a base **Exception** class and then the hierarchy continues, inheriting individual features of each class until you reach a specific exception. For example, the **ArithmeticError** exception handles errors in calculations. More specifically, the **ZeroDivisionError** exception is designed to identify calculations like the earlier example where division by zero was attempted.

Using objects and classes, you can build exception handlers based on generic errors or on very specific errors. For example, if you are calculating using data from an unknown source, you might want to trap just a basic arithmetic error; when using internal data, you'll want to know what sort of calculation error was raised.

What Happens When an Exception Occurs?

When an exception occurs, the default operation is for the Python interpreter to identify the error and then produce a stack trace about where the error occurred and how you got there. This is more useful than the typical error output produced by Perl or C where you normally see only the line where an error has occurred. This can make tracing the reason for the error very difficult.

To demonstrate the process, here's a simple script that tries to divide a number by zero:

```
print 24/0
```

Not surprisingly this raises an exception, since you cannot divide by zero:

```
Traceback (innermost last):
  File "t.py", line 1, in ?
    print 24/0
ZeroDivisionError: integer division or modulo
```

If you embed this calculation into a function call, you get a more detailed description of how the error occurred:

```
def divide(x,y):
    return x/y

def calc(x,y):
    return x*(divide(x,y))

print calc(24,0)
```

If you execute this script, you see a detailed description of where the error occurred, over and above the simple line number:

```
Traceback (innermost last):
  File "t.py", line 7, in ?
    print calc(24,0)
  File "t.py", line 5, in calc
    return x*(divide(x,y))
  File "t.py", line 2, in divide
    return x/y
ZeroDivisionError: integer division or modulo
```

You can see in the preceding example how the report is given in the form of a stack trace; you can backtrack from the actual error, the calculation in line 2, up to the original call that triggered the error, the call in line 7, which in turn, made a call through line 5. Note also that the stack trace includes the function name and the name of the source file in which the error occurred.

The trick is to try and trap these errors so that you can give the user a better idea of what error occurred. To do this, you embed the call into an exception handler made up of a **try** statement and the code to handle any errors. Let's rewrite the division script and include an exception handler:

```
def divide(x,y):
    return x/y
```

```
def calc(x,y):
    return x*(divide(x,y))

try:
    print calc(24,0)
except:
    print "Whoa!: Those numbers don't seem to work!"
```

Here you've created a simple exception handler that traps every type of exception and reports an error. Because you haven't specified which exception should be trapped, this script also reports an error if there is a syntax problem or if you supplied a string to the **calc** function. Python actually defines a number of different exceptions and exception classes to handle specific error types; we'll be looking at those in more detail later in this chapter.

The Python exception system works differently than most other languages. Normally in a situation like the preceding script, you'd check the values before trying the calculation to make sure that the information was correct and didn't raise an error during execution. For example, in Perl you'd do something like this:

```
print calc(24,0);

sub divide
{
    my ($x,$y) = @_;
    die "Cannot divide by zero with $y" if ($y == 0);
    $x/$y;
}

sub calc
{
    my ($x,$y) = @_;
    $x*(divide($x,$y));
}
```

The problem here is that you end up using lots of code to trap the different types of errors. What if you called the **calc** function with a string instead of a number? If you call **calc('Hello',1)** in Perl, the return value is 0 because Perl tries to convert the string into a number and fails, and therefore makes the assumption that the value of the string is 0. What you really want is for the invalid argument to be identified as an error. To do that, you'd need to insert yet another **if** statement to test the contents of the arguments and determine the type.

Let's try it in Python and report an error to the user if there is a problem with the numbers you are trying to use. The following example takes advantage of the Python's ability to identify specific error types:

```python
def divide(x,y):
    return x/y

def calc(x,y):
    return x*(divide(x,y))

try:
    print calc('Hello',1)
except ZeroDivisionError:
    print "Whoa!: Your trying to divide by zero and you can't!"
except TypeError:
    print "Whoa!: That doesn't look like a number!"
except:
    print "Whoa!: Some other kind of error occurred!"
```

If you run this script, you'll get the following output:

```
Whoa!: That doesn't look like a number!
```

Now you're identifying division by zero and invalid type errors, but you're still not modifying the functions, nor do you have to predict what the possible errors might be. Instead, you're handling errors that occur when calling the function, and then catching any possible exceptions that might occur. You can be as specific or as vague as you like; in the preceding example, you've got both specific (**ZeroDivisionError** and **TypeError**) and a generalized **Exception** error. The script doesn't care how the statement fails; we can trap it and act upon it.

Exception Handling

The exception process uses the **try** statement in two different forms: the **try…except…else** statement and the **try…finally** statement. You've already seen a few examples of the first format; the second format provides a simplified operation sequence when you want to act upon an exception, but not actually handle the exception. Let's look at some examples to make it clearer.

try...except...else

The first form of the **try** statement acts a bit like an **if** statement in reverse—you embed a block of code that is executed, and then a number of **except** statements account for an exception if it occurs. The basic format for this first form is:

```
try:
    BLOCK
except [EXCEPTION [, DATA...]]:
    BLOCK
else:
    BLOCK
```

When the Python interpreter encounters a **try** statement, it follows this basic procedure:

1. The **BLOCK** under the **try** statement is executed. If an exception is raised, execution returns immediately to the first **except** statement.

2. If the exception that was raised matches the **EXCEPTION** specified—or all exceptions if **EXCEPTION** is not defined—then the corresponding **BLOCK** is executed, with the objects defined in **DATA** being accessible to the handler.

3. If the exception does not match, execution jumps to the next **except** statement; you can have as many **except** statements as you like.

4. If no **except** statement matches, the exception is passed to the next highest **try** block that called this block.

5. If no exception occurred, the **else** block is executed.

There are a few core components in this process that deserve extra mention.

except Statements Support Multiple Formats

Although it may not be clear from the preceding procedure, you can trap errors and introduce a number of exception handlers in a number of different ways. The **except** statement accepts five different formats, as outlined in Table 7-1.

except Statements Are Checked in Sequence

In steps 2 and 3 of the exception-handling procedure, you can see that when the exception is raised, each **except** statement is examined to see if the specified exception matches the exception that occurs. The examination occurs in sequence; Python doesn't check all the **except** clauses in one go. This means that you can identify individual exceptions and also classes until you reach the top. You saw an example of this earlier.

Format	Description
except:	Catch all (or all other) exceptions.
except name:	Catch the exception specified by **name**.
except (name1, name2):	Catch all the exceptions listed.
except name, data:	Catch the exception and any additional data returned.
except (name1,name2),data:	Catch the exceptions listed and any additional data returned.

Table 7-1. *Formats Accepted by the except Statement*

The following script looks for a **ZeroDivisionError** exception and a **TypeError,** and traps everything else:

```
def divide(x,y):
    return x/y

def calc(x,y):
    return x*(divide(x,y))

try:
    print calc('Hello',1)
except ZeroDivisionError:
    print "Whoa!: Your trying to divide by zero and you can't!"
except TypeError:
    print "Whoa!: That doesn't look like a number!"
except:
    print "Whoa!: Some other kind of error occurred!"
```

The important thing to remember is to work from the most-specific exception to least-specific exception. If you'd placed **Exception**—the base class for all exceptions types—in the first **except** statement, the remaining handlers would not ever have been checked.

Exception Handlers Run Once

If you've executed the earlier script, you'll notice that it's the **TypeError** exception that is reported. Even though the general **Exception** would normally catch all exceptions, there's been a match—only one match by the **try...except...else** statement is allowed. As soon as the exception block has been executed, control returns to the statements immediately after the entire **try** statement, unless, of course, you've called another function or one of the **exit** functions.

else Only Runs When There Are No Exceptions

According to step 5 of the exception-handling procedure, the **else** statement is only executed if no exceptions occur. Normally you use this in the same way that you might use an **if** block:

```
try:
    file = open('file')
except EnvironmentError:
    print "Whoops: Can't seem to open the file"
else:
    lines = file.readline()
    file.close()
```

There is no exception to this rule. If you want to run similar statements in an exception handler, you'll either need to duplicate the statements or create a function to handle them.

Catching Data

Most exceptions include additional information about the cause of an exception in addition to the information about the error itself. For example, consider the following script:

```
def parsefile(filename):
    file = open(filename,'rw')
    print file.readline()
    file.write('Hello World!')
    file.close()

try:
    parsefile('strings')
except EnvironmentError,(errno,msg):
    print "Error: %s (%d) whilst parsing the file" % (msg,errno)
```

This script includes a single exception handler for an **EnvironmentError**; this is the base class used for problems encountered by Python when accessing information outside of the Python interpreter, such as the contents of a file. Instead of trying to trap all of the different errors that might occur such as nonexistent files, full file systems, or an end-of-file condition, you can just trap for the generic exception and use the additional information supplied by the exception to further describe the error to the user.

The **EnvironmentError** exception automatically returns the C library error number and the associated message (if there is one). For example, all of the following are perfectly valid error messages when calling the **parsefile** function:

```
Error: No such file or directory (2) whilst parsing the file
Error: Bad file descriptor (9) whilst parsing the file
Error: No space left on device (28) whilst parsing the file
```

If you specify a single object to catch the data, the built-in exceptions convert the information into string format and place the string into the reference pointed to by the variable. If you want to catch specific information, as in the preceding example, you need to supply a tuple. The exact format for the returned information is defined by each exception. (See the "Built-in Exceptions" section later in this chapter for more information on the data returned by the standard exceptions.)

try...finally

The other alternative to the **try...except...else** statement is the **try...finally** statement. The format for this version of the **try** statement is:

```
try:
    BLOCK
finally:
    BLOCK
```

The rules for executing the **try...finally** statement are as follows:

1. The statements in the **try BLOCK** are executed.

2. If an exception occurs, the **finally BLOCK** is executed before the exception is propagated up to the next level.

3. If no exception occurs, the **finally BLOCK** is executed and control continues as normal until after the entire **try** statement.

The **try...finally** statement is useful in those situations where you want to run a piece of code, irrespective of whether an exception occurs. For example, when communicating with a remote server over a network, you want to trap an error but still make sure that regardless of the error, the communication channel is closed. With a **try...finally** statement you can do that:

```
try:
    remote.send_data(destination,datastream)
finally:
    remote.close_connection()
```

Of course, on its own, a **try...finally** statement will only propagate the error up to the next level, so you'll probably want to embed the call within another **try** statement:

```
try:
    try:
        remote.send_data(destination,datastream)
    finally:
        remote.close_connection()
except NetworkError,errorstr:
    print "Error: Couldn't send data,",errorstr
else:
    print "Data sent successfully"
```

Now the connection is closed whether or not an exception occurs, while the outer **try** statement traps and handles the actual exception raised during the process.

Exceptions Nest

It should be pretty clear by now that exceptions are always handled by the enclosing exception handler, but what happens if your exception handler doesn't explicitly handle every possible exception?

The answer is quite simple; the exception is raised to the next highest level exception handler. For example, in the second **try...finally** example earlier, the exception raised by the **send_data** method was raised to the next exception, in this case, a **try...except...else** statement.

Exceptions are logically stacked during the execution of the script such that exceptions are removed from the stack if an exception handler catches them, or they are propagated up to the next level if the local exception handler doesn't know what to do with them. Consider the following script, a modification of the calculation script used earlier in this chapter:

```
def divide(x,y):
    try:
        result = x/y
    except ZeroDivisionError:
        print "Whoa!: You're trying to divide by zero and you
```

```
can't!"
        raise
    return result

def calc(x,y):
    return x*(divide(x,y))

try:
    print calc(1,0)
except TypeError:
    print "Whoa!: That doesn't look like a number!"
except:
    print "Whoa!: Couldn't complete the calculation"
```

If you run this script you should get two error messages—one is from the exception handler within the **divide** function and identifies the attempt to divide by 0. The handler also raises its own exception, which is then passed back to the main exception handler:

```
Whoa!: You're trying to divide by zero and you can't!
Whoa!: Couldn't complete the calculation
```

Alternatively, you can replace the main section with this version:

```
try:
    print calc('Hello',0)
except TypeError:
    print "Whoa!: That doesn't look like a number!"
except:
    print "Whoa!: Couldn't complete the calculation"
```

Now it's the local exception handler that catches the error. Note also the order—the **TypeError** exception is identified within the **calc** function, long before you reach the **divide** function that would raise the **ZeroDivisionError** exception.

Raising Exceptions

You can explicitly raise an exception using the **raise** statement. This has the same effect as if the exception had been raised by an internal error. The format for the **raise** statement is

```
raise [EXCEPTION [, DATA]]
```

where **EXCEPTION** is the name of the exception you want to raise, and **DATA** is the additional data you want to supply back to the exception handler.

The **EXCEPTION** can either be one of the built-in exceptions, or you can use an exception or exception class that you have already defined (see "Rolling Your Own Exceptions" later in this chapter). The **DATA** is passed to the exception handler as normal.

The assert Statement

Shorthand for a **raise** statement, the **assert** statement works in a similar fashion to the **ASSERT()** macro in C/C++. The **assert** statement works like a **raise** statement, but the exception is only raised if the interpreter has not optimized the code (i.e., the user has not specified the **-O** optimization flag). The general format for the **assert** statement is

```
assert TEST, DATA
```

which is essentially equivalent to

```
if __debug__:
    if not TEST:
        raise AssertionError, DATA
```

Note that the **__debug__** symbol is not available when the interpreter is optimizing the code.

Built-In Exceptions

As you've already seen, Python comes with a number of base exceptions and exception classes. All of these exceptions can be used and trapped within your scripts to indicate or identify an error. If you are creating new exceptions (described in "Rolling Your Own Exceptions" later in this chapter), consider using one of these exceptions as the base class. See Figure 7-1 for an illustration of the class structure for the exception system.

Exception

This is the root class used for all exceptions. Note that a string operation on the arguments returned from any exception should give a string representation of the error that occurred, irrespective of the number or type of arguments supplied. To obtain the individual arguments of any exception, use the data format of the **except** statement, passing a tuple of names into which the information should be placed:

```
try:
    pow(2,262)
except Exception,(args,):
    print args
```

```
                    Exception
                        StandardError
                            ArithmeticError
                                    FloatingPointError
                                    OverflowError
                                    ZeroDivisionError
                            AssertionError
                            AttributeError
                            EnvironmentError
                                    IOError
                                    OSError
                                            WindowsError
                            EOFError
                            ImportError
                            KeyboardInterrupt
                            LookupError
                                    IndexError
                                    KeyError
                            MemoryError
                            NameError
                                    UnboundLocalError
                            RuntimeError
                                    NotImplementedError
                            SyntaxError
                            SystemError
                            SystemExit
                            TypeError
                            ValueError
                                    UnicodeError
```

Figure 7-1.   *Python's class structure for the exception system*

Alternatively, if you fail to supply an explicit tuple of tuple, as in

```
except Exception,args:
    print args
```

then **args** now holds the tuple of values returned by the exception.

StandardError

StandardError is the base class used for all the built-in exceptions. **StandardError** inherits the facilities offered by the **Exception** root class.

ArithmeticError

For exceptions arising due to arithmetic errors, one of the specific arithmetic exceptions (**OverflowError**, **ZeroDivisionError**, or **FloatingPointError**) is raised. **ArithmeticError** is the base class used by all three exceptions to indicate a general arithmetical fault. Since it's the base class, you can use this exception to trap all three specific arithmetic errors.

AssertionError

AssertionError is the exception raised when an **assert** statement fails.

AttributeError

AttributeError is the exception raised when an attribute reference or assignment fails. Note that if the object type does not support attributes then a **TypeError** is raised.

EnvironmentError

EnvironmentError is the class for errors that occur outside of Python's control, but that can be traced to the environment in which Python is operating. Used **EnvironmentError** as the base class for **IOError** and **OSError** exceptions.

The standard arguments returned by this exception are a two- or three-element tuple. In the two-element format, the first element is the error number (**errno**) as returned by the operating system and the second element is the associated error string. In the three-element version, the third element is the filename used when the exception was raised.

For example

```
try:
    open('nosuchfile')
except EnvironmentError,(errno,string):
    print "Whoops!: %s (%d)" % (string, errno)
```

EOFError

EOFError is the exception raised when the end-of-file (eof) condition is detected by the built-in data-handling functions. Note that this exception is only raised if the eof is detected without any data being read from the source. Note also that the built-in **read** and **readline** methods return an empty string when the eof is detected.

FloatingPointError

The **FloatingPointError** exception is raised when a floating-point operation fails. This exception is only available if the interpreter has been compiled with floating-point signal handling enabled. If not compiled with this option, an **ArithmeticError** exception is raised instead.

ImportError

The **ImportError** exception is raised when an **import** statement fails to find the specified module or when **from** fails to find the specific symbol in the module. See Chapter 5 for more information on import methods and semantics.

IndexError

The **IndexError** exception is raised when you try to access a sequence element out of the range of the sequence's size. Note that a nonsequenced object returns **TypeError** if you try to access an element via the normal subscript notation.

IOError

The **IOError** exception is raised when an I/O operation fails, for example, trying to open a nonexistent file or trying to write to a device with no free space. The information supplied by the exception is the same as the information supplied by any exception based on the **EnvironmentError** class.

KeyError

The **KeyError** exception is raised when the dictionary or other mapping key requested does not exist within the mapping object.

KeyboardInterrupt

The **KeyboardInterrupt** exception is raised when the interrupt key combination (Ctrl-C on a PC or Command-. on a Mac) is pressed. This exception is raised even when the built-in **input** or **raw_input** functions have been called.

LookupError

LookupError is the base exception class for the built-in **IndexError** and **KeyError** exceptions. This exception is used to indicate an error when accessing information from a sequence (string, list, or tuple) or mapping (dictionary).

MemoryError

The **MemoryError** exception is raised when the interpreter runs out of memory while executing a specific option, but still thinks it can recover from the situation if some objects are deleted to free up memory. It may not always be possible to recover from this situation, but by raising an exception, a stack trace for the program is triggered. The data passed by the exception describes what kind of internal operation triggered the exception (although it may not always be possible).

NameError

The **NameError** exception is raised when the object specified cannot be found within either the local or global scope. The data passed by the exception indicates the name that failed.

NotImplementedError

The **NotImplementedError** exception is raised when an abstract, user-defined error requires methods that can't be found. This exception is derived from the **RuntimeError** exception.

OSError

The **OSError** exception is raised when an operating system error occurs, usually through the **os** module interface. This exception is derived from the **EnvironmentError** exception.

OverflowError

The **OverflowError** exception is raised when an arithmatical operation exceeds the limits of the Python interpreter. Note that when doing long-integer math, the interpreter raises a **MemoryError** instead of an **OverflowError**.

RuntimeError

The **RuntimeError** exception is raised when there has been a run-time error that cannot be represented by one of the other exception types. This exception is included for compatibility only, since most errors now have their own exception class. The data passed by this exception is a string indicating the error that occurred.

SyntaxError

The **SyntaxError** exception is raised when a syntax error occurs, either within the original script, during an **import** or **exec** statement, or within the built-in **eval** function.

The information returned by the **SyntaxError** exception is a simple string of the error message. If you are accessing the exception object directly, the object includes the attributes **filename**, **lineno**, the **offset** within the line, and the actual **text** of the line.

For a more detailed analysis, the data passed by the **SyntaxError** exception can be accessed as a tuple of the form **(message, (filename, lineno, offset, text))**. For example, the code

```
try:
    eval("print :")
except SyntaxError,(message,(filename,lineno,offset,text)):
    print "Error in line %d, from file %s: \n" % (lineno, filename),\
        text,"\n",\
        ' ' * offset+"^", message
```

generates the following output when executed:

```
Error in line 1, from file None:
print :
      ^ invalid syntax
```

SystemError

The **SystemError** exception is raised when a system error occurs. Note that this exception applies to internal Python errors that can be safely trapped and could, potentially, be recovered from. The data passed by the **SystemError** exception is a string representing the error that went wrong.

 *You should send **SystemError** exception information to the Python maintainers (see Appendix B) because it indicates a possible error in the interpreter.*

SystemExit

The **SystemExit** exception is raised when the **sys.exit()** function is called. Normally, the Python interpreter exits without any error or stack trace being printed.

TypeError

The **TypeError** exception is raised when a built-in operation or function is applied to an object of inappropriate type. The returned value is a string that gives details about the type mismatch.

UnboundLocalError

The **UnboundLocalError** exception is raised when a reference is made to a local variable within the scope of a function or method, but no value as been bound to that variable.

UnicodeError

The **UnicodeError** exception is raised when a Unicode-related encoding or decoding error occurs.

ValueError

The **ValueError** exception is raised when a built-in operation or function receives an argument that has the right type but an inappropriate value, and the situation is not described by a more precise exception such as **IndexError**.

WindowsError

The **WindowsError** exception is raised when a Windows-specific error occurs. This exception is also raised when the error number returned does not match a valid **errno** value. The actual values returned are populated using the **GetLastError** and **FormatMessage** Windows API calls.

ZeroDivisionError

The **ZeroDivisionError** exception is raised when the second argument of a division or modulo operation is 0. The returned value is a string that indicates the type of the operands and the operation.

Rolling Your Own Exceptions

You can roll your own exceptions by creating a new exception class, which you should inherit from one of the system exception classes. Alternatively, for backward compatibility, you can also create a string-based exception, as in the following example:

```
CustomError = 'Error'

raise CustomError
```

Note that exceptions match against values, so raising a string exception but checking against the object still works:

```
CustomError = 'Error'

def test():
    raise 'Error'

try:
    test()
except CustomError:
    print "Error!"
```

However, it's bad practice to rely on this, so you should instead raise one of the predefined error strings.

To create class-based exceptions, create a new class, including any initialization information. You can then raise the exception, with any additional information, for parsing by an exception handler. The additional data collected by an **except** statement is extracted from the **args** attribute of an exception object, as in the following example:

```
class MyNameException(Exception):
    def __init__(self, name, msg):
        self.args = (name, msg)

try:
    raise MyNameException('Marvin', 'Not my real name')
except MyNameException,(name, msg):
    print 'Sorry, but',name,'is',msg
```

You'll be seeing some other examples of object/class–based exceptions throughout this book.

Note   *Although Python doesn't currently enforce it, you should base your exception classes on one of the built-in exception classes. This will enable you and programmers using your code and exceptions to trace problems using one of the generic, higher level classes as a catch-all, rather than needing to explicitly specify your exception class. String-based exceptions are outside of this hierarchy and should be avoided.*

The Complete Reference

Part II

Applying the Python Libraries

The Complete Reference

Chapter 8

Python's Built-In Functions

The bulk of functionality that Python provides in its standard form is handled by a series of external modules. These modules cover everything from the basic mechanics of getting command-line arguments and system configuration and information right up to complex modules for talking to SMTP and HTTP servers and to other systems and APIs.

However, despite the large library that comes standard with Python, you still need some built-in functionality to create, manipulate, and otherwise determine information about the objects, types, and classes that make up the Python language. This chapter concentrates on these built-in functions, while the rest of this part is given over to looking at specific modules within the Python standard library.

   The information contained in this chapter is based on the documentation available for Python 2.0. Updated versions of the full documentation supplied with Python can be found on the Python and MCwords web sites. See Appendix A for details.

The functions in this part are part of the **__builtin__** module.

__import__ (name [, globals [, locals [, fromlist]]])

The **__import__**() function is invoked automatically by the **import** statement. For example, the statement

```
import module
```

results in the following call to **__import__**():

```
__import__('module',globals(),locals(),[])
```

while the call

```
from module import class
```

results in the following call to **__import__**():

```
__import('module',globals(),locals(),['class'])
```

The **__import__**() function exists mainly so that you can optionally replace it with your own import function. See the **ihooks** and **rexec** modules for more examples.

abs(x)

The **abs()** function returns the absolute value of a number (plain, long integer, or floating-point). If you supply a complex number, only the magnitude is returned. Here's an example:

```
>>> print abs(-2.4)
2.4
>>> print abs(4+2j)
4.472135955
```

apply(function, args [, keywords])

The **apply()** function applies the arguments **args** to **function**, which must be a callable object (function, method, or other callable object). The **args** must be supplied as a sequence; lists are converted to tuples before being applied. The **function** is called using **args** as individual arguments. For example,

```
apply(add,(1,3,4))
```

is equivalent to

```
add(1,3,4)
```

You need to use the **apply()** function in situations where you are building up a list of arguments in a list or tuple and you want to supply the list as individual arguments. This is especially useful in situations where you want to supply a varying list of arguments to a function.

The optional **keywords** argument should be a dictionary whose keys are strings; these strings will be used as keyword arguments to be supplied to the end of the argument list.

buffer(object [, offset [, size]])

The **buffer()** function creates a new buffer on **object**, providing that **object** supports the buffer call interface; such objects include strings, arrays, and buffers. The new buffer references **object** using a slice starting from **offset** and extending to the end of the object or to the length **size**. If no arguments are given, the buffer covers the entire sequence. The resulting buffer object is a read-only copy of the object's data.

Buffer objects are used to create a more friendly interface to certain object types. For example, the string object type is made available through a buffer object that allows you to access the information in the string on a byte-by-byte basis.

callable(object)

The **callable()** function returns true if **object** is callable, false if **object** is not callable. Callable objects include functions, methods, and code objects, and also classes (which return a new instance when called) and class instances that have the **call** method defined.

chr(i)

The **chr()** function returns a single character string matching the ASCII code **i**, as in the following example:

```
>>> print chr(72)+chr(101)+chr(108)+chr(108)+chr(111)
Hello
```

The **chr()** function is the opposite of the **ord()** function, which converts characters back to ASCII integer codes. The argument **i** should be in the range 0–255; a **ValueError** exception is raised if the argument is outside that limit.

cmp(x, y)

The **cmp()** function compares the two objects **x** and **y** and returns an integer depending on the outcome. The return value is negative if **x** < **y**, 0 if **x** == **y**, and strictly positive if **x** > **y**. Note that this specifically compares the values rather than any reference relationship, such that

```
>>> a=99
>>> b=int('99')
>>> cmp(a,b)
0
```

coerce(x, y)

The **coerce()** function returns a tuple consisting of the two numeric arguments converted to a common type, using the same rules used by arithmetic operations. Here's are two examples:

```
>>> a = 1
>>> b = 1.2
```

```
>>> coerce(a,b)
(1.0, 1.2)
>>> a=1+2j
>>> b=4.3e10
>>> coerce(a,b)
((1+2j), (43000000000+0j))
```

compile(string, filename, kind)

The **compile()** function compiles **string** into a code object, which can later be executed by the **exec** statement to be evaluated using the **eval** function. The **filename** should be the name of the file from which the code was read, or a suitable identifier if generated internally. The **kind** argument specifies what kind of code is contained in **string**. See Table 8-1 for more information of the possible values of **kind**.

For example:

```
>>> a=compile('print "Hello World"','<string>','single')
>>> exec(a)
Hello World
>>> eval(a)
Hello World
```

complex(real [, imag])

The **complex()** function returns a complex number with the real component **real** and the imaginary component **imag**, if supplied. If **imag** isn't supplied, the imaginary component is 0j.

kind Value	Code Compiled
exec	Sequence of statements
eval	Single expression
single	Single interactive statement

Table 8-1. *The Kinds of Code Compiled by the **compile()** Function*

delattr(object, name)

The **delattr()** function deletes the attribute **name** from **object**, providing that **object** allows you to. This function is identical to the statement

```
del object.attr
```

but **delattr()** allows you to define **object** and **name** programmatically, rather than explicitly in the code.

dir([object])

When supplied without an argument, the **dir()** function lists the names in the current local symbol table, as in the following example:

```
>>> import smtplib, sys, os
>>> dir()
['__builtins__', '__doc__', '__name__', 'os', 'smtplib', 'sys']
```

When supplied with an argument, the **dir()** function returns a list of attributes for that object. This can be useful for determining the objects and methods defined within a module:

```
>>> import sys
>>> dir(sys)
['__doc__', '__name__', '__stderr__', '__stdin__', '__stdout__',
 'argv', 'builtin_module_names', 'byteorder', 'copyright',
 'exc_info', 'exc_type', 'exec_prefix', 'executable', 'exit',
 'getdefaultencoding', 'getrecursionlimit', 'getrefcount',
 'hexversion', 'maxint', 'modules', 'path', 'platform', 'prefix',
 'ps1', 'ps2', 'setcheckinterval', 'setprofile',
 'setrecursionlimit', 'settrace', 'stderr', 'stdin', 'stdout',
 'version', 'version_info']
```

The information is built from the **__dict__**, **__methods__**, and **__members__** attributes of the given object and may not be complete. For example, methods and attributes inherited from other classes are not normally included.

divmod(a, b)

The **divmod()** function returns a tuple that contains the quotient and remainder of **a** divided by **b**, as in the following example:

```
>>> divmod(7,4)
(1, 3)
```

For integers, the value returned is the same as **a / b** and **a % b**. If the values supplied are floating-point numbers, the result is **(q, a % b)**, where **q** is usually **math.floor(a / b)** but may be one less than that. In any case, **q * b + a % b** is very close to **a**; if **a % b** is non-zero, it has the same sign as **b**, and **0 <= abs(a % b) < abs(b)**. The following examples show how **divmod()** works with floating-point numbers:

```
>>> divmod(3.75, 1.125)
(3.0, 0.375)
>>> divmod(4.99, 1.001)
(4.0, 0.98600000000000065)
>>> divmod(-3.5, 1.1)
(-4.0, 0.90000000000000036)
```

eval(expression [, globals [, locals]])

The **eval()** function evaluates the string **expression**, parsing and evaluating it as a standard Python expression. When called without any additional arguments, **expression** has access to the same global and local objects in which it is called. Alternatively, you can supply the global and local symbol tables as dictionaries (see the descriptions of the **globals()** and **locals()** functions later in this chapter).

The return value of the **eval()** function is the value of the evaluated expression, as in the following example:

```
>>> a=99
>>> eval('divmod(a,7)')
(14,1)
```

Any syntax errors are raised as exceptions.

You can also use **eval()** to compile code objects such as those created by the **compile()** function, but only when the code object has been compiled using the "eval" mode.

To execute arbitrary Python code incorporating statements and expressions, use the **exec** statement or the **execfile()** function to dynamically execute a file. See the section "Executing Arbitrary Statements" at the end of this chapter for more information.

execfile(file [, globals [, locals]])

The **execfile()** function is identical to the **exec** statement (see the section "Executing Arbitrary Statements" at the end of this chapter for more information), except that it executes statements from a file instead of from a string. The **globals** and **locals** arguments should be dictionaries containing the symbol tables that will be available to the file during execution. If **locals** is omitted, then all references use the **globals** namespace. If both arguments are omitted, the file has access to the current symbol tables at the time of execution.

filter(function, list)

The **filter()** function filters the items in **list** according to whether **function** returns true, returning the new list, as in the following example:

```
a=[1,2,3,4,5,6,7,8,9]
b=filter(lambda x: x > 6, a)
print b
```

If **function** is **None**, the identity function is used and all the elements in **list** that are false are removed instead.

float(x)

The **float()** function converts **x**, which can be a string or number, to a floating-point number.

getattr(object, name [, default])

The **getattr()** function returns the value of the attribute **name** of **object**. Syntactically the statement

```
getattr(x,'myvalue')
```

is identical to

```
x.myvalue
```

If **name** does not exist, the function returns **default** if supplied, or raises an **AttributeError** otherwise.

globals()

The **globals()** function returns a dictionary that represents the current global symbol table. This is always the dictionary of the current module. If **globals()** is called within a function or method, it returns the symbol table for the module where the function or method is defined, not the function from where it is called.

hasattr(object, name)

The **hasattr()** function returns true if **object** has an attribute matching the string **name**. Returns 0 otherwise.

hash(object)

The **hash()** function returns the integer hash value for an object. The hash value is the same for any two objects that compare equally. This function does not apply to mutable objects.

hex(x)

The **hex()** function converts an integer to a hexadecimal string that is a valid Python expression.

id(object)

The **id()** function returns an integer (or long integer)—the object's *identity*—which is guaranteed to be unique and constant during the lifetime of the object.

input([prompt])

The **input()** function is equivalent to **eval(raw_input(prompt))**. See the description of the **raw_input()** function later in this chapter for more information.

int(x [, radix])

The **int()** function converts the number or string **x** to a plain integer. The **radix** argument, if supplied, is used as the base for the conversion and should be an integer in the range 2–36.

intern(string)

The **intern()** function adds **string** to the table of interned strings, returning the interned version. *Interned strings* are available through a pointer, rather than a raw string, allowing lookups of dictionary keys to be made using pointer comparisons instead of string comparisons. This provides a small performance gain over the normal string-comparison methods.

Names used within the Python namespace tables and the dictionaries used to hold module, class, or instance attributes are normally interned to speed up the execution of the script.

Interned strings are not garbage collected, so be aware that using interned strings on large dictionary key sets increases the memory requirements significantly, even after the dictionary keys have gone out of scope.

isinstance(object, class)

The **isinstance()** function returns true if **object** is an instance of **class**. The determination follows the normal inheritance rules and subclasses. You can also use the **isinstance()** function to identify if **object** is of a particular type by using the type class definitions in the **types** module. If **class** is not a class or type object, a **TypeError** exception is raised.

issubclass(class1, class2)

The **issubclass()** function returns true if **class1** is a subclass of **class2**. A class is always considered a subclass of itself. A **TypeError** exception is raised if either argument is not a class object.

len(s)

The **len()** function returns the length of a sequence (string, tuple, or list) or dictionary object.

list(sequence)

The **list()** function returns a list whose items and order are the same as those in **sequence**, as in the following example:

```
>>> list('abc')
['a', 'b', 'c']
>>> list([1,2,3])
[1, 2, 3]
```

locals()

The **locals()** function returns a dictionary that represents the current local symbol table.

long(x)

The **long()** function converts a string or number to a long integer. The conversion of a floating-point number follows the same rules as **int()**.

map(function, list, ...)

The **map()** function applies **function** to each item of **list** and returns the new list, as in the following example:

```
>>> a=[1,2,3,4]
>>> map(lambda x: pow(x,2), a)
[1,4,9,16]
```

If additional lists are supplied, they are supplied to **function** in parallel. Lists are padded with **None** until all lists are of the same length.

If **function** is **None**, the identity function is assumed, causing **map()** to return **list** with all false arguments removed. If the **function** is **None** and multiple list arguments are supplied, a list of tuples of each argument of the list is returned, as in the following example:

```
>>> map(None, [1,2,3,4], [4,5,6,7])
[(1, 4), (2, 5), (3, 6), (4, 7)]
```

The result of the preceding example is identical to the result produced by the **zip()** function.

max(s [, args...])

When supplied with a single argument, the **max()** function returns the maximum value in the sequence **s**. When supplied a list of arguments, the **max()** function returns the largest argument from those supplied. See the description of the **min()** function for more details.

min(s [, args...])

When supplied with a single argument, the **min()** function returns the minimum value in the sequence **s**. When supplied a list of arguments, the **min()** function returns the smallest value of all the arguments. Note that sequences in a multi-argument call are not traversed—each argument is compared as a whole, such that

```
min([1,2,3],[4,5,6])
```

returns

```
[1, 2, 3]
```

and not the often expected 1. To get the minimum value of one or more lists, use concatenation:

```
min([1,2,3]+[4,5,6])
```

oct(x)

The **oct()** function converts an integer to an octal string. The result is a valid Python expression, as in the following example:

```
>>> oct(2001)
'03721'
```

Note that the returned value is always unsigned, such that **oct(-1)** yields '037777777777' on a 32-bit machine.

open(filename [, mode [, bufsize]])

The **open()** function opens the file identified by **filename**, using **mode** and the buffering type **bufsize**. This function returns a file object. (See Chapter 3 and Chapter 6 for more information on file objects.)

The **mode** is the same as that used by the system **fopen()** function; see Table 8-2 for a list of valid modes. If **mode** is omitted, it defaults to **r**.

Mode	Meaning
r	Open for reading.
w	Open for writing.
a	Open for appending (file position automatically seeks to the end during the open).
r+	Open for updating (reading and writing).
w+	Truncates (empties) the file and then opens it for reading and writing.
a+	Opens the file for reading and writing and automatically changes current file position to the end of the file.
b	When appended to any option, opens the file in binary rather than text mode. (This mode is available for Windows, DOS and some other operating systems only. Unix/MacOS/BeOS treat all files as binary, regardless of this option.)

Table 8-2. *File Modes for the* **open()** *Function*

The optional **bufsize** argument of the **open()** function determines the size of the buffer to use when reading from the file. Table 8-3 lists the supported **bufsize** values. If the **bufsize** argument is omitted, the system default is used.

ord(c)

The **ord()** function returns the ASCII or Unicode numeric code of the string of one character **c**. The **ord()** function is the inverse of the **chr()** and **unichr()** functions.

pow(x, y [, z])

The **pow()** function returns the value of **x** raised to the power of **y**. If **z** is supplied, this function calculates **x** raised to the power **y** modulo **z**. This calculation is more efficient than using

```
pow(x,y) % z
```

The arguments supplied to **pow()** should be numeric types, and the types supplied will determine the type of the return value. If the calculated value cannot be represented by the supplied argument types, an exception is raised. For example, the following call to **pow()** will fail:

```
pow(2,-1)
```

But

```
pow(2.0,-1)
```

is valid.

Bufsize Value	Description
0	Disable buffering.
1	Line buffered.
>1	Use a buffer that is approximately **bufsize** characters in length.
<0	Use the system default (line buffered for **tty** devices and fully buffered for any other file.

Table 8-3. *Buffer Sizes Supported by the **open()** Function*

range([start,] stop [, step])

The **range()** function returns a list of numbers starting from **start** and ending before **stop** using **step** as the interval. All numbers should be supplied and are returned as plain integers. If **step** is omitted, the step value defaults to 1. If **start** is omitted, the sequence starts at 0. Note that the two-argument form of the call assumes that **start** and **stop** are supplied; if you want to specify a **step**, you must supply all three arguments.

The following calls to **range()** use positive values of **step**:

```
>>> range(10)
[0, 1, 2, 3, 4, 5, 6, 7, 8, 9]
>>> range(5,10)
[5, 6, 7, 8, 9]
>>> range(5,25,5)
[5, 10, 15, 20]
```

Note that the final number is **stop** minus **step**; the range goes up to but not including the **stop** value.

If you supply a negative value to **step**, the range counts down rather than up. **stop** must be lower than **start**; otherwise the returned list will be empty. The following examples illustrate the use of **step** as a negative value:

```
>>> range(10,0,-1)
[10, 9, 8, 7, 6, 5, 4, 3, 2, 1]
>>> range (25,0,-5)
[25, 20, 15, 10, 5]
>>> range(0,10,-1)
[]
```

raw_input([prompt])

The **raw_input()** function accepts raw input from **sys.stdin** and returns a string. Input is terminated by a newline character, which is stripped before the string is returned to the caller. If **prompt** is supplied, it is written to **sys.stdout** without a trailing newline character and used as the prompt for input, as in the following example:

```
>>> name=raw_input('Name? ')
Name? Martin
```

If the **readline** module has been loaded, features such as line editing and history are supported during input.

reduce(function, sequence [, initializer])

The **reduce()** function applies **function** (supporting two arguments) cumulatively to each element of **sequence**, reducing the entire statement to a single value. For example, the following statement emulates the ! mathematical operator:

```
reduce(lambda x,y: x*y, [1,2,3,4,5])
```

The effect is to perform the calculation

```
((((1*2)*3)*4)*5)
```

which equals 120.

If **initializer** is supplied, it's used as the first element in the sequence:

```
>>> reduce(lambda x,y: x*y, [1,2,3,4,5],10)
1200
```

reload(module)

The **reload()** function reloads an already imported module. The reload includes the normal parsing and initializing processes employed when the module was imported originally. This allows you to reload a changed Python module without needing to exit the interpreter.

There are a number of caveats for using **reload()**:

- If the module is syntactically correct but fails during initialization, the import process does not bind its name correctly in the symbol table. You will need to use the **import()** function to load the module before it can be reloaded.

- The reloaded module does not delete entries in the symbol table for the old version of the module first. For identically named objects and functions this is not a problem, but if you rename an entity, its value remains in the symbol table after a reload.

- The reloading of extension modules (which rely on built-in or dynamically loaded libraries for support) is supported, but is probably pointless and may actually fail, depending entirely on how well behaved the dynamically loaded library is.

- If a module imports objects from another module using the **from...import...** form, the **reload()** function does not redefine the objects imported. You can get around this by using the **import...** form.

- Reloading modules that provide classes does not affect any existing instances of that class—the existing instances will continue to use the old method definitions. Only new instances of the class will use the new forms. This also holds true for derived classes.

repr(object)

The **repr()** function returns a string representation of **object**. This is identical to using back quotes (`) on an object or attribute. The string returned yields an object with the same value as that when passed to **eval()**, as in the following example:

```
>>> dict = {'One':1, 'Two':2, 'Many': {'Many':4, 'ManyMany':8}}
>>> repr(dict)
"{'One': 1, 'Many': {'Many': 4, 'ManyMany': 8}, 'Two': 2}"
```

round(x[, n])

The **round()** function returns the floating-point value **x** rounded to **n** digits after the decimal point, as in the following examples:

```
>>> round(0.4)
0.0
>>> round(0.5)
1.0
>>> round(-0.5)
-1.0
>>> round(1985,-2)
2000.0
```

setattr(object, name, value)

The **setattr()** function sets the attribute **name** of **object** to **value**. The **setattr()** function is the opposite of the **getattr()** function, which merely gets the information. The statement

```
setattr(myobj, 'myattr', 'new value')
```

is equivalent to

```
myobj.myattr = 'new value'
```

The **setattr()** function can be used in situations where the attribute is known pragmatically by name, rather than explicitly as an attribute.

slice([start,] stop [, step])

The **slice()** function returns a slice object that represents the set of indexes specified by **range(start, stop, step)**. If one argument is supplied, it's used as **stop**; if two arguments are supplied, they're used as **start** and **stop**. The default value for any unsupplied argument is **None**. Slice objects have three attributes (**start**, **stop**, and **step**) that merely return the argument supplied to the **slice()** function.

str(object)

The **str()** function returns a string representation of **object**. This is similar to the **repr()** function except that the return value is designed to be a printable string rather than a string that is compatible with the **eval()** function.

tuple(sequence)

The **tuple()** function returns a tuple whose items are the same and in the same order as the items in **sequence**. Here are two examples of the **tuple()** function:

```
>>> tuple('abc')
('a', 'b', 'c')
>>> tuple([1,2,3])
(1, 2, 3)
```

type(object)

The **type()** function returns the type of **object**. The return value is a type object, as described by the **types** module. Here's an example:

```
>>> import types
>>> if type(string) == types.StringType:
    print "This is a string"
```

unichr(i)

The **unichr()** function returns a Unicode string of one character whose code is the integer **i**. This function is the Unicode equivalent of the **chr()** function described earlier in this chapter. Note that to convert a Unicode character back to its integer form, you can use **ord()**; there is no **uniord()** function. A **ValueError** exception is raised if the integer supplied is outside the range 0–65535.

unicode(string [, encoding [, errors]])

The **unicode()** function decodes a given **string** from one form to another, using the encoding format codec. Any error in encoding is tagged with the string in errors. Typically used to convert between string and Unicode encoding formats. The default behavior (when **encoding** is not supplied) is to decode UTF-8 in strict mode, with **errors** raising the **ValueError** exception. See the **codecs** module for a list of suitable codecs. See Chapter 10 for more information on how Unicode in Python works.

vars([object])

The **vars()** function returns a dictionary corresponding to the current local symbol table. When supplied with a module, class, or class instance, the **vars()** function returns a dictionary corresponding to that object's symbol table. Do not modify the returned dictionary because the effects are undefined.

xrange([start,] stop [, step])

The **xrange()** function works the same as the **range()** function, except that **xrange()** returns an **xrange** object. An **xrange** object is an opaque object type that returns the same information as the list that was requested, without having to store each individual element in the list. This is particularly useful in situations where you are creating very large lists; the memory saved by using **xrange()** over **range()** can be considerable.

zip(seq1, ...)

The **zip()** function takes a series of sequences and returns them as a list of tuples, where each tuple contains the nth element of each of the supplied sequences. Here's an example:

```
>>> a=[1,2,3,4]
>>> b=[5,6,7,8]
>>> zip(a,b)
[(1, 5), (2, 6), (3, 7), (4, 8)]
```

Executing Arbitrary Statements

Python supports three constructs that allow you to execute some arbitrary file or a string of Python code. It can be useful to execute a statement that has either been dynamically built by the script, or perhaps provided by the user. The three constructs are the **exec** statement and the **execfile()** and **eval()** functions. However, make sure you are using the correct construct to execute the code or fragment because each statement is designed to perform a specific function.

exec Statement

The **exec** statement is designed to execute any piece of Python code that can use any combination of functions and statements. The code you execute has access to the same globally and locally defined objects, classes, and methods or functions. Here's a simple example using the **exec** statement:

```
exec "print 'Hello World'"
```

You can also restrict the available resources for the **exec** statement by supplying a dictionary containing the list of objects and their values, as in the example:

```
exec "print message" in mynamespace
```

where **mynamespace** is the dictionary you want to use.

You can also explicitly supply global and local dictionary namespaces using the statement

```
exec "print message" in myglobals, mylocals
```

You can use the **globals()** and **locals()** functions to get dictionaries of the current tables.

Note that the **exec** statement executes/evaluates expressions and statements, but it does not return a value. A syntax error is raised if you try to get a return value because **exec** is a statement, not a function:

```
>>> a=exec '3+4'
  File "<stdin>", line 1
    a=exec '3+4'
          ^
SyntaxError: invalid syntax
```

execfile() Function

The **execfile()** function, explained earlier in this chapter, performs the same operation as the **exec** statement except that it reads the statements to be executed from a file, rather than through a string or code object. In all other respects **execfile()** is identical to the **exec** statement.

eval() Function

The **eval()** function does not allow you to execute arbitrary Python statements; the **eval()** function is designed to execute a Python expression and return a value, as in the following example:

```
result=eval(userexpression)
```

or more explicitly in this statement

```
result=eval("99+45")
```

You *cannot* use the **eval()** function to execute a statement:

```
>>> a=eval('print "Hello world"')
Traceback (most recent call last):
  File "<stdin>", line 1, in ?
  File "<string>", line 1
    print "Hello world"
          ^
SyntaxError: invalid syntax
```

As a rule of thumb, use the **eval()** function to evaluate an expression to a return value, but use the **exec** statement in all other situations.

The
Complete
Reference

Chapter 9

Interfacing to the OS

The most basic operation of any programming language is to interact with the operating system under which it is running. With a command-line–based operating system, such as Unix or Windows, interaction should include the extraction of other elements and text supplied on the command line. While we're at it, it's probably a good idea to actually parse the contents.

Beyond these basics, there are other more complex operations, including starting new processes, executing external programs, and handling multithreaded operations on those systems that support them.

Python provides a unified entry point for most of these operations in the **sys** and **os** modules. There are also separate modules that handle other systems, such as **time** and **getopt**. We'll have a look at all of these modules in this chapter and provide pointers to other chapters in this section that handle similar systems.

Working with the System (sys Module)

In a strict sense, the **sys** module provides tools for communicating directly with the system under which Python is being executed. Although it does provide some generic functionality (including access to the command-line arguments), its primary purpose is to help the programmer determine the environment under which their script is being executed.

Getting Command-line Arguments

In Python the command-line arguments are available through the **sys.argv** array. As with other arrays, counting starts at zero, with the first element containing the name of the script and elements from index one onwards containing any arguments supplied to the script.

For example, the script

```
import sys
count=0
for argument in sys.argv:
    print "Argument %d is %s" % (count,argument)
    count += 1
```

generates the following output when executed:

```
$ python argv.py hello this is a test
Argument 0 is argv.py
Argument 1 is hello
Argument 2 is this
Argument 3 is is
Argument 4 is a
Argument 5 is test
```

Knowing the name of the script can be useful, especially if you want to report an error to the user.

Parsing Command-line Arguments

You may want to supply arguments to your script that can be parsed just like those supplied to other programs, such as:

```
process.py -y -g --debug --output=process.out myfile.txt
```

In this case you need to use the **getopt** module. The module provides a single function called **getopt** that processes the arguments, placing the information into some more convenient forms. The basic format of the function is

```
getopt(args, options [, long_options])
```

where **args** is the list of arguments you want to parse, and **options** is a string containing the single-letter arguments you want to interpret. If you append a colon to a letter within the **options** string, then the argument will accept an additional argument as data to the argument. If supplied, the **long_options** should be a list of strings defining the words, rather than single letters, which should be identified and parsed. Note that in the arguments list, word-based arguments must be prefixed with a double, rather than a single, hyphen. The = suffix to an argument in **long_options** causes **getopt** to interpret the following argument as additional data.

The **getopt** function returns two objects. The first is a list of tuples containing the parsed argument and its value (if it has one); the second object is a list of the remaining, unparsed arguments.

For example:

```
>>> import getopt
>>> args = ['-a','-x','.bak','--debuglevel','99','file1','file2']
>>> opts, remargs = getopt.getopt(args,'ax:', ['debuglevel='])
>>> opts
[('-a', ''), ('-x', '.bak'), ('--debuglevel', '99')]
>>> remargs
['file1', 'file2']
```

The **getopt** function raises an exception (**GetoptError**) if an unrecognized option is seen in the argument list, or if the argument is expecting additional data but doesn't receive it.

Standard Filehandles

All processes on all platforms potentially support three standard filehandles: those which can be used to communicate with the standard input (the keyboard or terminal), standard output (the monitor or terminal), or standard error (usually the monitor/terminal). For users of Unix, you can equate these handles to the **<**, **>**, and **2>** redirection operators. Under Mac OS, these filehandles are emulated by the Python interpreter.

You can access the standard filehandles in Python using the **sys.stdin**, **sys.stdout**, and **sys.stderr** objects. These are file objects, so you must use the file methods defined in Table 10.1 in Chapter 10.

The **print** statement sends its output to the equivalent of **sys.stdout** so the statements

```
print 'Busy doin nothin'
```

and

```
sys.stdout.write('Busy doin nothin\n')
```

produce the same result.

Redirecting Output

It's often useful to redirect the output of one of the standard filehandles to another location. For example, if you wanted to trace the execution of a script, and you were using **sys.stderr** to send messages to the usual error channel, you could redirect the output from within your script.

To redirect any filehandle you need to open a file using the built-in **open()** function to create a new file object and either assign it to a new object and then assign that object to one of the standard filehandles, or assign the object directly, which is what we do here:

```
import sys
sys.stderr = open('error.log','w')
sys.stderr.write('Error log!\n')
sys.stderr.close()
```

Original Filehandles

If you reassign any of the standard filehandles within Python, the original objects as they were at the start of the scripts execution are available using the **sys.__stdin__**, **sys.__stdout__**, and **sys.__stderr__** objects.

Assuming we'd redirected the output to another file using the trick in the previous example, we could put standard error back to normal using:

```
sys.stderr = sys.__stderr__
```

Terminating Execution

Your script naturally terminates when the Python interpreter sees the end of the script—when there are no more statements to execute, then the execution stops. You can also force the termination of a script using the **sys.exit()** function:

```
Python 2.1 (#2, Apr 29 2001, 14:36:04)
[GCC 2.95.3 20010315 (release)] on sunos5
Type "copyright", "credits" or "license" for more information.
>>> import sys
>>> sys.exit()
$
```

You can supply an optional argument to the function, which can either be an integer or an object. If it's an integer, then by convention zero indicates successful execution while any nonzero value indicates an error. If you supply an object, then the object is written (using **str()**) to **sys.stderr** and a value of 1 is returned to the caller. If the object is the special value **None** then a zero is returned instead.

The actual implementation of the **sys.exit()** function causes Python to raise a **SystemExit** exception. This forces any **finally** clauses of any outstanding **try** statements to be honored and executed, and it's possible to trap the exception in order to perform cleanup operations (closing files, network/database connections, etc.) before the script finally terminates.

Note *An alternative way to quit is to actually raise the **SystemExit** exception; it'll have the same effect as calling **sys.exit()**.*

Tracing Termination

Although you could use the **SystemExit** exception to trap a termination request and perform some cleanup functions, it's much better to use **sys.exitfunc()**. You use this to define the name of a function to be called when **sys.exit()** is called. For example:

```
import sys

def cleanup():
    print "Had enough, deciding to leave\n"

sys.exitfunc = cleanup
```

For a more extensive system, use the **atexit** module; see the online documentation for more information.

Interpreter Information

In addition to the functions and structures already seen, the **sys** module also provides an interface to a number of variables that hold various pieces of information about the current instances of the Python interpreter. These variables are summarized in Table 9-1.

Python sys **Variable**	**Description**
builtin_module_names	A tuple containing the names of the all the modules built into the Python executable.
copyright	The copyright message from the current Python interpreter.
exec_prefix	Directory where the platform-dependent Python library files are kept.
executable	Returns the path to the executable file holding the current Python interpreter.
maxint	The largest integer supported by the **integer** object type.
platform	The platform identifier string determined during installation/configuration. For example, 'sunos5' or 'mac'.
prefix	Directory where platform-independent Python library files are kept.
ps1, ps2	The strings containing the primary and secondary prompts used when using the interpreter interactively. By default these are set to **>>>** and **...** respectively.
version	The version of the interpreter running the current script. The return value is a string of the form "2.0 (#71, Oct 22 2000, 22:09:24) [CW PPC w/GUSI2 w/THREADS]". The string contains the major version, minor revision, the build date, and the platform and options configured when the interpreter was built.

Table 9-1.   *Interpreter and Other Variables Supported by the **sys** Module*

Module Search Path

Python modules are looked for within a standard search path that is determined during compilation time. For example, the following list comes from a Python 2.0 installation under Solaris 8:

```
['', '/usr/local/lib/python2.0',
'/usr/local/lib/python2.0/plat-sunos5',
'/usr/local/lib/python2.0/lib-tk',
'/usr/local/lib/python2.0/lib-dynload',
'/usr/local/lib/python2.0/site-packages']
```

The list of directories is stored within the **sys.path** array object. If you want to add other directories to the list of those searched when you use the **import** statement, then simply modify the **sys.path** array:

```
import sys
sys.path.append('/home/mc/lib')
import smtplib
```

To insert the paths so that they get searched in preference to the standard path, use the **insert()** method:

```
import sys
sys.path.insert(0,'/home/mc/lib')
import mymodule
```

Once loaded, you can determine which modules are currently loaded using the **sys.modules** object. This is a dictionary that lists the module name and where it was loaded. For example, here's a list from a Linux installation taken *before* any user modules have been imported:

```
{'os.path': <module 'posixpath' from
'/usr/local/lib/python2.1/posixpath.pyc'>,
'os': <module 'os' from '/usr/local/lib/python2.1/os.pyc'>,
'readline': <module 'readline' (built-in)>,
'exceptions': <module 'exceptions' (built-in)>,
'__main__': <module '__main__' (built-in)>,
'posix': <module 'posix' (built-in)>,
'sys': <module 'sys' (built-in)>,
'__builtin__': <module '__builtin__' (built-in)>,
'site': <module 'site' from '/usr/local/lib/python2.1/site.pyc'>,
'signal': <module 'signal' (built-in)>,
'UserDict': <module 'UserDict' from
'/usr/local/lib/python2.1/UserDict.pyc'>,
```

```
'posixpath': <module 'posixpath' from
'/usr/local/lib/python2.1/posixpath.pyc'>,
'stat': <module 'stat' from '/usr/local/lib/python2.1/stat.pyc'>}
```

Note that the format of each dictionary pair is specific: the key contains the name of the module, and the corresponding value contains information about the module's real name and whether it is a built-in module or loaded from an external file.

Working with the Operating System (os Module)

Interacting with the operating system includes everything from determining the environment in which the interpreter and your script are running, the user and process environment, and also controlling and communicating with external aspects such as files and file systems.

In Python most of this functionality is handled by the **os** module, although some other modules provide generic interfaces to other systems. The **os** module is not itself the provider of functionality—instead it creates the necessary links between the **os** namespace and built-in modules such as **posix** (for Unix/Windows NT and 2000) or **mac**, which provide the real functionality on a system-dependent basis. This allows the **os** module to act as a cross-platform module that provides all of the core APIs for communicating with the host system.

You can determine which of the various OS-dependent modules has been loaded by examining the **os.name** variable. For example:

```
Python 2.0 (#71, Oct 22 2000, 22:09:24)  [CW PPC w/GUSI2 w/THREADS] on mac
Type "copyright", "credits" or "license" for more information.
>>> import os
>>> os.name
'mac'
```

The **os.path** variable holds the name of the module that should be used for handling platform-independent pathname operations. You can import the module required directly using

```
import os.path
```

Manipulating Environment Variables

The **os.environ** dictionary provides access to the environment variables of the current process (the Python interpreter). The **os.environ** variable is actually a mapping object, which means that we can access the information just like a dictionary, and we can also modify the real environment values using standard dictionary statements and expressions. Changing the environment will affect the Python interpreter and any programs we start from the interpreter through **os.system()** or **os.exec()**, and it will also be used as the environment for any children we create using **os.fork()**.

During startup the contents of **os.environ** are populated with the current environment. You can access the information just as would a standard dictionary:

```
print os.environ['PATH']
```

You can also assign a value to specific keys within **os.environ** to create and/or set the value of an environment variable. For example, to modify the value of the environments **PATH** variable, which defines the list of directories used to search for an external program, we would use

```
os.environ['PATH'] = '/bin:/sbin:/usr/sbin:/usr/bin:/usr/local/bin'
```

Alternatively, you can set the value of an environment variable using the **os.putenv()** function:

```
os.putenv('PATH', 'C:\\Python;C:\\WINNT\\system32;C:\\WINNT')
```

Note that although assigning a value to the mapping object provided by **os.environ** automatically calls **os.putenv()**, the **os.putenv()** function does automatically update **os.environ**. This may mean that changes made to the environment using **os.putenv()** are not reflected in **os.environ** even though the real environment has actually been modified.

Line Termination

Because the **os** module is loaded on a system-dependent basis, it also provides a handy way for setting and providing information that is system dependent. Most of this functionality is handled through the different functions and other system-dependent modules loaded by **os**.

Line termination is a perennial problem with any cross-platform–compatible language. Python solves this by automatically setting the value of the **os.linesep** variable to the correct line termination used by the current platform. The actual value is a string, either the single character newline ('\n') for POSIX systems, carriage return ('\r') for Mac OS machines, or the carriage-return/newline sequence ('\r\n') used by Windows.

The value is used by **print** when outputting information to the screen and by the **readline()** method when reading information from a file. In most situations you won't need to refer to this value. But if you are writing a cross-platform script and using file objects and **write()** methods to output textual data, then you should use the **os.linesep** value at the end of each statement. For example:

```
file.write('Some other text' + os.linesep)
```

This will ensure that whatever operating system you are currently executing on you will be using the correct line termination.

Process Environment

To get user ID and other process-specific information, you need to use one of a series of functions from the **os** module. A list of these functions is in Table 9-2.

Python Function	Description
chdir(path)	Changes the current working directory to **path**.
getcwd()	Returns the path of the current working directory.
getegid()	Returns the effective group ID. Unix only.
geteuid()	Returns the effective user ID. Unix only.
getgid()	Returns the real group ID. Unix only.
getpgrp()	Returns the ID of the current process group. Unix only.
getpid()	Returns the process ID of the current process. Unix/Windows only.
getppid()	Returns the ID of the parent process. Unix only.
getuid()	Returns the real user ID. Unix only.
putenv(var, value)	Sets the value of the environment variable name **var** to **value**. See "Manipulating Environment Variables" earlier in this chapter for more information. Unix/Windows only.
setgid(gid)	Sets the group ID to **gid**. Unix only. Requires Superuser privileges.
setpgrp()	Creates a new process group for the current process. Returns the ID of the new process group. Unix only. Requires Superuser privileges.

Table 9-2.   *Process Information Functions in the **os** Module*

Python Function	Description
setpgid(pid, pgrp)	Assigns the process ID **pid** to be a member of the group **pgrp**. Unix only. Requires Superuser privileges.
setsid()	Creates a new session and returns the newly created session ID. Sessions are used with terminals and the shells that support them to allow multiple applications to be executed without the use of a windowing system. Unix only.
setuid(uid)	Sets the user ID of the current process. Unix only. Requires Superuser privileges.
strerror(errno)	Returns the error message associated with the error number in **code**. Unix/Windows only.
umask(mask)	Sets the umask of the current process to **mask**. Unix/Windows only.
uname()	Returns a tuple of strings containing the system name, node name, release, version, and machine for the current system. Unix only.

Table 9-2. *Process Information Functions in the* **os** *Module* (continued)

Process Execution and Management

You can execute and manage processes within Python. Execution involves either replacing the Python interpreter, starting a new process or communicating with a process either to read or write to the process, or both. We can also install signal handlers to control how our process reacts when it is sent a signal. Most of this functionality is handled in Python by the **os** module.

Running External Commands

Although we can do most things within Python using some form of module or extension, there are times when we need to communicate with the outside world by running some external command.

The os.exec*() **Functions** The basic Python function for execution an external command is **execv**. There are also variations on the same function that also allow you to supply a dictionary of environment variables (**execve()**, **execvpe()**) or to search the environment path in **os.environ['PATH']** for the specified application to execute (**execvp()**, **execvpe()**). The format for each function is shown below:

```
os.execv(path, args)
os.execve(path, args, env)
os.execvp(path, args)
os.execvpe(path, args, env)
```

The **path** should be the full path to the file that you want to execute. When using **os.execvp()** or **os.execvpe()**, the environment path directories are searched. Alternatively you can set a different path using the **os.defpath** variable. The **args** argument should be a list (or tuple) of arguments supplied to the program being called. The **env** argument should be a dictionary of environment variables: these will be used in place of the environment being used by the Python interpreter.

Here are some examples of running all of the above functions:

```
os.execv('/bin/ls', ('-la'))
os.execve('/usr/local/bin/cvs', ('commit'), {'CVSROOT':'/export/cvs'})
os.execvp('ls',('-la'))
os.execvpe('cvs', ('commit'), {'CVSROOT':'/export/cvs'})
```

Note that in *all* cases the **exec*()** series of commands entirely replace the Python interpreter. If you execute the following from within a Python script (without using **os.fork()**), the Python interpreter and your script will terminate and the **ls** program will execute in its place:

```
os.execv('/bin/ls', ('-la'))
```

If you want to start an additional process, you will need to use either **os.fork()** to start a new child process, **os.spawn*()** (Unix/Windows only) or use the **os.system()** command.

In addition to the base versions there are also multiple argument versions that can be used with a variable number of arguments rather than using a tuple or list argument.

os.execl(path, arg0, arg1, ...)	Equivalent to **os.execv(path, (arg0, arg1, ...)**
os.execle(path, arg0, arg1, ..., env)	Equivalent to **os.execve(path, (arg0, arg1, ...), env)**
os.execlp(path, arg0, arg1, ...)	Equivalent to **os.execvp(path, (arg0, arg1, ...))**

In all cases an **OSError** exception is raised if the program in **path** cannot be found, with additional arguments containing the precise error, for example:

```
>>> import os
>>> os.execv('nothing',('',))
```

```
Traceback (most recent call last):
  File "<stdin>", line 1, in ?
OSError: [Errno 2] No such file or directory
```

Starting a New Process   To start a new process, rather than replace the current process, you need to use the **system()** function:

```
import os
os.system('emacs')
```

The return value from **os.system()** is the exit status of the called program. Under Windows, however, the value returned is always zero. If you want to read the output from a program, then use the Python **os.popen()** function instead (see "Communicating with an External Process").

Alternatively, under Unix and Windows you can use the **os.spawn*()** functions. They work in a similar fashion to the **os.exec*()** function but create a new process, rather than replacing the existing process. There are two forms:

```
os.spawnv(mode, path, args)
os.spawnvw(mode, path, args, env)
```

where **path** is the location of the application you want to spawn, and **args** is a list or tuple containing the arguments for the application. When using **os.spawnve()**, the **env** argument is a dictionary that is used to populate the environment for the spawned application.

In both cases the **mode** is a constant, as defined by the **os** module and listed in Table 9-3.

Communicating with an External Process

To read the output from an external command you need to use the **os.popen()** function. It opens a pipe to a program call so that you can read the information output from the file or write the information to the file. For example, the code below opens a connection to the **ls** external command to get a list of files, which we then read and print out (for a better alternative, see the **glob** module in Chapter 11):

```
import os
dir = os.popen('ls -al','r')
while(1):
    line = dir.readline()
    if line:
        print line,
    else:
        break
```

The **os.popen()** function works exactly the same as the built-in **open** function, returning a file object that we can read from in bytes or lines, as we have here. The actual format for the **os.popen()** function is

```
os.popen(command [, mode [, bufsize]])
```

The **command** should be the string to be executed by the shell, which is started when the function is called. The **mode** should be "r" for reading or "w" for writing; it defaults to "r" if no **mode** is supplied. The **bufsize** is the buffer size to be used when reading from the command, just like the **bufsize** argument to Python's **open()** function. The **os.popen()** function is only supported under Unix and Windows.

Unfortunately the **os.popen()** function works only in one direction; you can only read or write to the program that you called, you cannot read and write to the process. For this, you need the **popen2()** function in the **popen2** module.

The **popen.popen2()** function spawns a new process and returns the child standard output and input filehandles:

```
(child_stdout, child_stdin) = popen2(cmd [, bufsize [, mode]])
```

popen3() returns the standard output, input and error filehandles:

```
(child_stdout, child_stdin, child_stderr)
                    = popen3(cmd [, bufsize, [, mode]])
```

Finally the **popen4()** function returns a combined stdout/stderr filehandle:

Constant	Description
P_WAIT	Executes the program and waits for it to terminate before returning control to the calling program.
P_NOWAIT	Executes the program and immediately returns a process handle.
P_NOWAITO	Identical to **P_NOWAIT**.
P_OVERLAY	Executes the program, replacing the current process—that is, it works like the **exec*()** functions.
P_DETACH	Executes the program and detaches from it; the new process continues to run but cannot use **wait()** to wait for the process to terminate.

Table 9-3. *Modes for Spawning New Applications*

```
(child_stdout_and_error, child_stdin) = popen4(cmd[, bufsize[, mode ] ])
```

Once opened we can read and write to/from **child_stdout**, **child_stdin** or **child_stderr** using the same methods as for a normal file.

The **popen2.Popen3()** function returns an instance of the **Popen3** class:

```
child = Popen3(cmd [, capturestderr [, bufsize]])
```

The **capturestderr** argument if true forces the instance to capture standard error as well as input and output. The default is not to capture standard error. The new instance has the following methods and attributes:

child.poll()	Returns the exit code of the child or –1 if the child is still running
child.wait()	Waits for the child process to terminate, returning the exit code
child.fromchild	The file object that captures the child's standard output
child.tochild	The file object that sends input to the child's standard input
child.childerr	The file object that captures the child's standard error

Finally, there's also a **Popen4** class that works in the same way as the **popen4()** function, returning a combined standard out/standard error filehandle.

```
Popen4(cmd[, bufsize ])
```

Creating Child Processes

Lots of servers and other processes create "children" during their execution. The parent is normally some kind of listening program or service dispatcher—for example a web server—and when it receives a request or network connection it then creates a child process to service the request. In this way it's easier to handle the requests of a number of clients without resorting to a round robin or loop approach to servicing requests.

The operating system **fork()** function creates a new child process. In Python the **os.fork()** function is just an alias for the operating system version. What actually happens when **os.fork()** is called is that the current process is duplicated, and the **os.fork()** function returns zero within the child process while returning the ID of the child process in the parent. Within Python, to handle this just check the return value:

```
pid = os.fork()
if not pid:
    # Start of child process
```

```
else:
    # Continuation of parent process
```

For example, the script below forks off a new process and sends a message:

```
import os,time

pid = os.fork()
if not pid:
    for step in range(10):
        print 'Hello from the child!'
        time.sleep(1)
else:
    for step in range(10):
        print 'Hello from the parent!'
        time.sleep(1)
```

When executed, this script generates the following output:

```
Hello from the parent!
Hello from the child!
Hello from the child!
Hello from the parent!
...
Hello from the parent!
Hello from the parent!
Hello from the child!
Hello from the child!
Hello from the parent!
```

As you can see, from within the same script we are effectively executing two different processes. In essence, we end up with a quasi-multithreaded system for executing multiple processes from within a single process. Note that any open filehandles—including network sockets—are duplicated when **os.fork()** is called. This can be useful in situations where you want to accept data on an open filehandle in the parent but provide the child with the information. Once the process has forked, close the filehandles in the parent and let the child deal with them.

Waiting for Children

When you fork new processes and they eventually die, you will need to wait for the processes to exit cleanly to ensure that they do not remain in the process table as "zombies." This process is called *reaping*. There are two functions that will wait for a process to terminate, **os.wait()** and **os.waitpid()**.

```
(pid, exitcode) = os.wait([pid])
(pid, exitcode) = os.waitpid(pid, options)
```

The **pid** should be the process ID of the process that you want to wait for. If you do not specify a **pid** to the **wait()** function, the process will wait until all of the children have died. For example, to wait for child processes to terminate at the end of a script you might simply use

```
os.wait()
```

Note that the parent process blocks (pauses) until the process you are waiting for has completed.

If you want to avoid this blocking, you need to use the **waitpid()** function. The **options** argument accepts either zero, which forces normal operation identical to calling **os.wait()**, or the **os.WNOHANG** if you want the call to immediately return. Using **waitpid()** in this manner allows you to call a reaping process as part of a standard loop within the parent. For example:

```
import os

while 1:
    # wait for a connection
    if accepted:
        pid = os.fork()
    if not pid:
        # do the child stuff
    else:
        os.waitpid(pid, os.WNOHANG)
```

In a true multiprocess environment, you'd probably add the process ID to an array and then process each in order.

A much better solution is to create a signal handler. Each child process sends a **SIGCHLD** signal to its parent when it terminates. You can trap this using a signal handler, which then calls **wait()** or **waitpid()** for you. For example, the following signal handler is probably the easiest way to reap old processes:

```
def child_handler(signum, frame):
    os.wait()
```

See "Signals" later in this chapter for more information on how to create and install different signal handlers.

Getting Exit States

Both the **wait()** and **waitpid()** functions return a tuple consisting of the process ID of the child that terminated and its exit status. The exit status is a 16-bit number; the low byte of this is the signal number that killed the process, and the high byte is the exit status.

```
(newpid, exitcode) = os.waitpid(pid, os.WNOHANG)
```

On its own, the **exitcode** is not very useful, but the **os** module defines a number of functions that check the **exitcode** against known values to determine how the child terminated. These functions are **WIFSTOPPED()**, **WIFSIGNALED()**, **WIFEXITED()**, **WEXITSTATUS()**, **WSTOPSIG()**, and **WTERMSIG()** and return true if the **exitcode** matches the given condition.

For example, to check if a child process terminated because it was sent another signal we might use

```
import os

while(1):
    (newpid, exitcode) = os.waitpid(pid, os.WNOHANG)
    if (WIFSIGNALED(exitcode)): break
```

Signals

Signals provide a method for signaling a particular event to a process. They are not a communication mechanism: you cannot transmit information—all you can do is signal a particular event. Signals are used on a variety of operating systems, primarily those that are Unix or POSIX 1003.1 compatible (including Windows NT/2000), and are usually used as a way of managing a process or its execution. For example, the **KILL** signal tells the operating system to terminate the process. Others can be used to initiate a particular function; For example, sending the **HUP** signal to the **named** DNS server forces it to reload its configuration file.

The exact list of signals supported on your system is entirely OS and even OS version dependent. As a rough guide I've included a list in Table 9-4 of POSIX signals that should be supported by most operating systems.

All signals have a default operation: the **SIGSEGV** signal usually produces a core dump of the process under Unix, for example. Some signals can also be trapped, as in the example given for **named** above. For more information on trapping signals see the section "Signal Handlers" later in this chapter. Support under non-Unix operating systems is very limited; for example Windows supports only the ABRT, FPE, ILL, INT, SEGV, and TERM signals.

POSIX 1003.1	
Name	**Description**
SIGABRT	Abnormal termination
SIGALRM	The timer set by the **alarm** function has expired
SIGFPE	Arithmetic exceptions; for example, divide overflow or divide by zero
SIGHUP	Hang-up detected on the controlling terminal or death of a controlling process
SIGILL	Illegal instruction indicating a program error
SIGINT	Interrupt signal (special character from the keyboard or signal from another application)
SIGKILL	Termination signal; cannot be caught or ignored
SIGPIPE	Attempt to write to a pipe with no application reading from it
SIGQUIT	Quit signal (special character from the keyboard or signal from another application)
SIGSEGV	Attempt to access an invalid memory address
SIGTERM	Termination signal (from another application or OS)
SIGUSR1	Application-defined (user-defined) signal
SIGUSR2	Application-defined (user-defined) signal
SIGCHLD	A child process terminated or stopped
SIGCONT	Continue the process if currently stopped
SIGSTOP	Stop signal; stops the specified process
SIGTSTP	Stop signal from special character from keyboard
SIGTTIN	A read was attempted from the controlling terminal by a background process
SIGTTOU	A write was attempted to the controlling terminal by a background process

Table 9-4.   *POSIX Signals*

Sending Signals

The Python **os.kill()** function sends a signal to an existing process:

```
kill(pid, signal)
```

The **signal** module contains the symbolic constants for the different signals with each constant in the form **SIG***. For example we could send the alarm signal to the current process using

```
kill(os.getpid(), signal.SIGALRM)
```

See Table 9-4 for a full list of the POSIX signals or see the **signal(5)** manual page under Unix or the MSDN library under Windows for information on which signals are supported on your system.

Signal Handlers

To trap a signal you must install what is known as a *signal handler*. This is just a function that will be called when the signal is received by the process. In Python we install a signal handler using the **signal.signal()** function. It accepts two arguments: the signal to be trapped and the function that will be called:

```
signal.signal(signal, handler)
```

For example, to install a system handler for the **SIGALRM** signal:

```
import signal,time,sys

def alarm_handler(signum, frame):
    print "Wake Up!"
    sys.exit()

signal.signal(signal.SIGALRM, alarm_handler)

signal.alarm(5)
print "Going to sleep... "
time.sleep(10)
print "Now I'm up. "
```

The **signal.alarm()** function installs an alarm timer for the given number of seconds. Once the time is up, the OS automatically sends a **SIGALRM** signal to the process. In this case we set an alarm for 5 seconds, while waiting for 10 seconds. If we run the script we should get the "Wake Up!" message after about 5 seconds, without seeing the "Now I'm up" message as the script terminates at the end of the signal handler function.

In all cases a signal handler must accept two arguments. The first argument are **signum**, the signal raised when the handler was called, and **frame**, which is a frame object describing the Python execution stack at the point the signal was raised. We'll be looking at frames in more detail in Chapter 24: they are used by the Python interpreter to manage the execution of a script.

If you don't supply a function that accepts two arguments when installing the signal handler, then a **TypeError** exception is raised.

Getting the Current Signal Handler   You can get the name of the current signal handler installed for a particular signal using

```
handler = signal.getsignal(signal.SIGALRM)
```

The returned object is callable, so we could immediately invoke the handler using

```
handler()
```

Disabling a Signal Handler   The **signal** module defines two standard handlers that can be used to modify the behavior of the signal handling process. The **signal.SIG_IGN** handler forces Python to ignore the specified signal, while the **signal.SIG_DFL** handler causes Python to invoke the default signal handler.

We can ignore a signal like this:

```
signal.signal(SIGALRM, signal.SIG_IGN)
```

or set the signal to its default operation (as defined by the operating system) using

```
signal.signal(SIGQUIT, signal.SIG_DFL)
```

Note that you cannot ignore signals such as KILL. They are always handled by your OS.

User/Group Information

The user and group information stored in the Unix **/etc/passwd** and **/etc/group{s}** files is available through the **grp** and **pwd** modules. In each case the functions raise a **KeyError** if the group does not exist. See Table 9-5 for a list of the supported functions.

For example, to get the home directory and shell for the current user we might use

Function	Description
grp.getgrgid(gid)	Returns a tuple containing the information for the group matching **gid**. The tuple consists of the group name, group password, group id, and a list of the members of the group. For example **grp.getgrgid(0)** returns: **('root', '', 0, ['root'])**.
grp.getgrnam(name)	Identical to **getgrgid()** but looks for a group matching **name**.
grp.getgrall()	Returns a list of tuples, where each tuple contains the information returned by **getgrgid()**.
pwd.getpwuid(uid)	Returns the user information for the user ID **uid**. Information is returned as a tuple containing username, password, user ID, group ID, gecos (full name and/or contact detail), home directory, and shell. For example **pwd.getpwuid(0)** returns **('root', 'x', 0, 1, 'Super-User', '/', '/usr/bin/bash')**.
pwd.getpwnam(name)	Identical to **getpwuid()** but looks for a user matching **name**.
pwd.getpwall()	Returns a list of tuples, where each tuple contains the information returned by **getpwuid()**.

Table 9-5. *Getting User and Group Entries with Python*

```
import pwd,os

pwinfo = pwd.getpwuid(os.getuid())
name = pwinfo[0]
fullname, homedir, shell = pwinfo[4:]
print "You are %s (%s)\nHome Directory is %s\nShell is %s" \
        % (name, fullname, homedir, shell)
```

You might also want to investigate the **getpass** and **crypt** modules, which provide a safe way of getting a password from a terminal and for encrypting a text password into the encrypted version that is stored in the **/etc/passwd** file. For example, the script below prompts and then checks the current user's password:

```
import getpass,pwd,crypt
```

```
password = getpass.getpass()
realpw = pwd.getpwnam(getpass.getuser())[1]
if realpw == crypt.crypt(password,password[:2]):
    print "Password validated"
else:
    print "Password invalid
```

Multithreading

Threads are a relatively new mode of operation for many platforms and programming languages. Threads are essentially a method for executing a number of different functions *simultaneously* within a given process without resorting to using **fork()** (which implies a serious overhead as the process is duplicated) or using less efficient methods such as the **select()** function (see Chapter 10). Before we look at the specifics of threads, though, it's worth taking a look at how modern multitasking operating systems operate.

How Multitasking Works

If you look at a typical modern operating system, you'll see that it's designed to handle the execution of a number of processes simultaneously. The method for employing this is either through *cooperative multitasking* or *preemptive multitasking*. In both cases, the actual method for executing a number of processes simultaneously is the same—the operating system literally switches between applications every fraction of a second, suspending the previous application and then resuming the next one in a round-robin fashion. So, if the operating system has 20 concurrent processes, each one will be executed for a fraction of a second before being suspended again and having to wait for 19 other processes to do their work before getting a chance to work again.

The individual processes are typically unaware of this switching, and the effects on the application are negligible—most applications couldn't care less whether they were working as a single process or as part of a multiprocessing environment, because the operating system controls their execution at such a low level.

The two different types of multitasking—cooperative and preemptive—describe how the operating system controls the applications that are executing. With *cooperative* multitasking, all processes are potentially given the same amount of execution time as all others. What actually happens is that a given process executes until it calls a system function, at which time the OS is able to switch to a different process. This means that it's possible for an application never to relinquish its control over the processor. Some operating systems are more specific and provide the "main" application with the bulk of the processor time (say 80 percent), and the "background" applications with equal amounts of the remainder (20 percent). This is the model used by the Mac OS (but not MacOS X), and it allows the GUI environment to give the most time to the application the user is currently employing.

Preemptive multitasking is much more complex. Instead of just arbitrarily sharing the processor time between all of the processes that are executing, an operating system with preemptive multitasking gives the most processor time to the process that requires it. The operating system does this by monitoring the processes that are running and manages the execution of each process; those with higher priorities get more time, and those with the lowest priorities get the least. Because we can control the priorities of the processes, we have much greater control over how different processes are executed. On a database server, for example, you'd want to give the database process the highest priority to ensure the speed of the database. Preemptive multitasking is one of the main features of many server-oriented operating systems, including Unix, Linux, and NT-based Windows implementations, including Windows 2000 and NT itself. It's also more commonly used in client-oriented operating systems; Windows 95/98/NT Workstation/2000 Professional, Mac OS X, and BeOS all support preemptive multiprocessing.

The different multitasking solutions also determine the different hardware types that can be used with an operating system. Cooperative multitasking is really only practical on a single-processor system. This is because of the round-robin approach, which requires that the process resides on the same processor for its entire duration. Although it's possible (and indeed frequently common) to find preemptive multitasking on single processor machines, they do not handle as well as you might expect. In fact in some quarters the requirement of a preemptive system has helped to drive processor design— the SPARC, SuperSPARC, and UltraSPARC processors used by Sun have all been specially designed with multitasking in mind. They employ multiple register sets to allow the processor to easily switch between multiple tasks.

With preemptive multitasking, multiprocessor solutions are the best hardware platform. Because the operating system knows how much time each process requires, it can assign individual processes to different processors depending on how busy each processor is. This helps to make the best use of the available processor capacity and to spread the load more effectively. However, the division of labor is only on a process-by-process basis, so if you have one particularly intensive process, it can only be executed on a single processor, even if it there is spare capacity on other processors in the system.

From Multitasking to Multithreading

With a multitasking operating system, there seem to be a number of processes all executing concurrently. In reality, of course, each process is running for a fraction of a second, and potentially many times a second, to give the impression of a real multitasking environment with lots of individual processors working on their own application.

For each process, there is an allocation of memory within the addressing space supported by the operating system that needs to be tracked, and for multiuser operating systems, such as Unix, there are also permission and security attributes and, of course, the actual code for the application itself. Tracking all of this information is a full-time job— under Unix there are a number of processes that keep an eye on all of this information, in addition to the core kernel process that actually handles many of the requests.

If an individual process wants to be able to perform a number of tasks concurrently, there are two possible solutions. The first solution is a round-robin approach, as used by the main operating system, but without the same level of control. Each function that needs to be executed is called in sequence in a loop, but because we can't arbitrarily terminate a function mid-execution, there are often problems with "lag-time"—if a function has a large amount of information to process, then its execution will hold up the entire loop.

For file processing, you can get around this by using **select** and parsing fixed blocks of information for each file. In this instance, we only process the information from the files that have supplied (or require) more data, and provided we read only a single line or a fixed-length block of data, the time to process each request should be relatively small.

For solutions that require more complex multitasking facilities, the only other alternative is to **fork** a new process specifically to handle the processing event. Because **fork** creates a new process, its execution and priority handling can be controlled by the parent operating system. This is usually the solution used by network services, such as Apache and IMAP or POP3 daemons. When a client connects to the server, it forks a new process designed to handle the requests of the client.

The problem with forking a new process is that it is a time-consuming and very resource-hungry process, and it doesn't really solve the problem: it gives the OS yet another process to manage and allot time to. Creating a new process implies allocating a new block of memory and creating a new entry in the process table used by the operating system's scheduler to control each process's execution. To give you an idea of the resource implications, a typical Apache process takes up about 500K. If 20 clients connect all at the same time, it requires the allocation of 10MB of memory and the duplication of the main image into each of the 20 new processes.

In most situations, we don't actually need most of the baggage associated with a new process. With Apache, a forked process doesn't need to read the configuration file—it's already been done for us, and we don't need to handle any of the complex socket handlers. We need only the ability to communicate with the client socket we are servicing.

This resource requirement puts unnecessary limits on the number of concurrent clients that can be connected at any one time—it is dependent on the available memory and ultimately the number of processes that the operating system can handle. The actual code required to service the client requests could be quite small, say 20K. Using multiprocessing on a system with 128MB might limit the number of clients to around 200—not a particularly large number for a busy website. To handle more requests than that, you'd need more memory and probably more processors: switching between 200 processes on a single CPU is not recommended because the amount of time given to each process during a single pass (executing each process once) would be very small, and therefore it could take minutes for a single process to service even a small request.

This is where threads come in. A thread is like a slimmed-down process—in fact they are often called "lightweight processes." The thread runs within the confines of the parent process and normally executes just one function from the parent. Creating a new thread doesn't mean allocating large areas of memory (there's probably room within the parent's memory allocation) or require additions to the operating system's schedule tables, either. In our web server example, rather than forking a new process to handle the client, we could instead create a new thread using the function that handles client requests.

By using multithreading, we can therefore get the multiprocessing capability offered by the parent operating system, but within the confines of a single process. Now an individual process can execute a number of functions simultaneously, or alternatively execute the same function a number of times, just as you would with our web server.

On an operating system that supports preemptive multitasking and multithreading, we get the prioritizing system on the main process and an internal "per-process" multitasking environment. On a multiprocessor system, most operating systems will also spread the individual threads from a single process across all of the processors. So, if we have one particularly intensive process, it can use all of the available resources and processors by splitting its operation into a number of individual threads. We no longer get into a situation where one process is tied to one processor, or into the situation where we have to create large numbers of duplicates to service the requests of a number of machines.

Threading is, of course, very OS-specific. Even now, there are only a handful of operating systems that provide the functionality to a reasonable level, and some require additional or different libraries to enable the functionality. Most of the operating systems that support threading are either Unix based (Solaris, AIX, HP-UX, some Linux distributions, BSD, Mac OS X) or Windows based (Windows 98/NT/2000/Me), but there are exceptions such as BeOS and even Mac OS.

Comparing Threads to Multiple Processes

The major difference between multithreaded and multiprocess applications is directly related to the relative resource cost, which we've already covered. Using **fork** to create duplicate instances of the same process requires a lot of memory and processor time. The overhead for a new thread is only slightly larger than the size of the function you are executing, and unless you are passing around huge blocks of data between threads, it's not inconceivable to be able to create hundreds or on a suitable system thousands of threads within a single process.

The only other difference is the level of control and communication that you can exercise over the threads. When you **fork** a process, you are limited in how you can communicate with the child. To exchange information, you'll need to open pipes to communicate with your children and this becomes unwieldy with a large number of children. If you simply want to control the children, you are limited to using signals to either kill or suspend the processes—there's no way to reintegrate the threads into the main process, or to arbitrarily control their execution without using signals.

Comparing Threads to select()

The **select** function provides an excellent way of handling the data input and output from a number of filehandles concurrently, but this is where the comparison ends. It's not possible, in any way, to use **select** for anything other than communicating with filehandles, and this limits its effectiveness for concurrent processing.

On the other hand, with threads you can create a new thread to handle any aspect of your process's execution, including, but not limited to, communication with filehandles. For example, with a multidiscipline calculation you might create new threads to handle the different parts of the calculation.

Threads and Python

Python supports threads on Windows, Solaris, BeOS, some Linux variants, and most other Unix variants that support the POSIX thread library (pthread). By default, threads are disabled in the Python source distribution: you'll need to manually add support by modifying the Python **Setup** file in the Extensions directory. Check the installation files that come with Python for more information.

The scheduling of threads and thread switching are controlled by an interpreter lock that controls thread execution. This ensures that only a single thread can be executed by the current instance of the interpreter at any time. We can also only switch between threads between the execution of individual byte codes. (See Chapter 23 for more information on byte code and how it affects execution.) You can control the number of bytecode instructions that are executed for each thread before execution switches to the next thread using the **sys.setcheckinterval()** function. The default is 10 bytecode instructions.

Also be careful when using Python extensions written in C/C++ that may or may not be written to be thread compatible. If they are not thread compatible, the process will block until the function call has completed, irrespective of the **sys.setcheckinterval()** settings.

You should also be aware of the effects of using signals when employing threads. Signals handlers can be caught and executed only by the main thread, not by any additional threads in the script. This obviously also implies that you cannot send a signal to an individual thread.

Basic Threads

The **thread** module provides a very simplified method for creating threads and managing locks on data structures. All threads in Python work by creating a new thread whose sole responsibility is to execute the function they are supplied with during execution. This means that if you have a piece of code that you executed within a separate thread, you will need to place it into a function before you create a thread to execute.

Creating New Threads

The core function is **start_new_thread()**:

```
start_new_thread(func, args [,keywordargs])
```

The function creates a new thread that starts executing the function **func**, which is called using the arguments **args** and the keyword arguments **keywordargs** by using the **apply()** function. The thread starts immediately; if you want to delay the execution of a given thread, you can do this using the **threading** module, covered later in this chapter in the "Advanced Threads" section. If there is an error in the function and the exception has not been handled, then a stack trace is printed and the thread exits, but other threads, including the parent, continue to execute. Exceptions are not propagated up to the parent.

However, when the parent thread terminates, the continued execution of the threads is entirely OS dependent. Some will allow the threads to continue until they reach the end of their function. Others will kill all the threads and terminate the entire program. Check your system's documentation to see how it treats parentless threads.

For example, here's a script that displays the time, updated every 10 seconds, using a thread to handle the update process.

```
import thread, time

def display_time(interval, prefix=''):
    while 1:
        print prefix,time.ctime(time.time())
        time.sleep(interval)

thread.start_new_thread(display_time, (10, 'The is now'))
while 1:
    pass
```

The function itself is just a loop that prints out the time (using an optional prefix) before pausing for the specified interval. Note that the arguments to the thread function have to be supplied as a tuple. We also have to set up a loop in the main thread that does nothing so that the parent process doesn't die, as this would also kill off the thread we created.

Thread Control

To terminate a thread, you either let the thread's function terminate with a return, or, to force termination, you can call the **thread.exit()** function. Also be aware that the **sys.exit()** function *when called from within a thread* calls the **thread.exit()** function, which terminates only the thread, not the entire script.

All threads are also given a unique integer identity number that you can determine within a thread using the **get_ident()** function. This is especially useful if you want to log thread execution. (We'll see an example of this when we look at object access across threads.) Note that thread IDs are not sequential and there is no relation between the threads of a process and the process ID.

Object Locking

Threads share and have access to all of the global objects and data structures within the parent, so you must use extreme caution when updating these structures from multiple threads. Although it's difficult to demonstrate, the effects of updating the same data structure at the same time in two different threads is unlikely to achieve the desired result. Although there are different methods of controlling access to individual variables within the thread system, they all rely on the same basic premise of a "lock." This is a thread-safe object that can be used to control access to another object from within multiple threads. The **thread** module provides only a very simple object locking mechanism, called a *mutex*, for mutual exclusion; for more advanced methods see "Advanced Threads" later in this chapter.

The **allocate_lock()** function creates a lock object (of type **LockType**) that can be used to set or determine the lock for a given object. The relationship between the lock and the object is not automatic; you need to know which lock object relates to each variable before using the system. For example, if we create a variable **counter** we might create a **counter_lock** object that we'll use to control access to that variable:

```
counter = 0
counter_lock = thread.allocate_lock()
```

If we want to make changes to **counter** we need to first acquire the lock handled by **counter_lock**. The **acquire()** method attempts this operation for us:

```
lock.acquire([waitflag])
```

By default **waitflag** is zero, indicating that the method should return immediately whether the lock could be acquired or not. If **waitflag** is nonzero then the thread will block until the lock has been acquired. In either case, you *must* supply a value if you want to check its return status. The method returns zero if the lock could not be acquired and 1 if it could. For example, to acquire a lock and then change the value of our counter we could use

```
if (counter_lock.acquire(0)):
    counter += 1
```

The **counter_lock** is now locked and requests by other threads to acquire the lock will always fail. Although it's possible for other threads to still modify the **counter** object, they would be doing so outside of the authority of the lock and could corrupt the information in the object. Mutexes are essentially just a protocol; all the threads need to follow the protocol for the system to work. To actually release the lock we need to

use the **release()** method on our **counter_lock** object so that other threads can acquire
the lock and change the value:

```
counter_lock.release()
```

If you want to check the status of a lock without using the **acquire()** method you can
also use the **locked()** method. This returns 1 if the object is locked or zero if not.

Putting this all together, the script below is a simple counter with three threads. The
first thread is the display thread that simply outputs the current counter value without
making modifications. There are also two threads, A and B, that acquire the lock on a
variable, increase its value and then hold on to the lock for a short period before
releasing it.

```
import thread, time

counter = 0

counter_lock = thread.allocate_lock()

def thread_incra():
    while 1:
        print "Thread A(%d): Executing" % (thread.get_ident(),)
        if (counter_lock.acquire(0)):
            global counter
            print "Thread A: Acquired lock...pausing..."
            counter += 1
            time.sleep(20)
            counter_lock.release()
        else:
            print "Thread A: Couldn't get lock"
        time.sleep(5)

def thread_incrb():
    while 1:
        print "Thread B(%d): Executing" % (thread.get_ident(),)
        if (counter_lock.acquire(0)):
            global counter
            print "Thread B: Acquired lock...pausing..."
            counter += 5
            time.sleep(10)
            counter_lock.release()
        else:
            print "Thread B: Couldn't get lock"
        time.sleep(5)

def thread_display():
```

```
    while 1:
        print "Display thread(%d): Counter is %d" % (thread.get_ident(), counter)
        time.sleep(5)

thread.start_new_thread(thread_display, ())
thread.start_new_thread(thread_incra, ())
thread.start_new_thread(thread_incrb, ())
while 1:
    pass
```

If we execute the script we get the following output:

```
Display thread(1026): Counter is 0
Thread A(2051): Executing
Thread A: Acquired lock...pausing...
Thread B(3076): Executing
Thread B: Couldn't get lock
Thread B(3076): Executing
Thread B: Couldn't get lock
Display thread(1026): Counter is 1
Thread B(3076): Executing
Thread B: Couldn't get lock
Display thread(1026): Counter is 1
Thread B(3076): Executing
Display thread(1026): Counter is 1
Thread B: Couldn't get lock
Display thread(1026): Counter is 1
Thread B(3076): Executing
Thread B: Acquired lock...pausing...
Thread A(2051): Executing
Thread A: Couldn't get lock
Display thread(1026): Counter is 6
Display thread(1026): Counter is 6
Thread A(2051): Executing
Thread A: Acquired lock...pausing...
Display thread(1026): Counter is 7
Thread B(3076): Executing
Thread B: Couldn't get lock
Display thread(1026): Counter is 7
Thread B(3076): Executing
Thread B: Couldn't get lock
```

You can see here how first thread A acquires the lock, updates the counter, and then holds on to the lock while thread B continues to try to execute and acquire the lock—then the process is reverse as thread B gets the lock and thread A fails to get the lock. Simultaneously, the display thread goes on outputting the current counter value.

Advanced Threads

Although the **thread** module should suffice for most thread implementations, it will not suit everybody. There is no way in the **thread** module, for example, to control the operation or execution of the threads from within the parent. It's also limited in the way in which we can control access to variables, including the way we communicate between threads without using a global variable or the resources or namespace of the parent thread.

The **threading** module solves this by providing a more advanced method of initiating a new thread and a number of lock systems, semaphores, and other interthread communication systems to better help you control and communicate between your parent and threads.

We'll have a look at the specifics shortly; all of the solutions are based on a number of new object classes, but there are general utility functions within the module to allow you to monitor the current situation. These functions are

activeCount()	Returns the number of currently active **Thread** objects.
currentThread()	Returns the **Thread** object for the currently executing thread. This can be useful within a thread as a method of determining information about the thread from within itself.
enumerate()	Returns a list of all the currently active **Thread** objects, regardless of their execution status.

The **threading** module and its classes are actually built on top of the main **thread** module. Although **threading** doesn't support any different solutions for the creation of threads or locking mechanisms, what it does do is augment the basic methods to support the functionality offered by many OS/language interfaces.

Thread Objects

The core of the system is the **Thread** class. This defines a separate thread and is used to execute a function in the same way as the **thread.start_new_thread()** function. The basic format for creating a new Class instance is

```
Thread(group=None, target=None, name=None, args=(), kwargs())
```

The **target, args**, and **kwargs** arguments are identical the **func, args**, and **keywordargs** arguments to **thread.start_new_thread()**. The **group** argument is reserved for future extension and for the moment can be safely ignored. The **name** argument is the name that you want to give to your thread. Names are merely notational and have no bearing on the execution or control of your threads. The default name is "Thread-N" where **N** is a sequential number.

For example, we could create a new **Thread** object for our counter thread in the earlier example using

```
my_display_thread = Thread(None, thread_display, None, (), {})
```

The result is a **Thread** object that supports the following methods:

t.start()	When a thread is created it is not immediately executed; you must call the **start()** method for the function to actually be executed. What actually happens is that **start()** calls the threads **run()** method, which itself calls the function you specified when the **Thread** object was created.
t.run()	Called when the thread starts. By default this calls the function specified when the object was created but you can also overload this method with the statements you want executed in new classes based on **Thread**.
t.getName()	Gets the name of the thread.
t.setName()	Sets the name of the thread.
t.isAlive()	Returns 1 if the thread is alive (that is, currently executing) or zero otherwise. Threads in which the **start()** method has not been called or that have terminated will return zero.
t.setDaemon()	You can daemonize a thread by calling the **setDaemon()** method *before* calling **start()**. Daemonized threads continue to execute in the same way that a daemonized program (as controlled by the **os.setpgprp()** function) continues to execute after the main program has finished. Using **setDaemon()** you can therefore start a multithreaded server just like the **named** or **httpd** daemons under Unix, or in a similar way to services under Windows NT/2000.

Lock Objects

The **threading** module augments the basic lock mechanism with two new lock objects, the primitive lock and the reentrant lock.

Primitive Locks   Primitive locks work in the same way as the basic lock mechanism in **thread**. They have two states, lock or unlocked, and you can acquire or release a lock using the **acquire()** and **release()** methods. To create a new primitive lock:

```
mylock = Lock()
```

The **acquire()** works in a similar way to the **acquire()** method on a **thread** lock, but by default the function blocks (as opposed to returning instantly). To change this behavior, supply a single argument of zero to the function. As before, the method returns 1 if the operation was successful or zero if the lock could not be acquired.

```
mylock.acquire(1)
```

To release the lock, use the **release()** method:

```
mylock.release()
```

Reentrant Locks   A reentrant lock is to the **Lock** class, but the same lock can be acquired and released a number of times within the same thread. Normally, once a lock has been acquired by a thread it cannot be acquired again until the lock has been released. Using a reentrant lock, we can release and acquire a lock within a nested set of statements. Only the outermost **release()** operation resets the lock to its unlocked state.

The way the system works is that calls to **acquire()** increment the lock state. If the lock is already acquired by the current thread, then calling **acquire()** again only increments the count and returns immediately with a true value to the caller. When you call **release()**, the counter is decremented—it's only when the counter reaches zero that the lock is properly relinquished.

To create a reentrant lock use the **RLock** class:

```
myrlock = RLock()
```

The **acquire()** and **release()** methods work the same as for the **Lock** class.

Condition Variables

Condition variables are a more advanced form of the locking mechanisms already described. Rather than simply providing a lock mechanism, a condition variable can be used to indicate a particular change of state or event to a thread. For example, in a situation where one thread generates output for another thread to process, the processing thread may be waiting to access the data in a shared variable. Meanwhile, the producer thread has to wait for the processor thread to complete before adding new data.

Using a simple **Lock** or **RLock** class in this case would be complex. The condition variable gets around this by simplifying the process for determining the state and for notifying a waiting thread that the variable is available to use.

You create a new condition variable using the **Condition** constructor:

```
mycondition = Condition([lock])
```

The optional **lock** argument should be an instance of the **Lock** or **RLock** classes. If none is specified, then a new **RLock** instance is created. The new object supports the following methods:

mycondition.acquire(*args)	Acquires the underlying lock, calling the correct **acquire()** method according to the underlying lock. The **args** if supplied are passed verbatim to the lock's **acquire()** method.
mycondition.release()	Releases the underlying lock.
mycondition.wait([timeout])	Waits for notification from another thread either for the period specified in **timeout** or indefinitely. Once called, the underlying lock is released, and the thread pauses until it receives a **notify()** or **notifyAll()** event from another thread for the given lock. Once the event has been received, the lock is reacquired and the method returns. If the operation times out, the lock is reacquired and execution continues as normal.
.mycondition.notify()	Sends a notification event to a thread currently waiting. Note that the operation does not actually release the lock; you need to call both **notify()** and **release()** to allow the other thread to continue.
mycondition.notifyAll()	Notifies all threads waiting.

As an example, the simple script below passes messages from one thread to another to be printed. We use **notify()** in the sending thread to indicate to a waiting thread that a new message is ready to printed. Obviously this is a simplistic example, but it demonstrates how easily we can communicate the status of a variable between two threads.

```
import threading, time

mycondition = threading.Condition()
mymessage = ''

def thread_send():
    global mymessage
    counter = 0
    while 1:
        mycondition.acquire()
```

```
        mymessage = 'New Message: '+str(counter)
        counter += 1
        mycondition.notify()
        mycondition.release()
        time.sleep(5)

def thread_receive():
    global mymessage
    while 1:
        mycondition.acquire()
        if mymessage:
            print "Display:",mymessage
            mymessage = ''
            mycondition.wait()
        mycondition.release()

threada = threading.Thread(None, thread_send, None)
threadb = threading.Thread(None, thread_receive, None)

threada.start()
threadb.start()

while 1:
    pass
```

Semaphores

A semaphore is a basic counter-based locking mechanism. Calls to **acquire()** decrement the counter and calls to **release()** increment the counter. If the counter ever reaches zero, then the **acquire()** method blocks until another thread calls **release()**. Semaphores can be used to indicate a particular status for a given thread or other object. For example, you might use a semaphore in conjunction with an array to indicate how many items are in the array—that way, once the number of items in the array reaches zero you can block a thread from executing and removing information from the array.

To create a semaphore use the **Semaphore** class:

```
mysemaphore = threading.Semaphore([value])
```

The option **value** argument indicates the initial value for the semaphore; the default is 1. The value should be a positive integer.

mysemaphore.acquire([blocking])	The **acquire()** method attempts to acquire the semaphore. If the semaphore's counter is larger than zero, **acquire()** decrements the count and returns immediately. If the counter is already at zero, then the method blocks until another thread calls **release()**. The **blocking** argument works as for other locks.
mysemaphore.release()	Increases the semaphore's internal counter. If the counter is zero, calling **release()** unblocks a waiting thread.

Events

Events are used to communicate between threads by signaling a specific event that other threads can wait for. An event object has an internal flag that can be set or cleared at will. In addition, a **wait()** method allows you to wait until the flag is set. To create an event object:

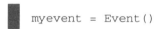

```
myevent = Event()
```

The internal flag is initially set to false. The methods supported by an **Event** instance are

myevent.isSet()	Returns true if the internal flag is true.
myevent.set()	Sets the internal flag to true.
myevent.clear()	Clears the internal flag, setting it to false.
myevent.wait([timeout])	Waits for the internal flag of **myevent** to become true. The methods waits indefinitely, or until the **timeout** (specified as a floating point value, treated as seconds) expires. Obviously if the flag is already set to true then the method returns immediately.

Queues

Although the different messaging methods we have already seen work adequately in most situations, they do not resolve all of issues, especially when dealing with threads that need to communicate large volumes of data between one another. Although we can share objects using one of the methods shown above (effectively sharing information), especially if the provider and consumer threads work at different rates, or deal with different volumes of data, then we end up in contention situations that become difficult to resolve.

The **Queue** module provides a solution. It provides a class that sets up a multiprovider and multiconsumer FIFO (First In, First Out) queue. Using the object we can add new requests to the queue, and process requests from the queue without worrying about processing rates, job sizes, or other limitations, and also proceed without the problems of manually dealing with object locks.

To create a new queue, we need to create an instance of the **Queue** class:

```
myqueue = Queue(maxsize)
```

The **maxsize** defines the maximum number of items that can be placed into the queue. If the **maxsize** is less than or equal to zero, then there is no upper limit. Choosing a suitable queue size is important, as choosing the wrong size could mean you end up with too few spaces available for new objects; or if the value is set very high, or infinite, then you run the risk of allowing your threads to consume ever increasing amounts of resource.

Although there are ways to control how many items are supplied to the queue it's probably best to size it according to about half the size of maximum number of items you expect to process. For example a program that processes about 10,000 elements should probably set a **maxsize** of about 5000. If the size of your queue elements is particularly large, then factor the size according to the maximum amount of space you want to allocate to your application.

An instance of **Queue** supports the following methods:

myqueue.qsize()	Returns the approximate size of the queue; an exact figure will always be difficult to determine since other threads may be updating the queue.
myqueue.empty()	Returns 1 if the queue is empty or zero if not.
myqueue.full()	Returns 1 if the queue is full or zero if not.
myqueue.put(item [, block])	Puts the object **item** into the queue. If **block** is supplied and is a positive value, then the caller blocks until a free slot is available. If not supplied, or if **block** is zero, then a **Full** exception is raised if the queue is full.
myqueue.put_nowait(item)	Equivalent to **myqueue.put(item, 0)**.
myqueue.get([block])	Gets an item from the queue. If **block** is supplied and a positive value, then the caller blocks until an item is available. If not supplied, or if **block** is zero, then an **Empty** exception is raised if the queue is empty.
myqueue.get_nowait()	Equivalent to **myqueue.get(0)**.

The Complete Reference

Python

Chapter 10

Processing Information

Most applications involve some form of data manipulation, whether it's simply adding a few numbers together or extracting the individual fields from a log file and creating a report. In either case, you need to manipulate information from one form or value into another.

Data manipulation in Python relies on a combination of the built-in operators and external modules that provide additional functionality. For example, the **math** module provides trigonometric functions so you can calculate the length of the side of a triangle given just the angle and the lengths of the opposite sides.

For manipulating text there are a number of solutions available, including the built-in operators and string functions. For more advanced operations you can use regular expressions to match elements with a remarkable degree of control.

This chapter looks at both aspects of data manipulation and explains how to handle special data types, including binary structures and Python's Unicode system.

Manipulating Numbers

Most numeric operations can be performed using the range of built-in operators that work directly with number objects. All of the basic math operations such as addition, subtraction, raising numbers to the power of another value, and so on, are supported natively by the Python operators.

For other mathematical and trigonometric functions you need the **math** or **cmath** (for complex numbers) modules. The **random** and **whrandom** modules provide different methods for generating random numbers. All of these modules are discussed in this section.

math

The **math** module provides the basic mathematical and trigonometric functions. Note that all the trigonometric operations function in radians, not degrees. You can convert degrees into radians by using the formula **d*((2*pi)/360)**, where **d** is the value in degrees. To convert the value back to degrees, use the formula **r*(260/(2*pi))**.

The **math** module provides two constants, **pi**, the ratio of the circumference of a circle to its diameter, and **e**, the natural logarithm.

Table 10-1 lists the functions supported by the **math** module.

The **ceil()** and **floor()** functions should be explained further. Both return a whole number, represented as a **float** type, which is either the integer component of the supplied expression or the next whole number. This is a similar principle to rounding up or down, except that **ceil()** always rounds up to the nearest whole number and

Function	Description
acos(x)	Returns the arccosine of **x**.
asin(x)	Returns the arcsine of **x**.
atan(x)	Returns the arctangent of **x**.
atan2(y, x)	Returns **atan(y/x)**.
ceil(x)	Returns the ceiling (the next whole number) of **x**.
cos(x)	Returns the cosine of **x**.
cosh(x)	Returns the hyperbolic cosine of **x**.
exp(x)	Returns **e ** x**.
fabs(x)	Returns the absolute value of **x**.
floor(x)	Returns the floor (the whole number) of **x**.
fmod(x, y)	Returns **x % y**.
frexp(x)	Returns a tuple containing the positive mantissa and exponent of **x**.
hypot(x, y)	Returns the result of Pythagoras' theorem, i.e., **sqrt(x**2+y**2)**.
ldexp(x, i)	Returns **x*(2 **i)**.
log(x)	Returns the natural logarithm of **x**.
log10(x)	Returns the base-10 logarithm of **x**.
modf(x)	Returns a tuple containing the fractional and integer parts of **x**. Both values have the same sign as **x**.
pow(x, y)	Returns **x ** y**.
sin(x)	Returns the sine of **x**.
sinh(x)	Returns the hyperbolic sine of **x**.
sqrt(x)	Returns the square root of **x**.
tan(x)	Returns the tangent of **x**.
tanh(x)	Returns the hyperbolic tangent of **x**.

Table 10-1. *Functions Supported by the **math** Module*

APPLYING THE
PYTHON LIBRARIES

floor() always rounds down to the nearest whole number. You can see the results of **ceil()** and **floor()** when using the functions interactively:

```
>>> from math import *
>>> ceil(9)
9.0
>>> ceil(8.9)
9.0
>>> ceil(8.1)
9.0
>>> floor(9.9)
9.0
>>>
```

cmath

The **cmath** module is identical to the **math** module except that it operates on complex numbers. The **cmath** module also provides complex number versions of the **pi** and **e** constants. Table 10-2 lists the functions supported by the **cmath** module.

Random Numbers

Calculating a random number can be useful in many areas of programming. Introducing a random element is a great way to add a unique or impossible-to-guess value to an ID or reference number and can also be used in applications such as games where you need an unexpected or unpredictable result.

True random number production is difficult, if not impossible, for a computer purely because computers are designed to work with precise and predictable numbers. Humans are, of course, much better at producing random numbers, but you can't always have a handy human to generate your random numbers!

Most random number generators are officially listed as pseudo-random number generators, and most rely on imperfections or minor differences in calculations to produce a random result. None of these should be relied on solely to produce a random number for a temporary ID. See the sidebar "Creating Random IDs" for methods of creating unique IDs using random and static elements.

The standard Python distribution includes two modules for random numbers, **random** and **whrandom**. The **random** module provides a number of different functions for calculating random numbers. In addition, the **random** module exports the functions

Function	Description
acos(x)	Returns the arccosine of **x**.
acosh(x)	Returns the arc hyperbolic cosine of **x**.
asin(x)	Returns the arcsine of **x**.
asinh(x)	Returns the arc hyperbolic sine of **x**.
atan(x)	Returns the arctangent of **x**.
atanh(x)	Returns the arc hyperbolic tangent of **x**.
cos(x)	Returns the cosine of **x**.
cosh(x)	Returns the hyperbolic cosine of **x**.
exp(x)	Returns **e ** x**.
log(x)	Returns the natural logarithm of **x**.
log10(x)	Returns the base-10 logarithm of **x**.
sin(x)	Returns the sine of **x**.
sinh(x)	Returns the hyperbolic sine of **x**.
sqrt(x)	Returns the square root of **x**.
tan(x)	Returns the tangent of **x**.
tanh(x)	Returns the hyperbolic tangent of **x**.

Table 10-2. *Functions Supported by the* **cmath** *Module*

APPLYING THE
PYTHON LIBRARIES

in **whrandom**. The **whrandom** module provides a more familiar interface for creating random numbers (using the Wichmann-Hull algorithm) with just four basic functions: **randint()**, **random()**, **seed()**, and **choice()**.

The **seed()** function seeds the random number generator and accepts three arguments:

```
seed(1,2,3)
```

Creating Random IDs

If you want to create a session ID that must be unique, you cannot use random numbers alone; although for a basic definition of random, the numbers generated will be random, the reality is that because of their nature, eventually a natural sequence will occur.

You can get around this by using a combination of the current time and a random number. You can calculate the current time to the nearest second (actually, you can calculate it more precisely, but accuracy to the second is supported on all platforms). So if the session is created fresh each time, it will require an exceedingly large number of requests at exactly the same instance in time in order for the entire ID string to be duplicated. Although there are many methods for this, the one I've used for years is as follows:

```
def make_session_id():
    from whrandom import randint
    from time import gmtime
    (a,b,c) = (randint(0,9999),
               randint(0,9999),
               randint(0,9999))
    (year, month, day, hour, minute, second) = gmtime()[0:6]

    session = "%02d%04d%02d-%02d%02d%04d-%d%d%d" % \
              (second,a,hour,month,minute,b,c,day,year)
    return session
```

The result of **make_session_id**, when called, is a string that looks something like 52854910-08398569-891732001, which while not guaranteed to be completely random and unique, is probably close enough given the current CPU limits. I've tested the result produced using the same physical time for 10,000,000 combinations and never found a duplicate, so it must be reasonably reliable.

If you don't supply any values or the three arguments have the same value, the current time is used as a seed value. The **seed()** function is automatically called if you haven't already called the function the first time you use one of the other three functions.

The **random()** function returns a random number in the range 0.0 to 1.0:

```
>>> whrandom.random()
0.44718597724016607
>>> whrandom.random()
0.93284180701215091
```

```
>>> whrandom.random()
0.03717170343673537
```

The **randint()** function accepts two arguments that indicate the range of the integer number to be generated. For example, to produce a random number between 1 and 256 (inclusive):

```
>>> whrandom.randint(1,256)
24
```

To produce a random number between 100 and 1000:

```
>>> whrandom.randint(100,1000)
291
```

Finally, the **choice()** function randomly selects one of the elements from the supplied sequence. Consider the following example:

```
>>> whrandom.choice([1,3,5,7,11,13,17,19,23,29])
23
```

Note that the item isn't removed from the sequence; it is only selected and returned.

The **random** module exports functions to generate random numbers using different distributions on real numbers. All of the functions are likely to produce numbers with a random deviation better than the base **randint()** and **random()** functions from the **whrandom** module, but with a slightly performance overhead. Table 10-3 lists the functions exported by the **random** module.

Function	Description
betavariate(alpha, beta)	Returns a value between 0 and 1 from the Beta distribution. **alpha** and **beta** should be greater than −1.
cunifvariate(mean, arc)	Returns a value between **(mean-arc/2)** and **(mean+arc/2)** from the circular uniform distribution.

Table 10-3. *Functions Exported by the **random** Module*

Function	Description
expovariate(lambda)	Returns a value between 0 and infinity from the exponential distribution.
gamma(alpha, beta)	Returns a value from the Gamma distribution where **alpha** should be greater than –1 and **beta** should be greater than 0.
gauss(mu, sigma)	Returns a value from the Gaussian distribution with mean **mu** and standard deviation **sigma**.
lognormvariate(mu, sigma)	Returns a value from the log normal distribution with mean **mu** and standard deviation **sigma**.
normalvariate(mu, sigma)	Returns a value from the normal distribution with mean **mu** and standard deviation **sigma**.
paretovariate(alpha)	Returns a value from the paretovariate distribution with shape parameter **alpha**.
vonmisesvariate(mu,kappa)	Returns a number from the von Mises variation, where **mu** is the mean angle radians between 0 and **2*pi** and **kappa** is a positive concentration factor.
weibullvariate(alpha, beta)	Returns a value in the Weibull variation with scalar parameter **alpha** and shape parameter **beta**.

Table 10-3. *Functions Exported by the* **random** *Module* (continued)

Text Manipulation

Strings in Python are objects, and because of Python's strong operator support, simple tasks like concatenating two strings together can be done easily using the + operator. Strings are also sequences, and that means that you can address a single character or a sequence of characters (a *slice*) without resorting to an additional function to extract the characters you want.

But what about other operations, like changing the case of a string or splitting a text record where fields are delimited by a single character into separate fields?

Here's an example: Let's say you want to replace a portion of text in a Python string with another portion of text, for example, replacing the word "cat" with "dog" in the expression "the cat on the mat". Although you can find the location of the word using the **index()** method, you cannot replace it. Strings are immutable—you cannot replace the characters in the sequence directly even if the replacement characters are the same length as the character you're replacing. You could do it by finding the location of the word, slicing out everything up to the word and everything after the word, and then reassembling the string.

Messy though, isn't it? What happens if the original expression is "the Cat sat on the mat", or "The Cat Sat on the Mat"? Worse still, what happens if you want to replace either "Cat" or "Mouse" with "Elephant"? You'd have to account for all the different cases of the words and all the different possible words in order to make the process work.

Alternatively, you could use regular expressions. Regular expressions are really just another language that allows you to specify what you want replaced. The language runs from the simple act of replacing "cat" with "dog", through to replacing "cat" or "mouse" with "elephant", irrespective, right up to replacing "cat" with "dog" but only if the cat is "sat" on the "mat", and only if it's all in lowercase.

For most of the basic string manipulations, you can rely on either the built-in functionality offered by the **string** object type, or you can use the **string** module. For regular expressions, you use the **re** module. This section discusses both of these modules.

Basic String Manipulation

The **string** module defines a host of useful functions for manipulating, extracting, and mutating strings. This section describes the **string** module in detail, including the built-in methods and operators for manipulating strings.

Throughout this section it's important to remember that you must capture the return values from all of these functions—Python does not change or modify a string except when you are using a method on a specific string object.

Finding String Segments

To find the location of a particular string within another string, use the **index()** function. For example, to find the string "cat" in the string "the cat sat on the mat" use

```
loc = string.index('the cat sat on the mat','cat')
```

The **loc** variable should now contain the value 4, since the word you are looking for appears at the fifth character in the string (remember that string indices start at 0).

The **index** function also accepts a third argument—the index within the string where the search should start. For example, if you are looking for "at", but aren't interested in the one in "cat", you could use

```
lastat = string.index('the cat sat on the mat', 'at', 8)
```

Finally, you can look for a string starting at the end of the string and working backwards, rather than starting from the beginning of the string using the **rindex** function. Note that the order of the string is not affected, only where you start looking for the text. For example, to pick up the word "on", starting from the end, use the following:

```
rloc = rindex('The cat sat on the mat', 'on')
```

Replacing String Segments

In Python, the **string** object does not support assignment, so the following command still does *not* work:

```
text[4:7] = 'tyrannosaurus rex'
```

A **TypeError** exception will be raised if you try this. Instead, the most straightforward solution is to use slices to extract the text before and after the portion of text that you want to replace and then use concatenation to reassemble the string, as follows:

```
text = text[:4] + 'tyrannosaurus rex' + text[7:]
```

Alternatively, if you can be sure that the string you are searching can be found without skipping over elements, you can use the **string** module's **replace()** function:

```
replace(text, old, new [, max])
```

This example replaces **old** with **new** in the string **text** either as many times as seen, or **max** times if the argument is supplied. You can therefore rewrite the preceding example as:

```
text = string.replace(text, 'cat', 'tyrannosaurus rex')
```

You can also use the **replace()** method directly on the string:

```
text.replace('cat', 'tyrannosaurus rex')
```

Note however that searches *always* start from the beginning of the string. Replacing "at" once changes "cat"; you can't start the search from anyplace other than the start. If you want to replace a word that appears at the end of a string, either use a regular expression or use slices to make the change only in the component of the original string that you want to modify. For example,

```
text = text[:-3] + string.replace(text[-3:], 'at', 'oon')
```

changes the **text** variable to read "the cat sat on the moon".

Splitting

The Python **split()** function comes as part of the **string** module and allows you to split a string by a single- or multi-character sequence. For example, you might want to split a list of fields separated by commas into a list of separate fields. The function splits a string into component parts, returning a list. The general format of the **split()** function is

```
split(text, [, expr [, max]])
```

The **text** argument is the string that you want to split and **expr** is the separator. If you do not supply **expr**, Python assumes you want to split by whitespace. For example, you can convert a sentence of text into a list of individual words as follows:

```
words = string.split('I pushed the button but nothing happened')
```

You can also use the **split()** function to extract individual fields from a character-delimited string such as

```
fields = split('rod:IA266:$23.99',':')
```

If the **max** argument is supplied, it operates in the same way as the Perl version, limiting the number of times that the split operation occurs.

If you want to perform a regular expression-based split, use the **split()** function that comes with the **re** module:

```
import re
fields = re.split(r'[\s,:;]+', text)
```

The preceding statement splits the characters in **text** whenever it sees one or more whitespaces, commas, colons, or semi-colons. See the section "Regular Expressions" later in this chapter.

Joining

Although you can concatenate two strings together in Python using the + operator, the process can be quite tedious if you have a number of strings that you want to join together using the same character or sequence. For example, imagine that you want to reassemble the sentence you split earlier. Because you don't know the length of the list of words, you'd ordinarily need to use a loop:

```
s = ''
for word in words:
    s += word + ' '
```

Using this technique, you end up with a useless space on the end of the string.

The solution is to use the **join()** function in the **string** module. The **join** function joins together all the elements in a list using the same separator, but it only places the separator between the elements that it's concatenating, as in the following example:

```
names = string.join(['martin', 'sharon', 'wendy', 'rikke'], ', ')
```

As you can see, the first argument is the list or tuple that you want to join together, and the second argument is the separator you want to place between each element pair. The value of **names** is:

```
'martin, sharon, wendy, rikke'
```

Trimming

You can trim the leading and/or trailing whitespace from a string in Python using the **lstrip()**, **rstrip()**, and **strip()** functions. The mnemonic here is that **lstrip()** strips the left whitespace and **rstrip()** strips the right whitespace:

```
string = '    leading space trailing    '
lstrip(string) # returns 'leading space trailing    '
rstrip(string) # returns '    leading space trailing'
strip(string)  # returns 'leading space trailing'
```

Changing Case

Python supports a range of case translation functions through the **string** module. These functions change the case and return the new version of the string. Table 10-4 lists these functions.

For example, to change a word to lowercase, use

```
lctext = string.lower(text)
```

Function	Description
string.lower(text)	Change all characters in **text** to lowercase.
string.upper(text)	Change all character in **text** to uppercase.
string.capitalize(text)	Change the first character in **text** to uppercase.
string.capwords(text)	Change the first character of each word in **text** to uppercase.
string.swapcase(text)	Swap the case of all characters in **text** (lowercase to uppercase/uppercase to lowercase).

Table 10-4.   *Case Translation Functions in Python*

Translating Characters

Although there are times when all you want to do is change the case of a string, there are also times when you want to translate individual characters. For example, imagine you have a string "ffffff" when you need the string "aaaaaa". You could do the translation manually, but there is an easier way—use the **translate** function in the **string** module.

The translate function accepts two arguments: a string and a translation table that maps the characters you want to find and the replacement characters you want to use. This mapping needs to be generated by the **maketrans()** function, which itself accepts two arguments: the list of characters to be translated from and the corresponding characters that you want them translated to.

For example, you can change all lowercase characters to uppercase using

```
string.translate(text, maketrans('abcdefghijklmnopqrstuvwxyz',
                                  'ABCDEFGHIJKLMNOPQRSTUVWXYZ'))
```

The two strings are used in sequence—in the preceding example, the first character in the first string is "a" and the first character in the second string is "A". When the string is translated, each occurrence of "a" is replaced with "A".

Let's consider a different example, translating lowercase characters to their opposite number, i.e., "a" to "z" and "z" to "a":

```
string.translate(text, maketrans('abcdefghijklmnopqrstuvwxyz',
                                  'zyxwvutsrqponmlkjihgfedcba'))
```

Using the preceding example, the result of translating "the cat sat on the mat" is "gsv xzg hzg lm gsv nzg"!

Standard Character Definitions

In addition to the functions you've already seen, the **string** module also defines some constant string sequences that can be used with many of the functions described in this section. Table 10-5 lists the constants that you can use within functions like **maketrans()** to refer to specific groups of characters.

Regular Expressions

Regular expressions are simply a way of describing the search criteria for searching the text in a function. At the simplest level, a regular expression can be composed of just raw text. But the power of regular expressions is that you can also specify wildcard elements so you can match any character or sequence of characters, repetitions, and more complex sequences. Ultimately, it's best to think of regular expressions as another language.

Perl Expression	Python Equivalent
[0-9]	digits
[0-9A-F]	hexdigits
[a-zA-Z]	letters
[a-z]	lowercase
[A-Z]	uppercase
[0-7]	octdigits
\s	whitespace

Table 10-5. *String Sequences*

There are two basic regular expressions operations:

- *Matching*, where you search, and hopefully match, a particular expression within a text string
- *Substitution*, where you search for and replace information in a string

For example, going back to the "cat" example, replacing "cat" with "dog" without using regular expressions was difficult, but not impossible. Using regular expression substitution, you can do that easily:

```
text = 'the cat sat on the mat'
text = re.sub(r'cat', 'slug', text)
```

Furthermore, you can make substitutions on the text without knowing the word you want to replace. For example, imagine you want to change the name of the animal in the statement, but don't necessarily know what the animal is. You can use regular expressions to make the change by identifying the word in between "the" and "sat" as in the following example:

```
text = 'the elephant sat on the mat'
text = re.sub(r'the.*?sat', 'the slug sat', text)
```

The regular expression here is "the.*?sat". The two words you can probably recognize, the bit in the middle, ".*?", is a regular expression fragment. The period signifies that it should match any character, the asterisk (*) indicates that the previous regular expression element (the period) should be matched zero or more times, and the question mark (?) indicates that the wildcard match ".*" should only swallow all of the characters up until the next statement ("sat"). The result is that you replace "the <something> sat" with "the slug sat", where <something> is matched by the regular expression fragment ".*?".

Regular Expression Components

Before learning about the specifics of the regular expression mechanism offered by the **re** module, you first need to look at the regular expression elements that are supported by the regular expression engine.

For a start, all raw text is matched exactly as it's seen—if you include the word "cat", the regular expression engine exactly matches the letter "c" followed by the letter "a" followed by the letter "t". If you include a period (.), the regular expression engine matches *any* single character in an expression, such that "c.t" matches "cat" and "cot" as well as "c!t" and any other combination.

Finally, there are two special operators that match the beginning or end of a string. For example, in "the cat sat on the mat", doing a substitution on the word "the" with "a" may not achieve the result you want. If you only want to replace the first "the", you can do it by specifying the search expression as "^the"; the "^" character matches only at the start of the string. You can also match the end of the string using the special "$" character, so you can replace the last "at" sequence using "at$". Table 10-6 summarizes the basic regular expression characters.

Any expression can also be further qualified by specifying the number of times the expression should be matched. For example, to match any word beginning with "d" and ending in "g", you can use "d.*g"; the period indicates to match any character, and the "*" indicates to match zero or more repetitions.

Unfortunately, as well as matching "debug", this would also match "debugging", and in fact, would match any sequence starting with "d" and ending in "g", so this would also match "do the right thing".

The ".*" is called as a *maximal match* because it matches as many characters as it can in the source string. Because this isn't always what you want, you can also use a *minimal match*. Minimal matches only swallow up characters up until the first occurrence of the following item, so in "debugging", ".*?" matches up to "debug", and in "do the right thing", it matches up to "do the rig".

As well as the zero or more quantifiers, there are also one or more, zero or one, and specific match quantifiers. Table 10-7 contains the full list of supported quantifiers.

For matching more complex items, you can use a number of character sequences to select specific characters. For example, you can match against a specific set of characters using the "[]" sequence. You can use this to match a character range; i.e., "[a-z]" matches only lowercase characters, "[!$?%]" only matches the symbols listed, and "[^0-9]" matches anything except the digit range 0–9.

You can also match alternatives. For example, you can match "cat" or "mouse" using "cat|mouse"; the vertical bar acts just like the | operator acting as a logical OR between the two items.

Character Sequence	Description
text	Matches the string **text**.
.	Matches any character except newline (unless the **s** flag is in use).
^	Matches the start of a string.
$	Matches the end of a string.

Table 10-6.   *Basic Regular Expression Characters*

Maximal	Minimal	Description
*	*?	Matches zero or more repetitions of the preceding expression, matching as many or as few repetitions as possible.
+	+?	Matches one or more repetitions of the preceding expression, matching as many or as few repetitions as possible.
?	??	Matches zero or one repetitions of the preceding expression, matching as many or as few repetitions as possible.
{m}	{m}?	Matches exactly **m** repetitions of the preceding expression, matching as many or as few repetitions as possible.
{m, }	{m,}?	Matches at least **m** repetitions of the preceding expression, matching as many or as few repetitions sas possible.
{m,n}	{m,n}?	Matches at least **m** and at most **n** repetitions of the preceding expression, matching as many or as few repetitions as possible.

Table 10-7.   *Match Quantifiers*

Finally, you can also use groups to match and extract specific elements. For example, given the sentence "the cat sat on the mat", imagine that you want to determine how the cat was situated on the mat. Using a regular expression you can certainly identify the element, but you need to know what the actual word was.

Using a group you can extract the word you want without knowing what it is. For example, the expression "the cat (.*?) on the mat". The parentheses create a new group, which you can extract after the regular expression has been executed. Groups can be used in other areas, too. For example, you can extract the elements from a date of the form "23/6/2001" using the expression "([0-9]+)/([0-9]+)/([0-9]+)".

Table 10-8 lists the group and set operators.

Beyond the special characters you've already seen, there are also special sequences that can be used to match against a specific character type or situation. For example, "\b" matches against a word boundary, so the expression "food\b" matches "food" and "zoofood" but not "foodies". Other sequences can be used to match against a specific type of character. You can match any whitespace using "\s" and you can match any number of whitespace characters by adding a qualifier to that expression.

Groupings	Description
[...]	Matches a set of characters; for example [a-zA-Z] or [,./;'].
[^...]	Matches the characters not in the set.
A | B	Matches either expression **A** or **B**.
(...)	Expression group.
\number	Matches the text in expression group **number**.

Table 10-8. *Set and Group Operators*

For example, the regular expression "^\S+\s+\S+$" basically matches any string containing two words separated by one or more whitespace characters, including any of the following fragments:

```
the cat
the   cat
the           cat
the\ncat
```

Table 10-9 lists the special characters supported by Python. Note also that the regular expression engine matches any of the backslash-qualified characters interpreted as normal in a string such as "\n" and "\t".

Character	Description
\A	Matches only at the start of the string.
\b	Matches a word boundary.
\B	Matches not a word boundary.
\d	Matches any decimal digit—equivalent to **r'[0-9]'**.
\D	Matches any non-digit character—equivalent to **r'[^0-9]'**.

Table 10-9. *Special Character Sequences*

Character	Description
\s	Matches any whitespace (space, tab, newline, carriage return, formfeed, vertical tab).
\S	Matches any non-whitespace character.
\w	Matches any alphanumeric character.
\W	Matches any non-alphanumeric character.
\Z	Matches only the end of the string.
\\	Matches backslash.

Table 10-9. *Special Character Sequences* (continued)

The final set of regular expression elements contains assertions that can be used to assert against specific events within a regular expression without actually affecting the processing of the rest of the expression. For example, if you have a list of numbers separated by a colon and you want to pull out blocks of six numbers—i.e., convert "1:2:3:4:5:6:1:2:3:4:5:6" into ["1:2:3:4:5:6:", "1:2:3:4:5:6"]—there is no easy way to do this. You could use **string.split** to split the entire string into individual components and then reassemble into six-element blocks, but that would be messy.

What you can do is use an assertion to create a regular expression group to match your size fields—i.e., the expression that matches six occurrences of "#:"—and then create a further group to hold the six-field sequence.

The actual assertion looks like this: "((?:[^:]*?:){6})". If you deconstruct it, the important part is "(?:[^:]*?:)"; this part creates a new regular expression group, but the group doesn't populate the group table normally populated by "()". The result is that you match "#:", then quantify the sequence six times, and place the "#:#:#:#:#:#:" into a standard regular expression group.

Table 10-10 contains the full list of assertions supported by the regular expression system.

We've really only scratched the surface here of what is possible with regular expressions. Entire books can and indeed have been written on the topic. The best such title is *Mastering Regular Expressions* by Jeffrey E. F. Friedl, (O'Reilly, 1997).

Regular Expression Modifiers

Most regular expressions also support a number of modifiers (also known as flags) that modify how the expression is executed. For reference, Table 10-11 lists these modifiers.

Assertion	Description
(?iLmsux)	The group matches the empty string, with the **iLmsux** characters matching the corresponding regular expression modifiers listed in Table 10-11. Note that these options affect the portion of the regular expression following the assertion, rather than the entire expression. They can also be used when you want the effects to be defined by the search expression, rather than by the regular expression function.
(?:...)	Matches the expression defined between the parentheses but does not populate the grouping table.
(?P<name>)	Matches the expression defined between the parentheses, but the matched expression is also available as a symbolic group identified by **name**. Note that the group still populates the normal group match variables. To refer to a group by name, supply it directly to the **match.end()** or **match.group()** methods or use **\g<name>**.
(?P=name)	Matches whatever text was matched by the earlier named group.
(?#...)	Introduces a comment; the contents of the parentheses are ignored.
(?=...)	Matches if the text supplied matches the next regular expression element, without consuming any text. This allows you to look ahead in an expression without affecting the rest of the regular expression parsing. For example, "Martin (?=Brown)" only matches "Martin " if it's immediately followed by "Brown".
(?!...)	Matches only if the specified expression doesn't match the next regular expression element (the opposite of **(?=...)**).
(?<=...)	Matches if the current position in the string is preceded by the supplied text, with the whole expression terminating at the current position. For example, **(?<=abc)def** matches "abcdef". Matching is precise to the number of characters preceding, so that **abc** and **a	b** matches but **a*** does not.
(?<!...)	Matches if the current position in the string is not preceded by the specified match (opposite of **(?<=...)**).

Table 10-10. *Regular Expression Assertions*

Modifier	Description
I or **IGNORECASE**	Ignores the case of the expression and matches the text.
L or **LOCALE**	Use locale settings for determining the \b, \B and \w, \W sequences.
M or **MULTILINE**	Makes ^ and $ apply to the start and end of lines rather than strings in multiline strings.
S or **DOTALL**	Forces . to match all characters, including newline.
X or **VERBOSE**	Allows regular expressions to ignore unescaped whitespace and comments.

Table 10-11.   *Flags Supported by Regular Expression Processes*

Basic Searches/Matches

You can perform a basic search (or match) using the **re.search()** function:

```
search(pattern, string [, flags])
```

For example, to determine whether the string "cat" is in **string**, do the following:

```
if re.search(r'cat', string): ...
```

The **search()** function returns **None**, and therefore a false value, if the regular expression could not be matched against the text you supplied. If it succeeds, it returns a **MatchObject** that can be used to extracted the text from the group. See the "Using MatchObjects" section later in this chapter for more information.

The **match()** function in the **re** module is a more restrictive version of **search()**, only matching expressions at the beginning of the supplied string, rather than anywhere within the string. This can be used to force a script to check for a match starting at the beginning of a string, irrespective of any user-supplied regular expression. In essence, this technique provides no advantages over preceding the search expression with \A.

Extracting Matched Components

If you want to find and match specific expressions, the simplest method is to use the **findall()** function. The **findall** function returns a list of the matches in a given expression, rather than in a **MatchObject**. The **findall()** function returns the matched text if no groups are used. If a group is used, the **findall()** function returns a list of all the matches, and if multiple groups are used, each item in the returned list is a tuple containing the text for each group. Consider the following example:

```
>>> import re
>>> string = 'the cat sat on the mat at ten'
>>> print re.findall(r'at',string)
['at', 'at', 'at']
>>> print re.findall(r'm.*?\b',string)
['mat']
>>> print re.findall(r'(at)',string)
['at', 'at', 'at']
>>> print re.findall(r'(cat)(.*?)(mat)',string)
[('cat', ' sat on the ', 'mat')]
```

Using MatchObjects

The **search()** and **match()** functions return **MatchObjects** that contain information both about the contents of the matched groups and about the locations within the original strings at which the matches occurred. Table 10-12 lists the methods available to the **MatchObject** indicated by **m**.

For example, you can extract the date and time from a string using the following script:

```
datetime = 'The date and time is 11/2/01 16:12:01 from MET';
dtmatch = re.match(r'((\d+)/(\d+)/(\d+)) ((\d+):(\d+):(\d+))',
datetime)
date = dtmatch.group(1)
time = dtmatch.group(5)
(day, month, year) = dtmatch.group(2,3,4)
```

Note here how the grouping works: Group numbers are actually assigned as each opening parenthesis is seen; in the preceding example, the first parenthesis denotes group 1 in the expression, which in turn contains groups 2, 3, and 4. (Note that regular expression indices start at 1, not 0). As a result, you can extract both the entire date string and the individual elements of the date string.

Substitution

The **sub()** function performs a substitution on a string. A substitution works in exactly the same way as a typical match, except that as well as a regular expression search string, there is also a replacement string. The replacement string is normally just basic text, but you can also refer to the text matched by any groups in the search expression.

MatchObject Method	Description
m.group([group, ...])	Returns the matched text for the supplied **group** or groups as defined by their index number, returning a tuple. If no group name is given, all of the matches are returned.
m.groups([default])	Returns a tuple containing the text matched by all the groups in the pattern. If supplied, **default** is the value returned for those groups that did not match the supplied expression. The default value for **default** is **None**.
m.groupdict([default])	Returns a dictionary containing all the subgroups of the match. If supplied, **default** is the value returned for those matches that didn't match; the default is **None**.
m.start([group])	Returns the starting location of the specified **group** or the starting location of the entire match.
m.end([group])	Returns the ending location of the specified **group** or the ending location of the entire match.
m.span([group])	Returns a two-element tuple equivalent to **(m.start(group), m.end(group))** for a given group or for the entire matched expression.
m.pos	The value of **pos** as passed to the **match()** or **search()** function.
m.endpos	The value of **endpos** as passed to the **match()** or **search()** function.
m.re	The regular expression object that created this **MatchObject**.
m.string	The string supplied to the **match()** or **search()** function.

Table 10-12.   *Methods for a Given MatchObject*

The basic format for the **sub()** function is:

```
sub(pattern, replace, string [, count])
```

Using the **sub()** function, you can replace "cat" with "slug" using the following commands:

```
text = 'the cat sat on the mat'
text = re.sub(r'cat', 'slug', text)
```

Note once again that the text or variable that you perform the substitution on is not modified in place; you must reassign the result of the function to the original variable to make the change.

The replacement can also contain group references in the form **\n**, where **n** is the group number. For example, you can convert an international date (*yyyymmdd*) into a British date using

```
date = '20010416';
date = re.sub(r'(\d{4})(\d{2})(\d{2})', '\3.\2.\1', date)
```

The **replace** argument also accepts a function that is supplied a single **MatchObject** argument. For example, to parse sequences of the form **%xx** as used in URLs with their single-character equivalent, you use

```
value = re.sub(r'%([a-fA-F0-9][a-fA-F0-9])',
               lambda x: chr(eval('0x'+x.group(1))), value)
```

To get the number of substitutions that took place, use the **subn()** function, which returns a tuple containing the substituted text and the number of substations, as in the following example:

```
text = 'the cat sat on the mat'
(text, subs) = re.subn(r'at', 'ow', text)
```

In this example, the **subn()** function sets the argument **subs** to 3.

Note that by default, all of Python's substitution functions replace all occurrences. To limit the number of modifications made, use the optional fourth argument **count**. For example, to change only the first occurrence of "at" to "oelacanth", use

```
text = 'the cat sat on the mat'
text = re.sub(r'at', 'oelacanth', text, 1)
```

which produces "the coelacanth sat on the mat".

Using Compiled Regular Expressions

When you use a regular expression, it is compiled into an internal language that is actually used to perform the match or substitution. If you do this a number of times using the same regular expression but different text elements—say when processing the individual lines of a file—you waste recompiling a regular expression that never changes.

You can get around this by precompiling the expression using the **compile()** function. It compiles a regular expression into a regular expression object. The basic form of the function is

```
compile(str [, flags])
```

where **str** is the regular expression you want to use and **flags**, as listed in Table 10-11, specifies the modifiers that you want to use on the new object. The new object has methods with the same name and purpose as the main functions in the **re** module.

For example, you can rewrite the Python fragment

```
text = 'the cat sat on the mat'
text = re.sub(r'at', 'oelacanth', text, 1)
```

as

```
text = 'the cat sat on the mat'
cvanimal = compile(r'at')
text = cvanimal.sub('oelacanth', text)
```

Table 10-13 lists the other methods supported by regular expression objects.

Escaping Strings

Sometimes you'll build a regular expression by using variable elements. The problem is that the variable you are using may contain characters that may otherwise be interpreted as regular expression components. For example, using "Martin (Brown)" in a regular expression when you specifically want to match against the parentheses causes a problem, because you already know that parentheses are used to indicate a group. If you were specifying the match by hand, you could escape those parentheses using the backslash (\) character.

If the information is being determined from elsewhere, you have no way to modify the text before it is used in the expression.

Regular Expression Method	Description
r.search(string [, pos [, endpos]])	Identical to the **search()**function, but allows you to specify the starting and ending points for the search.
r.match(string [, pos [, endpos]])	Identical to the **match()** function, but allows you to specify the starting and ending points for the search.
r.split(string [, max])	Identical to the **split()** function.
r.findall(string)	Identical to the **findall()** function.
r.sub(replace, string [, count])	Identical to the **sub()** function.
r.subn(replace, string [, count])	Identical to the **subn()** function.
r.flags	The flags supplied when the object was created.
r.groupindex	A dictionary mapping the symbolic group names defined by **r'(?Pid)'** to group numbers.
r.pattern	The pattern used when the object was created.

Table 10-13. *Methods/Attributes for a Regular Expression Object*

However, the **re** module defines the **escape()** function. The **escape()** function translates any characters in a string that would be identified as regular expression elements so that they are instead interpreted as raw characters, as follows:

```
string = re.escape(expr)
```

Time

When working with time values on any machine you have to understand how the machine treats the time value itself. For nearly all machines and operating systems, time information is stored in the form of a number. The number represents the number of seconds since the epoch—the epoch being some past point in time that you can use as a reference. Under Windows and Unix, the epoch is January 1, 1970, 00:00:00. On the Mac OS (but not on Mac OS X), the epoch is January 1, 1904, 00:00:00.

For example, at the time of this book's writing, the time value was 996853682.48452997, which translates to Fri Aug 3 16:48:02 2001. You can get the current epoch value by using the **time.time()** function:

```
>>> import time
>>> time.time()
996853682.48452997
>>> time.ctime(996853682.48452997)
'Fri Aug  3 16:48:02 2001'
```

The **ctime()** function converts an epoch value into a string. See the section "Time Formatting" later in this chapter for more information on how to format time values.

The rest of the **time** module provides functions and variables that hold information about the time information on the current host. Table 10-14 lists the variables defined by the **time** module.

Extracting Time Values

You can convert an epoch value into its individual time components—day, month, year, hours, minutes, etc.—using the **gmtime()** and **localtime()** functions. Both of these function accept a single argument, an epoch value, and return a tuple of individual time values, listed in Table 10-15.

The only difference between the two functions is that **localtime()** returns the time values according to your time current zone and **gmtime()** returns the time values

Variable	Description
accept2dyear	A Boolean value; if set to true, the time functions accept two-digit years in addition to four-digit years.
altzone	The time zone used when Daylight Savings Time (DST) is active in the current time zone.
daylight	Set to non-zero if a DST time zone is in effect.
timezone	The local non-DST time zone.
tzname	A tuple containing the name of the local time zone and the time zone used when DST is in effect.

Table 10-14. *Variables Defined in the* **time** *Module*

Element	Content	Value Range	Description
0	year	0–9999	The full year, i.e., 2001
1	month	1–12	The month number
2	day	1–31	The day of the month
3	hour	0–23	The hour of the day (24-hour format)
4	minute	0–59	The minute of the hour
5	second	0–59	The second of the minute
6	weekday	0–6	The day of the week (Sunday=0)
7	day	1–366	The day of the year
8	dst	-1, 0, 1	1 if Daylight Savings Time (DST) is in operation, 0 if it isn't, and –1 if no information is available

Table 10-15. *Tuple Elements Returned by the* **localtime** *and* **gmtime** *Functions*

according to GMT (Greenwich Mean Time, otherwise known as UTC, Universal Coordinated Time). Both functions use the current epoch value if none is supplied.

For example, to extract today's date, use

```
(year, month, day) = localtime()[0:3]
print "%d/%d/%d" % day, month, year
```

As a general rule, use **localtime()** when you want to display a time value, but use **gmtime()** when comparing or storing time values that you want to retrieve later. Because **localtime()** is subject to the local time zone, it returns different values in different locations, and most importantly, different values when used where Daylight Savings Time (DST, known in the UK as BST, British Summer Time) is in effect. If you store two time values recovered using **localtime()** and then compare the values, you'll end up with spurious results because of the time zone and DST differences.

Time Formatting

Although you can extract and format the time information for yourself, the **time** module actually provides a number of utility functions for generating date and time strings from raw values without requiring any manual intervention or formatting. The two basic functions, **asctime()** and **ctime()**, return a standard string using the number and date format defined by the current locale. The **asctime()** function generates the string based on the tuple returned by **localtime()** or **gmtime()**:

```
print time.asctime(time.localtime(epoch))
```

The **ctime(epoch)** function is just shorthand for **time.asctime(time.localtime(epoch))**, where **epoch** is the time value in seconds. On a British operating system, this generates:

```
'Fri Aug  3 17:30:52 2001'
```

For a more structured output you can use the **strftime()** function. It accepts two arguments: the first is a format string in much the same style as the formatting operator (%) for Python strings, except that the formatting options return a time value. The second argument should be a tuple as returned from **localtime** or **gmtime**. Table 10-16 lists the supported strings.

For example, to write the date in typical day/month/year format, use

```
print time.strftime('%d/%m/%Y', time.localtime())
```

To write the same string as generated by **asctime()** or **ctime()**, use the **%c** format:

```
print time.strftime('%c', time.localtime())
```

Creating Epoch Values

You can convert individual time values back into epoch values using **mktime()**, which accepts a tuple of values in the same order and range as that returned by **localtime()** and **gmtime()**.

So you can convert an epoch value back into itself using

```
current = time.time()
new = time.mktime(time.localtime(current))
if (new != current):
    print "The time stasis has leaked!!"]
```

If you have a more complex time string and want to extract the information, you need to use the **strptime()** function. This is identical to **strftime()** except that it works in reverse, parsing a given date/time string and returning a **localtime()** or **gmtime()** style

Format String	Description
%a	Locale's abbreviated weekday name
%A	Locale's full weekday name
%b	Locale's abbreviated month name
%B	Locale's full month name
%c	Locale's appropriate date and time representation
%d	Day of a month as a decimal (0–31)
%H	Hour as decimal (0–23, 24-hour clock)
%I	Hour as decimal (01–12, 12-hour clock)
%j	Day of the year as a decimal (001–366)
%m	Month as a decimal (01–12)
%M	Minute as a decimal (00–59)
%p	Locale's equivalent of A.M. or P.M.
%S	Seconds as a decimal (00–59)
%U	Week number of the year (00–53, Sunday as first day of the week)
%w	Weekday as a decimal number (0–6, Sunday as the first day of the week)
%W	Week number of the year (00–53, Monday as the day of the week)
%x	Locale's appropriate date representation
%X	Locale's appropriate time representation
%y	Year without century prefix as decimal (00–99)
%Y	Year with century as decimal
%Z	Name of the current time zone
%%	The % character

Table 10-16.   *Format Strings for the* **time.strftime()** *Function*

tuple. For example, to convert your day/month/year string back into something more manageable, consider the following:

```
import time
datestring = '23/3/2001'
datetuple = time.strptime(datestring, '%d/%m/%Y')
```

The default value for the second argument—the format string you want to parse the date/time string with—is "%a %b %d %H:%M:%S %Y".

Comparing Time Values

Although it's possible to compare time values on an individual basis, it does create some problems. For example, if you want to find the difference between two month/year combinations, you'd have to compare the months and then the years to get a figure:

```
montha,yeara = 11,1999
monthb,yearb = 04,2001
monthsdiff = ((yearb-yeara)*12)-montha+monthb
```

To find the difference in days, it gets even more complicated, because now you also have to account for the number of days in each month (since it's not constant) and perform leap year calculations for February. You can imagine how complex it gets for comparing down to the last second!!

The solution is to convert your date/time values into an epoch value, subtract one epoch from the other, and then use **gmtime()** to report the details. What **gmtime()** reports is a date, but because it's calculating the date based on the epoch value that's supplied to it, what you actually end up with is a summary of the differences in years, months, days, etc. between the two values.

For example, let's work with some known numbers and find out the number of days between August 1, 2001 and August 31, 2001. Using the **mktime()** function, you can convert those dates into epoch values, compare them, and get the difference, as follows:

```
import time

epocha = time.mktime((2001,8,1,0,0,0,0,0,0))
epochb = time.mktime((2001,8,31,0,0,0,0,0,0))
(year, month, day) = time.gmtime(epochb-epocha)[0:3]
print "Years: %d, Months: %d, days: %d" % (year,month,day)
```

APPLYING THE PYTHON LIBRARIES

You're expecting a value of 30 days, but if you run the script the result is

```
Years: 1970, Months: 1, days: 31
```

The reason for this is that you're comparing two values and then returning the difference with reference to your epoch value, which you know is January 1, 1970. Since a value 0 supplied to **gmtime()** returns the tuple (1970,1,1,0,0,0,0,0,0), you need to remove the base component of the epoch to get the true difference, as follows:

```
import time

epocha = time.mktime((2001,8,1,0,0,0,0,0,0))
epochb = time.mktime((2001,8,31,0,0,0,0,0,0))
(year, month, day) = time.gmtime(epochb-epocha)[0:3]
year-=1970
month-=1
day-=1
print "Years: %d, Months: %d, days: %d" % (year,month,day)
```

Now if you execute the script, you get the following result:

```
Years: 0, Months: 0, days: 30
```

If you try it with different values, say February 22, 1967 and today's date, August 3, 2001, you get:

```
Years: 34, Months: 5, days: 11
```

Pausing a Process

The **time.sleep()** function pauses the execution of the current process for a specified number of seconds. For example, to pause a process for 1.5 seconds, use the following command:

```
time.sleep(1.5)
```

Note that different machines use different granularity for the underlying **sleep** function. Although Python allows fractional amounts (the argument to **time.sleep** should be a floating-point number), the underlying operating system may only support integer sleep values. Furthermore, the entire system may be inaccurate, and the actual time that you sleep may be up to one second more than you requested.

Data Types and Operators

Beyond the basic methods already described for manipulating and working with different data types, there are also a series of modules that can be used either to identify particular object types, to create structures based on particular data types, or to manipulate binary structures.

Type Identity

If you want to identify the type of a particular object, you can use the **type()** built-in function:

```
>>> import time
>>> type(time)
<type 'module'>
```

However, there are times when you want to check the object type. In many instances you can just supply an empty object, as in the following example:

```
if (type(list) == type([])):
...
```

But there are types that can't easily be generated in this way. To get around this, use the **types** module. The **types** module defines variables of all the different types, allowing you to specify an object by name. For example, the **reverse()** function in the next example identifies the object type that it's supplied and reverses the different objects accordingly:

```
def reverse(x):
    import types
    if (type(x) == types.ListType):
        copy = x
        copy.reverse()
        return copy
    if (type(x) == types.StringType):
        y = ''
        i = len(x)-1
        while(i >= 0):
            y += x[i]
            i -= 1
        return y
    if (type(x) == types.DictionaryType):
```

```
        y = {}
        for key in x.keys():
            y[x[key]] = key
        return y
    raise(TypeError)
```

Now you can call the **reverse()** function with lists, strings, or dictionaries and get a reversed version of what you supplied returned to you:

```
>>> reverse('hello')
'olleh'
>>> reverse([1,2,3])
[3, 2, 1]
>>> reverse({'a': 1,'b':2})
{2: 'b', 1: 'a'}
>>>
```

Table 10-17 contains the full list of object types.

Variable	Alias For
BufferType	Buffer objects, as created by the **buffer()** function
BuiltInFunctionType	Built-in functions
BuiltinMethodType	Built-in methods
ClassType	Class definition
CodeType	Byte-compiled code
ComplexType	Complex numbers
DictionaryType	An alternate name for **DictType**
DictType	Dictionary objects
EllipsisType	Ellipsis objects (extended slices)
FileType	File objects

Table 10-17.   *Object Types Defined in the* **types** *Module*

Variable	Alias For
FloatType	Floating-point objects
FrameType	Execution frame
FunctionType	User-defined function
InstanceType	Class object instance
IntType	Integer objects
LambdaType	An alternate name for **FunctionType**
ListType	Arrays and lists
LongType	Long (arbitrary) integer
MethodType	Bound class method
ModuleType	Module
NoneType	The **None** value
SliceType	Objects returned by the **slice()** function
StringType	Strings objects
TracebackType	Stack tracebacks of an exception
TupleType	Tuple objects
TypeType	Type objects (as returned by the **type()** function)
UnboundMethodType	Unbound class method (**class.method**)
UnicodeType	Unicode character strings
XRangeType	Created by the built-in **xrange()** function

Table 10-17.   *Object Types Defined in the* **types** *Module* (continued)

Operators

The **operator** module provides functions that access the built-in operators and special methods of the interpreter that were covered back in Chapter 3. Table 10-18 lists the functions exported, their equivalent object methods, and the equivalent operators.

Function	Object Method	Equivalent Operator
add(a, b)	__add__(a, b)	a + b (numeric)
sub(a, b)	__sub__(a, b)	a - b
mul(a, b)	__mul__(a, b)	a * b (numeric)
div(a, b)	__div__(a, b)	a / b
mod(a, b)	__mod__(a, b)	a % b
neg(a)	__neg__(a)	-a
pos(a)	__pos__(a)	+a
abs(a)	__abs__(a)	Absolute value of **a**
inv(a) invert(a)	__inv__(a) __invert__(a)	Inverse of **a**
lshift(a, b)	__lshift__(a, b)	a << b
rshift(a, b)	__rshift__(a, b)	a >> b
and (a, b)	__and__(a, b)	a & b
or (a, b)	__or__(a, b)	a | b
xor(a, b)	__xor__(a, b)	a ^ b
not (a)	__not__(a)	Not **a**
truth(a)		Returns 1 if **a** is true, 0 otherwise
concat(a, b)	__concat__(a, b)	a + b (sequences)
repeat(a, b)	__repeat__(a, b)	a * b (sequence **a**, number **b**)
contains(a, b)	__contains__(a, b)	b in a
countOf(a, b)		Returns the number of occurrences of **b** in **a**.
indexOf(a, b)		Returns the index of the first **b** in **a**.
getitem(a, b)	__getitem__(a, b)	a[b]
setitem(a, b, c)	__setitem__(a, b, c)	a[b] = c
delitem(a, b)	__delitem__(a, b)	del a[b]

Table 10-18.   *Functions/Methods and Their Equivalents in the* **operator** *Module*

Function	Object Method	Equivalent Operator
getslice(a, b, c)	__getslice__(a, b, c)	a[b:c]
setslice(a, b, c, v)	__setslice__(a, b, c, v)	a[b:c] = v
delslice(a, b, c)	__delslice__(a, b, c)	**del a[b:c]**

Table 10-18.   *Functions/Methods and Their Equivalents in the* **operator** *Module* (continued)

Array Building

The standard Python array or list type is essentially a list of references to other objects. For most situations this is exactly what you want, since you are likely to need to store strings, integers, and floating-point values within a typical list. For complex structures you might also add sequences, tuples, and dictionaries. However, such free-form arrays and lists are not efficient at storing large quantities of simple data such as characters or numbers. For example, in a standard list, each **Integer** data type takes up a minimum of 12 bytes. Multiply that by say 200,000 elements and you've just used 2.3MB for one list!

The solution is to use the **array** module. The **array** module enables you to create a list that accepts and stores elements only of a single type. For example, if you know that you want to store floating-point values, use the **array()** function to create a new array using the argument **'f'**, to indicate a floating-point array:

```
myfparray = array.arry('f')
```

An optional second argument contains the initial values that you want assigned to the array that is created. Table 10-19 lists the other supported array types.

Once created, the list can be manipulated and used just like any other list. In addition, the new object has the methods and attributes listed in Table 10-20.

Binary Structures

The C language uses the **struct** system to construct a single entity from a number of distinct base types. To read these binary structures you need to use the **struct** module. The **struct** module provides two main functions: **pack()** and **unpack()**. The **pack()** function packs a series of values into a binary structure; the **unpack()** function converts a binary structure back into a list of values.

Both functions rely on a format string that defines the format of the packed structure. The format consists of a string of letters, where each letter defines a particular data type; for example, "i" represents an integer (the C **int** type). You can also prefix each letter

Array Type Code	Description	Equivalent C Type
c	8-bit character	**char**
b	8-bit integer	**signed char**
B	9-bit unsigned integer	**unsigned char**
h	16-bit integer	**short**
H	16-bit unsigned integer	**unsigned short**
i	integer	**int**
I	unsigned integer	**unsigned int**
l	long integer	**long**
L	unsigned long integer	**unsigned long**
f	double-precision float	**float**
d	double-precision float	**double**

Table 10-19.   *Type Codes for Creating Fixed Type Arrays*

Method/Attribute	Description
typecode	The typecode characters used to create the array.
itemsize	Size of each element.
append(x)	Append **x** to the array.
buffer_info()	Returns a tuple containing the address in memory and the length of the buffer being used to store the array.
byteswap()	Swaps the byte ordering of all the items in the array from big endian to little endian or vice versa. Only supported for integer arrays.
fromfile(f, n)	Loads **n** elements from the file object **f** into the current array.

Table 10-20.   *Methods/Attributes for a Fixed Type Array*

Method/Attribute	Description
fromlist(list)	Appends items from **list** to the array. Raises **TypeError** if any one item from **list** does not match the type of the array.
fromstring(s)	Appends the item from string **s** as if **s** is a string of binary values.
insert(i,x)	Inserts the item **x** at element **i**.
reverse()	Reverses the order of the array.
tofile(f)	Writes the array as a binary stream to the file object **f**.
tolist()	Converts the array to an ordinary list of values.
tostring()	Converts the array to a binary string.

Table 10-20.   *Methods/Attributes for a Fixed Type Array* (continued)

with a number to indicate a repetition of a value; for example, to extract four integers, you use **'4i'**. In the case of the **'s'** character, which defines a string, the number prefix determines the maximum length of the string to be extracted.

For example, you can read the following C structure:

```
struct clockin {
  short id;
  char name[20];
  unsigned long timestamp;
};
```

The pack format to read this would be **'h20sL'**. To pack data into the structure, use

```
import struct, time

binary = struct.pack('h20sL',239,'Martin',time.time())
```

To unpack the binary string back into separate variables, use

```
(id, name, timestamp) = struct.unpack('h20sL', binary)
```

Table 10-21 contains the full list of supported format characters.

You also prefix a format string to specify the byte order and alignment of the resulting binary structure. The characters listed in Table 10-22 show the supported

Format Character	C Type	Python Type
x	pad byte	No value
c	char	String of length 1
b	signed char	Integer
B	unsigned char	Integer
h	short	Integer
H	unsigned short	Integer
i	int	Integer
I	unsigned int	Integer
l	long	Integer
L	unsigned long	Integer
f	float	Float
d	double	Float
s	char[]	String
p	char[]	String with length encoded in the first byte
P	void *	Integer

Table 10-21.   *Characters for Packing/Unpacking C Structures*

Format Prefix	Byte Order	Size and Alignment
@	Native	Native
=	Native	Standard
<	Little endian	Standard
>	Big endian	Standard
!	Network (big endian)	Standard

Table 10-22. *Byte Ordering/Alignment Prefixes Packed Structures*

prefixes. Note that these prefixes must be specified only once and only as the first character of the format string. The default option, if a prefix is not supplied, is to use the native byte ordering used by the current platform and standard alignment—no alignment is required for any type.

Unicode Strings

Some of you may have come across Unicode elsewhere, and if you haven't, then it's highly likely that you will soon. Unicode has long been a part of the Windows operating system, having been officially introduced with Windows 98, although support existed in Windows 95 and NT. The Mac OS has had Unicode support for many years. Although support under Unix is currently a system-wide issue, most software that thinks it ought to be using Unicode comes with its own support.

Unicode solves an age-old problem relating to the representation of characters on screen and how they are physically stored as data within objects and external files. The format that most people are aware of is ASCII, which officially lists the main Latin letters, numbers, and grammatical marks in their uppercase and lowercase versions. Some ASCII extensions are also universally accepted and allow for accented characters that support most of the southern European languages. The actual characters are referred to by a number, using a range of 0–255, which enables you to store the numerical equivalent of the letter into a single eight-bit byte.

However, what happens when you migrate a system that uses the ASCII, and therefore Latin, character set to an environment that doesn't actually use Latin characters? In Greece, for example, they use letters from the Greek alphabet, which are not part of the ASCII standard. Traditionally, programmers and designers have gotten around this issue by developing a font that maps normal Latin characters into their foreign equivalents. In essence, you're still using a single byte to represent each character, but because the software knows you should be using a Greek rather than a Latin font, it displays the Greek character.

When you move to more complex graphical languages such as Chinese and Japanese, this method no longer works. The traditional Chinese writing system has over 30,000 characters in it—not directly representable by a single byte that limits you to 256 characters. For these languages, you need to use multibyte characters, a specification that allows you to refer to a character in an alphabet that fits in the range 0 to $(2^{32}-1)$ (or 0 to $(2^{64}-1)$ for 64-bit computers).

It's here Unicode fits in. The Unicode standard is designed to be the accepted set of rules that allow people to exchange textual information around the world. Because the Unicode standard includes information on the character set and the multibyte format of the data being exchanged, you should be guaranteed that the information you are reading is in the correct format and language.

Python 2.0 introduced the Python Unicode support. In addition to the basic capabilities of allowing you to introduce Unicode and raw Unicode strings, Python now includes facilities for encoding and decoding Unicode and for the translation of Unicode characters between different encoding formats.

In addition, most of the core modules are also Unicode compliant, so you can execute regular expressions on Unicode objects just as you would with normal strings. You can also use Unicode strings as identity and search terms in the regular expression itself.

Creating Unicode Strings

Rather than supporting Unicode strings natively—where all strings used in Python are automatically in Unicode format—Python instead supports a new data type: Unicode strings. You can create a new Unicode object by prefixing a string with the letter **u**, in the same way that you introduce raw strings, as in the following examples:

```
>>> u'Hello World'
u'Hello World'
>>> u'Hello\u0020World'
u'Hello World'
```

To include special (non-native) characters into the Unicode object, use the Unicode escape, **\u**. This introduces the character according to the supplied hexadecimal value. In the previous example, you introduced the Unicode character with the hexadecimal value of 20—the space character—which as you can see has been interpreted accordingly in the example. Here's another example, this time inserting a lower case **o** with a stroke or slash (in other words, **ø**) into a Unicode string:

```
message = u'J\u00f8rgensen'
```

All other characters are converted according to the Latin-1 encoding. See the section "Translating Unicode" later in this chapter for information on translating a Unicode string to another format. Note that on platforms and systems that support it, the Unicode string conversion can also translate non-ASCII characters into Unicode. For example, on a Mac, introducing accented and other foreign characters is a built-in part of the operating system, so you can insert these characters directly into a u-prefixed string:

```
>>> u'øåé'
u'\xbf\x8c\x8e'
```

To introduce a raw Unicode string—a Unicode string without any embedded Unicode translation—use the **ur** prefix when creating the Unicode object, as in the following example:

```
>>> ur'Rikke\u0020J\u00f8rgensen'
u'Rikke J\u00f8rgensen'
```

Raw Unicode strings work in the same way as their raw string cousins—they exist to enable you to introduce strings that may contain information you don't want translated or interpreted. As with raw strings, this is especially useful when using Unicode strings within regular expressions. In these instances, Unicode escape sequences are interpreted only when there is an off number of backslashes in front of a small **u** character. You can see this more clearly in the following example:

```
>>> ur'\\u0020'
u'\\\\u0020'
>>> ur'\u0020'
u' '
>>> u'\\\u0020'
u'\\\\ '
```

Translating Unicode

At the most basic level, you can mix and match Unicode and normal Python string sequences, but the result is always another Unicode object, as in this example:

```
>>> 'Hello ' + u'Miss J\u00f8rgensen'
u'Hello Miss J\xf8rgensen'
```

APPLYING THE PYTHON LIBRARIES

To convert a Unicode object back into a normal ASCII (seven-bit) string, use the built-in **str()** function:

```
>>> str(u'Hello World')
'Hello World'
```

Be careful, however, with Unicode strings that are not ASCII compatible. The **str()** function raises an error if you try to convert a string that contains non-ASCII characters, as in the following example:

```
>>> greet=u'Miss J\u00f8rgensen'
>>> str(greet)
Traceback (most recent call last):
  File "<stdin>", line 1, in ?
UnicodeError: ASCII encoding error: ordinal not in range(128)
```

Note that this applies however you access the string, even when extracting characters from a Unicode string individually. For example, the following code still raises an error:

```
for char in u'Miss J\u00f8rgensen':
    print char,
```

*Errors in encoding and/or decoding strings raise a **UnicodeError** exception, which can be trapped in the same way as any other exception. The **UnicodeError** exception supplies the error message as its only argument.*

Encoding to Unicode Formats

ASCII is not the most useful of formats. You can translate a Unicode string into one of a number of different formats using the **encode()** function. **encode()** changes the encoding used to represent the Unicode object directly into another character set, such as Latin-1 or UTF-8. The method takes a single argument—the encoding type that you want to translate the Unicode string to. In fact, the **encode()** method is what is called when the **str()** built-in function is used on a Unicode object, supplying the encoding type as ASCII.

Latin-1 encoding, which supports the first 256 characters provided in the eight-bit ASCII table, can be used for most string representations, as in the earlier example:

```
>>> greet = u'Rikke J\u00f8rgensen'
>>> greet.encode('latin-1')
'Rikke Jørgensen'
```

Reproduction of these characters on screen of course relies on you having a font, application, and operating system that adhere to the Unicode standard!

A classic example here is the Mac OS, which doesn't directly support the Unicode standard. To get the same effect when writing to a standard Mac document or to the screen, you'll need to use Mac Roman encoding.

The **encode()** method can also be used to encode your Unicode object into one of the native Unicode encoding formats, such as UTF-8 or UTF-16. For example, to encode the sample string in the earlier example, you'd use the following:

```
>>> greet.encode('utf-8')
'Rikke J\xc3\xb8rgensen'
>>> greet.encode('utf-16')
'\xfe\xff\x00R\x00i\x00k\x00k\x00e\x00
\x00J\x00\xf8\x00r\x00g\x00e\x00n\x00s\x00e\x00n'
```

Decoding to Unicode Formats

To translate an encoded string back into its Unicode format (that is, to reverse encode()), use the built-in **unicode()** function. This function was introduced with Python 2.0. The function accepts two main arguments: the byte stream that you want to decode and the format that you want it decoded into. For example, you can decode Rikke Jørgensen from Mac Roman format into a Unicode string as follows:

```
>>> unicode('Jørgensen','mac-roman')
u'J\xf8rgensen'
```

The return type is a Unicode object. Be aware that the **unicode()** function decodes a string object into its Unicode version using the format you supply—use the wrong format and you end up with the wrong Unicode object. For example, decode Jørgensen sourced from a Mac document using Latin-1 encoding and you get a different Unicode string:

```
>>> unicode('Jørgensen','latin-1')
u'J\xbfrgensen'
```

You can also use **unicode()** to translate directly from one encoding format into another. The UTF-8 stream of Jørgensen, for example, can be translated straight into UTF-16 using this:

```
>>> unicode('Miss J\xc3\xb8rgensen','utf-16')
```

The **unicode()** function also accepts a third argument that tells the interpreter how to handle errors that arise during the encoding process. For example, using **'strict'** forces the encoding mechanism to perform a strict encoding—characters that cannot be encoded raise a **ValueError** exception:

```
>>> unicode('Jørgensen','utf-8','strict')
Traceback (most recent call last):
  File "<stdin>", line 1, in ?
UnicodeError: UTF-8 decoding error: unexpected code byte
```

The error string is used by the codecs to translate Unicode characters to determine how the encoding and errors should be handled. The actual error strings and their effects depend on the codec that you are using, but there are some standard strings supported by the translation system.

You already know the **'strict'** option; using **'ignore'** allows the translation to continue, removing any special characters within encoded string, such as the following:

```
>>> unicode('Jørgensen','utf-8','ignore')
u'Jrgensen'
```

To replace an unknown character with a character that the codec thinks may be suitable, use an error string of **'replace'**. Python uses the official **\uFFFD** replacement character as defined by the codec being used.

Writing Your Own Codec

The **unicode()** function and the **encode()** method use the **codecs** module, which is part of the standard library. The **codecs** module provides the base classes required to translate between the different formats, but a separate set of modules within the encodings directory in the Python standard library does the actual work. For example, when you specify to translate to Mac Roman format, it's the **mac_roman** module within the encodings directory that does the actual work.

You can write your own codec by creating a new module. It needs to import the **codecs** module, and you then need to define a **Codec** class that should inherit from the codecs. The **Codec** class should include two methods: **encode()** and **decode()**. The easiest way to implement these two methods is to use the **charmap_encode()** function and **charmap_decode()** function within the **codecs** module.

Both these accept a character map—a dictionary that maps the character to encode or decode to or from. For example, look at this extract from the **mac_roman.py** module:

```
{
    0x0080: 0x00c4, # LATIN CAPITAL LETTER A WITH DIAERESIS
    0x0081: 0x00c5, # LATIN CAPITAL LETTER A WITH RING ABOVE
    0x0082: 0x00c7, # LATIN CAPITAL LETTER C WITH CEDILLA
```

```
    0x0083: 0x00c9, # LATIN CAPITAL LETTER E WITH ACUTE
    0x0084: 0x00d1, # LATIN CAPITAL LETTER N WITH TILDE
    0x0085: 0x00d6, # LATIN CAPITAL LETTER O WITH DIAERESIS
    0x0086: 0x00dc, # LATIN CAPITAL LETTER U WITH DIAERESIS
    0x0087: 0x00e1, # LATIN SMALL LETTER A WITH ACUTE
...
}
```

If you are updating an existing dictionary, use the **make_identity_dict()** function in the **codecs** module. This creates a base dictionary according to the range you supply. For example, to match the standard 256-character eight-bit ASCII map, use the following:

```
decoding_map = codecs.make_identity_dict(range(256))
```

You can then merge your updated map dictionary using the **update()** method:

```
decoding_map.update({
    0x0080: 0x00c4, # LATIN CAPITAL LETTER A WITH DIAERESIS
    0x0081: 0x00c5, # LATIN CAPITAL LETTER A WITH RING ABOVE
...
})
```

Remember that you'll need two maps: one for the encoding and one for the decoding. Assuming the two translations are opposites of each other (that is, an encode/decode pass on a string should return the original string), you can create the opposite map using

```
encoding_map = {}
for k,v in decoding_map.items():
    encoding_map[v] = k
```

Going back to the **encode()** and **decode()** methods, using the map you've just created, you can define those methods like as follows:

```
class Codec(codecs.Codec):
    def encode(self,input,errors='strict'):
        return codecs.charmap_encode(input,
                                     errors,
                                     encoding_map)

    def decode(self,input,errors='strict'):
```

```
        return codecs.charmap_decode(input,
                                     errors,
                                     decoding_map)
```

Your codec also needs to define the **StreamWriter** and **StreamReader** classes. These are used by the **codecs** module to read and write specific data stream types and convert them into a suitable character format. You probably won't need this for simple Unicode translations, so you can dummy-define them:

```
class StreamWriter(Codec,codecs.StreamWriter):
    pass

class StreamReader(Codec,codecs.StreamReader):
    pass
```

The final step in creating your codec is to register your code with the **codecs** module, which you do by defining a **getregentry()** function. This returns a four-element tuple containing the **encode()** and **decode()** methods from your class and the **StreamReader** and **StreamWriter** classes. In your case, this produces a definition like this:

```
def getregentry():
    return (Codec().encode,
            Codec().decode,
            StreamReader,
            StreamWriter)
```

After you've created your codec, drop the module into the encodings directory. The codec is ready to use.

Here's a complete codec example that performs the relatively useless operation of translating **a** characters into **e** characters and vice versa:

```
import codecs

# Create our Codec class

class Codec(codecs.Codec):
    def encode(self,input,errors='strict'):
        return codecs.charmap_encode(input,
                                     errors,
                                     encoding_map)
```

```
    def decode(self,input,errors='strict'):
        return codecs.charmap_decode(input, .
                                     errors,
                                     decoding_map)

class StreamWriter(Codec,codecs.StreamWriter):
    pass

class StreamReader(Codec,codecs.StreamReader):
    pass

# Register ourselves with the codec module:

def getregentry():
    return (Codec().encode,
            Codec().decode,
            StreamReader,
            StreamWriter)

# Create our decode and encoding maps

decoding_map = codecs.make_identity_dict(range(256))
decoding_map.update({
    0x0041: 0x0045,
    0x0061: 0x0065,
    0x0045: 0x0041,
    0x0065: 0x0061,
})

encoding_map = {}
for k,v in decoding_map.items():
    encoding_map[v] = k
```

Let's try this codec with **'mcb'**. If you start up Python, here are the results:

```
>>> unicode('ae','mcb')
u'ea'
>>> u'ae'.encode('mcb')
'ea'
```

Translating Character Numbers

The **ord()** built-in function returns the number that represents a particular character. The function is Unicode aware, so you can get the Unicode number for a character like this:

```
>>> ord('ø')
248
```

To translate that back into a Unicode character, however, you need to use the **unichr()** function rather than the **chr()** function:

```
>>> unichr(248)
u'\xbf'
```

As you can see, this returns a single-character Unicode object.

Accessing the Unicode Database

The **unicodedata** module provides a direct interface to the Unicode database as defined by the data file released by the Unicode consortium.

To look up a Unicode character by its description, use the **lookup()** function. For example, here's how to determine the Unicode character for the Greek capital letter pi:

```
>>> import unicodedata
>>> unicodedata.lookup('Greek capital letter pi')
u'\u03a0'
```

Note that in the character name, case is not important but the name is—you cannot leave out words that you consider optional, and the whitespace between descriptive words is required. If it can't find the word, describe a **KeyError** exception to be raised. To get the Unicode name for a specific Unicode character, use the **name()** function:

```
>>> unicodedata.name(u'\u03a0')
'GREEK CAPITAL LETTER PI'
```

Chapter 11

Working with Files

Y ou can't always rely on using information entirely within your application. Sometimes you need to read information from a file or write the information to a file. In other situations you need to be able to open and update an existing file in place. Editing the contents of a file is often only part of the problem. Sometimes you don't know the name of the file and need to offer the user a list of filenames. Other times you want to process a list of files matching a particular name or extension. On the periphery of these operations are requirements to make, delete, obtain, and modify files and directories, as well as their ownership and accessibility settings.

This chapter looks at all of these operations.

File Processing

The basic techniques for opening a file were described in Chapter 3 and Chapter 8. You open a file using the built-in **open()** function, which accepts at least one argument, the name of the file to open. The basic format of the **open()** function is

```
file = open(filename [, mode [, bufsize]])
```

By default, the file is opened in read mode, but an optional second argument can be used to specify the mode used to open the file, from basic reading to reading with update and binary modes. Table 11-1 lists the supported modes for opening a file.

Mode	Meaning
r	Open for reading.
w	Open for writing.
a	Open for appending (file position automatically seeks to the end during the open).
r+	Open for updating (reading and writing).
w+	Truncates (empties) the file and then opens it for reading and writing.
a+	Opens the file for reading and writing and automatically changes the current file position to the end of the file.
b	When appended to any option, opens the file in binary rather than text mode. This mode is available for Windows, DOS, and some other operating systems only. Unix/MacOS/BeOS treat all files as binary, regardless of this option.

Table 11-1.   *File Modes for the **open** Function*

Bufsize Value	Description
0	Disable buffering.
1	Line buffered.
>1	Use a buffer that is approximately **bufsize** characters in length.
<0	Use the system default (line buffered for **tty** devices and fully buffered for any other file).

Table 11-2. *Buffer Sizes Supported by the **open()** Function*

A third optional argument defines whether the file should use buffering and if so, what size the buffer should be. Table 11-2 lists the available settings, with the default being <0.

The function returns a new file object, and it's through this file object that you read and write information to the file. Table 11-3 lists the supported methods to the file object, but you'll learn about each method in more detail later in this chapter.

Method	Description
f.close	Closes the file.
f.fileno	Returns the integer file descriptor number.
f.flush	Flushes the output buffers.
f.isatty	Returns 1 if file is an interactive terminal.
f.read([count])	Reads **count** bytes from the file.
f.readline	Reads a single line, returning it as a string.
f.readlines	Reads all the lines, returning a list of strings.
f.seek(offset [, where])	Changes the file pointer to **offset** relative to **where**.
f.tell	Gets the current file pointer.
f.truncate([size])	Truncates file to **size**.
f.write(string)	Writes **string** to the file.
f.writelines(list)	Writes the lines in **list** (a list of strings) to the file. The information in **list** is written raw; each element is not processed in any way, and the **writelines()** method does not imply that linefeed or carriage return characters are added to the output.

Table 11-3. *Methods for a File Object*

Reading

Reading information from a file is handled in two basic ways: byte by byte or line by line. The byte-by-byte format is most useful when you're reading binary data or when you're not going to be processing the information on a line-by-line basis. The line-by-line mode is best used when you expect to process the information on a line-by-line basis—say when processing a log file. The line-by-line mode has two separate modes: either you read a single line from the file or you read all the lines in the file at one time.

Line by Line

The **readline()** method reads a single line from the file:

```
line = file.readline()
```

Different platforms use different line-termination characters, and Python recognizes the appropriate line-termination character for your platform when reading a file. However, be warned that Python does not recognize the line-termination character for platforms other than the current platform. For example, you can read a Unix file line by line on a Unix system, but on a Mac, the same Unix file would appear as one big line to the Mac version of Python. Because Windows uses two characters for line termination, you can read individual lines from a file under Mac OS or Unix, but you'll have a spurious characters at the end or beginning of the lines you read from the file. See Chapter 23 for more information.

The line returned by the **readline** method includes the trailing line-termination characters, so you'll need to use the **string.rstrip()** method to take the new line off in many situations. For example, the temptation is to use a loop like the following to print a file to the screen:

```
    line = myfile.readline()
if line:
        print line
    else:
        break
```

The problem is that the output will include double line terminations, and therefore blank lines in the output. Instead, change the **print** line to

```
print line,
```

or use **sys.stdout.write()** to ensure that a line-termination character isn't automatically appended to the output.

Getting All the Lines

You can read all of the lines from a file using the **readlines()** method on an active file object. For example, you can read the entire file into a list using

```
lines = myfile.lines()
```

To read the entire contents of a file into a single string object, use the **read()** method without any arguments, as in the following example:

```
myfiledata = myfile.read()
```

Byte by Byte

You can also use the **read()** method to read a specific number of bytes from a file. For example, to read a 512-byte record from a file, use a statement like this:

```
record = file.read(512)
```

End of File

Python does not support the notion of an "end-of-file" status for an open file object. Although an **EOFError** exception does exist, it's actually used by the **input()** and **raw_input()** built-in functions to identify when an end-of-file character has been identified while reading input from the keyboard.

Instead, the **read()** and **readline()** methods return an empty string when they reach the end of the file. To end the processing of a file, you therefore need to check the information that you read from the file and break out of the loop accordingly:

```
while 1:
line = myfile.readline()
    if !line: break
    print line,
myfile.close()
```

The **if** test breaks out of the loop when it sees an empty line.

The other alternative is to use a **for** loop and the **readlines()** method to step through each individual line:

```
for line in myfile.readlines():
print line,
myfile.close()
```

This script automatically terminates when the list of lines returned by the **readlines()** call is reached.

Processing Example

Processing a file in Python requires more than just the basic ability to read lines or data. Most of the time you'll need to be able to identify different portions of the line or data that you read, and in fact, you saw many examples of this in Chapter 10. When working with data on a line-by-line basis, the obvious solution is to use **string.split()** to extract elements or to use the regular expression system offered by **re** to identify the elements you want.

If you are reading binary data, use the **struct** module to extract binary information. Alternatively, you may want to employ the services of the **pickle** module and similar modules described in Chapter 12 to store and load objects permanently in a file.

As an example of what you can do, here's a simple script in Python that uses **string.split()** to compile a count of the hosts and URL access from a standard web log:

```python
import sys

def cmpval(tuple1, tuple2):
    return cmp(tuple2[1],tuple1[1])

hostaccess = {}
urlaccess = {}

if len(sys.argv) < 2:
    print "Usage:",sys.argv[0],"logfile"
    sys.exit(1)

try:
    file = open(sys.argv[1])
except:
    print "Whoa!","Couldn't open the file",sys.argv[1]
    sys.exit(1)

while 1:
    line = file.readline()
    if line:
        splitline = string.split(line)
        if len(splitline) < 10:
            print splitline
```

```
            continue
        (host,ident,user,time,offset,req,
         loc,httpver,success,bytes) = splitline
        try:
            hostaccess[host] = hostaccess[host] + 1
        except:
            hostaccess[host] = 1
        try:
            urlaccess[loc] = urlaccess[loc] + 1
        except:
            urlaccess[loc] = 1
    else:
        break

hosts = hostaccess.items()
hosts.sort(lambda f, s: cmp(s[1], f[1]))

for host, count in hosts:
    print host, ": ", count

urls = urlaccess.items()
urls.sort(cmpval)

for url, count in urls:
    print url, ": ", count
```

Writing to a File

Writing information to a file is usually just a case of calling the **write()** or **writelines()** methods.

Using write() **or** writelines()

The **write()** and **writelines()** methods are the most obvious way to write information to a file in Python. Both can be used to write binary data and unlike **print**, they do not automatically add a newline to each string written to the file. The **write()** method writes a single string, and despite the name, the **writelines()** method actually only writes a list of strings to the file. For example, to write a string to an open file, use this statement:

```
file.write('Some text')
```

You can write a list of strings using the following statement:

```
file.writelines(lines)
```

Using print

New in Python 2.0 is the ability to write directly to an open file without using the **write()** or **writelines()** methods. Instead, use a special operator that, in combination with the name of the file object that you want to write to, places the information between the **print** keyword and the string you want to write:

```
print >>file 'Some kind of error occurred'
```

Because you're using **print**, the newline character is automatically appended, so be careful when using **print** over **write()**—appending a comma stops Python from appending the line-termination sequence. Also be careful when supplying a list or dictionary to **print** because it writes a string representation of the list, tuple, or dictionary to the file, rather than emulating the **writelines()** method.

Changing Position

All file objects keep a record of their position within the file. This position is based on the number of bytes you have read or written to the file; a value 0 means you are writing at the start, before the first byte in the file. Position 1 defines the first byte of the file, position 2 defines the second byte, and position 512 defines the 512th byte in the file. If you add information to the file, it's added *after* your current position, so at position 1, you actually start writing information from byte 2 on. Note, of course, that whenever you write information to a file, you are *overwriting* the existing data, not inserting it.

You can determine your current position using the **tell()** method on an open file object. To change your position—outside of reading or writing the file of course—use the **seek()** method. The **seek()** method takes a single argument that specifies the location within the file in bytes that you want to move to. For example, to move to the start of the file, use

```
file.seek(0)
```

Moving to the end of the file is more difficult because you'd need to know the file's length in order to be able to move to the absolute position of the last byte in the file. There is a solution however. An optional second argument to the **seek()** method defines from where to take the location. The default is 0—all locations are assumed to be relative to the start of the file.

If the second argument to **seek()** is set to 1, the supplied first argument is taken as an addition to the current position. So, if you are at byte 512 and use the statement

```
file.seek(512,1)
```

you automatically move to byte 1024 (512+512). If the second argument is 2, the first argument is taken as relative to the end of the file. Therefore, you can move directly to the last byte in a file using the statement

```
file.seek(0,2)
```

You can also move back 512 bytes using the statement

```
file.seek(-512,2)
```

Table 11-4 summarizes these values.

Seek Value	Description
0	Relative to the start of the file (i.e., absolute). This is the default value.
1	Relative to the current position.
2	Relative to the end of the file.

Table 11-4. *Seek Position Values*

Controlling File I/O

Once you've opened a file, you may want to control how the file is accessed and shared. Under Unix you can do this using the **fcntl** module, which provides an interface to the underlying **fcntl.h** and **ioctl.h** header file and library interfaces in C.

File Control

To use file control, first get the file descriptor number from the file object you want to control. The **fileno** method does this for you.

Next, the **fcntl()** function in the **fcntl** module sets or gets the configuration information for the file. The basic format of the **fcntl()** function is

```
fnctl(fd, command [, args])
```

The **fd** argument is the file descriptor number returned by **fileno()**. The **command** argument is a constant that specifies the command you want to send to the file control system. Commands either set or get status and sharing information about the file. Table 11-5 contains a list of the valid commands and Table 11-6 contains a list of the supported options for the **F_SETFL** command. Note that the **FCNTL** module exports all of the constants in these two tables.

Command	Description
F_DUPFD	Duplicates a file descriptor. If **args** is supplied, it's used as the lowest possible number that should be used for the duplicate file descriptor; the actual value depends on the open file descriptors. The return value is the value of the new file descriptor.
F_SETFD	Sets the close-on-exec flag. If set to true (**args** is 1), the file descriptor is closed when an **exec*()** call is executed. If set to false (**args** is 0), the file descriptor remains open and is duplicated by the call (the default).
F_GETFD	Returns the current value of the close-on-exec flag.
F_SETFL	Sets the file status flag to **args**, which should be a bitwise OR of one or more of the constants defined in Table 11-6. Make sure to use the correct flag for your system type.
F_GETFL	Gets the file status flag.

Table 11-5. *fcntl* Commands

Command	Description
F_GETOWN	Gets the process ID or process group ID to receive the SIGIO signal (BSD only).
F_SETOWN	Sets the process ID to receive the SIGIO signal (BSD only).
F_GETLK	Gets the file lock structure. Not supported on all platforms.
F_SETLK	Locks a file. Returns –1 if the file is already locked. Not supported on all platforms.
F_SETLKW	Locks a file but blocks the execution of the current process until the lock can be acquired. Not supported on all platforms.

Table 11-5.   *fcntl Commands* (continued)

I/O Control

The **ioctl()** function is identical to **fcntl()** except that it provides an interface to the **ioctl** subsystem for control I/O on any valid file descriptor. Check the documentation for your system to see what configurable options are supported.

File Locking

When working with any file, especially when writing, you may need to ensure that the current process is the only process that has the ability to write to the file. Although

System V	BSD	Description
O_NDELAY	FNDELAY	Non-blocking I/O— execution does not stop while reading or writing from the file. This shouldn't be necessary for most platforms.
O_APPEND	FAPPEND	Append mode.
O_SYNC	FASYNC	Synchronous I/O—no buffering is used so writing to the file automatically writes the information to disk. Under BSD this causes a SIGIO signal to be raised to the process group when I/O is possible.

Table 11-6.   *Status Flag Constants for the* **F_SETFL fcntl** *Command*

Operation	Description
LOCK_EX	Exclusive lock. Other processes cannot even obtain a shared lock on the file.
LOCK_NB	Don't block the locking process. This causes the functions to immediately return with the status of the lock. If not specified, the processes block (wait) until the specified lock can be achieved.
LOCK_SH	Get a shared lock. This allows only your process to read the write to the file while allowing others to read.
LOCK_UN	Remove any lock.

Table 11-7. *File-Locking Options*

there are lots of potential solutions for this, the best way to handle the locking process is to use the operating system file-locking facilities. There are two functions for locking a file:

- **flock()** provides a simple whole-file locking mechanism.
- **lockf()** allows you to lock specific portions of a file.

Both functions support the same operations, which are listed in Table 11-7 and supported through the module by a number of constants defined in the **fcntl** module. Note that support for **fcntl** options is entirely OS dependent.

The **flock()** function is defined as follows:

```
flock(fd, op)
```

where **fd** is the file descriptor number and **op** is a bitwise OR of the file-locking options described in Table 11-7. The **fd** function locks the entire file until you unlock it or the process terminates.

The **lockf()** functions is defined as follows:

```
lockf(fd, op [, len [, start [, whence]]])
```

The **fd** and **op** arguments are the same as before but the **len**, **start**, and **whence** arguments define the length and duration of the lock. If not supplied with these arguments, the lock is set for the whole file. If **len** is specified, the **lockf()** function locks only the first **len** bytes of the file. The **start** and **whence** arguments work like the arguments to **seek** specifying the starting location and reference point of the lock. For example, you can lock the first 1,024 bytes with

```
fnctl.lockf(myfd, FCNTL.LOCK_EX, 1024)
```

or the last 1,024 bytes with

```
fnctl.lockf(myfd, FCNTL.LOCK_EX, 1024, -1024, 2)
```

Getting File Lists

Often you want to work with a list of files rather than a single file. For example, suppose you want to process all the **.html** files within the current directory. You can get around this by using the shell—under Unix, it is the shell (**sh**, **ksh**, **bash**, etc.) that actually expands a file specification such as ***.html** into a list of files that is then supplied directly to the application and available within Python as **sys.argv**.

If you want to get a list of files without using the directory, use the **glob** module. The **glob()** function within the **glob** module supports the same wildcard options as most Unix shells; Table 11-8 lists the supported wildcard specifications.

For example, to get a list of all HTML files, use

```
files = glob.glob('*.html')
```

The return value is a list of strings, with each element referring to a single file.

To perform more complex matches, use the regular expression module described in Chapter 10 to check each filename. For example, to find all the files with capital letters and a single number, for example, **THEFILE1.txt**, you might use something like this:

```
filelist = []
for file in glob.glob('./*'):
    if (re.search(r'[A-Z]*?[0-9].[a-z]*', file)):
        filelist.append(file)
```

Specification	Description
*	Matches anything and any quantity.
?	Matches a single character.
[seq]	Matches any character in **seq**.
[!seq]	Matches any character not in **seq**.

Table 11-8.   *Wildcard Specifications for Finding Files*

Basic File/Directory Management

Most of the functions for moving, renaming, and otherwise manipulating directories can be found in the **os** module. Most of these functions are self-explanatory; they are summarized in Table 11-9.

Function	Description
chdir(name)	Changes the current working directory to **name**.
getcwd()	Returns the path to the current working directory.
link(source, dest)	Creates a hard link between **source** and **dest**. This function is supported by all platforms/operating systems.
mkdir(path [, mode])	Makes the directory **path** using the mode **mode**. Under Python, **mode** defaults to **0777** if not supplied.
makedirs(path [, mode])	Identical to **mkdir()** except that the **makedirs()** function makes all of the directories defined in the path, such that **makedirs('/a/b/c')** creates **'/a'**, **'/a/b'** and **'/a/b/c'** if they didn't already exist.
remove(path) or unlink(path)	Removes a given file.
removedirs(path)	Removes the directory specified in path, including any subdirectories or files (identical to **rm -r**). Raises an **OSError** exception if the directory cannot be removed.
rename(source, dest)	Renames **source** to **dest**.
renames(source, dest)	Identical to **rename()** except that any directories specified in **dest** that do not exist are created in an identical fashion to that used by **makedirs()**.
rmdir(path)	Removes the directory **path**.
symlink(source, dest)	Creates a symbolic link between **source** and **dest**. Not supported on all platforms/operating systems.

Table 11-9. *Making, Renaming, and Deleting Files/Directories in Python*

For more high-level options such as copying files and directory trees, use the **shutil** module. The **shutil** module includes functions for basic file copies, mode and permission copies, and utilities for duplicating and deleting entire directory trees. Table 11-10 contains the list of functions supported. Support is provided for all operating systems.

Function	Description
copyfile(src, dst)	Copies the file specified by the path **src** to **dst**.
copymode(src, dst)	Copies the permission bits for **src** to **dst**.
copystat(src, dst)	Copies the permissions, modification, and access times from **src** to **dst**. Note that this function does not copy the file contents nor does it change the owner or group for the file.
copy(src, dst)	Copies the file from **src** to the file or directory in **dst**.
copy2(src,dst)	Copies the file from **src** to the file or directory in **dst** and also copies the access and modification times of the files.
copytree(src, dst [,symlinks])	Copies the entire directory tree of the directory **src** to the directory **dst**. Files are copied using **copy2()**. If **symlinks** is true, symbolic links are recreated in the destination as symbolic links. If **symlinks** is false or unspecified, the file contents are copied as per a normal file.
rmtree(path [, ignore_errors [, onerror]])	Removes the entire directory tree in **path**. If **ignore_errors** is true, any errors are ignored. If **ignore_errors** is false, errors are handled by the function specified by **onerror**, which must accept three arguments: **func**, **path**, and **excinfo**. **func** refers to the function that caused the error (i.e., **rmdir()** or **remove()**), and **path** refers to the file or directory that was being deleted. **excinfo** is a set of exception information as raised by **sys.exc_info()**.

Table 11-10. *Functions for Copying and Removing Directories in shutil*

Access and Ownership

Often you need to determine or set the file options and permissions for a given file. The **os** module provides a series of functions to get and set file permissions and other information. You can also use the output in combination with the **stat** module to provide a cleaner interface to the information returned, or for some statistics, the **os.path** module.

Checking Access

To check your ability to access a file, use the **os.access()** function:

```
os.access(path, accessmode)
```

path should be the path to the file or directory you want to check, and **accessmode** is a constant that specifies what sort of access you want to check. Valid values for **accessmode** are:

- **R_OK** (able to read)
- **W_OK** (able to write)
- **X_OK** (able to execute)
- **F_OK** (to test for existence)

For example, to check whether you have permission to read a file, use:

```
os.access('myfile.txt', os.R_OK)
```

Getting File Information

To get information about a file (i.e., its permissions, ownership, and access times), use the **os.stat** function (for files) or the **os.lstat** function (for links). Both functions return the same information in the form of a tuple of values containing the information for a file. Table 11-11 lists the values returned and their element reference along with the constant exported by the **stat** module for accessing the information by name rather than index.

Element Reference	stat Constant	Description
0	**ST_MODE**	File mode (type and permissions)
1	**ST_INO**	Inode number
2	**ST_DEV**	Device number of file system
3	**ST_NLINK**	Number of (hard) links to the file
4	**ST_UID**	Numeric user ID of file's owner

Table 11-11. *Elements Returned by* **stat()**

Element Reference	stat Constant	Description
5	**ST_GID**	Numeric group ID of file's owner
6	**ST_SIZE**	File size, in bytes
7	**ST_ATIME**	Last access time since the epoch
8	**ST_MTIME**	Last modify time since the epoch
9	**ST_CTIME**	Inode change time (*not* creation time!) since the epoch

Table 11-11.   *Elements Returned by **stat()** (continued)*

For example, to get the size of a file, use:

```
filesize = os.stat(file)[6]
```

You can use the output of the **stat()** commands with the **stat** module in order to get, set, or determine the file type and other information. The **stat** module exports constants to access the different elements of a **stat()** tuple, as shown in Table 11-11 in the **stat** Constant column. In addition, it provides the functions in Table 11-12, which return summary information for a given aspect of the file. Note that all the functions accept a single argument: the mode as returned by **os.stat(path)[stat.ST_MODE]**.

Function	Description
S_ISDIR(mode)	Returns true if the path is a directory.
S_ISCHR(mode)	Returns true if the file is a character special device file.
S_ISBLK(mode)	Returns true if the file is a block special device file.
S_ISREG(mode)	Returns true if the file is a regular file.
S_ISFIFO(mode)	Returns true if the path is a FIFO.
S_ISLNK(mode)	Returns true if the path is a symbolic link.
S_ISSOCK(mode)	Returns true if the path is a Unix socket.
S_IMODE(mode)	Returns the portion of the file's mode that can be set by the **os.chmod()** function.
S_IFMT(mode)	Returns the portion of the file's mode that describes the file's type.

Table 11-12.   *Test Functions Exported by the **stat** Module*

A quicker interface is available through the **os.path** module, which provides utility functions to obtain most of this information with a single function call. Table 11-13 lists the supported functions in **os.path** for determining file information.

Setting File Permissions

To actually set the file mode and ownership within Python, use the **os.chmod()** and **os.chown()** functions respectively. Note that these functions only apply to Unix-style operating systems (including QNX, BeOS, and MacOS X), but not to Windows or MacOS. For example, to set the permissions on a file, use

```
os.chmod('file.txt', 0666)
```

Note that the permissions must be specified as an octal number, just as you would when specifying the mode on the command line in Unix. The **os.chown()** function accepts three arguments: the path, the user ID, and the group ID. For example, to change **file.txt** to be owned by user 1001 and group 1000, use the following statement:

```
os.chown('file.txt', 1001, 1000)
```

To use names rather than numbers, use the **pwd** and **grp** modules to determine the numeric IDs for a given user or group.

For cross-reference purposes, Table 11-14 contains the format of the **os.chmod()** and **os.chown()** functions.

Function	Description
getatime(path)	Returns the time of last access as the number of seconds since the epoch.
getmtime(path)	Returns the time of last modification as the number of seconds since the epoch.
getsize(path)	Returns the size of the file in bytes.

Table 11-13.   *Alternative Methods for Getting File Information in Python*

Python Function	Description
os.chmod(path, mode)	Change the permission mode of **path** to **mode**.
os.chown(path, uid, gid)	Change the user ID and group ID of **path**.

Table 11-14.   *Setting Access Modes in Python*

Manipulating File Paths

When working with files, you'll inevitably need to manipulate the directories and files or the paths of the files and directories that you want to open. Manipulating this information is not easy, especially if you want to support different platforms. For example, the Unix platform uses the forward slash (/) character to separate directory components, but MacOS uses a colon (:) and officially Windows uses the backslash (\) character, although the forward slash (/) character is supported on Windows 95 and later versions.

To make the process easier, the **os** module exports variables that define the settings for the current platform. Table 11-15 lists the variables that hold this information.

Variable	Description
sep	The character used to separate path components: / on Unix, : on MacOS, and \ on Windows.
pathsep	The character used to separate each path within the **$PATH** environment variable: : for Unix and ; for Windows/DOS.
pardir	The character sequence used to describe the parent directory: .. on Unix/Windows and :: on MacOS.
curdir	The character sequence used to describe the current directory: . on Unix and Windows and : on MacOS.
altsep	The character used as an alternative separator. This really only applies to Windows where the forward slash (/) can be used.

Table 11-15.   *Directory Component Variables in the **os** Module*

Armed with this information, you can assemble a file's path using

```
fullpath = basedir + os.sep + dir + os.sep + file
```

However, this is messy and it doesn't actually account for such niceties as removing duplicate separators in the final path. A much better solution is offered by the **os.path** module, which provides a number of functions to assemble and disassemble a given path on any platform into the correct format. Table 11-16 lists these functions.

The **basename()** and **dirname()** functions both disassemble a path and return the directory and/or filename from a path, as in the following example:

```
>>> os.path.basename('/usr/local/lib/python2.1/os.py')
'os.py'
>>> os.path.dirname('/usr/local/lib/python2.1/os.py')
'/usr/local/lib/python2.1'
```

The **abspath()** function cleans up a path, resolving references to current and parent directories in order to arrive at a final, cleaned path:

```
'/var/adm/su.log'
```

Finally, the **join()** function joins together components, including the correct separators for the current platform and returns a clean and valid path:

```
'/usr/local/python2.1/os.py'
```

Python Function	Description
os.path.join(patha [, pathb ...])	Joins the components **patha**, **pathb** into a valid path using the correct path separators for the current platform.
os.path.abspath(path)	Returns a cleaned-up version of **path**, removing references to current and parent directories.
os.path.basename(path)	Extract the base name (filename or final directory) for a given path.
os.path.dirname(path)	Extract the directory name for a given path.

Table 11-16. *Path Manipulation Functions in Python*

Chapter 12

Data Management and Storage

W̶e looked in the previous two chapters at processing information and reading and writing information to and from files, but what if our information is more complex than a simple set of strings or words? And how we do store and process information in lists and dictionaries in an efficient manner?

Some of the problems you face will be related to how you manage and work with the internal objects that you are using to hold your information. We'll be looking at two specific areas: the sorting of sequences (a topic touched on briefly in other chapters) and how to properly copy objects rather than references.

In the second part of the chapter we'll be concentrating on the methods available to you for storing and loading objects and data from sources other than a plain text file.

Managing Internal Structures

Creating a variable, storing some information in it, and later using the values that come back is not really all there is to variable management. Python includes powerful sorting capabilities, but in order to use them you need to think about both the type of information that you are sorting—list, tuple, or dictionary—and also the type of data contained within the sequence that you are sorting. For example, a simple text or numerical comparison is straightforward, but things get more difficult when comparing dates or objects.

We also need to be careful when copying and using objects. Because Python uses references to objects, it's possible to add or update a reference rather than a copy. We can get around this problem by forcing Python to copy the object into a new object (and associated reference).

Sorting Sequences

Sorting information in Python requires a little bit of thought and planning in order to get the sequence of events correct. The list built-in object type supports a **sort()** method that sorts the contents in place. There are three things to be wary of when sorting Python lists:

- Calling **list.sort()** sorts the list permanently. Unless you make a copy of the list, there is no way to preserve the original order of the list.

- Dictionaries cannot be sorted without extracting their key or value lists and then sorting the list.

- Tuples cannot be sorted at all. If you've received a tuple as a return value from a function (and many do return tuples rather than lists), you need to make a copy in a list before sorting the values.

Luckily Python's methods have some advantages, too: number- and string-based lists are automatically sorted numerically and alphabetically, for example, and because we use a copy of an object to sort the information, we can also separately manipulate it to produce a customer sort order.

Sorting Tuples

Because a tuple is immutable, we cannot sort it in place—the tuple built-in object doesn't even support a **sort()** method. The solution is to use the built-in **list()** function to create a copy of the tuple as a list, and then sort the list. For example:

```
tuplecopyaslist.sort()
for item in tuplecopyaslist:
    print item
```

Sorting Dictionaries

We've already seen an example of this when looking at dictionaries in Chapter 3, but it's worth a quick recap. Essentially, we cannot get a sorted list of the keys from a dictionary that we can use directly from within another statement. For example, the following **for** statement just won't work:

```
for item in dict.keys().sort():
```

Instead, we need to get a list of keys into a new variable, before sorting that:

```
keylist.sort()
for item in keylist:
    print '%s is %s' % (item, dict[item])
```

Sort Functions

When sorting nonstandard data, or when you want to normalize the data to be sorted without affecting the contents of the list itself, we need to use functions—either anonymous or named—to do the sorting operating for us.

In either case, the function is supplied two arguments—the two elements that are being compared. In a list, this is simply the values of the two elements you are comparing; with a dictionary, it's the two keys or values that you previously extracted from the dictionary. For example, sorting textual information is always a problem because what actually happens is that the data is sorted according to the ASCII table. This unfortunately leads to A coming before a and Z also coming before a. To get around this, you can use a separate sort function to convert the elements to lower case during the compare, therefore turning everything into the same case and sorting the items correctly.

For example, we can do this with an anonymous function:

```
list.sort(lambda x,y: return cmp(string.lower(x), string.lower(y)))
```

Or, using a separate function:

```
      return cmp(string.lower(x), string.lower(y))

list.sort(noncasesort)
```

Note that when calling the sorting function, we supply the code object for the **noncasesort()** function rather than actually calling the function.

Copying Objects

One of the problems arising from Python always using references to data is that it can play havoc with data structures that use references, rather than copies of data from other variables. For example, the following fragment creates two variables, **alist** and **blist**:

```
>>> blist = alist
```

The **blist** variable is a reference to the same array object as **alist**, which means changing a value in the *variable* **alist** modifies the same list to which **blist** points, such that:

```
>>> alist
[25, 50, 75, 2000]
>>> blist
[25, 50, 75, 2000]
>>>
```

We get the same value: both **alist** and **blist** point to the same array, so modifying values in one modifies the values we get back from the other.

To make a copy of a list or other sequence, we can extract a full-length slice; for example:

```
>>> blist = alist[:]
```

By assigning the values from a slice of the list, we copy the individual objects from **alist** to **blist**, thus:

```
>>> blist
[25, 50, 75, 2000]
```

The above operation creates what is called a *shallow* copy and will not copy nested structures:

```
>>> blist = alist[:]
>>> alist.append(5)
>>> blist
[1, 2, [3, 4]]
>>> alist[2][1] = 5
>>> blist
[1, 2, [3, 5]]
```

To perform a *deep* copy, which copies all elements (included nested structures) to a completely new variable, you need to use the **deepcopy()** function in the **copy** module. For example:

```
>>> alist = [1,2 [3,4]]
>>> blist = copy.deepcopy(alist)
>>> alist[2][1] = 5
>>> blist
[1, 2, [3, 4]]
```

Object Persistence

Often you want to do more than just store and read basic text files. If you are dealing with any form of complex data structure, such as a list, dictionary, or nested structure, then you need something more substantial to store your information.

Object Storage

If you have created a structure in a Python application and want to record that structure permanently in a file, there are a few options available to you. The most suitable one will largely depend on the complexity of the object that you have created. At the simplest level, it's unlikely that you'll want to store single numbers or strings, but even if you do, the file reading and writing methods we covered in the previous chapter will handle the information easily.With lists and tuples, assuming you are storing other basic types such as strings and numbers, the information can easily be stored in files, just using multiple lines; each line refers to an elements of the array, so reading the information back is just a case of reading each line and adding it to the list. You'll have to be sure and convert any numbers from string form back into numeric format—the **string** module contains functions for converting strings to integers and floating-point values. Of course in an ideal world, you'd be better off working with a proper database system such as mySQL, which also provides methods for easily searching and obtaining the information you want without loading or parsing the entire file. See the "Commercial Databases" section later in this chapter for more information.

For dictionaries, things get more complicated, but information is still easily represented in a textual form—again assuming you're working with simple string and/or numeric keys and values. Using a standard text, we can just write the information to the file as individual lines; each key/value pair is on its own line, and a single character (colon or equals sign) separates the values. Dictionaries are often used to store configuration values, and if you look at the format of most configuration files you'll see they are in a relatively standard format, like this:

```
SaveLines = True
```

When reading the file back in, we only need to separate the key/value pairs again, which we can do with the **string.split()** function. Even easier still, you can use a DBM database to store dictionaries in their entirety: you never need to load the values or parse a text file. See the section "DBM Databases" later in this chapter for more details. Better still, you could write the information out as valid Python statements, and then you could just import the file directly!

Up to now, of course, we've just been dealing with fairly simple structures—strings, numbers, and simple sequences. When you start storing complex structures with nested structures—dictionaries of dictionaries or lists of lists, for example—the process gets more complex if you are using just a flat file. The process gets even more difficult when you start to store your own objects or binary information in a typical file. You can get around the problem by using a structured data format such as XML, but you still need to work through the problem of converting your structure to XML.

Python offers quite a few solutions to this problem through a number of standard modules which serialize just about any object into a file or string and then deserialize the generated information back into an object. The exact serialization process depends entirely on the module you are using, but most use the same basic principles that we've covered here, albeit in a more structured format in order to convert the internal object into a file or string-friendly format for permanent storage.

There are two modules in the standard distribution that support serialization of objects into files or strings, **marshal** and **pickle** (or its C implementation **cPickle**).

Using marshal

The **marshal** module supports only simple object types—that is numbers, strings, lists, tuples, dictionaries, and code objects. The sequence objects can use only one of the supported subtypes. Because **marshal** is not as flexible as **pickle**, it probably shouldn't be used in production systems; you'll also run into issues if you try to store an incompatible type.

However, if none of this has scared you off, using the **marshal** module is simplicity itself. To store an object in a file, you use the **dump()** function, which accepts two arguments: the object you want to dump and an open file object that you want to store the object in. For example:

```
names = { 'Martin' : 29,
          'Rikke' : '30',
          'Andy'  : '33', }
namesdb = open('names','w')
marshal.dump(names, namesdb)
```

A **ValueError** exception is raised if the object you supply is not one of the supported types. The information is written to the file just as if you were writing any data, so you can add new data and additional objects to the file before finally closing it. However, when reading the information back, you must have first located the position of the object that you want to load.

To load the object back, use the **load()** function, which accepts a single argument: an object and readable file object:

```
namesdb = open('names','r')
names = marshal.load(namesdb)
```

The function raises a **EOFError**, **ValueError**, or **TypeError** if the object should not be loaded from the file.

In addition to the two file-based functions, the module also supports two string-based functions. The **dumps()** function serializes an object, but rather than writing the object to a file, it returns the serialized object as a string. The **loads()** function will then load the object back from a string.

Using pickle/cPickle

The **pickle** module is the more capable of the two solutions. The **pickle** module will serialize any object, even classes, and write the information out to a file or string, just as the **marshal** module did. The **cPickle** module works with the **cPickle** extension to serialize objects significantly faster than **pickle;** its only limitation is that you can't inherit from the **cPickle** class

The module provides two basic classes, **Pickler** for serializing (pickling) objects and the **UnPickler** class for deserializing (unpickling) objects. To use, create a new instance of a **Pickler** object. The class constructor accepts two arguments, a file object and an optional binary argument. If the second argument is false or not supplied, the object is serialized into a textual format that can be read, but it is space inefficient since it relies heavily on text for the formatting and structure. If set to true, the serialization occurs using a binary format that is more space conscious but unreadable.

The resulting class instance supports two methods; **dump()**, dumps an object out to the file specified when the class instance was created. For example, to store our earlier dictionary:

```
names = { 'Martin' : 29,
          'Rikke' : '30',
```

```
              'Andy'  : '33', }
namesdb = open('names','w')
pickler = pickle.Pickler(namesdb)
pickler.dump(names)
```

The **Unpickler** class is used to load a pickled object and convert it back into an internal object. The unpickler automatically identifies whether the information was pickled using text or binary format, and therefore accepts only one argument: an open file object to read the data from. For example, to read our dictionary back:

```
namesdb = open('names','r')
unpickler = Unpickler(namesdb)
names = unpickler.load()
```

Note that as with **marshal** you can use any file and call **dump()** and **load()** as many times as you like, as long as you call the functions in the same order.

DBM Databases

DBM is probably short for Database Management, although nobody is really sure anymore. It uses the key/value pair, and it stores the data in one or two files on the file system. The original specification for DBM stated that you should be able to extract the value attached to a key in one disk access. This has led to DBM being a very fast, if somewhat simplified, database system.

Over the years the original DBM system has been improved on and has gone through a number of different incarnations, although the basic specification remains the same. Most of the different DBM systems are compatible with each other, to a greater or lesser extent depending on the platform and implementation involved. It should be noted as well that DBM files are not portable. The storage format used is specific to a particular hardware platform and operating system. In some cases, even different versions of the OS have incompatible DBM systems.

Because of the way information is stored, it's also difficult to copy the files using standard tools. A standard DBM database is composed of two files. One file is a directory containing a bitmap and has .dir as its suffix. The second file contains all the data and has .pag as its suffix. The data file is often full of holes where storage space has been allocated, but the area within the file actually contains no useful information. The downside to this method is that some implementations allocate too much storage space, thereby generating a file that is reported to be 10, 100, or even 1,000 times larger than the amount of useful information it stores. Other implementations, such as GDBM and Berkeley DB, use a single file; the space usage problems remain, but just in one file, instead of two.

With old implementations of DBM, there is a limitation on the storage size of each key/value pair, which is known as the *bucket size*. Entries larger than this will either cause the database to return an exception or truncate the information you attempt to store; it depends on how the database has been implemented at C level. The next few sections describe the common DBM implementations; you can also read the summarized information in Table 12-1.

DBM

DBM is the original implementation of the DBM toolkit. Although included as standard in most UNIX variants, it has been replaced almost entirely by NDBM as the DBM implementation of choice. The supported bucket size is 1K, but some systems have significantly less than this available.

NDBM

NDBM is the "new" replacement for the original DBM, with some speed and storage allocation improvements. It has replaced the standard DBM libraries, and in some cases it is the only implementation available. Depending on the OS, the bucket size is anything from 1K to 4K.

SDBM

SDBM stands for Substitute/Simple DBM; it is a speed- and stability-enhanced version of DBM. This version is only available with Perl, and although no standard interface to

Implementation	DBM/ODBM	NDBM	SDBM	GDBM	Berkeley DB
Bucket limit	1–2K	1–4K	1K (none)	None	None
Disk usage	Varies	Varies	Small	Big	Big
Speed	Slow	Slow	Slow	OK	Fast
Data files distributable	No	No	Yes	Yes	Yes
Byte-order independent	No	No	No	No	Yes
User-defined sort order	No	No	No	No	Yes
Wildcard lookups	No	No	No	No	Yes

Table 12-1.   *DBM Implementations*

it exists in Python, it's worth noting that it exists in case you come across it. You should be able to open SDBM files with NDBM or GDBM, but the compatibility is not guaranteed (or recommended). If you must use information from an SDBM file, use Perl to convert it to NDBM or GDBM first, using something like this script:

```perl
use GDBM_File;
use Fcntl;

die "Usage:$0 old new\n" if (@ARGV<2);

my($old,$new) = @ARGV;

tie (%oldhash, 'SDBM_File', $old, O_RDONLY, 0444)
    || die "$0: Error opening source $old: $!\n";
tie (%newhash, 'GDBM_File', $new, O_CREAT|O_RDWR|O_EXCL, 0666)
    || die "$0: Error opening dest $new: $!\n";

while(($key, $value) = each(%oldhash))
{
    $newhash{$key} = $value;
}

untie %oldhash || die "$0: Error closing old DBM file, $!\n";
untie %newhash || die"$0: Error closing new DBM file, $!\n";
```

SDBM supports a bucket size of 1K, but this can be modified at compile time.

GDBM

GDBM is the GNU/FSF implementation of DBM. Faster than all implementations except Berkeley DB, GDBM has also been ported to a larger number of platforms than other implementations. GDBM supports limited file and record locking within the DBM file, as well, which can be useful in a multiuser situation. There is no bucket size for a GDBM database—key/value pairs can be of arbitrary length.

Berkeley DB

Berkeley DB is a public-domain C library of database access methods, including B+Tree, Extended Linear Hashing, and fixed/variable length records. The **bsddb** module provides extensive support for using Berkeley DB files within Python, supporting both the B-tree and hash implementations, thus enabling it to be used like a DBM replacement. You can also access the Berkeley DB hash database interface directly using the **dbhash** module.

In the following script, we'll be using the **anydbm** module. This opens (or creates) a DBM database using the best available implementation. In order, it tries to use a Berkeley DB hash, GDBM, DBM or **dumpdbm** database. This means that it will open any one of those databases (provided your system supports them), or it will create one based on the best implementation available. On a modern system, you're unlikely not to have NDBM, and the use of GDBM or Berkeley DB requires the installation of a separate module. The **dumpdbm** database is merely a compatibility interface, and it should really be relied on for serious development. It is very slow, inefficient, and often inconsistent.

Using DBM

What you do with a DBM database is entirely up to you. At the simplest level it's just an on-disk dictionary that you can use to store information. You could use it to store configuration information, or if you've got a relatively simple database you could use it store all of your information.

If you are expecting to deal with large internal dictionaries, using a DBM database is a good way to lower the memory footprint of your application by shifting the storage of your dictionary into an external file.

For example, to open a GDBM database:

```
import gdbm

dict = gdbm.open('mydbmdatabase')
```

The **dict** object created by the process is just a normal dictionary, except that storing a value writes the information to an external file, and accessing a file reads the information from the file. In all other ways, the object acts like a normal dictionary.

However, be aware that you cannot use keys or values composed of anything other than numbers or strings: you cannot use nested objects, lists, or dictionaries unless you use **pickle** or similar to serialize the nested information. A more transparent solution is available through the **shelve** module. This works in a similar fashion to the DBM modules, providing a dictionary-like object—but unlike the DBM systems, it does support nested structures.

The other DBM modules work in the same way, providing the same **open()** function in each case; its general format is

```
open(file [, flag [, mode]])
```

The optional **flag** allows you to specify which mode to open the database; these follow the generic file opening modes used with the built-in **open()** function seen in Chapter 3 and Chapter 11. The default is read-only mode. The optional **mode** argument is the octal value used to create the database if it does not already exist; the default is 0666.

For example, to open a GDBM database, you would use something like:

```
dict = gdbm.open('mydbmdatabase, 'r', 0666)
```

APPLYING THE PYTHON LIBRARIES

If you don't know what type of DBM file you are opening, then using the wrong module to open the file may cause data corruption, or just a simple failure to read the contents. To get around this, you can use the **anydbm** Python module, which will identify the DBM database type and use the appropriate module to open and read the file; so we can rewrite the above as:

```
dict = anydbm.open('mydbmdatabase, 'r', 0666)
```

Commercial Databases

Although I've used the term "commercial," I'm really referring to any full-blown database system, such as the free mySQL and PostgreSQL or full commercial systems like Oracle and Sybase.

Unfortunately, there is no coherent and single interface to all these different systems at the moment, although the db-sig group are trying to produce a database interface that supports a consistent interface to just about any database system. Until then, you'll need to trawl the Vaults of Parnassus (http://www.vex.net/parnassus/) to find an interface module for the database system you want to use.

For example, the MySQL-Python module allows you to access a mySQL database. The script below demonstrates how to run an SQL query and print out the results.

```
import MySQLdb

dbh = MySQLdb.Connect(db='clients')
mycursor = mydb.cursor()

stmt = "select firstname, lastname from clients"
cursor.execute(stmt)
results = cursor.fetchall()

for firstname, lastname in results:
        print firstname, lastname

mydb.close()
```

Other modules are available for talking to other database systems. Check the Python site and the Vaults of Parnassus (see Appendix B for more information) where you can search the modules available.

The Complete Reference

Chapter 13

Communicating over a Network

There was a time when copying files between machines meant putting the files onto a disk and carrying it between the machines in question. This obviously isn't practical for large files, even when using a Jaz or other sizeable storage format. Instead, we have networks where the machines are connected to each other. The modern LAN (local area network) is a relatively simple beast: cables connect one machine to another or, for the most part when using Ethernet, cables connect to a central hub or router. With the invention of the Internet, the process works over even longer distances. Using a combination of routers, bridges, and other information, we can communicate between two machines that are located on opposite sides of the world.

In this chapter, we're going to look at the basics of network programming, from the mechanics of addressing and exchanging information through to the specifics of open network connections. Python also comes with an extensive library of client protocol modules for communicating directly with web servers, mail servers, and a variety of other services. We'll be covering all these topics in this chapter.

Networking 101

Most networking systems have historically been based on the ISO/OSI (International Organization for Standardization Open Systems Interconnection) seven-layer model. Each layer defines an individual component of the networking process, from the physical connection up to the applications that use the network. Each layer depends on the layer it sits on to provide the services it requires.

Most people now agree that the seven-layer model is no longer really applicable. There are too many exceptions and smudges of the rules for all protocols to fit within the model. Many protocols lie over two of the layers in the OSI model, rather than conveniently sitting within a single layer. Actually, the seven-layer model still has its place: a majority of the protocols we'll be look at in this chapter can still be slotted into the seven-layer model—it's the other generally local protocols like NetBEUI (used on PCs for LAN communication) and AppleTalk/EtherTalk (used by Macs on LAN) that don't fit.

Logical Connection Types

Regardless of the particular theoretical model, the same basic principles apply to all networking technology. You can characterize networks by the type of logical connection. A network can either be *connection oriented* or *connectionless*. A connection-oriented network relies on the fact that two computers that want to talk to each other must go through some form of connection process, usually called a handshake. This handshake is similar to using the telephone: the caller dials a number and the receiver picks up the phone. In this way, the caller immediately knows whether the recipient has received the message, because the recipient will have answered the call. This type of connection is supported by TCP/IP (Transmission Control Protocol/Internet Protocol) and is the main form of communication over the Internet and local area networks (LANs).

In a connectionless network, information is sent to the recipient without first setting up a connection. This type of network is also a *datagram* or *packet-oriented* network because the data is sent in discrete packets. Each packet will consist of the sender's address, recipient's address, and the information, but no response will be provided once the message has been received. A connectionless network is therefore more like the postal service—you compose and send a letter, although you have no guarantee that the letter will reach its destination, or that the information was received correctly. Connectionless networking is supported by UDP/IP (User Datagram Protocol/Internet Protocol).

In either case, the "circuit" is not open permanently between the two machines. Data is sent in individual packets that may take different paths and routes to the destination. The routes may involve local area networks, dial-up connections, ISDN routers, and even satellite links. Within the UDP protocol, the packets can arrive in any order, and it is up to the client program to reassemble them into the correct sequence— if there is one. With TCP, the packets are automatically reassembled into the correct sequence before they are represented to the client as a single data stream.

There are advantages and disadvantages to both types of networks. A connectionless network is fast, because there is no requirement to acknowledge the data or enter into any dialogue to set up the connection to receive the data. However, a connectionless network is also unreliable because there is no way to ensure the information reached its destination. A connection-oriented network is slow (in comparison to a connectionless network) because of the extra dialogue involved, but it guarantees the data sequence, providing end-to-end reliability.

Connectionless systems are used mostly for broadcast data or for sending out information that you don't necessarily expect back. For example, UDP can be used to check the availability of clients on a network—a UDP packet is sent out on the network, and all the machines that see that packet (since it has no fixed destination address) then reply to say they are up and running. UDP is also used by some Internet video streaming services; because the data is broadcast over UDP anybody can listen, since a multimedia stream is only one way the client never needs to respond to the server. In fact, probably the best way to think of UDP is as a radio or TV broadcast.

Connection-oriented systems are used in all those situations when a proper two-way communication between two machines is required. Email, web, and file transfer services all use connection-oriented systems, because the client connects to a specific server, sends some information, and expects some back. Connection-oriented systems are analogous to a phone call: you want to call or speak to someone with a specific telephone, even if the other end of the line provides a generic service such as web serving.

Network Names and Numbers

The IP element of the TCP/IP and UDP/IP protocols refers to the Internet Protocol, which is a set of standards for specifying the individual addresses of machines within a network. Each machine within the networking world has a unique IP address. This is made up of a sequence of 4 bytes typically written in dot notation, for example, 192.168.1.1. These numbers relate both to individual machines within a network and to entire collections of machines.

Because humans are not very good at remembering numbers, a system called DNS (Domain Name System) relates easy-to-remember names to IP addresses. For example, the name www.mcgraw-hill.com relates to a single IP address. You can also have a single DNS name pointing to a number of IP addresses, and multiple names point to the same address. It is also possible to have a single machine that has multiple interfaces, and each interface can have multiple IP addresses assigned to it. However, in all cases, if the interfaces are connected to the Internet in one form or another, then the IP addresses of each interface will be unique.

Network Ports

The specification for communication does not end there. Many different applications can be executed on the same machine; and so communication must be aimed not only at the machine, but also at a port on that machine that relates to a particular protocol, and ultimately a listening application. If the IP address is compared to a telephone number, the port number is the equivalent of an extension number.

The first 1,024 port numbers are reserved for the well-known Internet protocols, and each protocol has its own unique port number. For example, HTTP (Hypertext Transfer Protocol), which is used to transfer information between your web browser and a web server, has a port number of 80. To connect to a server application, you need both the IP address (or machine name) and the port number on which the server is listening. However, port numbers are merely extensions to the IP address. Although port 80 is reserved and the default used for HTTP communication, there is nothing stopping you from running an HTTP service on port 2000, 8000, or 8081. Note that Unix reserves the first 1,024 ports for specific protocols; if you are creating your own server, you'll need to use a number above this value unless you have superuser privileges.

Network Communication

Any form of network application needs to exchange information, but the mechanics behind that exchange require a little care. There are many different methods for controlling two-way communication, although no system is ultimately reliable. The most obvious is to "best-guess" the state that each end of the connection should be in. For example, if one end sends a piece of information, then it might be safe to assume it should then wait for a response. If the opposite end makes the same assumption, then it could send information after it has just received some information.

The best-guess situation is not the most reliable, because if both ends decide to wait for information at the same time, then both ends of the connection are effectively dead. Alternatively, if both ends decide to send information at the same time, the two processes will not lock; but because they use the same send-receive system, once they have both sent information, they will both return to the wait state, expecting a response. Sure, we could add timeouts to kill and reconnect, but they don't solve the underlying problem of getting the two ends to talk to each other at the right time and say the right things.

A better solution to the problem is to use a protocol that places rules and restrictions on the communication method and order. This is how Simple Mail Transfer Protocol (SMTP) and similar protocols work. The client sends a command to the server, and the immediate response from the server tells the client what to do next. The response may include data and will definitely include an end-of-data string. In effect, it's similar to the technique used when communicating by radio. At the end of each communication, you say "Over" to indicate to the recipient that you have finished speaking. In essence, it still uses the same best-guess method for communication. Provided the communication starts off correctly, and each end sends the end-of-communication signal, the communication should continue correctly.

FTP uses a slightly different solution. The File Transfer Protocol is used to exchange files between machines, but it also has an interactive interface that allows you to navigate through the directories of the remote machine from your client. The interactive element of FTP is called the control connection and usually works on port 25. When transferring any significant amount of information, such as a file or directory listing, the two ends open a data connection. If the data connection fails for any reason, you still have the control connection so you can try again.

The BSD Socket Interface

The BSD (Berkeley Systems Division, a "flavor" of Unix) socket system was introduced in BSD 4.2 as a way of providing a consistent interface to the different available protocols. A socket provides a connection between an application and the network. You must have a socket at each end of the connection in order to communicate between the machines. One end must be set to receive data at the same time as the other end is sending data. As long as each side of the socket connection knows whether it should be sending or receiving information, then the communication can be two-way.

The socket interface is now universally accepted as the interface between the operating system and the underlying hardware. Most operating systems, including Mac OS, Unix, Windows, BeOS, and a host of others, use the BSD socket libraries to support their network communication.

In Python, the base module for all our network communication is, unsurprisingly, the **socket** module. It more or less mirrors the functionality of the underlying C libraries. If you are used to writing socket systems under other languages, then using the **socket** module under Python will be familiar.

In addition, Python supports a host of modules built on top of the **socket** module that handle the main protocols such as HTTP, FTP, SMTP, NNTP, and one or two others. The standard also comes with server modules for providing either generic socket servers or HTTP servers. In fact, the standard library includes an entire web server written in Python called **BaseHTTPServer**, which supports the **BaseHTTPServer** class. For a CGI-compatible version, you can use the **CGIHTTPServer** module.

If you want more information on networking with sockets and streams under TCP, UDP, and IP, then I can recommend *The UNIX System V Release 4 Programmers Guide: Networking Interfaces* (Prentice-Hall, 1990), which covers the principles behind networking, as well as the C source code required to make it work.

Obtaining Networking Information

Before you can even start to communicate with remote machines, you need a way of determining the IP address of a machine. Manipulating IP addresses and names requires using a set of basic functions provided in the **socket** module. The list of functions supported by the module for address resolution are listed in Table 13-1.

Function	Description
gethostbyname(hostname)	Gets a host's IP address by its hostname.
gethostbyname_ex(hostname)	Gets extended information about a host by its hostname. The function returns a tuple containing the hostname, a list of aliases for the hostname, and a list of IP addresses.
gethostbyaddr(address)	Returns the same information as **gethostbyname_ex()**, but for a given IP address rather than a name.
getprotobyname(protocolname)	Gets a constant relating to a specific protocol name for use in the **socket** module. For example, **getprotobyname('icmp')** returns **IPPROTO_CMP**. May not be supported by all operating systems.
getservbyname(name, protocol)	Gets a given protocol number by the protocol and service name. For example **getprotobyname('tcp','http')** should return 80. May not be supported by all operating systems.
gethostname()	Returns the hostname of the current machine.

Table 13-1. *Python Network Information Functions*

For example, you can get the IP address for a given host using

```
address = gethostbyname('www.python.org')
```

Python returns the address as a string, in this case in the form of a dotted quad (xxx.xxx.xxx.xxx, for example 192.168.1.1) . The information is not packed into a single structure.

The **gethostbyname_ex()** function returns extended information that can be useful if you need to talk to a remote machine that has multiple servers and/or interfaces, and therefore multiple IP addresses. You can see this clearly below: www.python.org is served through a single IP address, but www.altavista.com is served by a number of addresses.

```
>>> socket.gethostbyname_ex('www.python.org')
('parrot.python.org', ['www.python.org'], ['132.151.1.90'])
>>> socket.gethostbyname_ex('www.altavista.com')
('altavista.com', ['www.altavista.com'], ['209.73.164.96',
'209.73.164.97', '209.73.164.98', '209.73.164.99', '209.73.180.1',
'209.73.180.2', '209.73.180.3', '209.73.164.93', '209.73.164.94',
'209.73.164.95'])
```

Basic Socket Functions

To actually use a socket from either the server or the client end requires a specific sequence. In the case of opening a socket to communicate with an existing TCP/IP service, the sequence is

1. Open the socket (using **socket()**).
2. Connect to the remote machine (using **connect()**).
3. Use **recv()** and **send()** to read and write information to and from the server.

The process within Python to do this is actually very simple—the **socket.socket()** function creates a new socket. The function accepts two arguments, the socket family and the socket type. There are two basic socket family types. The Unix socket family (available through the **socket.AF_UNIX** constant) creates a socket for communicating between two systems through a shared file (but is only available under Unix). Unix domain sockets are often used for communication between two processes on the same system—for example, some Unix print systems and system logging facilities actually operate through a Unix socket.

The Internet socket family (**socket.AF_INET**) is the socket family used for the TCP and UDP communication used by protocols like FTP, SMTP, and most other Internet-compatible protocols. Within the Internet socket family, there are also two major types of socket, both of which we've already discussed: UDP, which is a datagram socket type and can be specified using the **socket.SOCK_DGRAM** constant, and the TCP socket, which is stream based and therefore available using the **socket.SOCK_STREAM** constant. Internet sockets are used for just about everything; in general, you should probably use Internet sockets unless you are communicating with an existing Unix socket system.

For example, to open a TCP/IP socket, you would use

```
mysock = socket.socket(socket.AF_INET, socket.SOCK_STREAM)
```

The **socket()** function returns a socket object, so further options are made through a series of methods on our object. The next stage from our list is to connect to a remote server, which we do through the **connect()** method. This accepts a single argument, a tuple pair containing the hostname (or IP address) of the remote machine and the port number.

To get the port number, you can use the **getservbyname()** method on our objects. It accepts two arguments, the service name and the protocol name. For example, to get the port number for HTTP, a TCP service, you would use

```
httpport = mysock.getservbyname('http','tcp')
```

Now we can connect to a remote machine using

```
mysock.connect(('www.mcwords.com','httpport'))
```

Now that we've connected, we can use the **recv()** and **send()** methods to receive and send information to our remote server.

We can actually condense the entire process down into a single function:

```
import socket

def open_tcp_socket(remotehost,servicename):
    s = socket.socket(socket.AF_INET, socket.SOCK_STREAM)
    portnumber = socket.getservbyname(servicename,'tcp')
    s.connect((remotehost,portnumber))
    return s
```

We can now open a TCP socket, send a request to an HTTP server, and print out the results using

```python
mysock = open_tcp_socket('www.mcwords.com','http')
mysock.send('GET http://www.mcwords.com\n\n')
while (1):
    data = mysock.recv(1024)
    if (data):
        print data
    else:
        break
mysock.close()
```

A full list of the methods supported by a **socket** object are listed in Table 13-2. Constants exported by the **socket** module for socket options and message sending flags are listed in Tables 13-3 and 13-4, respectively.

Method	Description
S = socket(family, type)	Opens a socket with **family** and **type**, where **family** is one of **socket.AF_UNIX** or **socket.AF_INET**.
S.accept()	Accepts a connection from a remote hose.
S.bind(address)	Binds a socket to a particular address. You need to use **bind** when creating a server or when you need to bind to a particular address on a machine that supports multiple IP addresses for a network interface card.
S.close()	Closes a network socket.
S.connect((address,serviceport))	Opens a connection to the host at **address** on the port **serviceport**.
S.getpeername()	Gets the name of the remote host to which this socket is connected.
S.getsockname()	Gets the name of the local host to which this socket is connected.

Table 13-2.   *Socket Methods Supported by the **socket** Object*

Method	Description
S.getsockopt(level, option [, buflen])	Gets a socket option. Socket options set configurable values for an open socket. The **level** should be the level to which the option is applied—**socket.SOL_SOCKET** for socket-level options or a protocol number such as **socket.IPPROTO_IP** for protocol-specific options. The **option** specifies the option value that you want to obtain. The **buflen** specifies the maximum length of the information that should be returned. If unspecified, then all the data is returned. See Table 13-3 for a list of supported option values for all sockets. Note that the exact list of supported options is OS dependent.
S.listen(waitqueue)	Starts listening for new connections. The **waitqueue** is the number of connections to queue before additional connections are refused.
message = S.recv(buflen [, flags])	Reads data up to **buflen** bytes from a socket. The **flags** define how the information is to be received—see Table 13-4 for a list of system-dependent values supported through constants in the **socket** module.
(message, address) = S.recv(buflen [, flags])	Identical to **recv()** except that the return value is a tuple consisting of the data read from the socket and the address from which the data was received. Only really applicable to UDP sockets, although it will also work for TCP sockets.
S.send(message [, flags])	Sends **message** to the remote machine. The **flags** argument is identical to that for **recv()**.
S.sendto(message [, flags], (address, port))	Identical to **send()** except that the message is sent to the machine specified in the **(address, port)** tuple. Only really applicable to UDP sockets, but will also work with TCP sockets.

Table 13-2.   *Socket Methods Supported by the **socket** Object* (continued)

Method	Description
S.setsockopt(level, option, value)	Sets the socket **option** to **value**. See Table 13-3 for a list of possible values. Note that not all sockets support all options; check your socket documentation or the socketmodule.c file generated during the Python build for information on what is supported.
S.shutdown(how)	Shuts down a socket. If **how** is zero, the socket can no longer receive information. If **how** is 1, the socket can no longer send information, and if **how** is 2 the socket can be used neither to send nor receive. Useful when you want to use two sockets for communicating with a remote host—each socket can be used to send or receive, respectively.

Table 13-2.   *Socket Methods Supported by the **socket** Object* (continued)

Option	Valid Values	Description
SO_KEEPALIVE	0,1	If set to 1, the socket is kept alive by periodically probing the other end of the connection without actually sending any data. Useful for server sockets when you want to service multiple requests. Using one socket a number of times instead of multiple sockets once only increases the speed of access.
SO_RCVBUF	Integer	Specifies the size of the receive buffer in bytes.
SO_SNDBUF	Integer	Specifies the size of the send buffer in bytes.

Table 13-3.   *Socket Options Configurable through the **socket** Module*

Option	Valid Values	Description
SO_REUSEADDR	0,1	Allows the local address to be immediately reused. If set to zero (the default), the port will be blocked for a short time even after the server has been terminated.
SO_RCVLOWAIT	Integer	Number of bytes read before the **select()** call is notified.
SO_SNDLOWAIT	Integer	Number of bytes available in the send buffer before a **select()** call is notified.
SO_RCVTIMEO	Integer	Timeout value for receiving data in seconds.
SO_SNDTIMEO	Integer	Timeout value for sending data in seconds.
SO_OONINLINE	0,1	Places out-of-band data into the input queue.
SO_LINGER	0,1	If set to 1, the socket lingers after **close()** if there is still data waiting to be sent. Default is zero.
SO_DONTROUTE	0,1	If set to 1, the packets bypass the normal routing tables (send only).
SO_ERROR	Integer	Returns the error status.
SO_BROADCAST	0,1	If set to 1, the socket will allow the sending of broadcast datagrams (UDP sockets only).
SO_TYPE	Integer	Returns the socket type.
SO_USELOOPBACK	0,1	If set to 1, the sending socket receives a copy of the data it sends. Useful for verifying that the data that was actually sent matches what you thought you'd sent.

Table 13-3. *Socket Options Configurable through the **socket** Module* (continued)

If you want to be able to read and write to a network socket as if it was a file, then use the **fdopen()** function within the **os** module to create a new file object based on the file descriptor number. File descriptors are shared between files and sockets on most operating systems (Unix and Windows NT variants, but not BeOS or MacOS), and you can obtain the file descriptor number of any file or socket object using the **fileno()**

Message Flag	Description
MSG_PEEK	Allows you to read the data without removing the information from the buffer.
MSG_WAITALL	Don't return until the number of bytes requested in the call to **recv()** has been read from the socket.
MSB_OOG	Send or receive out-of-band data.
MSG_DONTROUTE	Outgoing packets bypass the normal routing tables (send only).

Table 13-4. *Available Flags When Sending/Receiving Data*

method. For example, we could rewrite the code we used earlier for reading from an SMTP server:

```
mysock = open_tcp_socket('mail.mchome.com','smtp')
message = mysock.recv(1024)
print message
mysock.close()
```

To

```
mysock = open_tcp_socket('mail.mchome.com','smtp')
file = os.fdopen(mysock.fileno())
line = file.readline()
print line,
file.close()
mysock.close()
```

This opens the socket, creates a file object based on the socket's file number, and then uses **readline()** to read the information. We can also do this automatically (without the need for **os**) using the **makefile()** method:

```
mysock = open_tcp_socket('mail.mchome.com','smtp')
file = mysock.makefile()
line = file.readline()
print line,
```

```
mysock.close()
file.close()
```

If you are communicating with one of the standard Internet services such as SMTP, HTTP, or FTP, then use one of the modules that comes with Python—we'll be looking at some alternatives later in this chapter.

Other functions supported by the **socket** module are listed in Table 13-5.

Creating a Network Server

When creating a network server, there is a slightly different process. Whereas with the client socket we were creating a connection to an existing machine, with a server socket we need to create the socket and then listen for incoming connections. Once the connections have been received, we can then read and write information again just like a client socket.

The actual sequence for a TCP/IP socket is

1. Create a socket object.

2. Bind the socket to a local address (using **bind()**).

3. Listen for connections (using **listen()**).

Function	Description
fromfd(fd, family, type [, proto])	Creates a socket object based on the open file descriptor in **fd** using the specified **family** and **type**. The file descriptor must be a socket, rather than a file handle. Not supported on all platforms.
ntohl(x)	Converts 32-bit integers from network (big-endian) to host byte order.
ntohs(x)	Converts 16-bit integers from network to host byte order.
htonl(x)	Converts 32-bit integers from host byte order to network byte order.
htons(x)	Converts 16-bit integers from host byte order to network byte order.

Table 13-5. *Other Functions in the **socket** Module*

4. When a connection request is received from the client, accept the connection (using **accept()**).

5. Use **read()** and **write()** to read and write information to and from the server.

If you want to relate the server-side process to the client side, see Figure 13-1.

The biggest different is in stages 2 and 3. The **bind()** process registers the socket against a specific IP address and port, actually in much the same way that **connect()** specifies the information on the client side. The **listen()** just puts the socket into a state where it's ready to accept connections, but a connection to a client socket is not actually completed until **accept()** is called.

We can do this in code using the following:

```
import socket

s = socket(socket.AF_INET, socket.SOCK_STREAM)
s.bind('', 8000)
s.listen(5)

while 1:
    client,addr = s.accept()
    print "Accepted a connection from", addr
    data = client.recv(1024)
    client.send("You said: " + data)
    client.close()
```

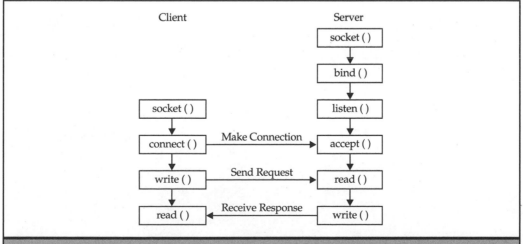

Figure 13-1.   *Server- and client-side interoperation*

However, there are a number of problems with this example: first and foremost, we have to do a lot of work for ourselves when there must be an easier way. Second, we don't handle multiple clients in anything but a round-robin situation. If five clients connected at the same time, we would process all the requests but only sequentially. For a simple server this is fine, but for a real-world server such a system would create a major bottleneck.

We can solve both problems by using the **SocketServer** module, which provides a class-based system for supporting network services.

Using SocketServer

You can use the usual methods of calling **os.fork()** or the **select** module, or even threads to support the multiple connections required by most network servers. If you are creating a network service, however, you might be better off using the **SocketServer** module, which provides a number of different classes designed to handle network communication. The module provides eight different classes, which provide all of the mechanisms required to support basic network services similar to HTTP, SMTP, and others. You can see a list of the classes supported in Table 13-6.

Class	Description
TCPServer(address, handler)	A basic TCP-based server. The **address** should be a tuple containing the hostname and port number to set up the service. If **hostname** is set to an empty string, then the server binds to the default address for the current host. The **handler** should be an instance of the **BaseRequestHandler** class—see the main text for information on how to create the handler required.
UDPServer(address, handler)	A basic UDP-based server.
UnixStreamServer(address, handler)	A server that uses the Unix domain sockets in stream mode for communication.
UnixDatagramServer(address, handler)	A server that uses the Unix domain sockets in datagram mode for communication.

Table 13-6. *Network Servers Supported by the **SocketServer** Module*

Class	Description
ForkingUDPServer(address, handler)	Identical to **UDPServer**, except that the server handles multiple requests by using **os.fork()**.
ForkingTCPServer(address, handler)	Identical to **TCPServer** except that the server handles multiple requests by using **os.fork()**.
ThreadingUDPServer(address, handler)	Identical to **UDPServer** except that the server handles multiple requests by using threads to set up multiple client handler threads.
ThreadingTCPServer(address, handler)	Identical to **TCPServer** except that the server handles multiple requests by using threads to set up multiple client handler threads.

Table 13-6.   *Network Servers Supported by the **SocketServer** Module* (continued)

In order to create a server using these base classes, you need to create a new subclass of the **BaseRequestHandler** class provided by the module. The class needs to define at the bare minimum the **handle()** method, which is called each time a connection from a client is obtained. The object instance (**self**) contains a number of different attributes, including the **socket** object used to communicate with the server as **request** and the address of the client that made the connection as **client_address**.

Once the new subclass has been created, all you need to do is create a new instance of the desired server class, passing the handler subclass you just created. Finally, you need to call either the **handle_request()** method, which handles a single request, or the **serve_forever()** method, which processes requests until you terminate the server process.

For example, the script below creates a handler called **TimeHandler**, which returns the date or time of the server, or its epoch value when requested from the client:

```
import SocketServer, socket, string, time

class TimeHandler(SocketServer.BaseRequestHandler):
    def handle(self):
        socketfile = self.request.makefile()
```

```
            self.request.send('Hello %s, What do you want?\r\n'
                            % (self.client_address,))
        while 1:
            line = socketfile.readline()
            print "Got %s\n" % (line,)
            line = string.strip(line)
            if not line:
                break
            if line == 'time':
                self.request.send("The time is: %s\r\n"
                                    % (time.strftime('%H:%M:%S',
                                        time.localtime(time.time()))),)
            if line == 'date':
                self.request.send("The time is: %s\r\n"
                                    % (time.strftime('%d/%m/%Y',
                                        time.localtime(time.time()))),)
            if line == 'datetime':
                self.request.send("The time is: %s\r\n"
                                    % (time.strftime('%d/%m/%Y %H:%M:%S',
                                        time.localtime(time.time()))),)
            if line == 'rawtime':
                self.request.send('%d\r\n' % (time.time(),))
        socketfile.close()

server = SocketServer.TCPServer(('', 8000), TimeHandler)
server.serve_forever()
```

Using this script, we can easily get the time of the remote machine:

```
$ telnet twinsol 8000

Hello ('198.112.10.135', 43712), What do you want?
time
The time is: 15:09:39
date
The time is: 14/04/2001
datetime
The time is: 14/04/2001 15:09:43
rawtime
987257386
```

This is a basic example, but you could extend the service to just about any
network-based solution you needed.

Running HTTP Services

If you want to provide an HTTP service, the standard distribution also includes a
number of modules and related base classes for supporting HTTP services. They are
actually based on the **SocketServer** module. There are three modules and classes:
BaseHTTPServer, which covers the basic interface of accepting requests; then there is
SimpleHTTPServer, which handles simple GET requests–this module is suitable for
providing a basic web server service.

The last module/class is **CGIHTTPServer**, which builds on **SimpleHTTPServer**
and also allows you to service CGI requests. The easiest way to use these modules is
actually to call the **test()** function in each module. For example, to start up an HTTP
server within the current directory is as simple as

```
Python 2.1 (#2, Apr 29 2001, 14:36:04)
[GCC 2.95.3 20010315 (release)] on sunos5
Type "copyright", "credits" or "license" for more information.
>>> import SimpleHTTPServer
>>> SimpleHTTPServer.test()
Serving HTTP on port 8000 ...
```

Client Modules

Python comes with a number of modules for communicating with network servers as a
client. For a list of the supported protocols and modules, see Table 13-7.

We'll take a look at some of the client modules in this section.

Working with SMTP

SMTP (Simple Mail Transfer Protocol) is used to send email from your machine and to
distribute email around a network and the Internet before it finally reaches the mailbox
of the user it was sent to. Using SMTP from Python to send your email is a more efficient
way than calling an external application like **mail** or **sendmail**, and it has the advantage
that it can be used on any platform.

Python's **smtplib** uses a class-based model: once we've create a new instance of the
smtplib class, we can use methods with the same name as SMTP commands to set up
and send the email. A quicker way, if all you want to do is send a quick email, is the

Client Protocol	Python Module	Description
SMTP (Simple Mail Transfer Protocol)	smtplib	Used to send email
FTP (File Transfer Protocol)	ftplib	Used to upload/download files
NNTP (Network News Protocol)	nntplib	Used to transfer Usenet news posts
POP (Post Office Protocol)	poplib	Used to access email mailboxes
IMAP (Internet Mail Access Protocol)	imaplib	Used to read and file email
HTTP/FTP	urllib	Used to download URLs to the local disk

Table 13-7. *Python Network Client Modules*

sendmail() method, which accepts three arguments, the sender, recipient, and email message, which we can use like this:

```
import smtplib

server = smtplib.SMTP('localhost')
server.sendmail('mc@mcwords.com','mc@mcwords.com',
            "Subject: Reminder\nDon't Mail Self\n")
server.quit()
```

Here's a more extensive example that also gets input from the user. This fragment is taken from the bottom of the **smtplib** module:

```
import sys, rfc822
from smtplib import *

def prompt(prompt):
    sys.stdout.write(prompt + ": ")
    return string.strip(sys.stdin.readline())

fromaddr = prompt("From")
```

```
toaddrs  = string.splitfields(prompt("To"), ',')
print "Enter message, end with ^D:"
msg = ''
while 1:
    line = sys.stdin.readline()
    if not line:
        break
    msg = msg + line
print "Message length is " + `len(msg)`

server = SMTP('localhost')
server.set_debuglevel(1)
server.sendmail(fromaddr, toaddrs, msg)
server.quit()
```

Working with FTP

The **ftplib** module provides a class-based interface to a remote FTP server. You can create a new instance of the **ftplib** class using the **FTP** class:

```
import ftplib

remote = ftplib.FTP('ftp.python.org')
```

The new instance of the **FTP** class should now be used by submitting the commands that you want to send to the remote server, using methods that specify the type of information that you expect to receive. For example, when getting a list of remote files, you use the **retrlines()** method to accept multiple lines of output:

```
remote.retrlines('LIST')
```

To actually receive a file, use the **retrbinary()** method, supplying the command and an object pointing to a suitable file object method. For example,

```
remote.retrbinary('RETR pytcrsrc.tgz',
open('pytcrsrc.tgz','w').write())
```

Working with HTTP

HTTP (Hypertext Transfer Protocol) is the protocol used by your web browser and web servers to transfer web pages. Unlike FTP, which offers directory browsing and two-way file transfer, HTTP is designed to support a simple request from the client—usually the URL or the path component of a URL that the client is requesting—and then to simply have the file returned to client. There's no other processing, and no way for the client to request file lists or other information—all the HTTP server can do is return the file that was requested.

Although there is a separate **httplib** module for communicating over HTTP, in all likelihood all you want to do is download a specific URL to your machine. The **urllib** module provides a very simple interface to download a particular URL to a local file:

```
import urllib

urllib.urlretrieve('http://www.python.org', 'pythonhomepage.html')
```

If you want to process the information you are downloading without temporarily storing that information in an external file, you can use **urlopen**. This opens the remote URL and returns a file object so we can process the information returned from the server as if it was a local file.

For example, at the simplest level, we could rewrite the **urlretrieve()** function like this:

```
import urllib

url = urllib.urlopen('http://www.python.org')
file = open('pythonhomepage.html','w')

while 1:
    line = url.readline()
    if len(line) == 0:
        break
    file.write(line)
```

If you actually want to parse the information in an HTML page that you download, you need to use the **htmllib** module. We'll be covering the parsing of HTML in Chapter 20, but as a rough guide to what you can do, the script below downloads a page, processes the HTML within it to extract a list of images, and then downloads each of the images from that page:

```
import htmllib, sys,formatter, urllib, urlparse, os.path

# Create a new parser class to read handle the HTML
class ImgParser(htmllib.HTMLParser):
    def __init__(self, formatter):
```

```
            htmllib.HTMLParser.__init__(self, formatter)
            self.imglist = []
# Extract the information from an image tag when seen
    def handle_image(self, src, alt, ismap, align, width, height):
            self.imglist.append((src, alt, ismap, align, width, height))

# Get the URL from the command line
try:
    url = sys.argv[1]
except:
    print 'You must supply a URL'
    sys.exit(1)

# Open the URL as a file
try:
    urlfile = urllib.urlopen(url)
except IOError, msg:
    print "Error:", url, ":", msg
    sys.exit(1)

# Create a new parser based on our parser class, and then
# read each line from the file and pass it on to the parser
# for processing
parser = ImgParser(formatter.NullFormatter())
while(1):
    line = urlfile.readline()
    if line:
        parser.feed(line)
    else:
        break

urlfile.close
parser.close()

# Based on the list of images extracted from the file,
# get the full URL of each image, then the filename
# and download each to disk
for img in parser.imglist:
    imgurl = urlparse.urljoin(url,img[0])
    imgfile = os.path.basename(urlparse.urlparse(imgurl)[2])
    urllib.urlretrieve(imgurl,imgfile)
```

Working with IMAP

The Python **imaplib** module provides a class-based interface to an IMAP (Internet Mail Access Protocol) server. IMAP is an alternative to POP3 that allows you to store not only your incoming email but also your filed email on a central server. As such, the IMAP protocol is much more complicated than POP3.

The sample below is a slightly modified version of the script included in my *Python Annotated Archives* title. It downloads the email from a single email account, displaying the results as HTML so that I can check my incoming email from a browser without having to fire up an email client.

```
#!/usr/local/bin/python

import imaplib
import sys,os,re,string

# Set up a function that we can use to call the corresponding
# method on a given imap connection when supplied with the
# name of an IMAP command
def run(cmd, args):
    typ, dat = apply(eval('imapcon.%s' % cmd), args)
    return dat

# Get the mail, displaying the output as HTML

def getmail(title,login,password):
# Login to the remote server, supplying the login and
# password supplied to the function
    run('login',(login,password))

# Use the select method to obtain the number of
# messages in the users mail account. The information is returned
# as a string, so we need to convert it to an integer
    nomsgs = run('select',())[0]
    nomsgs = string.atoi(nomsgs)

# Output a header for this email account
    print "<p><font size=+2><b>"+title+"</b></font></p>"

# Providing we've got some messages, download each message
# and display the sender and subject
    if nomsgs:
# Output a suitable table header row
        print "<table border=0 cellpadding=0 cellspacing=0>"
```

```
        print "<tr><td><b>Sender</b></td><td><b>Subject</b></td></tr>"
# Process each message
        for message in range(nomsgs,0,-1):
            subject,sender,status = '','','U'
# Send the fetch command to the server to obtain the
# email's flags (read, deleted, etc.) and header from the email
            data = run('fetch', (message,'(FLAGS RFC822.HEADER)'))[0]
            meta,header = data
# Determine the email's flags and ignore a message if it's
# marked as deleted
            if string.find(meta,'Seen') > 0:
                status = ''
            if string.find(meta,'Deleted') > 0:
                continue
# Separate the header, which appears as one large string, into
# individual lines and then extract the subject and sender fields
            for line in string.split(header,'\n'):
                if not line:
                    sender = re.sub(r'\<.*\>','',
                                re.sub(r'\"','',sender))
# If the message is unread, then mark the subject and sender
# in red
                    if (string.find(status,'U') == 0):
                        subject = '<font color=red>'
                                  + subject + '</font>'
                        sender = '<font color=red>'
                                 + sender + '</font>'
                    print "<tr><td>%s</td><td>%s</td></tr>"
                                % (sender,subject)
                    break
# Extract the sender/subject information by looking for the field
# prefix
                if line[:8] == 'Subject:':
                    subject = line[9:-1]
                if line[:5] == 'From:':
                    sender = line[6:-1]
        print "</table>"
    else:
        print "No messages"
# Logout from the server
    run('logout',())

# Set the server information
server='imap'
```

```
# Print out a suitable HTTP header and HTML page header
print "Content-type: text/html\n\n"
print """
<head>
<title>Mail</title>
</head>
<body bgcolor="#ffffff" fgcolor="#000000">
"""

# Connect to the server, and then call getmail to get the mail
# from the server
try:
    imapcon = imaplib.IMAP4(server)
except:
    print "Can't open connection to ",server
    sys.exit(1)
getmail('MC','mcmcslp','PASSWORD')
```

You can see the results of using the script in Figure 13-2.

Handling Internet Data

Beyond the standard text and graphics formats supported by the Internet, there are also a number of additional standards that are used to represent multifile documents. Other formats are used to encode binary 8-bit data into 7-bit formats for transfer by email. Although on most modern email systems this isn't actually required, it's a carryover from the older UUCP system that only supported the 7-bit character set.

base64

The **base64** module is used to encode and decode data using the base64 encoding format. This is often used in MIME and other multipart messages to encode binary information in a cross-platform way. Functions supported by the module are listed in Table 13-8.

binascii

Provides functions for encoding/decoding a number of different ASCII formats. The functions supported by the module are listed in Table 13-9.

The module supports two different exceptions, as shown in Table 13-10.

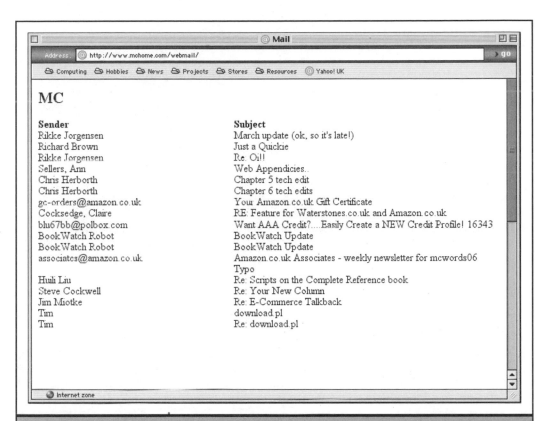

Figure 13-2.   *Checking your email using IMAP*

Function	Description
decode(input, output)	Decodes the base64 data in the file or file object in **input** to the file or file object **output**.
decodestring(s)	Decodes **s** from base64 format. Returns the decoded data stream.
encode(input, output)	Encodes the file or file object in **input** to base 64 in the file or file object **output**.
encodestring(s)	Encodes **s** into base64 format. Returns the encoded data stream.

Table 13-8.   *Functions in the **base64** Module*

APPLYING THE
PYTHON LIBRARIES

Function	Description
a2b_base64(string)	Converts the ASCII base64 encoded **string** to binary format.
a2b_hqx(string)	Converts the ASCII binhex **string** to binary format.
a2b_uu(string)	Converts the uuencoded **string** to binary format.
b2a_base64(data)	Converts the binary **data** to base64 ASCII format.
b2a_hqx(data)	Converts the binary **data** to binhex ASCII format.
b2a_uu(data)	Converts the binary **data** to uuencoded ASCII format.
rlecode_hqx(data)	Compresses **data** using the RLE algorithm, returning the compressed string in ASCII binhex format.
rledecode_hqx(data)	Decompresses the RLE (Run Length Encoding) compressed **data** in ASCII binhex format.
xcrc_hqx(data,crc)	Creates a CRC (Cyclic Redundancy Check) sum for **data**. The **crc** argument should be the starting value for the CRC.

Table 13-9. *Functions Supported by the binascii Module*

binhex

The binhex format has for a long time been used on the Mac to encode and decode files because it encodes both the resource and data fork of a given file. On platforms other than Mac OS, the module only encodes/decodes the data fork. Functions supported by the module are listed in Table 13-11.

Exception	Description
Error	The exception raised for a generic error.
Incomplete	The exception raised when there is incomplete data to finish the decoding.

Table 13-10. *Exceptions in the binascii Module*

Function	Description
binhex(input, output)	Encodes the binary file or file object **input** to the file or file object **output**.
hexbin(input [, output])	Decodes the binhex data in the file or file object **input** to the file or file object **output**. If **output** is not supplied, the name is determined from the binhex file.

Table 13-11.   *Functions Supported by the **binhex** Format*

mailcap

The **mailcap** module provides functions for reading data from mailcap files (see Table 13-12). Mailcap files tell mail readers and web browsers how to process different files with different file types by matching extensions and MIME types to known applications and operations.

Function	Description
getcaps()	Reads all the available mailcap files and returns a dictionary mapping MIME types to a mailcap entry. By default, mailcap files are read from **$HOME/.mailcap**, **/etc/mailcap**, **/usr/etc/mailcap**, **/usr/local/etc/mailcap**.
findmatch(caps, mimetype [, key [, filename [, plist]]])	Searches the dictionary **caps** (as returned by **getcaps()**) for the MIME type matching **mimetype**. The **key** if specified should indicate the desired action; **filename** is the file that we want to process; and **plist** is a list of named parameters to the operation. Returns a tuple containing the command from the **mailcap** file and the raw **mailcap** entry.

Table 13-12.   *Functions Supported by the **mailcap** Module*

mimetools

The **mimetools** module provides functions for manipulating MIME-encoded messages. MIME (Multipurpose Internet Mail Extensions) is a recognized standard for sending multiple files over Internet email. MIME is also used for multipart requests and responses from web servers. The functions supported by the module are shown in Table 13-13.

Function	Description
Message(file [, seekable])	Parses **file** as a mail message and returns a **Message** object that is itself derived from the **rfc822.Message** class. The **seekable** argument should specify whether the file object in **file** is a seekable object (such as a normal file) or nonseekable (network socket). See Table 13-14 for a list of supported methods.
choose_boundary()	Creates a unique string that can be used as a part boundary in a MIME file. The format of the returned string matches hostipaddr.uid.pid.timestamp.random.
decode(input, output, encoding)	Decodes the MIME data in **input** and writes the decode data to **output**. The **input** and **output** arguments should be previously opened file objects. The **encoding** should be the encoding method used to decode the data. Should be one of "base64," "quoted printable," or "uuencode."
encode(input, output, encoding)	Encodes the file in **input** and writes a MIME-formatted file to **output**. The **input** and **output** arguments should be previously opened file objects. The **encoding** should be the encoding method used to decode the data. Should be one of "base64," "quoted printable," or "uuencode."

Table 13-13. *Functions Supported in the **mimetools** Module*

Function	Description
copyliteral(input, output)	Reads lines from the file object **input** and writes them to the file object **output** without translation.
copybinary(input, ouput)	Reads blocks of binary data from the file object **input** and writes them to the file object **output** without translation.

Table 13-13.   *Functions Supported in the **mimetools** Module* (continued)

A **Messsage** object (as returned by the **Message()** class in the module) has the methods shown in Table 13-14.

Method	Description
getplist()	Returns the parameters (in the form **key=value**) from the content-type header in the message. Note that only parameters are returned, not the actual MIME type. Also note that the return format is a list of strings, not a dictionary, and that **key** is converted to lowercase.
getparam(name)	Returns the value of the last parameter from the content-type header.
getencoding()	Returns the encoding specified in the content-transfer-encoding message header. Returns "7bit" if no such header exists.
gettype()	Returns the message type from the content-type header. Returns "text/plain" by default.
getmaintype()	Returns the primary type from the content-type header. Returns "text" by default.
getsubtype()	Returns the subtype from the content-type header. Returns "plain" by default.

Table 13-14.   *Methods Supported by the **mimetools.Message** Class*

mimetypes

The **mimetypes** module provides functions that attempt to identify the type or extension of a file according to the MIME type. The functions supported by the module are shown in Table 13-15.

MimeWriter

The **MimeWriter** module defines a class, **MimeWriter**, that can be used to generate MIME-encoded files. To create a new object, you use

```
MimeWriter(file)
```

Function/Object	Description
guess_type(filename)	Guesses the MIME type of a file by examining its filename.
guess_extension(type)	Guess the extension of a file by identifying the MIME **type**.
init([files])	Initializes the extension/MIME type table by reading information from a file in the form mimetype: extensions. The extensions should be supplied as a list of space-separated extensions, without a leading period. For example, text/html: htm html.
read_mime_types(filename)	Reads MIME types from **filename**.
knownfiles	Returns a list of the common names for MIME files as used by default by the **init()** function.
suffix_map	Returns a dictionary mapping extensions to matching extensions; for example, ".htm" would be mapped to ".html."
encodings_map	Returns a dictionary mapping filename extensions to encoding types.
types_map	Returns a dictionary mapping encoding types to filename extensions.

Table 13-15. *Functions/Objects Supported by the **mimetypes** Module*

where **file** is an existing file object into which the output will be written. Alternatively, you can use a **StringIO** object. The resulting object has the methods listed in Table 13-16.

multifile

The **multifile** module defines a class, **MultiFile**, that can be used to read multipart files such as text messages. An instance of the **MultiFile** class can be created using

```
MultiFile(file [, seekable])
```

Method	Description
addheader(key, value [, prefix])	Adds a header to the file of the form "key: value." The **prefix** defines where the header is inserted. If zero (default), it's appended to the end of the existing headers. If 1, it places the header before the existing headers.
flushheaders()	Write all the headers to the file.
startbody(ctype [, plist [, prefix]])	Returns a file-like object that can be used to insert information into the final file. The **ctype** should specify the content type; **plist** lists the parameters for the file content; and **prefix** has the same meaning as for **addheader()** except that the default value is 1.
startmultipartbody(subtype [, boundary [, plist [, prefix]]])	Indicates the start of a multipart body element. Returns a file-like object that we can use to write the content of the message. The **subtype** defines the multipart subtype, such as mixed; **boundary** is used as the separator between file; **plist** is a list of parameters for the file; and **prefix** has the same meaning as for **addheader()**.
nextpart()	Returns the new instance **MimeWriter** that represents an individual part in a multipart message.
lastpart()	Indicates the last part of a multipart message.

Table 13-16. *Methods Supported by a **MimeWriter** Class*

where **file** is an existing file object from which we can read information. The **seekable** argument should specify whether the file is seekable (a normal file) or unseekable (a network socket).

The methods for the class instance are listed in Table 13-17.

Method/Attribute	Description
push(str)	Pushes a boundary string into the reader. This method indicates an end of section or end of message. You can push more than one boundary marker, but pushing a boundary other than the most recently read value raises an error.
readline()	Reads a line of text from the file. If the line matches the most recently pushed boundary, an empty string is returned. If the boundary corresponds to an end marker, then the **last** attribute is set to 1.
readlines()	Returns all the lines remaining in the current part as a list of strings.
read()	Returns all the lines remaining in the current part as a single string.
next()	Skips to the next section.
pop()	Pops a section boundary, indicating the start of a new file section.
seek(pos [, whence])	Seeks new position within the current section. **pos** should be specified in bytes, and **whence** indicates the base location to perform the move relative to. 0 means from the start of the section; 1 means from the current location; 2 means from the end of the part.
tell()	Returns the current location.
level	The nesting depth of the current part.
last	True if the last end-of-file was an end-of-message marker.

Table 13-17. *Methods/Attributes for a **MultiFile** Object*

quopri

The **quopri** module converts text to/from the quoted-printable format. The quoted-printable format is used to encode text files in a compatible format. See Table 13-18 for its functions.

rfc822

The **rfc822** module provides a class-based system for reading/writing the header content from email messages. A typical email message looks like this:

```
Return-Path: <cyrus@twinsol>
X-Sieve: cmu-sieve 2.0
Return-Path: <mc@mcslp.com>
Received: from punt-21.mail.demon.net (punt-21.mail.demon.net [194.217.242.6])
    by mcslp.pri (8.11.2/8.11.2) with SMTP id f6VHW7Z21877
    for <mcslp@prluk.demon.co.uk>; Tue, 31 Jul 2001 18:32:07 +0100 (BST)
Received: from punt-2.mail.demon.net by mailstore for mcslp@prluk.demon.co.uk
        id 996600381:20:25406:0; Tue, 31 Jul 2001 17:26:21 GMT
Received: from smaug.dreamhost.com ([216.240.148.26]) by punt-2.mail.demon.net
        id aa2025334; 31 Jul 2001 17:26 GMT
Received: from mcslp.pri (prluk.demon.co.uk [158.152.8.40])
        by smaug.dreamhost.com (8.12.0.Beta7/8.12.0.Beta7/Debian
8.12.0.Beta7-1) with ESMTP id f6VHPcKJ007697
        for <mc@mcslp.com>; Tue, 31 Jul 2001 10:25:38 -0700
Received: from [192.168.1.129] (atuin.mcslp.pri [192.168.1.129])
    by mcslp.pri (8.11.2/8.11.2) with ESMTP id f6VHPZZ21840
    for <mc@mcslp.com>; Tue, 31 Jul 2001 18:25:35 +0100 (BST)
User-Agent: Microsoft-Entourage/9.0.1.3108
Date: Tue, 31 Jul 2001 18:25:32 +0100
Subject: Reminder
From: Martin C Brown <mc@mcslp.com>
To: Martin C Brown <mc@mcslp.com>
Message-ID: <B78CA89C.32ACC%mc@mcslp.com>
Mime-version: 1.0
Content-type: text/plain; charset="US-ASCII"
Content-transfer-encoding: 7bit

Just a reminder to make that meeting...
```

Everything up to the first blank line is treated as a header, where the header format is "field: value." For example, the message's subject is defined as "Subject: Reminder."

Function	Description
decode(input, output)	Decodes from quoted-printable format from the file object **input** to the file object **output**.
encode(input, output, quotetabs)	Encodes from raw text to quoted-printable from the file object **input** to the file object **output**. If **quotetabs** is 1, then tabs are quoted; if zero, tabs are included as standard.

Table 13-18.   *Functions Supported by the **quopri** Module*

You can parse the headers for a message by creating a new instance of the **Message** class:

```
Message(file [, seekable])
```

where **file** is an existing file object from which we can read information. The **seekable** argument should specify whether the file is seekable (a normal file) or unseekable (a network socket).

For an example of the module in action, see "Working with SMTP," earlier in this chapter.

The resulting object instance behaves like a dictionary, aside from the notes and additional methods listed in Table 13-19.

Method/Attribute	Description
m[name]	Returns the value for the header **name**.
m[name]=value	Sets the value for the header **name**.
m.keys()	Lists all the header fields in the message.
m.values()	Lists all the header values in the message.
m.items()	Returns a list of two-element tuples containing the header field name and value.

Table 13-19.   *Methods Supported by the **Message** Class*

Method/Attribute	Description
m.has_key(name)	Returns true if the message has the header **name**.
m.get(name [, default])	Gets the value for the header field **name** or returns **default** if specified when the header cannot be found.
len(m)	Returns the number of headers.
str(m)	Returns a string representation of the headers that should be valid as an RFC822-compatible message header.
m.getallmatchingheaders(name)	Returns all the headers matching **name**.
m.getfirstmatchingheader(name)	Returns the first header matching **name**.
m.getrawheader(name)	Returns the raw string from a header line from the field **name**.
m.getheader(name [, default])	Like **getrawheader()** but removes all leading and trailing spaces.
m.getaddr(name)	Returns a tuple consisting of the name and email address from an address header matching **name**.
m.getaddrlist(name)	Returns a list of tuples containing the addresses for the header matching **name**.
m.getdate(name)	Returns a nine-element tuple for the date found in the header **name**.
m.getdate_tz(name)	Returns a ten-element tuple that includes the offset from the UTC time zone for the date found in the header **name**.
m.headers	Returns a list of all the header lines.
m.fp	Returns the file-like object used when the object instance was created.

Table 13-19. *Methods Supported by the **Message** Class* (continued)

Other functions supported by the **rfc822** module are listed in Table 13-20.

Function	Description
parsedate(date)	Parses an RFC822-formatted date such as "Tue, 31 Jul 2001 18:34:03 +0000" and returns a nine-element tuple containing the parsed data. The tuple is compatible with **time.mktime()**.
parsedate_tz(date)	Parses an RFC822-formatted date such as "Tue, 31 Jul 2001 18:34:03 +0000" and returns a ten-element tuple containing the parsed data including the time zone offset from UTC. The tuple is compatible with **time.mktime()**.
mktime_tz(tuple)	Converts a ten-element tuple back into a UTC timestamp.
AddressList(addrlist)	Converts a string containing a list of email addresses into an **AddressList** object. The new object supports two methods, **len()** and **str()**, which return the number of addresses in the object and a string representation of the object, respectively. The **+** and **−** operators add and subtract the individual addresses within two **AddressList** objects.

Table 13-20. *Other Functions Supported by the **rfc822** Module*

uu

The **uu** module encodes and decodes files to/from the UUCP uuencode format. The functions supported by the module are shown in Table 13-21.

Function	Description
encode(input, output [, name [, mode]])	Encodes the filename or file object in **input** into uuencoded format into the filename or file object in **output**. The **name** should be the name to use for the file, and **mode** is the file mode (in octal) for the file when it is decoded.
decode(input [, output [, mode]])	Decodes the uuencoded data in **input** (a filename or file object). The output name and mode are automatically determined from the file, or they can be overridden by **output** and **mode**.

Table 13-21.   *Functions Supported by the **uu** Module*

xdrlib

The **xdrlib** module provides a whole suite of functions for converting data to/from the Sun XDR (External Data Representation) format. XDR is used in the RPC (Remote Procedure Call) system to encode data in a machine/network-neutral format, although XDR can also be useful for exchanging information between systems, assuming your system supports the XDR and RPC libraries. See the online documentation for more information on this module.

Chapter 14

Using Python for Multimedia

P ython may not seem the obvious choice for multimedia development, but actually it's pretty well suited to the task. Python's strong mathematical abilities, coupled with its object orientation and typing, make it a good choice for all sorts of multimedia data.

In this chapter, we're going to have a look at the different modules that come as part of the standard distribution that you can use to manipulate audio and image files.

Audio Modules

The standard library comes with a number of modules for reading and writing different audio formats, along with a variety of functions for manipulating sound information.

All the audio formats we'll cover here—and, in fact, most audio formats in general—work on the same basis. Audio is encoded into a digital format by recording the frequency and volume of a sound at a particular instant in time. These two numbers are recorded over a period of time in order to represent a segment of sound. Each pair of numbers, volume and frequency, is called a sample, and the length of each sample and the number of samples each second help determine the quality of the audio that is created. For example, a sample rate of once a second would only be good enough to represent a single tone for one second—now imagine playing a tune with that! Sound is normally sampled thousands of times a second. For example, your music CDs are recorded at a rate of 44,100 times every second.

Other terms we'll be covering include

■ **Sampling rate** or **frame rate** is the number of samples of the sound that are taken each second. For example, CD audio takes 44,1000 samples a second, or 44.1 KHz. The higher the number, the better the quality.

■ **Bits per sample** is the number of bits used to quantize the sound that has been digitized. CD quality audio uses 16-bit samples, whereas digital phone systems use 8-bit samples. The larger the number of bits per sample, the better quality output.

■ There are from one to many **channels** stored in the audio. Stereo uses two channels, mono one channel. Some formats allow you to supply multiple channels simultaneously, which can be useful for multitrack data or for surround sound systems, which use 4, 5.1, or 8.1 channels. The DVD format, for example, typically uses 5.1 channels (front left/right, rear left/right, center, and subwoofer).

■ A **frame** is a single data block used to store the data from one sample. The size of the frame can be calculated by multiplying the bits per sample and the number of channels. For example, CD audio uses 2 channels and 16-bit sampling, so each frame would be 4 bytes in size.

We can, therefore, calculate different pieces of information about a particular file given certain pieces of information:

■ Provided with the number of frames in a file and the sampling rate, you can calculate the duration of the file:

```
Duration = noofframes/samplerate
```

■ Provided with the number of frames, sampling rate, bits per sample, and number of channels, you can calculate the size of the audio component of a file:

```
filesize = noofframes*samplerate*channels*(bitspersample/8)
```

■ Finally, to calculate the data rate required to transfer audio, you need to know the number of channels, bits per sample, and sampling rate:

```
datarate = samplerate*channels*(bitspersample/8)
```

sndhdr

For manipulating sound files of any kind, you should use one of the other modules, but if you need to know what sound format a particular file is using, beyond identifying the file's extension, you can use the **sndhdr** module.

The **what()** and **whathdr()** functions perform the same operation, returning a tuple containing information about a specific file. For example, the script

```
import sys, sndhdr
print sndhdr.what(sys.argv[1])
```

will output the tuple returned for the file supplied on the command line. For example, when supplied a stereo AIFF file of a track ripped from a CD, you get

```
('aiff', 44100, 2, 10248840, 16)
```

You can see a list of the elements returned in Table 14-1 and the list of supported audio formats in Table 14-2.

Tuple Element	Description
type	The data type identified from the file. See Table 14-2 for a list of returned formats.
samplingrate	The sampling rate in Hertz (number of samples per second). May return 0 if the rate cannot be identified or is difficult to determine.
channels	The number of channels: 2 for stereo, 1 for monaural.
frames	The number of frames (data blocks). May be –1 if the number of frames cannot be determined or is not stored by the file type.
bitspersample	The number of bits in each sample, or "A" for "A-LAW" and "U" for "u-LAW" formats.

Table 14-1. *Elements Returned by **imghdr.what()** and **imghdr.whathdr()***

Format	Description
aifc	Compressed AIFF
aiff	Audio Interchange File Format
au	NeXT/Sun au format
hcom	Macintosh HCOM format
sndr	Amiga 8-bit
sndt	Amiga 8-bit
voc	Creative (maker of the SoundBlaster cards) voice format
wav	Windows WAVE format
8svx	Amiga sound sample, a modified version of AIFF
sb	Raw signed 8-bit
ub	Raw unsigned 8-bit
ul	US 8-bit format—uses exactly 8,000 samples a second (used in telephony)

Table 14-2. *Sound Formats Supported by **sndhdr***

aifc

The **aifc** module allows you to read and write audio files in the AIFF and the compressed AIFC formats. The **open()** function opens an audio file (including creating a file if necessary) and follows the same format as the standard **open()** function:

```
open(file, mode)
```

The **file** should be either the name of the file to open or create, or a file-like object. The **mode** should be one of "r" or "rb" for reading from an existing file, or "w" or "wb" for writing and creating a new file. For example, to open a file for reading,

```
myaiff = open('myaiff.aiff', 'rb')
```

Once opened in read mode, you can use the methods to the returned object shown in Table 14-3.

Method	Description
getnchannels()	Returns the number of audio channels in the file.
getsampwidth()	Returns the size in bytes of the sample rate.
getnframes()	Returns the number of frames in the audio stream.
getframerate()	Returns the frame rate—the number of samples per second.
getcomptype()	Gets the compression type used to compress the data in an AIFF-C or AIFC file.
getcompname()	Gets the textual description of the compression type used to compress data in an AIFF-C or AIFC file.
getparams()	Gets the parameters for the file. Returns a tuple (channels, sample width, number of frames, frame rate, compression type, compression name).
getmarkers()	Gets a list of the markers in the audio file. Returns a list of tuples, where each tuple contains three elements, the marker ID, the marker position, and the marker name.

Table 14-3.   *Reading Methods for AIFF Files*

Method	Description
getmark(id)	Returns the tuple for the marker **id**.
readframes(nframes)	Reads **nframes** relative to the current position from the file.
rewind()	Rewinds to the beginning of the file.
setpos(pos)	Sets the current position of the file to **pos**. Note that **pos** should be specified in frames, not bytes.
tell()	Returns the current position (in frames) from the start of the audio stream.
close()	Closes the file.

Table 14-3. *Reading Methods for AIFF Files* (continued)

If you've opened the file for writing, you can use the methods shown in Table 14-4. Trying to use these methods on a file not opened for writing will raise an exception.

Method	Description
aiff()	Creates an AIFF file. The default operation is to create an AIFF-C (or AIFC) file unless the file ends in **.aiff** when an AIFF file is created.
aifc()	Creates an AIFF-C file. The default operation is to create an AIFF-C (or AIFC) file unless the file ends in **.aiff** when an AIFF file is created.
setnchannels(channels)	Specifies the number of channels in the file.
setsampwidth(width)	Specifies the size of the sample rate in the file.
setframerate(rate)	Specifies the sampling frequency in frames per second.
setnframes(nframes)	Specifies the number of frames to be written to the audio file.

Table 14-4. *Methods Supported for Writing Data to AIFF Files*

Method	Description
setcomptype(type, name)	Specifies the compression type to be used for compressing the audio; only suitable for AIFF-C files. The **name** should be a human-readable description of the compression format, and **type** should be a four-character string. The module currently supports "None," "ULAW," "ALAW," and "G722."
setparams(nchannels, sampwidth, framerate, comptype, compname)	Sets all the parameters for the file at once.
setmark(id, pos, name)	Adds a mark with the ID **id** at the position **pos** (as returned by **tell()**), using the name **name.**
tell()	Returns the current location (in frames) within a file.
writeframes(data)	Writes the frames in **data** to the file. Only supported after the parameters for the file have been set.
writeframesraw(data)	Identical to **writeframes()** except that the file header is not updated to reflect the additional frames written to the file.
close()	Closes the file and updates the file header to reflect the true size of the file.

Table 14-4.   *Methods Supported for Writing Data to AIFF Files* (continued)

In order to create the frames that you want to write out, you need to create a sine wave calculated using the frequency and sample rate over the period of a number of frames. The raw value calculated is then converted into a 2-byte value (for 16 bits per sample audio). If you are working from notes, rather than frequencies, you can use the handy details in Table 14-5 to work out the frequency for a given octave and note.

We can combine all of this together to create an audio file using the **afic** module. The example below creates the sound sequence from a famous sci-fi film:

```
import aifc
import math

def write_note(freq, length, sample_rate, bitspersample, aifcfile):
    reallength = length*sample_rate
```

```
        max = (2**bitspersample) / 2
        pos = 0
        notedata = ''
        while (pos <= reallength):
            note = int(math.sin(
                math.pi*(float(pos)/
                        (sample_rate/freq)))*max)
            notedata += chr((note >> 8) & 255) + chr(note & 255)
            pos += 1
        aifcfile.writeframesraw(notedata)

sample_rate = 44100
bitspersample = 16
channels = 1

aifcfile = aifc.open('ceottk.aiff','wb')
aifcfile.setframerate(sample_rate)
aifcfile.setsampwidth((bitspersample/8))
aifcfile.setnchannels(1)

write_note(493.9, 0.5, sample_rate, bitspersample, aifcfile)
write_note(261.7, 0.5, sample_rate, bitspersample, aifcfile)
write_note(440,   0.5, sample_rate, bitspersample, aifcfile)
write_note(220,   0.5, sample_rate, bitspersample, aifcfile)
write_note(261.7, 0.5, sample_rate, bitspersample, aifcfile)

aifcfile.close()
```

The clue to the film's title is in the name of the ceottk.aiff file that is created when executed.

audioop

The **audioop** module is a generic tool for operating on the frames contained within different sound streams, as represented by strings using samples that are 8, 16, or 32 bits wide. The format used is the same as that used by the **al** and **sunaudiodev** modules, and the functions supplied support u-LAW and Intel/DVI ADPCM encodings. You will need to convert AIFF/AIFC or MP3 formats before making use of the functions in this module.

The list of supported functions is shown in Table 14-6. Note that nearly all the functions need to be supplied with the width of the samples in the data stream you are using in bytes, rather than bits.

NOTE/OCTAVE	C,,	C,	C	C	C'	C''	C'''	C''''
C	16.35	32.70	65.41	130.8	261.7	523.3	1046.6	2093.2
C#	17.32	34.65	69.30	138.6	277.2	554.4	1108.8	2217.7
D	18.35	36.71	73.42	146.8	293.7	587.4	1174.8	2349.6
D#	19.44	38.89	77.79	155.6	311.2	622.3	1244.6	2489.3
E	20.60	41.20	82.41	164.8	329.7	659.3	1318.6	2637.3
F	21.82	43.65	87.31	174.6	349.2	698.5	1397.0	2794.0
F#	23.12	46.25	92.50	185.0	370.0	740.0	1480.0	2960.1
G	24.50	49.00	98.00	196.0	392.0	784.0	1568.0	3136.0
G#	25.95	51.91	103.8	207.6	415.3	830.6	1661.2	3322.5
A	27.50	55.00	110.0	220.0	440.0	880.0	1760.0	3520.0
A#	29.13	58.27	116.5	233.1	466.2	932.3	1864.6	3729.2
B	30.86	61.73	123.5	246.9	493.9	987.7	1975.5	3951.0

Table 14-5. *Octave, Notes, and Corresponding Frequencies*

Function	Description
add(fragment1, fragment2, width)	Adds **fragment1** to **fragment2** returning a single fragment. Both fragments should be of the same length and the same **width**.
adpcm2lin(adpcmfragment, width, state)	Converts the ADPCM fragment in **adpcmfragment** to a linear fragment suitable for manipulation with the routines in this module. Returns a tuple containing the sample data stream and the new **state** of the returned code.
adpcm32lin(adpcmfragment, width, state)	Identical to **adpcm2lin()**, but operates on 3-bit ADPCM code.

Table 14-6. *Functions in the **audioop** Module*

Function	Description
avg(fragment, width)	Returns the average sample level for all the samples in the fragment.
avgpp(fragment, width)	Returns the average peak-to-peak level for all the samples in the fragment.
bias(fragment, width, bias)	Returns **fragment** with **bias** added to each sample.
cross(fragment, width)	Returns the number of zero crossings in **fragment**.
findfactor(fragment, reference)	Returns a factor such that **fragment** could be transmuted into as close an approximation of **reference** as possible. Both fragments should use 16-bit samples.
findfit(fragment, reference)	Attempts to find the portion of **fragment** that most closely matches **reference**. Returns a tuple containing the offset of the location in **fragment** and the required factor.
findmax(fragment, length)	Finds the portion of the audio stream **fragment** that contains the highest energy (volume) for the given **length**. Returns the location of the first sample within the fragment.
getsample(fragment, width, index)	Returns the value of the sample **index** from **fragment**.
lin2lin(fragment, width, newwidth)	Converts **fragment** from the sample **width** to **newwidth**. Used for translating fragments between sample widths.
lin2adpcm(fragment, width, state)	Converts samples to the 4-bit Intel/DVI ADPCM encoding. The **state** should be a tuple containing the state of the coder. You should pass **None** initially. The return value from the function is a tuple containing the ADPCM fragment and the new state of the encoder.
lin2adpcm3(fragment, width, state)	Identical to **lin2adpcm(fragment, width, state)** except that conversion is to 3-bit rather than 4-bit ADPCM encoding.

Table 14-6.   *Functions in the **audioop** Module* (continued)

Function	Description
lin2ulaw(fragment, width)	Converts samples from **fragment** into the u-LAW encoding format and returns this as a Python string.
minmax(fragment, width)	Returns a tuple containing the locations of the minimum and maximum values of **fragment**.
max(fragment, width)	Returns the maximum of all the values in **fragment**.
maxpp(fragment, width)	Returns the maximum peak-to-peak value in **fragment**.
mul(fragment, width, factor)	Returns **fragment** where each sample in fragment has been multiplied by **factor**.
ratecv(fragment, width, nchannels, inrate, outrate, start [, weighta [, weightb]])	Converts the frame rate of **fragment** from **inrate** to **outrate**, returning a tuple containing the new fragment and the new state. The **weightA** and **weightB** are parameters for a simple digital filter, and default to 0 and 1, respectively.
reverse(fragment, width)	Returns all of the samples in **fragment** in reverse order.
rms(fragment, width)	Returns the root mean square of a fragment. This is a measure of the power output of an audio signal (RMS is often used to describe amplifier output).
tomono(fragment, width, lfactor, rfactor)	Converts a stereo (two-channel) fragment into a mono (single-channel) fragment. The **lfactor** and **rfactor** are used to multiply the left and right channels in the resultant output. For example, **tomono(fragment, width, 1, 1)** would produce a balanced mono fragment, while **tomono(fragment, width, 0, 1)** would effectively return a mono fragment containing only the right-hand channel from the stereo fragment.

Table 14-6.   *Functions in the **audioop** Module* (continued)

Function	Description
tostereo(fragment, width, lfactor, rfactor)	Converts a mono fragment into a stereo fragment. The **lfactor** and **rfactor** are used as multipliers on the resulting output from the mono signal to apply their value to the left and right channels of the resulting stereo fragment.
ulaw2lin(fragment, width)	Converts sound fragments in u-LAW format to linearly encoded sound fragments.

Table 14-6. *Functions in the **audioop** Module* (continued)

chunk

The **chunk** module reads data stored in IFF chunks, as used by the AIFF, AIFF-C, and WAV formats. IFF chunks store information using a variable-length record; the format is detailed in Table 14-7.

To use the module, you need to create a new instance of the **Chunk** class that reads information from a given file object as if the data were stored in IFF chunks. The format for creating a new chunk is

```
Chunk(file [, align, bigendian, inclheader])
```

Offset	Length	Contents
0	4	Chunk ID
4	4	Chunk Size (in big-endian order)
8	n	Chunk data, where **n** is the chunk size stored in the previous fragment
8+n	0 or 1	Pad byte required when **n** is odd and chunk alignment is used

Table 14-7. *IFF Chunk Format*

The **file** argument should be a file-like object, such as an object previously created through the built-in **open()** function. The optional **align** argument specifies whether chunks are aligned to 2-byte boundaries if true (therefore triggering the pad byte shown in Table 14-7) or no alignment if false; the default value is true. If **bigendian** is false, then the chunk size is assumed to be in little rather than big-endian order; the default is true. If **inclheader** is true, the size given in the chunk's header includes the size of the header itself; the default is false.

The resulting **Chunk** object supports the methods in Table 14-8. Note that methods other than **getname()** and **getsize()** raise the **error** exception if called after a **close()**.

Note that because IFF chunks may be stored in the file as multiple chunks, you'll need to first open the file and read any format header (such as that used by AIFF) until you read the point of the first chunk. Then you'll need successive calls to create new **Chunk** instances and **read()** method calls in order to obtain all the IFF data from a given file. For an example of how this works in practice see the **aifc** module.

Method	Description
getname()	Returns the ID of the chunk, as stored in the first 4 bytes of the chunk's header.
getsize()	Returns the size of the chunk in bytes.
close()	Closes and skips to the end of the chunk, without closing the underlying file.
isatty()	Returns 0.
seek(pos[, whence])	Sets the chunk's current position. The **pos** should be specified in bytes; and **whence,** if supplied, uses the same values as the underlying file object (0 absolute, 1 relative, 2 relative to end).
tell()	Returns the current position within the chunk.
read([size])	Reads up to **size** bytes from the chunk. If **read** is not supplied, then reads all remaining bytes until the end of the chunk. Chunk data is returned as a Python string.
skip()	Skips to the end of the chunk. Further calls to **read()** will return an empty string.

Table 14-8. *Methods Supported by **Chunk** Objects*

sunau

The **sunau** module provides an interface to the Sun AU audio format. It is interface compatible with the **aifc** and **wave** modules.

All Sun AU files have a header in the format shown in Table 14-9.

You can use the constants listed in Table 14-10 for the encoding and magic word fields in the header.

The basic mode of operation is identical: you must first open an existing file or create a new one through the **open()** function. The methods supported by an opened object are identical to those supported by the **wave** and **aifc** modules, with the following additional notes:

- The **readframes()** method returns a string of audio data in linear format. Data in u-LAW format is converted on the fly.

- The **getmarkers()** method returns **None**, and the **getmark()** method raises an exception when called.

See Tables 14-11 and 14-12 in the next section for a list of supported methods.

wave

The **wave** module allows you to read and write Windows WAVE (WAV) files. The basic methods used here are identical to those used with the **aifc** module, covered earlier in this chapter.

Field	Description
magic word	The magic header foe a Sun AU file
header size	Size of the header in bytes
data size	Size of the data in bytes
encoding	The encoding format used for the data
sample rate	The sampling rate
# of channels	The number of channels
info	Description of the audio file

Table 14-9.   *The Header Format for Sun AU Files*

Constant(s)	Description
AUDIO_FILE_MAGIC	The integer that every Sun AU format file starts with, which is actually the string .snd in integer format
AUDIO_FILE_ENCODING_MULAW_8 AUDIO_FILE_ENCODING_LINEAR_8 AUDIO_FILE_ENCODING_LINEAR_16 AUDIO_FILE_ENCODING_LINEAR_24 AUDIO_FILE_ENCODING_LINEAR_32 AUDIO_FILE_ENCODING_ALAW_8	Values for the encoding field supported by the module
AUDIO_FILE_ENCODING_FLOAT AUDIO_FILE_ENCODING_DOUBLE AUDIO_FILE_ENCODING_ADPCM_G721 AUDIO_FILE_ENCODING_ADPCM_G722 AUDIO_FILE_ENCODING_ADPCM_G723_3 AUDIO_FILE_ENCODING_ADPCM_G723_5	Values for the encoding field not supported by this module

Table 14-10. *Constants Defined by the sunau Module*

The basic method of operation is to open a WAV file, either an existing file or a new one, through the **open()** function:

```
open(file [, mode])
```

As with the **aifc** module, the **file** argument should either be an existing file object or the filename of the file to open or create. The **mode** defines the mode of opening, "r" or "rb" for reading and "w" or "wb" for writing.

All methods raise a **wave.Error** exception when an error occurs.

When a file has been opened for reading, the methods in Table 14-11 are supported to the open object.

Note that the **setpos()** and **tell()** methods return values that are compatible only with themselves. Use of the values returned or used with these methods with a normal file object is not recommended.

Method	Description
close()	Closes the file stream. Further method calls raise an exception.
getnchannels()	Returns the number of channels in the audio file.
getsampwidth()	Returns the width of each sample.
getframerate()	Returns the frame rate in frames per second.
getnframes()	Returns the total number of audio frames in the file.
getcomptype()	Returns the compression type. Currently only supports None.
getcompname()	Returns the human-readable compression name. Currently returns only None.
getparams()	Returns the parameters for the audio in the file in the form of a tuple containing, in order, the number of channels, sample width, frame rate, number of frames, compression type, and compression name.
readframes(n)	Reads at most **n** bytes from the file and returns it as a string.
rewind()	Rewinds the file pointer to the beginning of the audio stream.
getmarkers()	Returns None. Remains for compatibility with the **aifc** module.
getmark(id)	Raises an error. Remains for compatibility with the **aifc** module.
setpos(pos)	Sets the file pointer to the specified position.
tell()	Returns the current file pointer position.

Table 14-11. *Read Methods for **wave** Objects*

When a **wave** object is opened for writing, you can use the methods in Table 14-12. For an example of how to write frames to a file, see the earlier example in the **aifc** section in this chapter, or see the **morse.py** example in the Python distribution.

Method	Description
close()	Closes the file and updates the frame information within the header. Automatically called when a **Wave** object is destroyed.
setnchannels(n)	Sets the number of channels.
setsampwidth(n)	Sets the sample width to **n** bytes.
setframerate(n)	Sets the frame rate to **n** frames per second.
setnframes(n)	Sets the number of frames within the file to **n**. Automatically updated when frames are written.
setcomptype(type, name)	Sets the compression type and description.
setparams(tuple)	Sets the parameters for the file all at once. The supplied tuple should contain, in order, number of channels, sample width, frame rate, number of frames, compression type, and compression name.
tell()	Returns the current position within the file.
writeframesraw(data)	Writes the frames in **data** to the file, without correcting the number of frames in the file.
writeframes(data)	Writes the frames in **data** to the file and updates the number of frames for the entire file.

Table 14-12.   *Writing Methods for **Wave** Objects*

Graphics Modules

Python supports a small number of basic image manipulation and identity modules. Most of these were developed for use with a number of SGI-specific modules not covered in this book. However, the modules that are covered here are not platform specific and can, therefore, be used under any platform.

imghdr

The **imghdr** module performs the same action as **sndhdr,** but on image files. The **what()** function returns a single string defining the image form. For example,

```
>>> import imghdr
>>> imghdr.what('mcslplogosm.gif')
'gif'
```

A full list of the strings and image files identified by the module are shown in Table 14-13.

colorsys

The **colorsys** module allows you to convert between the different color space definitions. The module allows you to convert between RGB (red, green, blue), YIQ (a European color space format), HLS (hue, lightness, saturation), and HSV (hue, saturation, value). The list of functions supported by the module are shown in Table 14-14.

Format	Description
rgb	SGI ImgLib files
gif	GIF 87a and 89a files
pbm	Portable Bitmap files
pgm	Portable Graymap files
ppm	Portable Pixmap files
tiff	TIFF files
rast	Sun Raster files
xbm	X Bitmap files
jpeg	JPEG data in JFIF format
bmp	BMP files
png	Portable Network Graphics files

Table 14-13. *File Formats Identified by the **imghdr** Module*

Function	Description
rgb_to_yiq(r, g, b)	Converts the color from RGB coordinates to YIQ coordinates
yiq_to_rgb(y, i, q)	Converts the color from YIQ coordinates to RGB coordinates
rgb_to_hls(r, g, b)	Converts the color from RGB coordinates to HLS coordinates
hls_to_rgb(h, l, s)	Converts the color from HLS coordinates to RGB coordinates
rgb_to_hsv(r, g, b)	Converts the color from RGB coordinates to HSV coordinates
hsv_to_rgb(h, s, v)	Converts the color from HSV coordinates to RGB coordinates

Table 14-14. *Functions for Converting Colorspace Values in* **colorsys**

Note that values are expressed as a floating-point value between 0 and 1. If you are used to using 8-bit values—values in the range 0–255—you will need to convert the numbers before supplying them to these functions.

imageop

The **imageop** module supports a number of functions for manipulating images that use 8 or 32 bits for storing image data. All functions return the **imageop.error** exception when an error occurs. The list of supported functions is shown in Table 14-15.

Function	Description
crop(image, psize, width, height, x0, y0, x1, y1)	Returns the **image** or **psize** bytes and **width** by **height** in size cropped using the coordinates of a bounding box defined from lower left (**x0, y0**) to top right (**x1, y1**). The bounding rectangle is included in the cropped image. If **x0** or **y0** are greater than **x1** or **y1**, the image is returned mirrored vertically and/or horizontally.

Table 14-15. *Functions Supported by* **imageop**

Function	Description
scale(image, psize, width, height, newwidth, newheight)	Scales **image** (of **psize** bytes and **width** by **height** in size) to **newwidth** and **newheight**. Image is scaled by duplicating or deleting pixels; no interpolation occurs.
tovideo(image, psize, width, height)	Filters **image** of **psize** bytes and **width** by **height** dimensions suitable for output on a device that uses interlacing.
grey2mono(image, width, height, threshold)	Converts an 8-bit monochrome image to a 1-bit monochrome image.
dither2mono(image, width, height)	Converts an 8-bit monochrome image to a 1-bit monochrome image using dithering.
mono2grey(image, width, height, p0, p1)	Converts a 1-bit monochrome image into an 8-bit monochrome image. The arguments **p0** and **p1** are used as the values for 0 and 1 valued bits, respectively. To get a grayscale image, use values of 0 and 255.
grey2grey4(image, width, height)	Converts an 8-bit grayscale image to a 4-bit grayscale image without dithering.
grey2grey2(image, width, height)	Converts an 8-bit grayscale image to a 2-bit grayscale image without dithering.
dither2grey2(image, width, height)	Converts an 8-bit grayscale image to a 2-bit grayscale image with dithering. As for **dither2mono()**, the dithering algorithm is currently very simple.
grey42grey(image, width, height)	Converts a 4-bit grayscale image to an 8-bit grayscale image.
grey22grey(image, width, height)	Converts a 2-bit grayscale image to an 8-bit grayscale image.

Table 14-15. *Functions Supported by* **imageop** (continued)

rgbimg

The **rgbimg** module allows you to read and write SGI **imglib** files using the **.rgb** extension. The functions support only the 4-byte RGBA, 3-byte RGB, and 1-byte grayscale images. The module supports the functions listed in Table 14-16. All functions raise the **rgbimg.error** exception on error.

Function	Description
sizeofimage(file)	Returns a tuple containing the width and height of the image in **file**.
longimagedata(file)	Reads the image from **file** and returns it as a Python string. The bottom-left pixel is the first in the string, and all pixels are represented in the 4-byte RGBA format.
longstoimage(data, x, y, z, file)	Writes the RGBA image in **data** to **file** using the width and height defined in **x** and **y**, respectively. The **z** argument defines the output format: 1 for grayscale, 3 for RGB, and 4 for RGBA.
ttob(flag)	Sets whether the module works with images from the bottom line to the top (**flag** should be zero, the default), or top to bottom (**flag** should be 1).

Table 14-16.   *Functions Supported by **rgbimg***

The Complete Reference

Python

Chapter 15

Interface Building with Tk

Making your program do everything you want is relatively easy, but actually making it usable requires that you create a suitable and easy-to-navigate user interface. There are many ways in which you can create an interface to the user. For simple utilities, the obvious solution is simply a set of command-line options that allow you to enter a command telling the application what you want it to do. One example is the **getopt** module, described in Chapter 9, which parses command-line arguments for you.

For more complex applications, especially if you want them to be used across a network and a variety of platforms, the best solution is to use HTML and CGI through an Internet or intranet site. Chapter 19 looks at the specifics of producing web sites with Python.

If your application fits somewhere in between these two, then you are probably looking for a "desktop" solution. This solution will be in the form of a stand-alone application that either uses local information or gathers information from a number of remote sources over a network.

Either way, your application needs an interface. It could be relatively simple—for example, a nice form to allow data entry into a database—or it could be more complex—for example, a web browser or an office application.

However complicated the application, you need to build an efficient interface that is comprised of windows, buttons, text entry points, and other widgets that allow the user to interact with and control your application through a familiar GUI (graphical user interface). You could design and develop the interface yourself, but getting many of the different systems working is very difficult. Even the simple operation of getting a button to click becomes a complex sequence. It's also highly likely that you'll be developing on a platform that already has a GUI—you just need to know how to interact with that GUI to allow you to develop your application.

There are no standard toolkits for developing these applications, but Tk is a good choice. It removes a lot of the complexity of implementing an interface, while the individual design remains your responsibility.

Tk is cross-platform compatible and there are versions that work on Unix (through the X Windows system), Windows, and MacOS. Python supports an interface to the Tk API called **Tkinter** that comes standard with all Python distributions.

Tk was originally developed by Dr. John Ousterhout, who was at the University of California, Berkeley, before moving to Sun Microsystems. A new company called Scriptics was created by Ousterhout to help develop Tk and Tcl in preparation for a commercial release. Scriptics has now been bought by Interwoven, although development of Tcl and Tk continues under the Scriptics name. The original Tcl and Tk projects are still free, while Scriptics also develops commercial products such as TclPro.

The role of Tk is to simplify the process of designing a user interface. The core of the Tk windowing system provides the methods and basis for simple operations and events such as opening windows, drawing lines, and accepting input and actions from the keyboard and mouse.

Creating even a simple on-screen element like a button or a simple text pane originally involved hundreds of lines of code. The result was the development of individual elements of a GUI environment called *widgets.* A single widget can define a core element of the interface, such as a button, scroll bar, and even more complex elements like scales and hierarchical lists, which themselves can be composed of other simpler widgets. Within Unix and the X Windows system, a number of different widget toolkits have been produced, including Qt, Gnome, Motif, Athena, OpenWindows, and, of course, Tk.

Because of the natural relationship between widgets and objects, developing GUIs within a scripting language is incredibly easy, and Tk was originally developed in cooperation with the Tcl language. Tcl (short for Tool Command Language) is essentially a macro language for simplifying the development of complex programs within the shell. However, Tcl is itself difficult to use compared to Python and other scripting languages, so efforts were made to support the Tk widgets directly within these languages.

Tkinter works on the same basis as pTk, which is a generic porting layer that sits on top of the real Tk libraries. The pTk system is now used by a number of different languages including Perl, Guile, Scheme, and of course, Python. **Tkinter** provides a complete interface to the underlying Tk libraries.

If you are serious about developing interfaces with Tk or any other system, I suggest, for the benefit of you and your users, that you read a suitable human-computer interface book. I can heartily recommend all of Apple's texts; they are the basis for many of the best interfaces you will find. You may also want to check out Alan Cooper's *About Face: The Essentials of User Interface Design* or the excellent introductory guide *The Elements of User Interface Design*, by Theo Mandel.

Installing Python/Tk under Unix

Your first step is to obtain the latest versions of the Tcl and Tk libraries. You can download the sources for these from the Scriptics web site (**www.scriptics.com**). If you're running Linux, you may find that Tcl and Tk are already installed on your system. You need to extract both packages into the same directory and then compile the Tcl libraries before you build the Tk libraries. On most systems the installation command sequence is something like this:

```
$ gunzip -c /export/contrib/archive/tcl8.3.2.tar.gz |tar xf -
$ bunzip2 -c /export/contrib/archive/tk8.3.2.tar.gz |tar xf -
$ cd tcl8.3.2/unix
$ ./configure
$ make
$ make install
$ cd ../..
$ cd tcl8.3.2/unix
```

```
$ ./configure
$ make
$ make install
```

Now you need to modify the module setup information in the Python sources so that you can build the **Tkinter** module and the extensions required for Python to communicate with the Tk libraries.

Go to your source directory for Python and open the **Setup** file in the **Modules** directory. In there you'll find the necessary lines that you'll need to uncomment and modify to enable Tk. For example, here are the lines required under Solaris using Tcl/Tk 8.3.2:

```
_tkinter _tkinter.c tkappinit.c -DWITH_APPINIT \
-L/usr/local/lib \
-I/usr/local/include \
-I/usr/openwin/include \
-ltk8.3 -ltcl8.3 \
-L/usr/openwin/lib \
-lX11
```

Now go back to the base directory for Python and run **make** to rebuild Python (if necessary) and set up the libraries. Run a **make install** command and you're ready to go.

Installing Python/Tk under Windows

The standard Python installer available from the main Python web site actually includes the Tk libraries and an installer is automatically initiated during the installation process to set up Tk and **Tkinter** for you.

Installing Python/Tk under MacOS

The MacOS installer includes the Tcl/Tk libraries that are required to use Tk under MacOS. They are automatically installed during installation.

Introduction to Tk

Developing a user interface with Tk is a case of creating a number of nested objects. The first object you create is the main window for your application. The nested objects are the individual widgets that make up the user interface. A widget is a button, text box, menu, or any of a variety of other components that are used to create your interface within the main window.

Once you have defined the individual widgets that make up the main window, the script then goes into a loop, called the *event loop.* The script accepts events from the user and performs the commands and actions that are defined when the widgets are created. This is different from most other Python scripts, which follow a logical process. However, unlike many Python scripts, users control the execution and choose a number of different options, depending on which button, text box, or other widget they manipulate.

The basic steps for creating a Tk-based GUI application are as follows:

1. Create a window to hold all of your objects. The main window is generally known as *main* or *top-level*, although it can be called anything.

2. Create a number of widgets, defining their contents, actions, and other elements. In the example that follows, a label to hold a simple message and a button that when pressed exits the script, are created.

3. Display and arrange the widgets within the window. This task is frequently handled by the Pack geometry manager, although there are other geometry managers available. The geometry manager supplies a method that allows you to control the orientation and spacing of the widgets within the window. Although you can exercise a certain amount of control, the geometry manager actually does a lot of the work for you. It makes decisions based on your recommendations about how to lay out the individual components.

4. Start the event loop. The main execution of the script has now finished, and the rest of the script is driven by the events configured for individual widgets.

Here is a short Python/Tk script that demonstrates these steps:

```
import sys
from Tkinter import *

def main():
    root = Tk()
    button = Button(root,
                    text = 'Hello, world',
                    command = quit_callback)

    button.pack()
    root.mainloop()

def quit_callback():
    sys.exit(0)

main()
```

The result, when run, looks like this on a Windows 98 machine:

You can see the effects of the script quite clearly. As a comparison, here's the same script executed on a Red Hat Linux machine:

Finally, to show the true cross-platform nature of Python and Tk, here's a version in MacOS:

The contents of the two windows are identical. It is only the window manager dressing for resizing the window, minimizing or maximizing the window, or closing it altogether that are different. The window decorations are specific to each platform and window manager, and any window you create within Tk will have these decorations.

There are five important elements that you should remember when developing Tk interfaces:

- windows
- widgets
- nesting
- geometry management
- callbacks

Windows

The window is the main container for all widgets and the only way in which you can develop an interface with Tk. Without a window, you cannot create a widget. It's possible to create a number of different main windows within the same application; you are not restricted to only one main window. This makes Tk much more practical from an application development point-of-view—you can actually develop most of the basic artifacts that you would expect from a GUI interface. This includes not just the basic windows, but also floating palettes, pop-up boxes, and warning messages.

Widgets

It's important to pay attention to how the individual widgets are created. You cannot create a widget outside of a window; a widget must be created within a container of some kind. Most containers are windows, although you can have widgets that are containers for other widgets. For example, the **Frame** widget can contain other widgets and is used to help confine one or more widgets within certain areas of your window. Furthermore, because the **Frame** is a widget itself, you can nest multiple frames to produce complex layouts.

Nesting

The nesting of widgets is another important principle. Within Microsoft Windows applications, each application window generally consists of two main areas. The very top of the window contains the menu bar, and the remainder of the window contains either a single frame of other components or an interface that allows multiple windows to exist within the larger frame. For example, within Microsoft Word, you can have multiple documents open that all share the same menu bar.

> **Note** *The inclusion of a per-window menu bar is different in other environments. MacOS is a prime example; there is one menu bar at the top of the screen, and all applications share this menu bar. When you switch applications, the contents of the menu bar change to match the active application. This makes the menu bar a completely separate item to deal with, almost as if it's within its own window.*

The contents of a menu bar within a Windows application are somewhat limited. Although some applications feign certain abilities, most Windows menus are limited to simple lists of options. The menu bar is, in fact, a container widget. There is nothing special about the **MenuBar** object—in fact, it's largely based on the **Frame** widget. You place **MenuButton**s into a **MenuBar** widget, and each **MenuButton** is made up of a number of menu items. However, unlike a your typical Windows application, a Tk-based application can put anything into the menu item: buttons, checkboxes, radio buttons, in fact, any other widget you like.

Furthermore, because a **MenuBar** is just another widget, you can place menus anywhere within the window—you're not tied to just producing the menu at the top of the window. The combination of flexible menus and nested widgets within those menus is great for tool and color palettes, or when you want to introduce a complex list of possibilities within a confined space.

I would be willing to argue that the nesting ability of the Tk interface system is perhaps its most powerful feature, after Tk's cross-platform compatibility.

APPLYING THE PYTHON LIBRARIES

Geometry Management

Do not dismiss the need for a geometry manager. The geometry manager actually does a lot more than just organizing the layout of the individual widgets within the window. Because the geometry manager is also ultimately responsible for drawing the widgets on the screen (since only it knows where they should be drawn), it's the geometry manager that actually displays each widget.

If you don't call the geometry manager, then no widgets are displayed because Tk doesn't inherently know where within the window the widget should appear. The geometry manager sets this information for you according to how you want to configure your layout.

Callbacks

In the demonstration script earlier in this section, the main **Button** widget has a **command** property. This property points to the method **exit** via an anonymous subroutine. This command is what's called a *callback*—it calls back a piece of code from another part of the script when you perform a certain action. In this example, when you click on the button, the script ends.

To fully understand callbacks and how the other elements of the Tk window work, you need to understand event loops.

Event Loops

The **mainloop** method executes a simple loop that dispatches requests from the underlying windowing system to the corresponding widgets. For each event, the method defined in the **command** property is executed. However, it's the responsibility of the called method to perform its job and relinquish control as soon as possible so as to allow other waiting events to execute.

For complex systems that are CPU intensive, you also need to make sure that you can effectively multitask between the different threads of execution so that you don't lock up the process while servicing an earlier event loop. For some applications and some systems, this requires you to manually divide a task into manageable chunks, allowing the event loop to send requests to other callback methods. An alternative solution is to use a multithreaded application model.

Any system call that blocks is generally a bad idea within a GUI interface since events in the event stack are processed while the system blocks. This is a particular problem on Windows where the process blocking can actually freeze the whole machine (even though it's not supposed to). The best method is to use something like **select**, which does the job of multiplexing between open filehandles for you. Unfortunately, this doesn't get around the problem of handling GUI and file events for you—you might want to consider using threads for this purpose (see Chapter 9 for more information on multithreading).

The **mainloop** method is not configurable; it's impossible to supply your own version. The main loop only exits when users click on the close box within their windowed environment, or when a call to **sys.exit()** is made, or when an exception is raised that has not otherwise been handled by the system.

Event Bindings

Beyond the basic event bindings handled by the **command** property, it is possible to bind specific events such as keypresses and mouse clicks to other methods. This is how you make keys equate to specific method calls and provide shortcuts to commands and methods. Tk provides the **bind** method, which allows you to map these low-level events to corresponding methods. It is also the method employed by individual widgets when you define the **command** property. The format for the method is

```
widget.bind(event, callback)
```

The **event** is the name of the event you want to bind and it can include keypresses or a mouse click (which is defined as a press and release). The **bind** method also supports more complicated events, such as a mouse click and drag, general mouse motion, the mouse pointer entering or leaving a window, and whole-window events, like resizing and iconifying/minimizing or hiding.

The **event** is defined as a string containing the sequence you want to map, which can be made up of one or more individual events called *event sequences*. For example, the code

```
widget.bind("<z>", pressed_z);
```

maps the user pressing the CTRL key, without any modifier, to the **pressed_z** method. Other possible values for **event** are

```
widget.bind("<Control-z>", undo);
```

which occurs when the CTRL key and Z are pressed at the same time, and

```
widget.bind("<Escape><Control-z>", redo);
```

which calls **redo** when the ESC key is pressed, followed by CTRL and Z. For mouse clicks, you use

```
widget.bind("<Button1>", redo);
```

Individual events are grouped into different classes called *modifiers*, *types*, and *details*. A modifier is a special key, such as **Escape**, **Control**, **Meta**, **Alt**, and **Shift**. Mouse buttons are also grouped into this class, so you get **Button1**, **Button2**, **Double** (for a double-click), and **Triple** (for a triple-click). There is also a special modifier, **Any**, that matches all of the modifiers, including none. Obviously, care needs to be taken if you are developing a cross-platform Tk environment because multibutton mice are not standard on the Macintosh, and three-button mice, though common on Unix workstations, are not common on Windows or Macintosh computers.

The type of event is one of **KeyPress**, **KeyRelease**, **ButtonPress**, **ButtonRelease**, **Enter**, **Leave**, and **Motion**. Note that you can identify both a keypress and its release, so you can configure a game, for example, to accept a certain keypress and only stop processing when the key is finally released. The same is true of button presses and releases. The **Leave** option identifies when the pointer leaves the confines of a widget (useful for tear-off menus and palettes), and **Motion** identifies when the pointer has been moved while a button and/or keyboard combination is pressed.

The detail class is only used for keyboard bindings and is a string defining the character that has been pressed. In addition, the detail class also supports **Enter**, **Right**, **Delete**, **Backspace**, **Escape**, **F1**, and the basic ASCII characters, A–Z, punctuation, and so on.

To make life easier, the Tk library also allows you to use abbreviations of the most common keypresses so that **<KeyPress-z>** can be specified simply as **<z>** and **<Button1-ButtonPress>** as **<1>**.

In addition, the **Text** and **Canvas** widgets allow an even finer granularity on individual bindings, allowing you to attach a binding to a specific tag. The format of **bind** changes accordingly: The first argument now defines the tag to identify, and the second and third arguments define the binding and method to be called. As a result, you can create a binding for pressing the second button on a piece of tagged text, as in this example:

```
text.bind('word', '<2>', synonym_menu);
```

Obtaining Event Details

The callback you configure for an event is passed a single argument when the event occurs. This argument is an **Event** object and contains information about the event that was raised. The attributes for a given **Event** instance are shown in Table 15-1.

For example, it's possible to get the mouse location within a window by accessing the **x** and **y** properties, so you can set up a callback like this:

```
def callback(event):
    print "You clicked on", event.x, event.y
```

Attribute	Description
widget	The widget that generated this event. This is a valid **Tkinter** widget instance, not a name. This attribute is set for all events.
x, y	The current mouse position, in pixels.
char	The character code (keyboard events only).
keysym	The key symbol (keyboard events only).
keycode	The key code (keyboard events only).
width, height	The new size of the widget, in pixels (Configure events only).

Table 15-1.   *Event Attributes*

Using Widgets

To understand how the Tk system works, let's take a brief look at the most commonly used widgets. There are many other widgets that are not listed in this chapter due to space constraints. For more information, check out *An Introduction to Tkinter*, written by Fredrik Lundh and downloadable from the Python web site (**www.python.org/topics/tkinter/doc.html**).

The Core Widgets

The Tk library comes with a number of predefined widgets. Some are the basic building blocks of your typical GUI application, such as **Button** and **Label**. Others are composites of other widgets. Table 15-2 lists the basic widgets supported by the Tk system.

Widget Class	Description
BitmapImage	A subclass of the **Image** widget for displaying bitmap images
Button	A simple push-button widget with similar properties to the **Label** widget
Canvas	A drawing area into which you can place circles, lines, text, and other graphic elements (You need to build these elements yourself, or you can provide widgets to allow the end user to do this for you.)

Table 15-2.   *The Basic Widget Set*

Widget Class	Description
Checkbutton	A multiple-choice button widget, where each item within the selection can be selected individually
Entry	A single-line text entry box
Frame	A container for arranging other widgets
Image	A simple widget for displaying bitmaps, pixmaps (color bitmaps), and other graphic elements
Label	A simple box into which you can place message text (non-editable)
Listbox	A multiline list of selection choices
Menu	A list of menu selections that can be made up of **Label**, **Message**, **Button**, and other widgets
Menubutton	A menu (within a single menu bar) that lists the selections specified in a **Menu** object
Message	A multiline **Label** object (non-editable)
OptionMenu	A special type of **Menu** widget that provides a pop-up list of items within a selection
PhotoImage	A subclass of the **Image** widget for displaying full-color images
Radiobutton	A multiple-choice button widget, where you can choose only one of multiple values
Scale	A slider that allows you to set a value according to a specific scale
Scrollbar	A slider for controlling the contents of another widget, such as **Text** or **Canvas**
Text	A multiline text widget that supports editable text that can also be tagged for display in different fonts and colors
Toplevel	A window that will be managed and dressed by the parent window manager

Table 15-2. *The Basic Widget Set* (continued)

One of the advantages of Tk is that because it supports such basic levels of widgets, they can be combined or modified to build other widgets. For example, the **ScrolledText** widget is a combination of the **Scrollbar** and **Text** widgets that allows you to control what part of the **Text** widget's text is displayed, according to the position of the **Scrollbar**.

At first, this makes Tk look far less practical than other more feature-rich toolkits. For example, unlike Windows and some of the Unix-based toolkits, Tk doesn't support a standard dialog box widget—you have to make one yourself. On the other hand, because you have to make it yourself, you can produce a customized version, perhaps including an error or reference number—something that the predefined toolkits wouldn't be able to support. The downside is that the development process can take longer—you spend a long time introducing the standard artifacts of a good GUI—but the flexibility wins out in the end.

Let's take a closer look at some of the more commonly used widgets.

Generic Widget Properties

The configuration of individual widgets is controlled through a series of *properties*. All widgets have a set of properties that define everything from the existence of borders and colors to font styles and sizes. Specialized widgets also have properties for the unique elements that make up that widget. For example, a **MenuButton** widget has a property called **state**, which indicates whether the menu is active or disabled.

The generic properties that are configurable for all widgets are shown in Table 15-3.

Property	Description
font	The font name in X or Windows format (see the section "Specifying Fonts" later in this chapter).
background, bg	The color of the background, specified either by a name or a hexadecimal RGB value.
foreground, fg	The color of the foreground, specified either by a name or a hexadecimal RGB value.
text	The string to be displayed within the widget, using the foreground and font values specified.
image, bitmap	The image or bitmap file to be displayed within the widget.
relief	The style of the widget's border, which should be one of raised, sunken, flat, ridge, or groove.

Table 15-3. *Generic Widget Properties*

Property	Description
borderwidth	The width of the relief border.
height	The height of the widget; specified in the number of characters for labels, buttons, and text widgets, and in pixels for all other widgets.
width	The width of the widget; specified in the number of characters for labels, buttons, and text widgets, and in pixels for all other widgets.
textvariable	The name of a variable to be used and/or updated when the widget changes.
anchor	Defines the location of the widget within the window, or the location of the text within the widget; valid values are **n**, **ne**, **e**, **se**, **s**, **sw**, **w**, **nw**, and **center**.

Table 15-3. *Generic Widget Properties* (continued)

Setting Widget Properties

When you define a widget, you set the properties by specifying the property name and value as keyword arguments to the widget class you are creating, as in the following example:

```
button = Button(root, text = 'Hello, world', command = quit_callback)
```

Alternatively, if you want to change the properties of a widget after it has been created, you have two options. The first option is to use each widget object as a dictionary so you can update values directly by setting the corresponding property, as in this example:

```
button['text'] = 'Hello, world'
```

The second option uses the **configure()** method:

```
Button.configure(text = 'Hello, world',
                 command = quit_callback)
```

Getting Widget Properties

To get the property settings for a given widget you have two options. The first is to use the **cget()** method:

```
buttontext = button.cget('text')
```

But it's probably easier to get the dictionary element directly, as follows:

```
buttontext = button['text']
```

Specifying Fonts

Font values are traditionally specified in the XLFD (X Logical Font Description) format. This is a complex string consisting of 14 fields, each separated by a hyphen. Each field defines a different property. For example, the font

```
-sony-fixed-medium-r-normal--16-120-100-100-c-80-iso8859-1
```

defines a font from the sony foundry, the fixed family, of medium weight. It's a regular (rather than italic) font—identified by the "r"—and the width is normal. The size of the font is 16 pixels or 12 points high (point size is specified in tenths of a point, so the size specified is 120 rather than 12). The next two fields specify the resolution—in this instance, 100 pixels wide and 100 pixels high—with an overall character ("c") width of 80. The last field is the registry or character locale name.

Usually, however, you can get away with specifying an asterisk or question mark as wildcards in particular fields so that you can request a more general font and then let the Tk and windowing interface determine the correct font. You should be able to get away with specifying the foundry, family, weight, slant, and points fields. For example, to use 12-point Helvetica, you might use

```
label.configure(font = '-adobe-helvetica-medium-r-*--*-120-*-*-*-*-*')
```

Obviously this is quite a mouthful, and it doesn't really apply to the Windows font system, which is much simpler. The Tk libraries also accept the simpler Windows and MacOS-style definition, which is also backwards compatible with the Unix Tk libraries. This definition includes the font name, point size, and weight, as in the following example:

```
label.configure(font = 'Helvetica 12 regular');
```

Specifying Colors

The X Windows system supports a file called **rgb.txt**, which maps red, green, and blue intensities to color names. This allows you to specify a color with a simple name. Here's a short extract from the beginning of a sample **rgb.txt** file:

```
255 250 250          snow
248 248 255          ghost white
248 248 255          GhostWhite
47   79  79          DarkSlateGray
0   191 255          DeepSkyBlue
46  139  87          SeaGreen
178  34  34          firebrick
147 112 219          MediumPurple
```

Obviously, Windows does not use X Windows, but it still has access to the core set of colors supplied with the majority of X Windows installations. If you want to be more specific, you can explicitly specify the RGB values precisely in the form **#RGB**, **#RRGGBB**, **#RRRGGGBBB**, and **#RRRRGGGGBBBB**, where the **R**, **G**, and **B** refer to an individual hexadecimal digit of the corresponding color's intensity.

For example, the **GhostWhite** color could be described as **#F8F8FF**. For many situations, it may be easier to use Python format operator to create the string, as follows:

```
color = "#%02x%02x%02x" % (142,112,219)
```

Specifying Sizes

When specifying the size for a specific widget parameter, there are a number of choices available to you, depending on which widget you are using. If the widget is of a graphical, rather than textual, base—for example, **Canvas**—then the size specification accepted by the **height** and **width** properties is in pixels. This also extends to labels and buttons that have a graphical, rather than textual, value. For all widgets that are text based, the specification is in characters, according to the size of the font being used to display the text.

Images and Bitmaps

Certain widgets support the use of images rather than text. For example, you can use an image in place of the text that would normally appear on a button. There are essentially two types of images: a two-color bitmap and a multicolored pixmap. In an effort to help improve performance, Tk considers an image to be a unique element. If it needs to be displayed in more than one place, you render it once and use the rendered image object as the source for the widget image. This means there are two steps to using an image within a widget.

The first step is to create the rendered image object. You use a different method to render individual image formats, although the return value from each method is always of the same type. To create an image object from X Bitmap (XBM), use the following code:

```
image = label.Bitmap(file = 'icon.xbm')
```

For an X Pixmap (XPM), use this code:

```
image = label.Pixmap(file = 'icon.xpm')
```

For a GIF or Portable Pixmap (PPM) format, you need to use the **Photo** constructor:

```
image = label.Photo(file = 'icon.gif')
```

When you want to configure a particular widget with an image object, use the **image** property:

```
label.configure(image = image)
```

For bitmaps, the **foreground** and **background** properties of the widget control the foreground and background color of the bitmap.

Widget Variables

Some widgets use a separate variable to hold their value. For some widgets this is used merely as a method for displaying information. For example, you might display the value of a variable within a **Label** widget. For other widgets, the variable is used as a link that both sets and receives the value of a particular widget. A good example is the **Scale** widget, which provides you with a slider. When you change the value of the variable tied to the **Scale** widget, you change the position of the slider. Conversely, changing the value of the slider also changes the value of the variable.

You cannot, unfortunately, use standard variables for these special values. Instead, you need to use a **Tkinter** type class to create a suitable object, as in the following example:

```
cbvar = IntVar()
cb = Checkbutton(master, text="Expand", variable=cbvar)
```

Tkinter actually defines a number of different variable types you can use; these include **IntVar()**, **FloatVar()**, **StringVar()**, and **BooleanVar()**. You cannot access or modify the value of these objects directly; instead, you need to use the **get()** and **set()** methods, as follows:

```
cbvar.set(99)
print "The value of the checkbutton is",cbvar.get()
```

Labels

A **Label** widget is the basic widget and it provides a simple way of displaying a small text label within a window. It supports all the basic properties listed in Table 15-3. Because labels are such a basic element, they often form parts, or the basis, of many of the other widgets in the Tk toolkit.

Buttons

Button widgets are essentially just labels with an additional property, **command**, that is a pointer to a method that will be called when the button is clicked. Additional properties and methods beyond the base list are listed in Table 15-4.

You saw an example of both the label and button in the "Hello, world" script earlier in this chapter.

Radio Buttons

The **Radiobutton** widget is used to provide either a simple on/off button or to act as a toggle between several different options. The valid properties and methods for a radio button are listed in Table 15-5.

Property	Description
command	A reference to the Python method or function to be called when the button is clicked with mouse button 1.
Method	
flash	Flashes the button briefly by reversing and resetting the foreground and background colors.
invoke	Starts the subroutine defined in the **command** property.

Table 15-4.   *Properties and Methods for Buttons*

Property	Description
command	A reference to the Python method or function to be called when the button is clicked with mouse button 1. The variable referred to by the **variable** property is updated with the value in the **value** property before the referenced subroutine is invoked.
variable	Takes a reference to a variable and updates it with the **value** property when the button is clicked. When the value of the referenced variable matches the **value** property, the button is selected automatically.
value	Specifies the value to store within the variable pointed to by the **variable** property when the button is selected.

Method	
select	Selects the radio button and sets the **variable** to **value**.
flash	Flashes the button briefly by reversing and resetting the foreground and background colors.
invoke	Starts the subroutine defined in the **command** property.

Table 15-5.   *Properties and Methods for Radio Button*

Remember that you must use one of the **Tkinter** variable types to actually hold the value from the radio button. Also note that radio buttons are grouped according to which variable they update.

For example, in the following example, two separate radio button sets are created, one for the first name and another for the last name, each of which updates its own variable:

```
from Tkinter import *

root = Tk();

firstname = StringVar()
lastname = StringVar()

radio1a = Radiobutton(root,text  = 'Martin',
```

```
                            value = 'Martin', variable = firstname)
radio1b = Radiobutton(root, text   = 'Sharon',
                            value = 'Sharon', variable = firstname)
radio1c = Radiobutton(root, text   = 'Rikke',
                            value = 'Rikke', variable = firstname)
radio1a.pack(side = 'left')
radio1b.pack(side = 'left')
radio1c.pack(side = 'left')

radio2a = Radiobutton(root, text   = 'Brown',
                            value = 'Brown', variable = lastname)
radio2b = Radiobutton(root, text   = 'Penfold',
                            value = 'Penfold', variable = lastname)
radio2c = Radiobutton(root, text   = 'Jorgensen',
                            value = 'Jorgensen', variable = lastname)
radio2a.pack(side = 'left')
radio2b.pack(side = 'left')
radio2c.pack(side = 'left')

root.mainloop()
```

Note that the same variable is used in each property definition, so the information is shared. A change to the value updates the corresponding radio button family with the correct selection. The resulting window is shown here:

Check Buttons

A **Checkbutton** widget, also known as a *checkbox*, depending on your background, is like a radio button, except that it is normally used to allow the user to select multiple check buttons for a single option. The possible properties and methods for a **Checkbutton** widget are shown in Table 15-6.

Text

A **Text** widget is a simple text box used for displaying multiple lines of text, unlike a label, which is really only useful for a small number of words on a single line. A **Text**

Property	Description
command	A reference to the Perl method to be called when the check button is clicked with mouse button 1. The variable referred to by the **variable** property is updated with the value in the **value** property before the referenced subroutine is invoked.
variable	Takes a reference to a variable and updates it with the **value** property when the check button is clicked. When the value of the referenced variable matches the **value** property, the button is selected automatically.
onvalue	Specifies the value to store within the variable pointed to by the **variable** property when the button is selected.
offvalue	Specifies the value to store within the variable pointed to by the **variable** property when the button is not selected.
indicatoron	If false (0), then rather than displaying the check button indicator, it toggles the **relief** base property of the entire widget, effectively making the whole widget the check button.
Method	
select	Selects the check button and sets the **variable** to **value**.
flash	Flashes the check button briefly by reversing and resetting the foreground and background colors.
invoke	Starts the subroutine defined in the **command** property.
toggle	Toggles the selection state and values of the check button on and off.

Table 15-6. *Properties and Methods for Check Buttons*

APPLYING THE
PYTHON LIBRARIES

widget becomes an editable entry box for information. It supports the **emacs** keyboard shortcuts for data entry and for moving around the box. In addition to the editing features of a **Text** widget, you can also "tag" individual pieces of text and change their properties. This allows you to create a full-featured text editor with multiple font, point size, and color support without any additional programming.

Text widget methods take one or more index specifications as arguments. An argument can be an absolute number (base) or a relative number (base and modifier), and both are specified as strings. Supported base index specifications are listed in the following table. Items in italics indicate the components of the index specification that you can modify. Anything else is a keyword.

line.char	Indicates the character at **char** characters across (left to right) and **line** lines down (top to bottom). The specification starts at 0 for characters within a line and 1 for lines within a text box.
end	The end of the text, as defined by the character just after the last newline.
insert	The location of the insertion cursor.
mark	The character just after the marker whose name is **mark**.
tag.first, tag.last	Used to specify the **first** and **last** characters of a tag.

The following index specifications can also be qualified with an additional modifier:

+count chars, -count chars, +count lines, -count lines	Adjust the base index specification by **count** characters or lines.
wordstart, wordend, linestart, lineend	Adjust the index to point to the first character on the word or line specified by the index (**wordstart**, **linestart**) or to the character immediately after the word or line (**wordend**, **lineend**).

Some of the supported properties and methods for the **Text** widget are listed in Table 15-7.

Property	Description
tabs	The list of tab stops for the **Text** widget. Specification should be as a reference to a list of strings. Each string should be comprised of a number that defines the character location within the line, followed by **l**, **c**, or **r** for left, center, or right justification for the specified tab.

Table 15-7. *Properties and Methods for **Text** Widgets*

Property	Description
state	One of **normal** for a standard editable text box, or **disabled** for an unmodifiable text box.
Method	
insert(index [, string [, tag]] ...)	Insert **string** with an optional **tag** at the specified **index**.
delete(index1 [,index2])	Delete the character at **index1** or the text from **index1** to **index2**.
get(index1 [,index2])	Get the character at **index1** or the text from **index1** to **index2**.
index(index)	Returns an absolute index for the corresponding **index** supplied.
see(index)	Returns true if the text at **index** is visible.
markSet(name, index)	Gives the text at **index** the bookmark name **name**.
markUnset(name)	Unsets a bookmark **name**.

Table 15-7. *Properties and Methods for **Text** Widgets (continued)*

For example, to insert a piece of text at the end of a text box, use the following code:

```
text.insert('Beginning!', 'end')
```

To insert the same piece of text at character 20 on line 5, use the following code:

```
text.insert('Beginning!', '5.20')
```

To specify and configure the tags, you need the methods and properties listed in Table 15-8.

For example, to create a simple tag, use the following code:

```
text.tagAdd('tagged', '1.0', '3.0')
```

This creates a tag called **tagged** from lines 1 through 3 inclusive. The tag name should be unique because you need it when configuring the options on an individual tag.

Property	Description
-foreground, **-background**, **-font**	As for the basic properties.
-justify	Justification for the tagged text, one of **center**, **left**, and **right**.
-relief, -borderwidth	The border width and relief style.
-tabs	As for basic text widget properties (see Table 15-7), but applies only if the first character in that line also belongs to the same tag. You cannot add "subtabs" to a tagged block.
-underline	Underlines the tagged text.
Method	
tagAdd(name [,index1[.index2]] ...)	Adds the tag **name** at the position specified in **index1** or bounded by **index1** and **index2**.
tagRemove(name [,index1[.index2]] ...)	Removes the tag **name** from the character or range specified by **index1** and **index2**, but does not delete the actual tag definition.
tagDelete(name)	Removes and deletes the tag **name**.
tagConfigure	Configures one or more properties for a tag.

Table 15-8.   *Tag Methods and Properties*

Therefore, to change the text tagged with the name **tagged** to 24-point Times, boldface, use the following code:

```
text.tagConfigure('tagged', font = 'Times 24 Bold')
```

Entry

An **Entry** widget is essentially a single-line text box, and it inherits many features and methods from the **Text** widget. However, because it's only a single line, the indexing and methods are much simpler. The indexing options are as follows:

number	An index into the widget's contents, starting with 0 as the first character
end	The end of the text
insert	The position immediately after the insertion cursor
sel.first, sel.last	The first and last characters of a tag

The supported properties and methods for the **Entry** widget are listed in Table 15-9.

List Boxes

A **Listbox** widget enables you to create a list, from which you can select an individual item. It displays a list of strings, one per line, and all the strings displayed have the same characteristics. When creating the list, the easiest way to populate it is to create

Property	Description
show	A simple Boolean option. If set, it displays * for each character entered and is primarily used for password entry. Note that although the characters are displayed in this manner, copying and pasting the contents of a hidden field reveals the real contents.
Method	
get(index)	Gets the string starting at **index**.
insert(index, string)	Inserts **string** at **index**.
index(index)	Returns an absolute index from a relative one.
selectionFrom(index)	Sets the selection from **index** to the end of the field.
selectionTo(index)	Sets the selection from the beginning of the field to **index**.
selection(from, to)	Sets the selection to the characters starting at **from** and ending at **to**.
selectionClear	Clears the selection.
selectionPresent	True if a selection is currently active.

Table 15-9.   *Properties and Methods for the **Entry** Widget*

the widget and then use the **insert** method to add items to the list. The **width** and **height** properties for the **Listbox** widget define the width of the list box and the height in characters. Alternatively, you can specify values of 0, which will cause the list box to grow to display all of the objects.

Here is an example of a script that uses the **Listbox** widget:

```
from Tkinter import *

root = Tk();

list = Listbox(root, height = 5, width = 0)
list.insert('end', 'Martin','Sharon','Wendy','Sharon','Chris')
list.pack()

root.mainloop()
```

The result is shown here:

Note that you need to use the **bind** method shown earlier in this chapter to bind a particular operation, such as a double-click, to a method. Within the method, you need to use the **get** method to obtain the current selection.

You can refer to individual elements within a **Listbox** widget similarly to selecting text within a **Textbox** widget. You specify a string that defines the row, the row selection, or the relative location within the list. The details are as follows:

number	The index of the row, starting with 0 for the first element.
end	The end of the current row.
active	Where the location cursor is currently positioned; the active location appears underlined in the list view.
anchor	The anchor point of the selection.

The properties and methods supported by the **Listbox** widget are listed in Table 15-10.

Property	Description
height, **width**	The height and width of the list in rows and characters. If either is 0, the widget resizes to incorporate all of the list elements.
selectMode	Defines the selection mode of the list; one of **single**, **browse**, **multiple**, or **extended**.
Method	
get(index)	Gets the string, starting at **index**.
insert(index, string)	Inserts **string** at **index**.
delete(index [, last])	Deletes the row at **index** or the rows between **index** and **last**.
see(index)	Brings the element **index** into the current view.
selectionFrom(index)	Selects all the rows from **index** to the end of the list.
selectionTo(index)	Selects all the rows from the beginning of the list to **index**.
selection(from, to)	Selects the rows starting at **from** and ending at **to**.
selectionClear	Clears the selection.
selectionPresent	Returns true if there is an active selection.
curselection	A list of the index values of all the selected items.

Table 15-10.   *Properties and Methods Supported by the **Listbox** Widget*

Menus

Menus are logically split into **MenuButton** widgets, which are the menu names. The **MenuButton** widget then becomes a container that holds the individual menu item widgets, which are split into different types to allow you to add normal menu items (actually just labels), buttons, check buttons, and radio buttons to your menus.

The normal method for creating a menu is as follows:

1. Create a menu bar frame using the **Frame** widget to hold individual menu buttons.

2. Create the individual menu buttons within the new frame. Each menu button defines each menu, so you need to create a menu button for File, Edit, and Help, for example, to keep within normal style guidelines.

3. Use the **MenuButton** widget methods to create a new **Menu** widget.

4. Use the **Menu** widget methods to create the individual menu options.

5. Once all of the individual menus and buttons have been created, call the **tk_menuBar()** method on your menu frame to create the final menu layout.

Properties and methods for the **Menu** widget are listed in Table 15-11.

The configurable **options** supported for the methods in Table 15-11 work like the properties and are listed in Table 15-12. Note that because you can have hierarchical menus, individual items can use further methods from Table 15-11.

The individual properties supported by the individual **Menu** entries are shown in Table 15-12.

Property	Description
indicatorOn	If true, shows a small diamond to the right of the menu.
state	The state of the menu, either **normal**, **active**, or **disabled**.
Method	
add_command(options)	Creates the corresponding type of menu item; the normal type for a standard menu entry.
add_radiobutton(options)	Adds a radio button menu item.
add_checkbutton(options)	Adds a check button menu item.
add_cascade(options)	Inserts a new cascading (hierarchical) menu.
add(type, options)	Adds a new menu of **type** with **options**.
delete(index1 [, index2])	Deletes the menu item **index1** or the items from **index1** to **index2**.
entryconfig(index, options)	Changes the properties of the menu item pointed to by **index**.
index(item)	Returns the **index** number of the item specified by the string **item**; the string should match the menu item's label.

Table 15-11.   *Properties and Methods for the **Menu** Widget*

Property	Description
indicatorOn	If true, places a small diamond next to the menu option, which allows an option to be toggled on and off by a menu.
selectColor	The color of the indicator, if **indicatorOn** is true.
tearOff	If true, the first element of the menu is a separator. Clicking on the separator "tears off" the menu into a separate top-level window. This feature is not always supported on all implementations.
label	The text to use for the menu item. This should be used in place of the normal **text** property.
underline	The index of a character to underline. This is used in combination with the **accelerator** property to indicate which keyboard shortcut should be used for this menu.
accelerator	Shows the string to be displayed, right justified, as the keyboard equivalent for the menu option. This doesn't bind the key to the command for you; you have to do that separately.
state	Status, which is one of **normal**, **active**, or **disabled**.
command	The name of the function to call when the menu item is selected.
value	The value of the attached radio button (see Table 15-5).
variable	The variable used to store **value**.
onvalue, offvalue	Identical to the options in Table 15-6 for check button style entries.

Table 15-12. *Generic Menu Item Properties*

For example, to create a simple command menu, you might use a script like this:

```
from Tkinter import *

def new_file():
    print "opening new file"

def open_file():
    print "opening OLD file"

def print_something():
```

```
        print "picked a menu item"

def makeCommandMenu():
    Command_b = Menubutton(mBar,
                           text='Simple Button Commands',
                           underline=0)
    Command_b.pack(side=LEFT, padx="2m")
    Command_b.menu = Menu(Command_b)
    Command_b.menu.add_command(label="Undo")
    Command_b.menu.entryconfig(0, state=DISABLED)
    Command_b.menu.add_command(label='New...', underline=0,
                               command=new_file)
    Command_b.menu.add_command(label='Open...', underline=0,
                               command=open_file)
    Command_b.menu.add_command(
        label='Different Font',
        underline=0,
        font='-*-helvetica-*-r-*-*-*-180-*-*-*-*-*-*',
        command=print_something)

    Command_b.menu.add_command(bitmap="info")
    Command_b.menu.add('separator')
    Command_b.menu.add_command(label='Quit', underline=0,
                               background='red',
                               activebackground='green',
                               command=Command_b.quit)


    Command_b['menu'] = Command_b.menu

    return Command_b

root = Tk()

mBar = Frame(root, relief=RAISED, borderwidth=2)
mBar.pack(fill=X)

Command_b      = makeCommandMenu()

mBar.tk_menuBar(Command_b)

root.title('menu demo')
root.iconname('menu demo')

root.mainloop()
```

Frame

A **Frame** widget is simply a container for other widgets. It's used when you need to create a complex layout that requires more advanced geometry management than you can normally do with the available tools. The way it works is that you divide individual areas of the window into frames and pack the collection of objects into the frame. For example, you might create a new frame that contains the menu bar, which you gravitate to the top of the window, while the actual menu buttons within the menu bar are arranged horizontally. You'll see an example of this later in this chapter when you learn about the **Scale** widget.

Scroll Bars

Scroll bars are available either as separate widgets, in which case you are responsible for managing the corresponding widget you are scrolling or they can be automatically added to any suitable widgets.

Let's discuss the automatic scroll bars first. To create an automatically scrolled widget, you use the special **Scrolled** widget method and then specify the type of widget to create with a scroll bar. For example, here's the line from the text viewer that creates a scrolled **Text** widget:

```
maintext - Scrolled(root, 'Text');
```

Internally, this creates a **Frame** widget that contains the main **Text** widget and the horizontal (and vertical) scroll bars. The return value actually refers to the newly created **Frame** widget.

Alternatively, you can create and manage your own scroll bars using the methods and properties in Tables 15-13 and 15-14. The methods in Table 15-13 allow you to set

APPLYING THE
PYTHON LIBRARIES

Property	Description
command	A reference to a subroutine used to change the view in the widget.
Method	
set(first, last)	Indicates the current view. The **first** and **last** elements should be fractions between 0 and 1. For example, a value of 0.1 and 0.2 should indicate that the area between 10 percent and 20 percent of the item should be shown.
get	Returns the current scroll bar settings.

Table 15-13. *Properties and Methods for Scroll Bars*

the current view within the widget to which you want to associate the scroll bar. The **set** method controls the current view, and the **command** property is called when the scroll bar is moved.

All widgets that are scrollable also support the methods and properties shown in Table 15-14. The properties define the methods and increments that the scroll bars control. The scroll bar widget automatically calls the correct method (**xview** or **yview**) to modify the display of the linked widget.

Scale

Scales are like thermometers. You define a size and range and the widget displays a horizontal or vertical slider. The slider automatically has a label (if you've defined one)

Property	Description
xscrollincrement, yscrollincrement	The scrolling in the x and y axis are determined by the supplied increment.
xscrollcommand, yscrollcommand	A reference to the method used to reposition the widget when the scroll bar is moved.
Method	
xview('moveto', fraction) **yview('moveto', fraction)**	Moves the scroll bar to the location specified by **fraction**. The new value indicates the leftmost, or topmost, character or pixel of the scroll bar tab. Note that the first argument is a constant.
xview('scroll', number, what) **yview('scroll', number, what)**	Indicates that the view should be moved up or down, or left or right, for **number** increments. If **what** is "units," then it is scrolled according to the increment in the **xscrollincrement** and **yscrollincrement** properties. If **what** is "pages," then the widget is scrolled **number** pages.

Table 15-14.   *Properties and Methods for Scrollable Widgets*

and tick marks to indicate individual divisions. In this section we'll see the code used
to build this slider, a widget for converting feet into meters:

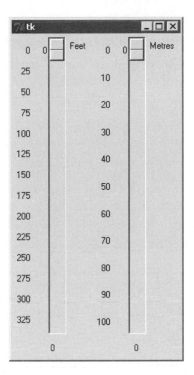

The supported properties and methods for the **Scale** widget are listed in Table 15-15.

Property	Description
command	Reference to a subroutine that will be called when the scale's value is changed.
variable	Reference to a variable to be updated whenever the slider moves. Works like the **variable** base property; updating this value also sets the slider position.
width, length	The **width** and **length** of the scale in pixels (not characters).

Table 15-15.   *Properties and Methods for **Scale** Widgets*

APPLYING THE
PYTHON LIBRARIES

Property	Description
orient	Allows you to select **horizontal** or **vertical** orientation.
from, to	The real range of values that the widget should scale **from** and **to**.
resolution	The value displayed and set into **variable** is always a multiple of this number. The default is 1.
tickinterval	The spacing, in real values, between tick marks on the scale.
label	The label to be displayed to the top (horizontal) or left (vertical) of the scale.
Method	
set(value)	Identical to modifying the value of **variable**.

Table 15-15. *Properties and Methods for **Scale** Widgets* (continued)

Here's the script that generated Figure 15-1. It provides a simple tool for converting feet into meters and vice versa.

```
from Tkinter import *

def main():
    main = Tk();

    global feetscale, metrescale
    feetscale = IntVar()
    metrescale = IntVar()
    feetframe = Frame(main)

    Scale(feetframe,
          command     = update_feet,
          variable    = feetscale,
          width       = 20,
          length      = 400,
          orient      = 'vertical',
          from_       = 0,
          to          = 328,
          resolution  = 1,
          tickinterval = 25,
```

```
            label        = 'Feet'
            ).pack(side = 'top')


    Label(feetframe,
          textvariable = feetscale
          ).pack(side = 'top',
                 pady = 5)


    feetframe.pack(side = 'left')


    metreframe = Frame(main)


    Scale(metreframe,
          command      = update_metre,
          variable     = metrescale,
          width        = 20,
          length       = 400,
          orient       = 'vertical',
          from_        = 0,
          to           = 100,
          resolution   = 1,
          tickinterval = 10,
          label        = 'Metres'
          ).pack(side = 'top');


    Label(metreframe,
          textvariable = metrescale
          ).pack(side = 'top',
                 pady = 5)


    metreframe.pack(side = 'left');


    main.mainloop()

def update_feet(self):
    global metrescale, feetscale
    metrescale.set(int(feetscale.get()/3.280839895))

def update_metre(self):
    global metrescale, feetscale
    feetscale.set(int(metrescale.get()*3.280839895))

main()
```

We saw the Windows version of this code at the beginning of the section. Here are the results of running this script under MacOS:

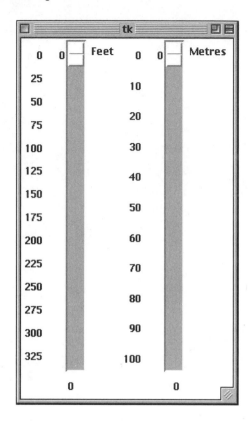

Here are the results of running this script under Unix/X Windows:

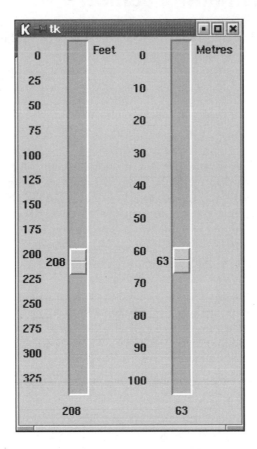

Controlling Window Geometry

Throughout this chapter, you've seen examples of the **pack** method, and you already know it is a required element of the window-building process. However, there are some tricks you can do with **pack** to aid in the arrangement of individual widgets within a window. Tk also supports two other methods of arranging widgets: the placer and the grid. You must use the same geometry manager within a single parent, although it's possible to mix and match individual geometry managers within multiple frames within a single window to suit your needs.

The placer requires some careful planning to use properly, since you must specify the location of each widget within the window using x and y coordinates. This is the same system used within the **Bulletin Board** widget under Motif and Visual Basic, so people moving from those systems may be more comfortable with this system.

The grid geometry manager uses a simple table layout, as you might use within a word processor or when designing web pages with HTML. Each widget is placed into a table cell, and you specify its location by defining the row and column in which the widget should appear. Individual widgets can span multiple rows and columns if necessary. As with the placer geometry manager, you need to give careful thought to how you want to lay out your widgets in this system.

The packer geometry manager is the one we've been using in this chapter, and it's the most practical geometry manager if you do not want to think too much about the geometry management process. As such, it's the one we'll pay the most attention to in this chapter. If you want details on the systems, please see the **Tkinter** documentation that is downloadable from the main Python web site.

Packer

The packer geometry manager is similar to Motif's **Form** widget and uses a much simpler system for defining the location of widgets within a frame of a window. Remember that the **pack** method is just that—it only provides the algorithm used to organize the layout of widgets. Individual calls to the **pack** method pack the corresponding widget into the next available space within the frame or window. This means that widgets are added to the window or frame in the order in which they are packed. This is similar to how you would pack a bag or fill a shelf: You start from a single point and add items until the space is all used up.

The algorithm works like this:

1. Given a frame, the packer attaches a widget to a particular side (top, bottom, left, or right).

2. The space used up by the widget is taken off from the space available in the frame, an area called the *parcel*. If the widget does not fill the parcel completely (if the parcel is wider or taller than the area sliced for the widget), then that space is essentially wasted. This is, in fact, the reason for supporting additional **Frame** widgets to make the best use of the space.

3. The next widget is then placed into the remaining space, and once again the widget can attach itself to the top or bottom or one of sides to use up the available space.

4. Note that all widgets that specify a particular anchor point will be grouped together and share that space. Thus, if you specify multiple widgets with a left anchor, they will be organized left-to-right within the frame. If you want to do more complex layouts (as in the **Scale** widget example), you need to create separate frames.

The available options to the packer method are listed in Table 15-16. Like other elements of the Tk system, options are specified as a dictionary to the **pack** method. If you do not specify an option, the packer geometry manager inserts widgets from top to bottom.

The **padx**, **pady**, **ipadx**, and **ipady** properties accept a string, rather than a numeric value. Depending on the value's suffix, the value is interpreted either as pixels, centimeters, inches, millimeters, or points. For values other than pixels, the geometry manager interrogates the window manager and determines the screen resolution and

Property	Description
side	The side of the frame to which the widget should be added. Should be one of **left**, **right**, **top**, or **bottom**.
fill	Specifies whether the widget should fill up the space in the parcel in the x or y direction. You can also specify **both** to fill in both directions or **none** to prevent filling altogether. The **ipadx** or **ipady** options can be used to specify some additional blank padding space around the widget within the parcel.
expand	Specifies whether the widget should expand to take up all of the remaining space after the other widgets have been placed. This is useful for **Textbox** widgets where you are defining an outer menu and toolbar and you want the main widget to take up all the remaining space.
padx, pady	The spacing between widgets, specified in pixels, millimeters, inches, or points (see also Table 15-17).
ipadx, ipady	The spacing around a widget that is "filling" the space provided by the parcel. Specified in pixels, millimeters, inches, or points (see also Table 15-17).

Table 15-16. *Options to the **pack** Method*

density to decide how many actual pixels to use. For example, on a typical Windows screen running at 96dpi, a specification of "1i" would introduce padding of 96 pixels. The valid suffixes are listed in Table 15-17.

Grid

The Grid geometry manager works in an identical fashion to tables within HTML. Individual widgets are placed into a grid of rows and columns. Individual widgets are confined to each cell within the grid, but individual cells can be made to span more than one row or column if required.

The **grid** method is the interface to the Grid geometry manager. You specify the location of each widget according to the row and column in which it should appear. The final size of the grid is based on the maximum row and column size that you specify. The properties for the **grid** method are listed in Table 15-18.

Placer

The placer works slightly differently than the other two geometry managers. Whereas the packer and grid work on the basis of aligning widgets according to the other widgets on the page, the placer allows you to specify very precisely where you want a widget to be placed. The specification is based on the location and size of the window into which the widget is placed. If you consider each window to be similar to a cell within the grid manager, you should get the idea. The widget is then placed into the window that is created through this process. Because of the explicit location specification, you must be careful to ensure that you don't inadvertently overlap widgets.

Suffix	Description
none	Size is calculated in pixels.
c	Size is interpreted as on-screen centimeters.
i	Size is interpreted as on-screen inches.
m	Size is interpreted as on-screen millimeters.
p	Size is interpreted as printer's points (1 point is approximately 1/72 inch). This is the same unit as the point size used when specifying font sizes.

Table 15-17.   *Padding Character Suffixes*

Property	Value
column	The column in which to insert the widget.
columnspan	The number of columns that the widget should span within the grid.
row	The row in which to insert the widget.
rowspan	The number of rows that the widget should span within the grid.
sticky	Defines the side of the parent widget to which the widget will stick. Should be specified as 0 or more of the characters **n**, **s**, **e**, or **w**. If none are specified, the widget becomes centered within its cell. If both **n** and **s** (or **e** and **w**) are specified, then the widget stretches to fill the height (or width) of the cell. If all four are specified, then the widget grows to fill the entire cell.
padx, pady	The spacing between widgets, specified in pixels, millimeters, inches, or points (see Table 15-17).
ipadx, ipady	The spacing around a widget that is "filling" the space provided by the parcel. Specified in pixels, millimeters, inches, or points (see Table 15-17).

Table 15-18.   *Properties for the Grid Geometry Manager*

The specification for the size of the window itself is defined in relation to the widget's parent (either a **Window** or **Frame** or other container widget). Armed with this principle, you can specify one of the following:

1. The location (in pixels) and size of the window within the parent.
2. The location and size of the window in relation to the parent.
3. A combination of the two, so you can have a fixed size but a variable location, or a fixed location but a variable size.

Thus, you can have a widget centered within a parent that expands with the parent, increasing both the border and widget size. These options are incredibly useful for **Canvas**, **Text**, and other widgets where you want to expand the display area without affecting the other widgets within the window.

The interface to the placer manager is via the **place** method to your widgets. The key/value pairs accepted by the method are listed in Table 15-19.

Property	Description
in	The widget (object) that the widget should be placed relative to. The value must be a valid widget object and must either be the window parent or a descendant of the window parent. You must also ensure that the widget and its parent are both descendants of the same window.
x, y	The *x* (horizontal) and *y* (vertical) coordinates to use as the anchor point for the widget. See Table 15-17 for a list of valid qualifiers for the number.
relx, rely	The relative *x* (horizontal) coordinate within the parent window. The number should be specified as a floating-point number, where 0.0 refers to the left edge of the parent and 1.0 refers to the right edge. Thus the setting 0.5 would center the widget in the parent.
anchor	Defines which point of the window should be treated as the anchor point. Uses the normal **n**, **ne**, **e**, **se**, **s**, **sw**, **w**, and **nw** values.
width, height	Specifies the width or height of the window. See Table 15-17 for a list of valid qualifiers for the values. Note that in both cases the measurement defines the outer width of the window, including any border.
relwidth, relheight	The relative width or height of the window compared to the size of the parent, where 0.5 means the window is half as big as the parent and 1.0 means that the window and parent are the same width or height.
bordermode	One of **inside** (default), **outside**, or **ignore**. If set to **inside**, then the area for the window is calculated less any border on the parent. If **outside**, it includes the area set by the parent's border. If set to **ignore**, then the calculations are taken irrespective of the border size, making the entire parent window available for use.

Table 15-19.   *Properties for the Placer Geometry Manager*

Note   *The x, relx, y, and rely settings can be combined. A value of 0.5 for relx and 5 for x would place the widget five pixels to the right of the center of the parent. The same is true for width, relwidth, height, and relheight, where a specification of 1.0 for relwidth and 5 for width would produce a window five pixels smaller than the parent.*

For more examples of using Tk, see Chapter 4 of *Python Annotated Archives*. The code from this book is downloadable from my web site (**www.mcwords.com**).

The Complete Reference

Python

Part III

Application Development

The
Complete
Reference

Chapter 16

Using Python
as a RAD Tool

Developing applications is a cutthroat business, especially now with the explosion of the Internet. In the time it takes you to have an idea and discuss it with someone, somebody else could already be two steps ahead of you. The quicker you can convert your idea into an application, the faster you can get to market or get exposure for your application so it becomes the standard by which all similar applications are judged.

The problem is that programming is a complex task. No matter how competent a programmer you are, there will always be algorithms that need to be developed and sequences and steps that need to implemented—and all of this code needs to be typed in by someone as well!

As if that weren't enough to cope with, you've also got to debug and optimize the code to make sure your application runs at a reasonable speed and doesn't fall over when a user clicks in the wrong place, enters the wrong value, or forgets to make space on their disk for storing some data.

There are no easy solutions: we're still not in the realm of "Star Trek" where we can ask the computer to write a program to reconfigure the warp engine for greater efficiency, but there are certain programming languages out there today that are more capable than others, and within those languages there are tools, extensions, and facilities that we can use to make the whole development process easier.

What RAD Really Is

RAD, Rapid Application Development, is all about developing an application in the shortest possible time while still creating an application that is stable, usable, and good enough for alpha, beta, or even the final product delivery. Ultimately, RAD is about making all applications easier to develop, and that requires a specific type of language and environment.

RAD-developed applications tend to follow a slightly different route than your typical application. Often development is done "on the hoof" using a combination of interactive sessions, small tests on algorithms and procedures, and using as much reusable content as possible. Although it's likely that a lot of work goes into thinking about the development design and process, in all likelihood there's probably not much more than a few notes on a piece of paper and gratuitous use of comments within the code to describe what's going on.

That's not to say in any way that a RAD application is substandard or badly developed. Having been involved in many different projects over the years, from those heavily planned and designed to those coded using RAD techniques, I'd have to side with the latter method when it comes to the quality of the finished product. This is probably because the amount of testing that goes into each individual component is heavier than may be applied to a finished application as a whole (see "Development Lifecycle" later in this chapter).

RAD Requirements

There are no hard and fast rules or international standards on how, or what, makes an environment applicable for RAD, but here are a few of the key components that I found make RAD programming easier, irrespective of the underlying language:

- **Library and extension availability.**   One of the most obvious areas where you can aim to increase the speed of development is through the use of external libraries and modules. It should be obvious that using **smtplib** and adjusting your code accordingly is much quicker than redeveloping the SMTP interface that matches how you want it to work.

  Also part of the library/extension problem is the issue of interfaces. Whether you are developing a stand-alone application that needs its own GUI (built on Tk/Gnome/Qt/X Windows/Cocoa/Carbon, etc.) or through a web interface, it's still an element that needs to be addressed. The quicker you can develop that interface, the quicker you can get your product out the door.

- **Object orientation.**   I may have alienated a large number of you just by mentioning this term. OO *isn't* the solution to everybody's programming needs, in much the same way that Python doesn't suit all tasks. But OO does lend itself well to the RAD experience because it can make adding new methods, classes, and extensions to your applications significantly easier. OO also makes reuse of your code at a later stage much easier, especially useful on your next RAD project.

- **Code reuse.**   Over the years you'll produce countless functions, classes, and extensions that can be useful in all sorts of applications beyond the original application that you developed. Being able to easily reuse this code, without it taking additional time to convert it into a suitable module or to make it publicly available as an extension or library, should help to improve your development time on new projects.

- **Transparent programming.**   Many languages give you the ultimate in flexibility when it comes to managing the environment in which your application works. You can control everything from how objects and variables are destroyed, through to the allocation of suitable memory for the information you want to hold in memory. All of this is very useful, but it also becomes a major requirement. Getting that memory allocation figure right is vital: too much and you waste memory and slow your application; two little and you risk crashes.

  With RAD applications, you need a language that handles all these elements for you, so you don't need to worry about how much memory you need, or how to delete variables to free up memory when you've finished with them (called garbage collection). All you want to worry about is handling and processing the information you have and achieving your goal.

- **Ease of use.**   Programming is not fun if you have to spend time working out how to do different actions in the language. An experienced programmer will obviously have an advantage, but even programmers who know the language forward and backward can be tripped up by odd interfaces or unspecific semantics that provide too much flexibility and not enough structure. Others can be slowed down just by figuring out the method required to achieve a result. Sorting arrays or handling data by keywords are classic examples that in some languages are quick and in others time consuming. Documentation can help, as can simple comments.

- **Fast development lifecycle.**   Developing any application is a time-consuming process, so the last thing you want is to have to spend time waiting for your source code to be compiled into the application before you can test whether the changes you've made have worked. An average application even on a fast machine will take a few minutes to compile. A large application could take hours, and huge applications the size of Microsoft Word or Mozilla could take days. Can you imagine waiting for days before testing whether a few bug fixes have worked?

Any or all of the above have the potential to reduce the development time and ultimately make life easier for the average programmer. Remember, we're talking here purely about easing the steps between the idea in the brain the final product, and wherever possible reducing the effects of any bottlenecks on that process.

Possible RAD Solutions

Given the list that we worked out in the previous section, a number of languages automatically suggest themselves as possibilities for RAD. Don't skip this section. One size does not fit all, and one language does not suit all programmers or, more importantly, all solutions. The focus in this chapter is why Python is better than others for RAD, so let's compare abilities and facilities between Python and some of the other top solutions out there.

Pascal/Modula-2

Pascal is often the first language that people are exposed to, as it's easy to learn. Pascal actually has a good history as an application development language: much of the Mac OS was written in Pascal, and it remained one of the most popular language alternatives for programming right up until support by Apple was dropped at about the same time as Mac OS 8 was developed.

Modula-2 has a much lower profile. It was developed in the 1980s as a heavily object-oriented version of Pascal, along with some other changes including a real-time environment and multithreading ability, even on platforms that didn't normally support multithreading.

Both languages have huge libraries and, to a greater or lesser extent, object-orientation capability. They also handled variable management and garbage collection for most situations, which was one of the reasons they were so heavily pushed for new users.

However, both suffer from the long development cycle in common with other compiled languages, and neither offers the advanced interface or systems programming abilities of languages like C/C++ or even Perl or Python. One success story in the Pascal RAD arena is Delphi, a Windows-only development environment—but therein lies a limitation compared to Python, which offers transparent cross-platform development.

C/C++/Objective C

Can we really call C/C++ a RAD alternative? Well, some would argue yes. Armed with some of the tools available, such as Microsoft's Visual Studio or the new development environment offered by Cocoa (the new interface builder for Mac OS X), you can see why some consider it a viable alternative.

Using Cocoa or Visual Studio, for example, we can build an interface visually and add the necessary hooks, callbacks, and event handlers afterwards to complete the application. In fact, with Cocoa it's possible to develop a complex application in a very short space of time, simply by dragging and dropping the components into the windows and dialog boxes and adding a very small amount of code. Cocoa and the development environment add all of the bells and whistles, including resizable elements, automatic scrollbars, and other artifacts without the need to write a single line of code.

At the end of the day, however, it still suffers from some of the more significant problems mentioned in our list of requirements. The lifecycle is too long, and even with the tools and libraries offered by Microsoft, Apple, GNU, and others we still have to manage our own variables and garbage collection—all of which add at least 50% to the development schedule, no matter how good you are at programming in C's various forms.

Perl

I've been told that Perl is the language that non-Perl programmers love to hate. Skipping over semantic details for the moment, theoretically there is not a lot of difference between Perl and Python programming. They are both scripting languages; both offer a quick turnaround in development time; and they both have a huge collection of extensions and interfaces and other enhancements.

Perl's downside is that despite all the work put in by an army of developers, it still remains largely a systems, administration, and text-processing language. Object orientation is available, but it's not an integrated or required part of the programming process. Also, over time, Perl becomes more difficult to maintain and support, as the language itself is not the most readable. The Perl slogan, "There Is More Than One Way To Do It" (TIMTOWTDI), becomes a curse, not an advantage, when you realize just how much the Perl interpreter makes up its own mind on what it thinks you were doing.

APPLICATION DEVELOPMENT

Tcl

Tcl is an often forgotten language even though it has a very popular following. Tcl was primarily developed as an extension to the traditional Unix shell. The structure actually closely follows your typical shell script, and if you need access to GUI you have the Tk interface, which is also used and supported by Python.

Also, Tcl can be embedded into traditional C/C++ applications, like Perl and Python, to provide scripting facilities. However, data handling is not one of Tcl's strong points. The strong data types supported by Python are much more powerful and flexible, and the object-oriented interface is not one of the most intuitive.

Tcl also suffers from a distinct personality problem: it's never really shrugged off the advanced shell script image, and it's therefore not as practical for many programming jobs because the flexibility of the language just isn't there.

BASIC

BASIC is probably one of the best known languages, as many of the first computers came with a BASIC interpreter built into the machine so you could start writing programs immediately. However, although BASIC allows for very quick development times, most versions do not support classes, object orientation, strong data types, or the high level of programming offered by Python. Extending BASIC is also not easy; it was never really designed to reuse code from somewhere else.

Why Python?

We've looked at what RAD environments need and what languages are available that may or may not fit the bill. Although I've painted a slightly negative picture for some of these languages, there's no reason why you couldn't use any of them for developing applications, either traditionally or using RAD techniques.

In many cases, Python has actually borrowed many of the features and advantages of the languages that we looked at—as well as some others—in order to provide the functionality that you may be familiar with. Python won't always fit the bill: it was never designed to replace all these other languages for every situation. As much as I love Python, I still use Perl for a significant part of my development projects, and there are projects for which I use C or C++ just for the improvement in speed it has over Perl or Python.

However, RAD has specific requirements, and ultimately it's about making the programming process easier, and none of the languages we've looked at so far fit the bill precisely. For some, Python won't fit the bill either, but it does tackle some of our major points:

■ Fast development lifecycle

■ Easy to use and program

- High-level, object-oriented approach
- Easy code reuse and large extension library

Python also provides a few extras that, while not vital to RAD, do help the process along.

Development Lifecycle

The most important aspect of a RAD environment is the speed with which you can develop your applications. Ignoring all the elements we've already or are about to discuss, one of the most significant time wasters is the language itself. If you have a language and environment that imposes a naturally time-wasting development cycle, you're already in negative equity when it comes to rapidly developing an application.

Compiled Languages

Languages such as C/C++, Pascal, and many others are compiled languages, which means that we have to write the source, compile, link, and then execute. The full sequence is as follows:

1. Edit the source code.
2. Compile the code into object files.
3. Link the objects files and standard library into an executable file.
4. Start the application.
5. Test its behavior.
6. Start the debugger.
7. Debug the application.
8. Stop the application.
9. Go back to step 1.

The process gets even longer when you consider that a typical application will be made up of a number of source files, one or more of which will need to be compiled before we can link and execute them into the final application.

Also, the final application is executable, so if something goes wrong in the application we can't quickly drop out and find out what went wrong. We'd probably have to start it off in a debugger, and even then we can't make changes to the code as it executes—we can only identify the part that went wrong before going back and editing the start file back at step 1.

Scripting Languages

Scripting languages like Perl, Python, Tcl, and many others offer a different solution. Scripting languages are so called because an interpreter executes a script. In essence, our script does nothing without the abilities of the interpreter—the interpreter provides all of the functionality, from the interfaces with the user and system through to the basics of variables and storing information.

The major benefit of a scripting language is that we can eliminate those compilation stages to shorten our lifecycle. In fact, the scripting language development looks something like this:

1. Edit the source code.

2. Start the application.

3. Test it's behavior.

4. Stop the application.

5. Go back to step 1.

With Python, we can actually go one stage further. Python's parser is available within any running application. We can drop into a command-line instance of the interpreter and edit and try out statements without going back and editing the original code. Furthermore, using **eval**, **exec**, or **execfile** we can make modifications to the code without ever terminating the application.

If you are using external modules to support your application, you also have the ability to reload the external module while the application is still running through the **reload** function. We can make changes to classes, functions, and methods all without ever stopping the application. For single-run applications this doesn't make a lot of difference, but for those applications that are perpetually running, say a network server or a CGI application, we'll never need to physically stop the service to make any changes to how it operates.

In practice, therefore, we can shorten the development lifecycle of a Python application to just three steps:

1. Start the application.

2. Test its behavior.

3. Edit program code and return to step 2.

What generally happens with Python is slightly more complex but ultimately provides quicker development, which obviously helps when it comes to rapid application development.

With Python you tend to prototype and try and out different methods and techniques interactively. You also tend to test the individual components of a Python application in more or less isolation before bonding them together into the final application. Because of the object-based operation, it's very easy to integrate the components into the final application without worrying about compatibility.

We therefore end up with a two-tiered development process that looks like this:

1. Test the components.

2. Edit the program code.

3. If the unit is complete, go to step 4; otherwise go to step 1.

4. Test the application; return to step 2

High-Level Programming

Languages like C/C++, and to a lesser extent Perl, sit closer to the system than they do to the user. They all allow you to get very close to the operating system on which they are running, which is great for people dealing with such low levels of operability.

We're dealing with applications, and while we don't necessarily want to be completely shielded from the lower levels, we don't want to have to cope with them either. For example, when getting a list of files in a directory according to a pattern, we don't want to process the filenames ourselves—we want a function that returns exactly what we want, a list of matching files.

At the top level it's the simplicity of Python that makes it so easy to use and understand. We don't have to worry about the underlying complexities of variables, garbage handling, or memory management. We also get access to a large library of extensions and interfaces to the underlying system that makes solving problems in Python so much easier.

Easier code generation makes for short programs. Python programs are often a fraction of the size of their C/C++ and even Perl equivalents. Shorter, clearer programs mean faster programming times, easier support and modification, and less opportunity for errors, all of which shorten the development process even further.

Instant Cross-Platform Compatibility

It's not everybody's primary concern, but for some of us cross-platform capability is as important to the development process as the interface you provide to your users. Many languages are cross-platform compatible: C/C++ is available for nearly all platforms, and you can get Perl, Tcl, and one version or another of BASIC for a similarly large number of other platforms.

However, most languages suffer from some form of incompatibility or limitation. C/C++ is the obvious weak link. Because it produces binary executables, we need to recompile the software for each platform we want to support the application for. And that's only half the story: there's also no common interface for building applications for a particular GUI. You'll almost certainly need to redevelop the application for a given platform just to make use of the platform's interface.

The other languages we've mentioned have got a head start. BASIC, Perl, and Tcl are all interpreted languages. Since we're not dealing with binary source, we can more or less take the application from one platform and execute it on the other. We still run into the same interface troubles; even with Python there is no one interface. The Tk toolkit is supported under Python on Windows, Mac OS, and Unix, which covers most bases and offers more integration than Perl, which currently supports Tk only under Windows and Unix.

APPLICATION DEVELOPMENT

The benefit with Python is that so many of the other problems are already solved for us. The development time for a native UI will be just as long as for C/C++, but we don't have to worry about the other aspects.

Python and OOP

Python does offer one of the strongest, most flexible, and, more importantly, easiest to use object oriented systems. OOP with C++ is very powerful, but it's complex, especially for new users who often have trouble grasping the basics of object orientation, let alone the complexities of the C++ implementation. Python's OOP implementation is much simpler than that offered in C++ and therefore offers the power without the complexity.

OOP is also an integral part of the language, and there's no reason why you shouldn't use it for all the areas of your application. Because of its simple implementation you shouldn't ever have to worry about how to achieve OOP in Python, helping to shorten that development time even further. We can also very easily reuse Python's objects without the baggage associated with making C++ objects cross-platform compatible.

Crossbreeding with Python

Python can be extended using C and C++ to provide additional functionality, to improve speed or just to provide an interface to a system not otherwise accessible from the native Python interpreter. We can also embed Python into a C/C++ application to enable us to provide a scripting component similar to Visual Basic or the macro languages supported by some applications.

This "crossbreeding" of C/C++ and Python leads to some advanced opportunities. Imagine, for example, developing your Python application using RAD techniques, only to find a performance bottleneck. You could rewrite that portion of your application in C and incorporate the extension into your application without making any other changes, while still reaping the benefits of much faster execution.

Python: RAD on Steroids

So what does this chapter really mean?

At the end of the day I like to think of Python as RAD on steroids. It has all the right ingredients and in all the right proportions. We can use Python to quickly produce an application that's automatically supported on a number of platforms, that took little time to write and even less time to debug and later support and update.

For those bits that need a speed boost, we can rewrite them in C, and in fact if we need to we could easily migrate the majority of the application to C or C++ and still use Python as the glue code that binds everything together to make our stand-alone application.

We'll be looking at the best ways to approach RAD generally and specifically in Python in the next chapter. We'll also look at how to make decisions about migrating Python applications into C/C++ hybrids. If you want more information on extending and embedding Python, see Chapters 26 and 27.

Chapter 17

Application Development with Python

405

Anything that helps the development process is a bonus—never look a gift horse in the mouth! Whether it's RAD specific or just a useful addition to the overall process that shaves off a few minutes, hours, or days from your schedule, or that prevents brain drain and late-night caffeine-fueled sessions, an off-the-shelf tool in any form is likely to make your life easier. Integrated Development Environments (IDEs) offer a unified editing/execution/debugging environment that can help to reduce the amount of time spent switching between applications and environments to test different elements.

Also useful are the various extensions and additional modules available from central repositories such as the Vaults of Parnassus or one of the many commercial development shops like PythonWare. If these don't suit you, then you could try rolling your own extensions or, if you're coming from the C/C++ side, embedding Python into your own application to add instant functionality to your application. If your application is web or Internet based, then another solution is to use Zope or Jython.

In the previous chapter we looked at some of the goals and requirements for RAD and how Python solved some of the bottlenecks to rapid application development. In this chapter we're going to take a more general look at some of the available solutions for aiding in the development process when using Python.

It's also worth thinking about how you program and develop your ideas. Do you build it bit by bit and make stuff as you go along, or do you try and plan it out? We'll be looking at the different alternatives and other issues you should be thinking about when writing Python applications.

The aim here is to demonstrate just what goes into typical Python and what steps are involved, along with where to get help when you want it. If you want a quicker guide to additional Python information, check Appendix B.

Integrated Development Environments

Anything that helps to improve the speed at which you write your applications can be seen as a solution to the RAD problem. How you program is as important as what you include and use within the application you are building.

At the end of the day, choosing your programming environment comes down to personal taste and to a greater or lesser extent the platform on which you are working. For Unix/Linux users, the frequently used environment is EMACS or vi, sometimes in association with a shell and other times using the built-in development environment. Within Windows you'd be amazed at how many use Notepad or Wordpad and a command-tool window for their development. Others prefer a programmer's editor such as Kedit or UltraEdit, and others will use the Windows port of EMACS. On the Mac, you'll probably use BBEdit, EMACS, or Pepper.

All of these options suffer from a lack of integration with Python itself. Sure, some of them can mark up Python scripts and highlight the different components. Some will even let you execute the Python script from within the editor without changing to a command window or opening the Python application. None, however, lets us interactively modify the code while it's running, or offers debug facilities or the ability to view Python modules, classes, and objects in a structure format.

For those sorts of features you need an IDE, an integrated development environment. There are quite a few possible solutions available, depending on what platform you are using to develop your Python applications.

IDLE

IDLE is a fairly basic IDE written entirely in Python, making use of the **Tkinter** GUI building interface that we looked at in Chapter 15. Because IDLE is written in Python and Tk, you should be able to run it on any platform that supports both systems. Initially you are offered a slightly enhanced interactive shell window, similar to what you'd get on the command line but with the addition of scrollback and cut and paste. You also get a fully Python-aware editor that adds code highlighting and completion, a class browser for viewing the classes and class components in a module, and an interactive debugger. You can see a sample of the major components in Figure 17-1.

Note	*One of the nice features of the IDLE interface is that its menus are Tk "tear-off" menus, so we can take the debugger and editing menus off and use them as toolbars.*

The IDLE debugger offers a similar set of features as the core debugger offered by the interactive debugger interface, so we can step through, set breakpoints, and set

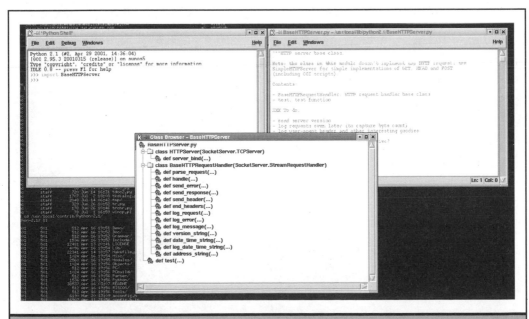

Figure 17-1.   *The IDLE IDE in action*

variable watches. What we can't do is look at specific locations in memory or the contents of variables. There is also no way to monitor timings or use the profiler, but these are all minor annoyances rather than major problems.

That doesn't mean that IDLE is devoid of problems. You can easily lock the IDE up by running a script or application that doesn't terminate—you can't use Control-C to stop the execution of a loop or a web server as used in our example. Also, the windows occasionally fail to redraw if they become hidden in any way, and updates stop entirely if the script you are executing does not terminate normally.

PythonWin

PythonWin, as the name suggests, is an IDE for Python supported only under Windows. It offers a slightly better interface than that offered by IDLE, although the basics of debugger, class browser, interactive window, and editor are available. The editor is very useful as it allows you to autocomplete module, class, method, and function names during typing, in much the same way that Microsoft Word offers autocomplete. You can see a sample of PythonWin in Figure 17-2.

The debugger is more extensive than that offered in IDLE, providing watches, code inspection, and an interactive window that can be used to modify and change

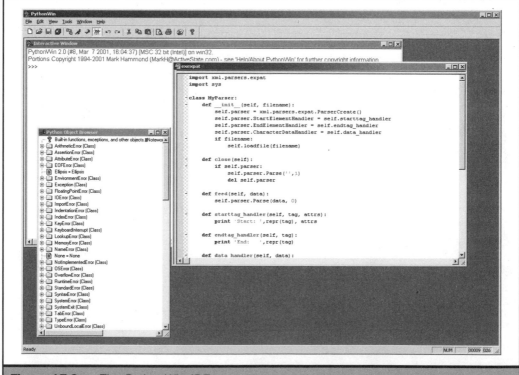

Figure 17-2.   *The PythonWin IDE*

components in situ while executing your application. Execution is still not ideal, however, and it's not impossible to end up in a situation where the IDE locks up and requires a forced termination to allow you to continue.

MacPython IDE

The MacPython IDE is naturally Mac OS specific and comes with the standard MacPython distribution. Written by another member of the Python family, literally, in the form of Just van Rossum, MacPython offers a very Mac-like alternative to IDLE while still providing most of the IDLE functionality.

The IDE incorporates an interactive session along with a basic editor, debugger, and code profiler. The editor *is* basic, offering simple indentation and editing facilities but without the element highlighting, coloring, or autocomplete features seen in the other IDEs we've looked at in this section. Programmers used to editors like EMACS and BBEdit will be somewhat disappointed, but the rest of the IDE's benefits more than compensate. Especially useful is the module browser—one of the best of those offered. You can see a sample of the IDE in action in Figure 17-3.

Figure 17-3. *The MacPython IDE*

Komodo

Komodo is a commercial IDE from ActiveState, the people behind the original port of Perl to Windows and of the ActivePython product and other Perl and Python tools, as well as other development tools primarily for the Windows platform. Komodo itself is available for Windows, Linux, and Solaris, but you must get the ActiveState Perl, Python, and Tcl distributions to make use of these in the IDE.

Komodo is an attempt to address the needs of the modern programmer by offering an interactive development environment that accommodates more than one language. Komodo 1.0 supports Perl, Python, JavaScript, XML, and Tcl with a project manager, editor, debugger, and execution environment. In addition Komodo also supports intelligent editing for HTML, XML, XSLT, C, C++, C#, IDL, Java, JavaScript, Lua, Makefile, PHP, Pascal, and ordinary text. In addition to the normal indentation, formatting, and code highlighting, you can also have the code marked up for possible errors as you work. As in Microsoft Word, suspect areas are underlined in red, and you can continue typing and go back and make the changes later.

You can see from the screenshot in Figure 17-4 that Komodo offers a very slick interface, and the package is in fact based on the Mozilla browser that came out of the Netscape development team. A browser may not seem the obvious choice for a development environment, but many of the core components of Mozilla actually lend themselves very well to any interface. Mozilla also allows for extensions and plug-ins that are used by Komodo to support more languages in the interactive environment.

Unfortunately, Komodo is a commercial product. Although you can obtain a free license, it's for noncommercial use only. A full development license with Komodo costs $295, with free updates and usage for a year—you'll need to renew that each year to continue using it. You'll also need a development license for ActivePython and any other languages you want to use. This position is understandable: ActiveState is a commercial company that pays the likes of Mark Hammond (Python, and author of PythonWin) and Gurusamy Sarathy (Perl) to develop the Windows extensions for the different languages.

However, Mozilla is free, as are Perl, Python, Tcl, and the XML standard, and the costs for developing with ActiveState tools are quite high. Personally, I use Komodo for much of the Windows development I do because it offers a much more coherent interface, although I continue to use EMACS and the Interactive tools under Unix/Linux and BBEdit or Pepper on the Mac.

Visual Studio/VisualPython

Microsoft's Visual Studio.NET initiative includes a number of innovative new features, including supporting a new intermediary language that applications can be compiled to from more or less any other language. You can then share the components that you've written in all these languages in your final application. For example, you could combine a text processor written in Perl with a network service written in Python with a front

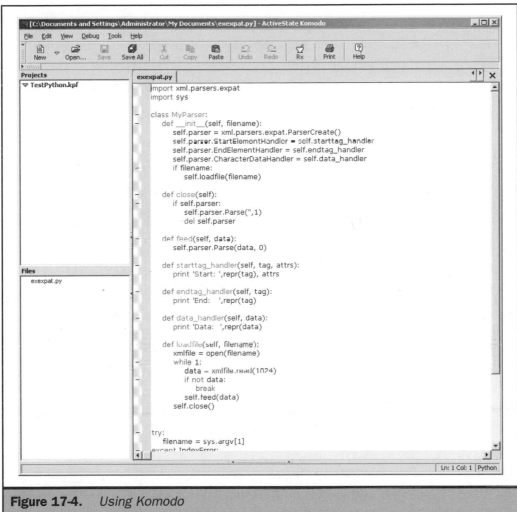

Figure 17-4. *Using Komodo*

end developed using C/C++ or the new C#, and then bond all of the elements together to make the final application.

As part of the new framework, the new Visual Studio development environment that previously supported only C/C++ and Visual Basic can now be updated with support for other languages. ActiveState, who also develop the Komodo system we've already looked at, also supports a new VisualPython component for the .NET framework. Still in beta at the beginning of July, and still with much of the .NET framework to be worked out on Microsoft's side, VisualPython does provide a tempting alternative to both Komodo and other IDEs.

The final version will include support for all of the current Visual Studio functions, including a syntax-aware editor with code completion, a project management tool for handling multifile applications, and a debugger. Based on past experience of ActiveState's tools, especially in the Perl arena, VisualPython is certainly a product to keep an eye on.

BlackAdder

BlackAdder is a fully commercial IDE (costing around $400) written using the QT GUI environment used by window managers such as KDE. QT itself is supported under Windows and Unix and provides an editor with syntax highlighting and code folding, however you have no code completion. The debugger offers the same basic tools as those available through the standard Python distribution tools, but without the ability to set watches on functions and variables.

The interface is the strong point with BlackAdder. Being based on QT you get a much more professional-looking interface, and you can customize the interface with your own buttons and toolbars as you can with Visual Studio. Also included is a visual form-designer, allowing you to click and drag window components—buttons, text boxes, scrollbars, and so on—onto a form and have the backing code written for you. The form designer works with QT and requires you to use the PyQT interface system, but QT is arguably better than Tk and offers a more OS-consistent interface.

BlackAdder is not without problems, though. The interface, while powerful, is not perfect—some oddities seem designed to drive you mad. There is also no way of executing a script without using the debugger, so there's no way to quickly run the application and go back to the editor. The IDE also locks up occasionally, and the editor will, for no apparent reason, decide that the file you are loading is not valid Python, even though it probably is.

WingIDE

The WingIDE is another commercial product, and in terms of its aims it sits at about the same level as Komodo. It supports an IDE for a number of different languages and includes an editor with command completion and syntax highlighting, as well as a very handy tool for navigating straight to the definition of different functions within your modules. You also get a useful module browser for navigating through modules, either by entity definitions or docstrings, and a reasonable debugger, albeit without watches.

WingIDE is certainly one of the better of the tools available, but you can occasionally suffer from "window glut" as too many windows fill the screen with no way to control their appearance. It also suffers from the same bug as IDLE, where a simple script can lock up the entire application. However, it's certainly promising if you want a serious environment for development.

Python Standard Library

Beyond unpacking and compiling your latest Python distribution, did you actually look at the contents? Guido and the rest of the development team have done a stunning job in providing a combination of a rich extension library—many of examples of which we've already seen—and a great combination of examples, samples, and additional tools.

While I don't condone plagiarism, looking at somebody else's code is often the quickest way to work out how to solve a particular problem. Documentation is always useful, but it's also just as useful to see samples and examples of the different modules in action. There really is no point in reinventing the wheel if somebody has already done a lot of the work for you.

In this section I want to give you some quick pointers as to what's provided in the standard Python distribution in the form of examples and demos, along with information on the standard module set and how to configure your Python distribution to support additional extensions and modules not enabled in the base package.

Demos, Examples, and Samples

The first place you should start looking for more information is actually within a specific module. For example, if you want to know how to use the IMAP library, checking the **imaplib** module will reveal a test function at the end of the module. You can use this as a basis for your own scripts. Other modules follow suit with many of the extensions (as opposed to the base modules such as **sys** and **os**) including test sections.

Within the standard Python distribution on any platform you'll also find demos and examples for the following areas:

- **Classes (Demo/classes):** Examples of how to build classes, handle class inheritance, and overload operators. All of the examples here provide classes for operating on special data types, including rational numbers, vectors, and dates.

- **Curses (Demo/curses):** How to build interfaces using the text-based curses system. Most of the scripts in here are fun rather than practical, but all help to explain how to build a curses-based application. Alternatively, they can provide a useful diversion in the form of **life.py** or a more seasonal demonstration in the form of **xmas.py**.

- **DNS utilities (Demo/dns):** A DNS client module and some sample scripts for retrieving information from the DNS system.

- **Remote Procedure Calls (RPC) (Demo/rpc):** The RPC system is a toolset for calling a function from a client that is actually executed on a remote server. For example, you could use RPC to query the status of a remote server without having to physically log in and check the information. The scripts in this section provide an interface to the Sun RPC system and could be useful if you are dealing with data structures that need to be serialized for interaction with another system.

RPC in its original format was platform and OS specific; even when used with the XDR (eXternal Data Representation) problems could occur. The SOAP (Simple Object Access Protocol) and XML-RPC use XML to naturalize the request and response, allowing you to use SOAP and XML-RPC on any platform.

- **Sample scripts (Demo/scripts):** A host of different scripts that do everything from factorizing numbers and summarizing your inbox through to creating an audio file in Morse code format from a string.

- **Sockets (Demo/sockets):** Socket programming is not just a case of opening the connection, sending some data, and closing the link. If you want to actually exchange information with a remote client, you'll need to handle problems like line termination and developing a protocol for communication. You'll find examples for building clients and servers using sockets as well as core network operations like multicasting and even a Telnet protocol client.

- **Threads (Demo/threads):** We looked at threads back in Chapter 9. Threads are easy, once you understand the basics, which are demonstrated here. You'll also find a useful example by Tim Peters that enables you to perform multiple calculations and obtain the results through the use of threads.

- **Tkinter (Demo/tkinter):** Everything from the basic application through to menus and even a Unix man page viewer are included here. You also get the progressive workings of a web viewer written entirely in HTML.

- **XML processing (Demo/xml):** How to parse and process XML documents. Much of the information here can be used for generic processing of any tag-based languages including XML, HTML, and SGML. We'll be looking at markup language processing in Chapter 20.

Alternatively, you can try looking at the applications in the Tools directory, which include the following:

- **Python compiler (Tools/compiler):** Looking over this module you'll get a good idea about the internal workings of the Python interpreter. The module provides a generic interface into the internal workings that allows you to sift through and find information in a script. The **demo.py** script in the tools directory, for example, will traverse an application, distilling a list of classes and methods.

- **FAQ Wizard (Tools/faqwiz):** A web/CGI-based interface for building and managing a FAQ (Frequently Asked Questions) document. The interface provides both a reader (end-user) interface for viewing and searching and a management interface for building a multilayered structure.

- **Python Freezer (Tools/freeze):** The **freeze** utility takes a Python project and bonds the Python source with the Python executable in order to make a stand-alone executable that can then be distributed to users without requiring them to have the Python interpreter. If you are creating applications under Mac OS, you might want to use the **BuildApplication** applet in the Python distribution.

- **IDLE (Tools/idle):** We looked at IDLE, a completely Python-derived IDE, earlier in this chapter. Looking over the code will tell you a lot about how to develop a Tk-based interface and how to execute and debug Python scripts.

- **Web checker (Tools/webchecker):** The web checker tool will traverse a directory tree or a URL and extract the links from the document to determine whether the site has any linking or other problems. It's a great tool to run over your website and do a sanity check, but it's not infallible, as any website that uses dynamic elements may fail to work properly. The scripts give some excellent background on processing HTML and accessing remote sites. They also give a good example about how to structure nested objects, which are used in the tool to record URLs and error information for different pages.

If you still can't find what you are looking for, then check the Vaults of Parnassus (see below) and Appendix B for a list of Python resources.

Standard Modules

Python comes with a huge standard module set that includes everything from the basics of interfacing to the OS through to different Internet protocols and text and XML processing systems. Although it's inevitable that you'll use some of these modules, it's worth checking through the modules that are supplied to see if one of them offers you an existing solution to your problems.

We've already covered most of these modules elsewhere, and a list of some of those supported by C extensions is shown later in this chapter. For a full list of the modules supported by Python see Appendix B.

Configuring the Standard Extensions

If you are compiling the standard distribution for yourself, you may want to modify the setup of the extension modules to enable additional functionality. For example, although the standard Python distribution comes with the necessary interfaces for integration with Tk, called Tkinter, they are not enabled by default.

You can configure which extensions are included by using the **Setup** file within the Modules directory in the Python distribution. The file is a standard text file similar in format to a Makefile. To enable different extension modules you'll need to uncomment lines and occasionally provide the locations of the libraries and include files required by the module in question. For example, to enable GDBM support, you need to uncomment and modify the line starting **gdbm** in the fragment shown below:

```
# Anthony Baxter's gdbm module.  GNU dbm(3) will require -lgdbm:
#
# First, look at Setup.config; configure may have set this for you.

gdbm gdbmmodule.c -I/usr/local/include -L/usr/local/lib -lgdbm
```

Many of the modules are preconfigured by the **configure** script used during the build process; others need to be manually enabled for them to work.

The exact list of modules varies from distribution to distribution, but for reference Table 17-1 lists the extension modules that are configured through this file, along with a description of the modules purpose and any notes that may be useful when enabling the module.

Module	Description
posix	Provides POSIX (Unix) system calls. Automatically enabled on POSIX-compatible operating systems, including Windows. Don't use this module directly; use the **os** module, which provides links through to the supported **posix** module functions.
sre	The Secret Labs regular expression library developed by Fredrik Lundh.
readline	Provides support for the GNU readline library, which provides line-by-line editing, input, command-line history, and other extensions useful when developing an application that either parses input on a line basis or uses line input. Remember that **readline** is covered by the GNU General Public License (GPL); if you supply a version of Python that is statically linked to the **readline** library, then you must abide by the GPL license. The alternative is to dynamically link to **readline** or supply the Python source with the binary. See the Python documentation for more details.

Table 17-1.   *Configurable Modules in the Python Distribution*

Module	Description
array	Support for fixed data type array objects.
math	Additional mathematical functions (**sin()**, **cos()**, **tan()**). Uses the standard C math library, normally enabled by default.
cmath	Additional mathematical functions (**sin()**, **cos()**, **tan()**) with support for complex numbers. Uses the standard C math library, normally enabled by default.
struct	Support for packing and unpacking binary structures such as those created through the C/C++ **struct** statement.
time	Standard time access and formatting functions. Enabled by default.
operator	Allows you to access the functions for supporting internal operators by name—for example, **add(a,b)** for **a+b**.
weakref	Basic weak reference support.
codecs	Used to provide access to the built-in codecs and codec registry used for translating text strings between Unicode, ASCII, and other character formats.
testcapi	Python C API test module.
unicodedata	Interface to the Unicode registry database to allow you to look up Unicode characters by name and also to devolve a Unicode string into its Unicode character descriptions.
locale	Access to the ISO C locale support functions for controlling string sorting algorithms and message output languages.
fcntl	File and I/O control interface to the fcntl and ioctl systems. Should be supported under most platforms.
pwd	Provides access to the Unix /etc/passwd database through the OS pwd calls. Only supported under Unix, BeOS through **cygwin** under Win32, and MacOS X.

Table 17-1.   *Configurable Modules in the Python Distribution* (continued)

Module	Description
grp	Provides access to the Unix /etc/group{s} database through the OS grp calls. Only supported under Unix, BeOS through **cygwin** under Win32, and MacOS X.
errno	POSIX errno values and corresponding strings. Only supported under POSIX-compatible operating systems.
select	Module for multiplexing I/O from different sources using the select() system. Support limited to Unix variants (but not all).
mmap	Interface to the Unix **mmap()** system call for mapping directly into memory. Supported under Unix and Win32.
xreadlines	Dynamic readline library support.
socket	Interface to the OS **socket()** network communication. The setup file provides lines suitable for non-SSL and SSL support, but you'll need the ssl and crypto libraries for it to work. The non-SSL variant should work on all platforms that implement the standard BSD socket system. Unix also allows support for SSL.
crypt	Interface to the crypt() system call under Unix for encrypting user passwords. You'll need to enable the **crypt** library under Linux and FreeBSD variants.
nis	Support for Sun's Network Information System(NIS), but not NIS+.
termios	Support for the POSIX tty I/O system. Support is limited to Unix variants.
resource	Handles the interface to the **rlimit** system for limiting resource usage. Support is limited to specific Unix variants.
audioop	A generic audio processing library; it should be supported under all platforms.
imageop	A generic image processing library; it should be supported under all platforms.

Table 17-1. *Configurable Modules in the Python Distribution* (continued)

Module	Description
rgbimg	A generic library for reading and writing SGI RGB image files. Although the file format supported is SGI specific, the library should be supported under any platform.
tkinter	The interface to the Tk Gui builder. You'll need to have the Tcl and Tk libraries installed first. You can download them from Scriptics (http://www.scriptics.com). You must compile Tcl first and then Tk. You can also add in support for the Python Image Library (PIL).
rotor	A Enigma machine–inspired encryption algorithm.
syslog	Interface to the syslog system logging daemon. Note that syslog is Unix specific.
dbm	Interface to the standard DBM library implementation. You'll need to use either the dbm or ndbm libraries. Unix only.
gdbm	Interface to the GDBM database library. You'll need the GNU gdbm library for it to work.
zlib	An interface for reading and writing files compressed using the gzip and compress tools. You'll need the zlib library, which is available from http://www.cdrom.com/pub/infozip/zlib/.
pyexpat	The Expat XML parser. You need the expat library from James Clark, http://expat.sourceforge.net. This provides the interface to the **xml.parsers.expat** module.
bsddb	Support for the BSD db database library. Note that support is currently limited to the old v1.85 version of the BSD libraries. A version supporting the new v3.x libraries can be found at http://electricrain.com/greg/python/bsddb3/.

Table 17-1.   *Configurable Modules in the Python Distribution* (continued)

You can find the active copy of the module in the **Config** directory in the main Python directory (usually /usr/local/lib/python#.#). To actually make any changes, you'll need to modify the Setup file in the source distribution and then run **make** within the Modules directory, or **make** in the parent to rebuild Python.

The individual modules and extensions will then be built and incorporated into the main Python library. If you have a dynamic Python installation, then the modules will be rebuilt for dynamic loading. For a static platform, the main Python library will be rebuilt and then the Python executable will be relinked to the new library.

Vaults of Parnassus

The Vaults of Parnassus (http://www.vex.net/parnassus/) is a website that was originally devoted to collating all of the module, example, and extension posts sent to the Python newsgroup (comp.lang.python). It's since become the focal point for new modules and extensions for Python, as well as a source of example scripts and demonstration applications that use Python either exclusively or in combination with other tools.

The vaults are best used as a method for finding a particular module or extension. For example, you can use the vaults to find interfaces to MySQL or PostgreSQL, XML parses, and many other extensions. Programmers coming from Perl may find the range of modules somewhat smaller than CPAN, but I think that can easily be countered by the fact that the Python standard library already contains many of the modules that you would otherwise have to download from CPAN.

That doesn't mean, however, that they are not looking for new submissions. If you have a module that you think others would find useful, make it available to the vaults.

Zope and Jython

If you are developing a web application, you could save yourself a significant amount of development time by using Zope. Zope publishes objects, so all you have to worry about is creating the classes and methods required to expose your information; Zope handles all of the CGI and database access for you. Since, from experience, designing the mechanisms for inputting and exporting information to/from a database makes up about 40% of the development process of the entire application, you can see where the savings can be made.

Jython attacks a similar problem from a different perspective. Jython is a complete Python interpreter, but it's written within the confines of Java. This allows you to create Python applications within Java so they can be executed on a client's machine—even if they don't have Python—and also to mix Python and Java elements into the same application.

See Chapter 21 for more information on these and other Web solutions written in and supported by Python.

The Complete Reference

Chapter 18

Distributing Python Modules

Once you've assembled your Python project, whether it's a full-blown application or a simple module, you'll need to package it in a format that will allow you to distribute it to other people.

There are two basic types of end-user, public and private. For a public version, you are creating a package that will be used by the public, either in a free or open source project or a piece of shareware or a commercial product. Alternatively, you can create a package that will be installed only by a select number of people, either as part of a custom (rather than mass-produced) commercial application or as part of another larger project. For example, you might be supplying Python CGI scripts as part of a website.

For private solutions, you can probably get by with creating a custom installation, or within reason by doing the installation by hand. In fact, when putting in a highly customized solution, this is probably the only solution available to you.

For stand-alone applications, you've got a bit more flexibility; although the exact solution will largely depend on how the package works, you can probably get away with just allowing people to copy it to a folder or directory on their machine. For more complex installations, you'll need to write some form of installation script. Herein lies the first problem. First, you need to worry about things like destination folders, then you need to worry about the installed location of Python itself—not everybody installs Python in /usr/local or C:\Python. Furthermore, things are complicated, but in different ways, if you want to support the application on the Mac as well (especially now that there are Mac OS and Mac OS X versions of the OS, which work very differently).

If you're supplying a module or extension to extend the capabilities of Python, things get even more complicated. For a standard (pure Python) module, all you need to do is copy the module into the right location. Finding that right location is the problem. When it comes to a C/C++ extension that also needs compiling before it's installed, you have a whole new set of problems to add to the location problem. Although there are techniques for compiling extensions under different platforms (see Chapter 26), they all rely on getting access to a file that is unique for each machine.

For a long time, to be honest, many of these problems were ignored. For those of you familiar with Perl, this may come as something of a shock. Fairly early on, Perl gained CPAN (the Comprehensive Perl Archive Network) and a companion module that would interface to and download modules and extensions to the language. CPAN itself also relies on a tool called MakeMaker, which is used within a Perl script and is full of configuration information in order to build a traditional Makefile. The Makefile is then responsible for building and ultimately installing the module into the Perl distribution.

Python has the Vaults of Parnassus, which provides a central repository for some of the Python modules and extensions available, but you still need to manually download the package and often do the installation manually, too.

The situation is getting better on the last point. Within the last year, work has been started by the dist-sig (special interest group) to produce a system called **distutils** (Python Distribution Utilities). This is a package of individual modules that, when used together, can produce the necessary steps to build and if necessary install modules and extensions onto a user's system simply by running a Python script.

The system is still very much in development as of May 2001, and I've deliberately avoided going into detail in this chapter about this system because of its developmental state. Check either my website (http://www.mcwords.com) or the Python website (http://www.python.org) to get the the current development status of the package since the release of this book.

In this chapter, we'll have a brief look at the system, the basic mechanics of how it works, and what we can expect in future versions.

Using distutils

The entire distutils system works through the use of a single file, setup.py, which contains all the information about the modules that are going to be installed. Then, when the user has downloaded your package, all they need to do is execute setup.py and give it an instruction to install your module—everything else happens automatically.

For example, given the simple setup.py file:

```
from distutils.core import setup
setup(name="mymodule",
      version-"1.0",
      py_modules=["mymodule"])
```

The user could install the module **mymodule** using:

```
$ python setup.py install
```

Easy!

The real power is in the backend **distutils** package and how you've written the setup.py file.

Supported Modules

The distutils package is designed to handle three basic module types:

- *Pure Python module:* This is a module written entirely in Python in its source (.py) form, along with the optional .pyc and .pyo files.

- *Extension module:* This is a C/C++ extension. Work is underway to support Jython extensions through Java classes.

- *Packages:* These are the collections of Python modules put into a single directory structure. See Chapter 5 for more information on packages.

Writing setup.py

The setup.py script is the core of the entire process. Essentially the script can do whatever you want. For example, you could ask the user questions about the module/application configuration and other information, but ultimately the entire process is handled through a single call to the function **setup()**, which is imported from the **distutils.core** module.

The arguments to **setup()** are supplied as a list of keyword arguments and contain a mixture of metadata and configuration information. For example, in our earlier example the metadata consisted of the version number. Other supported metadata fields include a description, author, email addresses, and URLs—and more information is being added all the time.

The configuration information includes the list of modules/packages to be installed, the names of extension source files, and even preprocessor and linker information required to build a specific extension.

For example, when writing the setup script for installing a C extension you might use something like:

```
from distutils.core import setup, Extension
setup(name="mymodule",
      version="1.0",
      description="Demonstration for C extensions",
      author="Martin C Brown",
      author_email="mc@mcwords.com",
      ext_modules=[Extension("mymodule", ["mymodule.c"])])
```

The **Extension** class is used to create a new extension instance, with the supplied arguments forming the detail for building the extension and the source files required to build the extension. Other arguments to **Extension** include **include_dirs** for a list of directories to be used when compiling, **define_macros** and **undef_macros** for defining and undefining C macros when building, and **library_dirs** and **libraries** to specify the library modules required to build the final extension.

Future Features

We've merely touched on distutils's current capabilities and on what's planned for the system long term. Already in the time it's taken to write this chapter, more features have been added to the system; watching the messages on the dist-sig mailing list, it's obvious that new features, suggestions, and extensions are being added on a daily basis. Hopefully by the end of 2001, the distutils package will be completed to the point that it becomes the standard system for distributing and installing all extensions to Python.

The Complete Reference

Part IV

Web Development

The
Complete
Reference

Chapter 19

Web Development Basics

ooking back over just a few years, it's hard to imagine a world without the Internet and the World Wide Web. I first started writing HTML for websites back in 1993, not long after HTML itself had been invented. It didn't take long for people to latch onto the abilities of HTML and the dynamic capabilities of the technology that would allow you to do more than just serve up static pages.

In this chapter we're going to look at the basics of generating HTML and manipulating URLs before looking at the specifics of creating dynamic websites using Python. We'll also look at the use of cookies, which allow you to store information on a user's browser, and we will look at the security aspects of your website that you should be aware of when writing scripts for the web.

In the rest of this section we'll look at how to parse HTML, XML, and SGML documents so that we can extract information and data from them. We'll also look at some of the more advanced web development solutions available with Python in Chapter 22.

Writing HTML

Before leaping into writing dynamic scripts with Python, it's worth going over the mechanics of how to write pages and how the web environment works. We'll start by looking at HTML (Hypertext Markup Language). HTML is a language that allows you to mark up the different elements within a text document so that they can be formatted.

Without HTML, websites would be boring: there'd be no way of highlighting or formatting different elements, and no way of incorporating images or linking to other documents.

HTML works by introducing 'tags' into the text. The tags define to an HTML viewer, such as a browser, how the text should be formatted onscreen. For example, to boldface a phrase, you use the **<b>** tag:

```
<b>Hello World!</b>
```

The opening tag, **<b>** starts the boldfacing, and the **</b>** end tag stops it. Other tags include those for building tables and changing fonts and text sizes, as well as those for introducing images and *anchors,* which provide links to external documents and therefore enable the hypertext element of the language.

However, this is a book about Python—if you want to learn more about HTML check out the World Wide Web Consortium website (www.w3c.org), which contains tutorials and reference manuals for all web-based standards, including HTML.
You might also want to check out *HTML: The Complete Reference* by Thomas Powell (Osborne/McGraw-Hill, 2000).

Within Python, generating HTML is as easy as using a **print** statement or using the **write()** or other methods on an open file. Remember, HTML is just marked-up raw text: it's not a binary file format, and there are no strict rules for how the information should be output. For example, we could output our earlier HTML example within Python using

```
print "<b>Hello World!</b>"
```

This method works for any quantity of HTML and is almost certainly the way you'll produce a large proportion of the HTML you need. We can also use the same techniques in Python CGI scripts.

However, using this method is not ideal in all situations. For a start, there is no structure to what you output: what would happen if you forget to print out the closing tag for a boldfacing instruction? Even worse, forgetting a closing **</table>** tag may well cause the entire table to disappear! There is no quick way to get around these problems; you just need to be vigilant about the HTML that you produce.

You can ease the process, however, by using the **HtmlKit** module. The **HtmlKit** module (available from http://www.dekorte.com/Software/Python/HtmlKit/) provides methods for creating most of the HTML tags that you'll ever need, while using a standard and structured interface that helps you to produce valid HTML without forcing you to manually check every line of HTML you produce.

For example, we could produce a table in HTML using the **HtmlKit** like this:

```
import HtmlKit

table = HtmlKit.Table()
row = table.newRow()
row.newColumn('Name')
row.newColumn('Title')
row.newColumn('Phone')
row = table.newRow()
row.newColumn('Martin')
row.newColumn('MD')
row.newColumn('01234 567890')
print str(table)
```

You can see here that we've built up the **table** object, first by creating it as an instance of the **Table()** class defined in **HtmlKit**, and then by adding rows and then columns to create the tables structure. Once we've finished, we can generate the final table by evaluating the **table** object through the **str()** function. The above code generates the following HTML:

```
<table border="0" cellpadding="3" cellspacing="1" width="100%">
<tr>
<td nowrap bgcolor="#dddddd">Name</td>
<td nowrap bgcolor="#dddddd">Title</td>
<td nowrap bgcolor="#dddddd">Phone</td>
</tr>
<tr>
<td nowrap bgcolor="#dddddd">Martin</td>
<td nowrap bgcolor="#dddddd">MD</td>
<td nowrap bgcolor="#dddddd">01234 567890</td>
```

WEB DEVELOPMENT

```
</tr>
</table>
```

You can see here that you should be careful when creating HTML with **HtmlKit** as it automatically adds attributes to the different elements that you may not want. These can of course be modified when you create the table with **HtmlKit**; check the documentation for more details.

Uniform Resource Locators

You've probably used a URL (uniform resource locator) and never thought much about what it actually is. A URL is an address for a resource on the Internet that consists of the protocol to be used, the address of the server, and the path to the file that you want to access. For example, the address

```
http://www.mcwords.com/index.shtml
```

indicates that you want to use the HTTP protocol, that you are connecting to the machine known as www.mcwords.com, and that you want to retrieve the file index.shtml.

URLs can also incorporate login names, passwords, and optional service port number information:

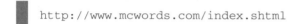
```
http://anonymous:password@ftp.mcwords.com:1025/cgi/send.py?file=info.zip
```

The preceding example shows downloading information from the server "ftp.mcwords.com," using service port "1025," with a login of "anonymous" and a password of "password."

This example also shows us accessing the object on the server called **send.py**. The information after the question mark is the data sent as part of the request. In this case we're sending a key/value pair on to a script called **send.py**. We'll look at how to handle this information later.

Parsing URLs

If you want to parse an existing URL, either to extract the individual components or to join a relative and absolute URL together, then the Python distribution comes with the **urlparse** module.

The module provides only three functions: **urlparse()**, **urlunparse()**, and **urljoin()**. The **urlparse()** function accepts a URL and returns a tuple defining the different components of the URL. The basic format of the function is

```
urlparse(urlstring[, default_scheme[, allow_fragments ] ])
```

The **urlstring** is the name of the string that you want to parse as a URL. For example, we could obtain a tuple of the components of our earlier sample URL like this:

```
>>>
urlparse.urlparse('http://anonymous:password@ftp.mcwords.com:1025/cgi/send.p
y?file=info.zip')
('http', 'anonymous:password@ftp.mcwords.com:1025', '/cgi/send.py', '',
'file=info.zip', '')
```

The format of the returned tuple is

```
(scheme, host, path, parameters, query, fragment)
```

Note that the user and password are not extracted for you; you'll need to do this yourself—which in turn leads to

```
scheme://host/path;parameters?query#fragment
```

The **default_scheme** argument should be used when you have an incomplete URL (for example www.mcwords.com) and need to resolve the URL within a given scheme (protocol). For example, the www.mcwords.com URL is actually a web address so it would need to be parsed within the 'http' scheme. Certain schemes don't support all the elements of a given URL. For example, an FTP schemed URL doesn't have either parameters or a query.

The **allow_fragments** argument specifies whether fragments are allowed in the URL that has been supplied. Setting this option overrides the settings for the supplied scheme.

The **urlunparse()** methods accepts a tuple in the same order as returned by **urlparse()** and rebuilds the given elements into a single URL string.

```
>>> urlunparse(('scheme', 'host', 'path', 'parameters', 'query', 'fragment'))
'scheme://host/path;parameters?query#fragment'
```

The **urljoin()** function takes two arguments, an absolute URL and a relative URL, and joins the two URLs together to make one absolute URL. For example, the URL of my website is http://www.mcwords.com, and the section on this book is defined within the contents page as /projects/books/pytcr. We can generate a full URL to point to this book using

```
>>> urljoin('http://www.mcwords.com', '/projects/books/pytcr')
'http://www.mcwords.com/projects/books/pytcr'
```

WEB DEVELOPMENT

It'll also work for more complex URLs. For example, deep within the site, the Perl Complete Reference page at http://www.mcwords.com/projects/books/pcr2e might refer to this book as ../pytcr, which we can also join together:

```
>>> urljoin('http://www.mcwords.com/projects/books/pcr2e/', '../pytcr')
'http://www.mcwords.com/projects/books/pytcr'
```

*If you want to download the file defined by a URL, you should use the **urllib** module. See Chapter 13 for more information.*

Dynamic Websites Using CGI

CGI, the Common Gateway Interface, is a method for exchanging information between the web server software and an external script. When you submit a form from within your browser to a web server, the data that you have filled in is supplied through a conduit to an external script, and then any output that the script provides is routed back by the web server to the user's browser.

CGI defines both how the web server talks to and executes an external application, as well as the methods used to transfer information between the external script and the server itself. The external script can, incidentally, be written in any language. We will, of course, use Python here, but it could just as easily be an AppleScript, C/C++ application, or Java Servlet. There are actually two basic methods for exchanging information between the web server and the CGI script that you are calling. The two methods are GET and POST, and which method you use is dependent on the information you are transferring. The GET method is useful for short requests and has the advantage that the fields and data can be appended to a URL. The POST method is best used for large volumes of text. We'll be looking at how the two methods affect the CGI side of the equation below.

Here is a more detailed overview of the process behind submitting data to a CGI script and getting the information back:

1. The user's browser (the client) opens a connection to the server.

2. The user's browser requests a URL from the server.

3. The server parses the URL and determines whether the URL points to a static HTML file or if it refers to a valid CGI script that should be executed separately. We will of course assume the latter for this example!

4. The external application is called. Any valid executable is valid at this point.

5. Any data (from a form, or from a suitably formatted URL) is supplied to the external application. If the information is sent as a GET request, then the information is made available in an environment variable that the script must

read. If the information is supplied using the POST method, data is sent to the standard input of the CGI application.

6. The CGI script now processes the information.

7. Any information generated by the CGI application and sent to the application's standard output is picked up by the web server and sent verbatim back to the client's browser. Valid responses must consist of an HTTP header that defines the format of the response and the actual HTML page that you want to supply back. The two elements should be separated by a blank line.

This is a very simplified outline to show how the basic process works. The important steps as far as we are concerned when developing CGI scripts are steps 4, 5, and 6.

In step 4, you need to think about the environment in which an application is executed. The environment defines the physical and logical confines of the Python script you want to run. In addition to the standard environment variables, such as **PATH**, there is also some web-specific information. In step 5, you have to extract any information supplied by the browser, either from one of the environment variables, which requires the **GET** method, or from the standard input, using the **POST** method. These names, **GET** and **POST** are the methods used to transfer the information from the browser—according to the configuration of the form—when it sends the form data to the server. In step 6, you have to know how to communicate information back to the user's browser.

We'll take a look at each of these issues separately in the next few sections of this chapter.

The Web Environment

The environment in which a script is executed does not normally affect the script's operation, except where otherwise noted in the general operation of Python. For example, a Python script executed within an environment that defines an alternative **PATH** will affect which programs the script can execute through the **exec*()** functions. On the whole, the environment doesn't change how the script executes, but it may affect certain operations of the script itself.

Most web servers populate the environment of the CGI script with a host of useful information about the client, it's browser, and information about the web server and the location of files and other information. You can see a list of the environment variables available on most web servers running under Unix in Table 19-1.

The exact list of environment variables supported depends on your web server, and also on the instance in which the URL was requested. For pages that are displayed as the result of a referral, you will also get a list of "referrer" information—the site from which the reference to the requested URL was made.

Environment Variable	Description
DOCUMENT_ROOT	The root document directory for this web server.
GATEWAY_INTERFACE	The interface name and version number.
HTTP_ACCEPT	The formats accepted by the browser. This information is optionally supplied by the browser when it first requests the page from the server. In the example shown in the main text, the default types accepted include all of the major graphics types (GIF, JPEG, X bitmap), as well as all other MIME types (*/*).
HTTP_ACCEPT_CHARSET	The character sets accepted by the browser.
HTTP_ACCEPT_ENCODING	Any special encoding formats supported by the browser. In the example, Netscape supports Gzip-encoded documents; they will be decoded on the fly at the time of receipt.
HTTP_ACCEPT_LANGUAGE	The languages accepted by this browser. If supported by the server, then only documents of a specific language will be returned to the browser.
HTTP_CONNECTION	Any HTTP connection directives. A typical directive is "Keep Alive," which forces the server to keep a web-server process and the associated network socket dedicated to this browser until a defined period of inactivity.
HTTP_HOST	The server host (without domain).

Table 19-1. *Web Server Environment Variables for CGI Scripts*

Environment Variable	Description
HTTP_USER_AGENT	The name, version number, and platform of the remote browser. In the example CGI output shown in the main text, the browser used was the Mozilla 4.0–compatible browser (actually the browser is really Microsoft Internet Explorer 5.0), for Macintosh PPC. Don't be fooled into thinking that the name Mozilla applies only to Netscape Navigator; other browsers, including Microsoft Internet Explorer, also report themselves as being Mozilla browsers—this helps with compatibility identification, even though all browsers render HTML differently.
PATH	The path for the CGI script.
CONTENT_LENGTH	The length of the query information. It's available only for **POST** requests, and it can help with the security of the scripts you produce.
QUERY_STRING	The query string, used with **GET** requests.
REMOTE_ADDR	The IP address of the browser.
REMOTE_HOST	The resolved name of the browser.
REMOTE_PORT	The remote port of the browser machine.
REQUEST_METHOD	The request method; for example, **GET** or **POST**.
REQUEST_URI	The requested URI (uniform resource identifier).
SCRIPT_FILENAME	The full path to the CGI script.

Table 19-1. *Web Server Environment Variables for CGI Scripts* (continued)

WEB DEVELOPMENT

Environment Variable	Description
SCRIPT_NAME	The name of the CGI script.
SERVER_ADMIN	The email address of the web-server administrator.
SERVER_NAME	The fully qualified domain name of the server.
SERVER_PORT	The server port number.
SERVER_PROTOCOL	The protocol (usually HTTP) and version number.
SERVER_SOFTWARE	The name and version number of the server software that is being used. This can be useful if you want to introduce a single script that makes use of specific features of multiple web servers.
TZ	The time zone of the web server.

Table 19-1.   *Web Server Environment Variables for CGI Scripts* (continued)

You can find this information using a CGI script like the one that follows. Don't worry too much about the details of this script at this stage.

```
#!/usr/local/bin/python

from os import environ

print "Content-type: text/html\n\n"
print "<h1>Environment:</h1>"

for key in environ.keys():
    print "%s =&gt; %s<br>" % (key, environ[key])
```

On my web server, which is Apache 1.3.20 running under Solaris 8, the following ends up being displayed within a browser window (Microsoft Internet Explorer for Mac 5.01):

```
DOCUMENT_ROOT => /export/http/webs/test
SERVER_ADDR => 192.168.1.1
QUERY_STRING =>
SERVER_PORT => 80
```

```
REMOTE_ADDR => 192.168.1.1
HTTP_VIA => 1.0 http-proxy.mcslp.pri:8080
PATH =>
/usr/local/bin:/usr/bin:/usr/games:/export/home/root/usr/etc:/export/home/
root/usr/bin:/usr/lib:/usr/ccs/bin:/usr/sbin:/usr/local/sbin:/usr/lib/
lp/postscript:/export/data/bin:/opt/NSCPcom:/usr/openwin/bin:.
HTTP_ACCEPT_LANGUAGE => en
GATEWAY_INTERFACE => CGI/1.1
SERVER_NAME => test.mcslp.pri
TZ => GB
HTTP_USER_AGENT => Mozilla/4.0 (compatible; MSIE 5.0; Mac_PowerPC)
HTTP_ACCEPT => */*
REQUEST_URI => /pyecho.cgi
HTTP_UA_CPU => PPC
HTTP_EXTENSION => Security/Remote-Passphrase
SCRIPT_FILENAME => /export/http/webs/test/pyecho.cgi
HTTP_HOST => test.mcslp.pri
REQUEST_METHOD => GET
SERVER_SIGNATURE =>
Apache/1.3.20 Server at test.mcslp.pri Port 80

HTTP_IF_MODIFIED_SINCE => Tue, 10 Jul 2001 13:37:05 GMT
SCRIPT_NAME => /pyecho.cgi
SERVER_ADMIN => mc@test.com
SERVER_SOFTWARE => Apache/1.3.20 (Unix) PHP/4.0.6 mod_perl/1.25
SERVER_PROTOCOL => HTTP/1.0
REMOTE_PORT => 51868
HTTP_UA_OS => MacOS
```

You can glean lots of useful information from this that you can use in your script. For example, the **SCRIPT_NAME** environment variable contains the name of the CGI script that was accessed by the client. The most important fields as far as a CGI program is concerned, however, are the **REQUEST_METHOD**, which defines the method used to transfer the information (request) from the browser, through the web server, to the CGI application.

The **CONTENT_LENGTH** defines the number of bytes contained in the query when using the **POST** method. This is useful primarily for verifying that some data has been supplied (and therefore needs processing). The **CONTENT_LENGTH** environment variable is not provided by all web servers and shouldn't be your only way of verifying whether any query has been sent. However, if used properly, it can also aid in the security of your web scripts. See the "Security" section later in this chapter for more information. The **QUERY_STRING** is the environment variable used to store the data from the client's browser when using the **GET** method.

Extracting Form Data

We already know that information supplied from a form or defined direct in a URL is made available either through the standard input or by populating the

QUERY_STRING environment variable. Accessing these two pieces of information is not difficult, but decoding the information is less straightforward.

Information from the form is supplied as a series of key/value pairs, where the key is the name of the form field and the value is the value of the field when the form was submitted. These key/value pairs are split by an equal sign, and more than key/value pair is split by ampersand characters.

As if that wasn't bad enough, the key/value information can often be encoded, since we obviously can't include either equal signs or ampersands in the string; otherwise the CGI script would get confused. Other characters are also encoded—in fact just about all characters apart from the letters (upper and lower case) and numbers are generally translated into their hex equivalents and prefixed by a percent sign. For example, the string "Martin Brown" would be translated into "Martin%20Brown."

Sound complicated?

The easiest way to get all of the form information is to use the standard **cgi** module. This parses the form data supplied to a CGI script for you and makes the information available either through a series of function calls or with a single function call you can place all of the information directly into a dictionary.

For example, the script below provides a simple form asking for your name. When you enter your name and submit the form the script then returns and says hello:

```
from cgi import *

print "Content-type: text/html\n\n"

print """
<html>
<head><title>Greeting</title></head>
<body bgcolor="White">
<h1>Please enter your name</h1>
<form method=get action="/pyform.cgi">
<b>Name: </b><input type=text name=name size=40></br>
<input type=submit>
<hr>
"""

form = FieldStorage()

if (form.getvalue('name')):
    print "<h2>Hello",form.getvalue('name'),"</h2>"

print "</html>"
```

The primary part of the process is creating an instance of the **FieldStorage** class. The result object is a structure containing the fields and their values, which we can access in a number of different ways.

If we use dictionary notation on the **form** object, it returns a **MiniFieldStorage** instance containing a list of the fields matching the supplied name. For example, the line

```
print form['name']
```

yields

```
MiniFieldStorage('name', 'MC')
```

This method is useful when you have a number of fields on a form that supply information to the same field name. For example, if you had a series of checkboxes listing possible options, you'd use one form field to hold all of the values when each box has been checked.

More useful for standard forms, and the method we use here, is the **getvalue()** method to our **form** object. The method returns the information in more familiar format, in this case as a string. Had we used checkboxes, the return value from **getvalue()** would have been a list of those values.

This is of course just the tip of the iceberg: what you do with the data that you've retrieved from the form is entirely up to you. You might want to send the information to a database, send the user an email, or use the information to build a news page customized to the users preferences.

Other function supported by the **cgi** module are listed in Table 19-2.

Sending Information Back

When you want to send information back to the client, you simply send output to the standard output of your script; the web server will pick this up and pass it back to the client over the network socket used by the client to submit the request.

There are two parts to your response: an HTTP header and the document that you want to send back. The HTTP header is used to tell the client about the information you are sending back. At the bare minimum you must include the **Content-type** header, which tells the client the format of the information that you are sending back. For HTML, as we've already seen, this should the type **text/html**. For example:

```
print "Content-type: text/html\n\n"
```

Function	Description
parse(fp)	Parses a query string (as from the **QUERY_STRING** environment variable, or **sys.stdin** if this is empty).
parse_qs(string [, keep_blank_values, strict_parsing])	Parse the query string in the argument **string**. The resulting fields and values are returned to the caller as a dictionaries, with the keys as the field names and the value as a list of the values for the field. If set to true **keep_blank_values** creates keys for empty fields. The default is for blank fields to be ignored. The **string_parsing** argument if set will raise a **ValueError** exception if there are any errors in the supplied string. The default operation is to ignore such errors.
parse_qsl(string [, keep blank values, strict parsing])	Same as **parse_qs()** but returns the field names and values as a list of field name/value pairs.
parse_multipart(fp, pdict)	Parse the input from the file object **fp** as multipart form data. The **pdict** should be a dictionary of the parameters that we supplied in the Content-type header by the client. Returns a dictionary like **parse_qs()**.
parse_header(string)	Parse a MIME header into a main value and dictionary of parameters.
test()	Writes back minimal HTTP headers and displays environment and form information back to the client. Useful for debugging.
print_environ()	Prints the shell environment in HTML format. Useful for debugging.

Table 19-2.   *Functions Supported by the cgi Module*

Function	Description
print_form(form)	Prints the form data in HTML format using the supplied **form** object. Useful for debugging.
print_directory()	Prints out the current directory from which the script was executed in HTML format.
print_environ_usage()	Prints a list of useful environment variables in HTML. Note that it only displays the environment variables names, not the data.
escape(s[, quote])	Converts the special HTML characters &, <, and > in the string **s** to HTML-safe sequences. If **quote** is true, then it also converts double quotes. See also the "Escaping Special Characters" section later in this chapter for details on a more extensive toolset for translating unsafe characters.

Table 19-2. *Functions Supported by the cgi Module* (continued)

WEB DEVELOPMENT

The header and the body of the document you are sending back should be separated by a single blank line, introduced above by including a linefeed character. There's some more information included about HTTP headers and what they can be used for below.

The body of the document can then contain what you like. You are not restricted to HTML—you could send back an image, sound file, or even a compressed archive.

HTTP Headers

The HTTP header information is returned as follows:

```
Field: data
```

The case of the **Field** name is important, but otherwise you can use as much white space as you like between the colon and the field data. A sample list of HTTP header fields is shown in Table 19-3.

Field	Meaning
Allow: list	A comma-delimited list of the HTTP request methods supported by the requested resource (script or program). Scripts generally support **GET** and **POST**; other methods include **HEAD**, **POST**, **DELETE**, **LINK**, and **UNLINK**.
Content-encoding: string	The encoding used in the message body. Currently the only supported formats are Gzip and compress. If you want to encode data this way, make sure you check the value of **HTTP_ACCEPT_ENCODING** from the environment variables.
Content-type: string	A MIME string defining the format of the file being returned. For an HTML page this will be text/html. Check the section later in this chapter for more information.
Content-length: string	The length, in bytes, of the data being returned. The browser uses this value to report the estimated download time for a file.
Date: string	The date and time the message is sent. It should be in the format 01 Jan 1998 12:00:00 GMT. The time zone should be GMT for reference purposes; the browser can calculate the difference for its local time zone if it has to.
Expires: string	The date the information becomes invalid. This should be used by the browser to decide when a page needs to be refreshed. Should be specified in the same format as the **Date:** header.

Table 19-3.   *HTTP Header Fields*

Field	Meaning
Last-modified: string	The date of last modification of the resource. This is used by the browser to determine whether the remote version is more up to date than that in the cache. Should be specified in the same format as the **Date:** header.
Location: string	You can use this to define the URL that should be visited by the browser, instead of continuing to read information from the requested URL. This can be useful when you want to redirect the user to another location. The URL should be absolute; relative URLs will not work.
MIME-version: string	The version of the MIME protocol supported. Check the MIME resource page at http://www.oac.uci.edu/indiv/ehood/MIME/MIME.html for more information.
Server: string/string	The web server application and version number.
Title: string	The title of the resource.
URI: string	The URI that should be returned instead of the requested one.

Table 19-3. *HTTP Header Fields* (continued)

WEB DEVELOPMENT

The only required field is Content-type, which defines the format of the file you are returning. If you do not specify anything, the browser assumes you are sending back preformatted raw text, not HTML. The definition of the file format is by a MIME string. MIME is an acronym for Multipurpose Internet Mail Extensions, and it is a slash-separated string that defines the raw format and a subformat within it. For example, text/html says the information returned is plain text, using HTML as a file format. Mac users will be familiar with the concept of file owners and types, and this is the basic model employed by MIME. MIME is rapidly becoming a generic method for describing the file type. It's used by email and Internet file transfer, and on some operating systems (notably BeOS, but Linux and others are expected to follow suit) it's used to describe the file content of files on the file system.

Other examples include application/pdf, which states that the file type is application specific binary and that the file's format is pdf, the Adobe Acrobat file format. Others you might be familiar with are image/gif, which states that the file is a GIF file, and application/zip, which is a Zip archive.

This MIME information is used by the browser to decide how to process the file. Most browsers will have a mapping that says they deal with files of type image/gif so that you can place graphical files within a page. They may also have an entry for application/pdf, which either calls an external application to open the received file or passes the file to a plug-in that optionally displays the file to the user.

Both client and server also map extensions to MIME types. For example, we know that the .doc extension refers to Microsoft Word documents, and ergo to the application/msword MIME type. On the server side, the extension of a file is used to send the MIME type to the client. On the client side, the mapping is used to identify the file type of files that do not come attached with a MIME type.

For more examples of MIME types, you can look at a fragment of the MIME type file supplied with the Apache web server:

```
application/mac-binhex40         hqx
application/mac-compactpro       cpt
application/macwriteii
application/msword               doc
application/news-message-id
application/news-transmission
application/octet-stream         bin dms lha lzh exe class
application/oda                  oda
application/pdf                  pdf
application/postscript           ai eps ps
application/powerpoint           ppt
application/remote-printing
application/rtf                  rtf
application/slate
application/wita
application/wordperfect5.1
application/x-bcpio              bcpio
application/x-cdlink             vcd
application/x-compress
application/x-cpio               cpio
application/x-csh                csh
application/x-director           dcr dir dxr
```

It's important to realize the significance of this one, seemingly innocent field. Without it, your browser would not know how to process the information it receives. Normally the web server sends the MIME type back to the browser, and it uses a lookup table that maps MIME strings to file extensions. Thus, when a browser requests myphoto.gif, the server sends back a Content-type field value of image/gif.

Failure to return the Content-type HTTP header will almost certainly render the output generated by your CGI script as plain text and will be displayed as such by the browser.

The Document Body

The document body is all about what you want to send back. If it's HTML, then use **print** statements or the **HtmlKit** module we saw at the beginning of this chapter to format the data that you want to send back.

As an example, here's a script that gets a list of email from an IMAP server and then formats it as HTML before supplying it back to the client.

```python
#!/usr/local/bin/python

import imaplib
import sys,os,re,string

# Set up a function that we can use to call the corresponding
# method on a given imap connection when supplied with the
# name of an IMAP command
def run(cmd, args):
    typ, dat = apply(eval('imapcon.%s' % cmd), args)
    return dat


# Get the mail, displaying the output as HTML

def getmail(title,login,password):
# Login to the remote server, supplying the login and
# password supplied to the function
    run('login',(login,password))

# Use the select method to obtain the number of
# messages in the users mail account. The information is returned
# as a string, so we need to convert it to an integer
    nomsgs = run('select',())[0]
    nomsgs = string.atoi(nomsgs)

# Output a header for this email account
    print '<p><font size="+2"><b>'+title+'</b></font></p>'

# Providing we've got some messages, download each message
# and display the sender and subject
```

```
        if nomsgs:
# Output a suitable table header row
            print '<table border="0" cellpadding="0" cellspacing="0">'
            print "<tr><td><b>Sender</b></td><td><b>Subject</b></td></tr>"
# Process each message
            for message in range(nomsgs,0,-1):
                subject,sender,status = '','','U'
# Send the fetch command to the server to obtain the
# email's flags (read, deleted, etc.) and header from the email
                data = run('fetch', (message,'(FLAGS RFC822.HEADER)'))[0]
                meta,header = data
# Determine the email's flags and ignore a message if it's
# marked as deleted
                if string.find(meta,'Seen') > 0:
                    status = ''
                if string.find(meta,'Deleted') > 0:
                    continue
# Separate the header, which appears as one large string, into
# individual lines and then extract the subject and sender fields
                for line in string.split(header,'\n'):
                    if not line:
                        sender = re.sub(r'\<.*\>','',
                                        re.sub(r'\"','',sender))
# If the message is unread, then mark the subject and sender
# in red
                        if (string.find(status,'U') == 0):
                            subject = '<font color="red">'
                                       + subject + '</font>'
                            sender = '<font color="red">'
                                       + sender + '</font>'
                        print "<tr><td>%s</td><td>%s</td></tr>"
                                  % (sender,subject)
                        break
# Extract the sender/subject information by looking for the field
# prefix
                    if line[:8] == 'Subject:':
                        subject = line[9:-1]
                    if line[:5] == 'From:':
                        sender = line[6:-1]
            print "</table>"
        else:
            print "No messages"
# Logout from the server
        run('logout',())

# Set the server information
server='imap'
```

```
# Print out a suitable HTTP header and HTML page header
print "Content-type: text/html\n\n"
print """
<head>
<title>Mail</title>
</head>
<body bgcolor="#ffffff" fgcolor="#000000">
"""

# Connect to the server, and then call getmail to get the mail
# from the server
try:
    imapcon = imaplib.IMAP4(server)
except:
    print "Can't open connection to ",server
    sys.exit(1)
getmail('MC','mcmcslp','PASSWORD')
```

Escaping Special Characters

Because we have to transfer data to the CGI script using text, there are limitations in what we can supply safely over a given connection. We've already seen that characters beyond the standard letters and numbers have to be converted back when we are reading the information from a client. If you want to supply information that's encoded in this way, you need to use the **quote()** function from the **urllib** module. To convert a quoted string back into it's original format, use **unquote()**; note that this is normally handled by the **cgi** module, and it automatically decodes quoted strings into their real versions as part of it's parsing process. You can the details of the two functions and their cousins **quote_plus()** and **unquote_plus()** in Table 19-4.

For example we would convert the string "file=/path/to/an/odd file" using

```
import urllib
print urllib.quote_plus('file=/path/to/an/odd file')
```

If you want to change the list of characters that are escaped during this process, you can supply a second argument to the function, the second argument defines which characters are safe, and therefore do not need to be escaped:

```
urllib.quote(url,'a-zA-Z0-9')
```

For more complex translations, you'll need to be more careful about which characters you do (or more importantly don't) include.

Function	Description
quote(string)	Escapes characters in **string** with URL-compatible formats. Note that the Python **quote()** does not convert spaces to + characters by default. Use the **quote_plus()** function if you also want translate the plus sign.
unquote(string)	Converts a string that has URL escape sequences embedded into it into a normal string. Note that the **unquote()** function does not convert + characters back to spaces; use **unquote_plus()** to encode spaces to plus signs.

Table 19-4.   *Converting URL to/from Escaped Versions*

Debugging

Care needs to be taken when debugging CGI scripts of any kind because there are a number of locations where errors can occur. The primary point is a fault in the CGI script itself. If the script raises an exception that you haven't otherwise trapped, then the script will terminate mid-execution and may have returned very little information to the client.

Although standard output is passed on to the client, standard error is not—that information is written out to the web server's error log. You can improve on this simply by diverting standard error to the standard output filehandle using

```
import sys
sys.stderr = sys.stdout
```

Beyond that, it really comes down to ensuring that your exceptions are as complete as possible and that you can trace the errors properly.

We'll actually be looking at debugging in more detail in Chapter 24, and we'll also look at some general and CGI specific techniques in that chapter.

Cookies

A cookie is a small, discrete piece of information used to store information within a web browser. The cookie itself is stored on the client end, rather than the server, and it can therefore be used to store state information between individual accesses by the browser, either in the same session or across a number of sessions. In its simplest form, a cookie might just store your name; in a more complex system, it provides login and password information for a website. This can be used by web designers to provide customized pages to individual users.

In other systems, cookies are used to store the information about the products you have chosen in web-based stores. The cookie then acts as your "shopping basket," storing information about your products and other selections.

In either case, the creation of a cookie and how you access the information stored in a cookie are server-based requests, since it's the server that uses the information to provide the customized web page, or that updates the selected products stored in your web basket. There is a limit to the size of cookies, and it varies from browser to browser. In general, a cookie shouldn't need to be more than 1,024 bytes, but some browsers will support sizes as large as 16,384 bytes, sometimes even more.

A cookie is formatted much like a CGI form-field data stream. The cookie is composed of a series of field/value pairs separated by ampersands, with each field/value additionally separated by an equal sign. The contents of the cookie is exchanged between the server and client during normal interaction. The server sends updates back to the cookie as part of the HTTP headers, and the browser sends the current cookie contents as part of its request to the server.

Besides the field/value pairs, a cookie has a number of additional attributes. These are an expiration time, a domain, a path, and an optional secure flag.

- The expiration time is used by the browser to determine when the cookie should be deleted from its own internal list. As long as the expiration time has not been reached, the cookie will be sent back to the correct server each time you access a page from that server.

- The definition of a valid server is stored within the domain attribute. This is a partial or complete domain name for the server that should be sent to the cookie. For example, if the value of the domain attribute is ".foo.bar," then any server within the foo.bar domain will be sent the cookie data for each access.

- The path is a similar partial match against a path within the web server. For example, a path of /cgi-bin means that the cookie data will only be sent with any requests starting with that path. Normally, you would specify "/" to have the cookie sent to all CGI scripts, but you might want to restrict the cookie data so it is only sent to scripts starting with /cgi-public, but not to /cgi-private.

- The secure attribute restricts the browser from sending the cookie to unsecure links. If set, cookie data will only be transferred over secure connections, such as those provided by SSL.

In Python there is a third-party module called **Cookie** that will build a new cookie suitable for sending back to the client. For example, we could rewrite the above using the **Cookie** module like this:

```
import Cookie
cookie = Cookie.SmartCookie()
```

```
cookie['sample'] = 'login=%s; other=Other' % (login)
cookie['sample']['path'] = '/'
cookie['sample']['domain'] = 'mcwords.mchome.com'
cookie['sample']['expires'] = 365*24*3600
print cookie
```

Note that we have to actually calculate the future value ourselves (in seconds) rather than using the relative strings that you may be familiar with when using Perl or JavaScript. The resulting cookie should be sent back to the client as part of the HTTP headers, so it should be placed before the single blank line separating the header and body.

Cookies are automatically sent back to the browser when the browser accesses a URL matching the domain and path defined when the cookie was created. Note that the client only sends back cookies matching the domain and path; it doesn't send all cookies to the client.

The web server then places the cookie information into the **HTTP_COOKIE** environment variable. The easiest way to parse a cookie supplied by a client back into an internal structure is to use the **load()** method on a **SmartCookie** object:

```
import Cookie, os

cookie = Cookie.SmartCookie()
cookie.load(os.environ['HTTP_COOKIE'])
print cookie['sample']
```

Cookies are a great way of storing information about a client that is pertinent to your website. For example, you might use a cookie to hold a reference value that refers to the user's login on your site. That way when they visit your site, you will automatically know who they are and therefore be able to provide them with a customized view.

But be careful: don't store user names and passwords in a cookie. Although the cookie is not sent to any CGI script other than that matching it's domain and path, users can still read the cookie data stored on a machine to determine user names and passwords. A better solution is to store a randomly generated string in a database and use that as the cookie value. When the user visits the site, you look up the random string in the database and identify the user that way. That makes it impossible for someone to determine the user's login name or password from looking in the cookies on the user's machine.

It doesn't protect them completely of course—they could copy the cookie, or use the machine to visit your site. As a double protection, therefore, make sure that any major operations, such as changing the user's preferences or submitting/accessing their credit card details, requires the user to enter their full password.

Security

The number of attacks on Internet sites is increasing. Whether this is due to the meteoric rise of the number of computer crackers, or whether it's just because of the number of companies and hosts who do not take it seriously is unclear. The fact is, it's incredibly easy to ensure that your scripts are secure if you follow some simple guidelines. However, before we look at solutions, let's look at the types of scripts that are vulnerable to attack:

- Any script that passes form input to a mail address or mail message
- Any script that passes information that will be used within a subshell or through a call to **system()** or **exec*()**
- Any script that blindly accepts unlimited amounts of information during the form processing

The first two danger zones should be relatively obvious: anything that is essentially executed on the command line is open to abuse if the attacker supplies the right information. For example, imagine an email address passed directly to **sendmail** that looks like this:

```
mc@foo.bar;(mail mc@foo.bar </etc/passwd)
```

If this were executed on the command line as part of a **sendmail** line, the command after the semicolon would mail the password file to the same user—a severe security hazard if not checked. The easiest way to trap this is to always check the information that you supply on to any external command of any kind.

There is a simple rule to follow when using CGI scripts: don't trust the size, content, or organization of the data supplied.

Here is a checklist of some of the things you should be looking out for when writing secure CGI scripts:

- Double-check the field names, values, and associations before you use them. For example, make sure an email address looks like an email address, and that it's part of the correct field you are expecting from the form.
- Don't automatically process the field values without checking them. As a rule, come up with a list of ASCII characters that you are willing to accept and filter out everything else with a regular expression.
- It's easier to check for valid information than it is to try to filter out bad data. Use regular expressions to match against what you *want*, rather than using it to match against what you *don't want*.
- Check the input size of the variables or, better still, of the form data. Mail addresses don't need to be more than 256 characters, and anybody supplying more data to a field that you know has been configured to support only

40 characters is probably up to no good. You can use the **CONTENT_LENGTH** environment variable, which is calculated by the web server to check the length of the data being accepted on **POST** methods, and some web servers supply this information on **GET** requests, too.

■ Don't assume that field data exists or is valid before use; a blank field can cause as many problems as a field filled with bad data.

■ Don't ever return the contents of a file unless you can be sure of what its contents are. Arbitrarily returning a password file when you expected the user to request an HTML file is open to severe abuse. Ensure that file requests point to a file that you are happy to return, or use **os.chroot()** to restrict what the user has access to.

■ Don't accept that the path information sent to your script is automatically valid. Choose an alternative **PATH** environment value that you can trust, hardwiring it into the initialization of the script. While you're at it, use **del** to remove any environment variables you know you won't use.

■ If you are going to accept paths or file names, make sure they are relative, not absolute, and that they don't contain **..**, which leads to the parent directory. An attacker could easily specify a file of ../../../../../../../../etc/passwd, which would reference the password file from even a deep directory.

■ Always validate information used with **os.system(), os.fork(),** or **os.exec*()**. If nothing else, ensure any variables passed to these functions don't contain the characters **;, |, (,** or **)**. Alternatively, avoid using these altogether.

■ *Never* use an untreated value with **os.popen()**, **os.exec*()**, or any function that otherwise runs an external command.

■ Ensure your web server is not running as **root**, which opens up your machine to all sorts of attacks. Run your web server as **nobody**, or create a new user specifically for the web server, ensuring that scripts are readable and executable only by the web server owner, and not writable by anybody.

■ Don't assume that HTML fields with a type of "hidden" are really hidden—users will still see them if they view the file source. And don't rely on your own encryption algorithms to encrypt the information supplied in these hidden fields. Use an existing system that has been checked and is bug free. Solutions are available for most encryption systems; check the Vaults of Parnassus for suitable modules.

If you follow these guidelines, you will at least reduce your risk from attacks, but there is no way to completely guarantee your safety. A determined attacker will use a number of different tools and tricks to achieve his goal.

Oh, and did I mention that you shouldn't trust the size, content, or organization of the data supplied?

The Complete Reference

Python

Chapter 20

Standard Markup Language Processing

There are a number of different markup languages used for creating documents: some, such as SGML and HTML, have been around for a while, and others, such as XML, are relatively new on the scene. Technically they are all based on the same fundamental system, and XML and HTML are really just examples of SGML applications.

Markup languages offer a way of structuring and laying out a document that allows you to identify individual portions of the document, such as headers and footers, chapter markers, and other elements, along with the ability to mark up individual words or phrases. For example, a very simple HTML document that includes the document title, some paragraph text—including some elements in bold—and list of items might look like this:

```
<html>
<head><title>Some Old Document</title></head>
<body bgcolor='#ffffff' fgcolor='#000000'>
<p>Here's a list of the items that I'd like today from
<b>Sainbury's</b>. Please remember your <i>credit cards</i></p>:
<ul>
<li>Sugar
<li>Redbush Tea
<li>Red Mountain Coffee
<li>Milk
</ul>
</body>
</html>
```

The individual components and elements of the document are marked up using *tags*, which are the elements with angle brackets. Within HTML they have special meaning—for example the **** tag indicates that the text following the tag should be marked in bold and a corresponding closing tag, ****, stops the bold rendering on the text. Other marks need only one tag; for example, the **<li>** tag indicates a list item, but we don't need to specify the end tag (except in XHTML).

SGML, XML, and HTML, work in the same way, using the same style of tags. Other markup languages, such as TeX or the *roff family, use a similar tag-based markup language, but they do not conform to the same format. Because the documents are text, creating them is not a problem—all we need to do is output the necessary information using **print**. We saw some examples of this in Chapter 19.

However, sometimes you want to read the information that you've placed into these documents, or use a document that you've obtained elsewhere to extract different elements. For example, in Chapter 19 we looked at the **urllib** module, which allows us to download any Internet object. If we could understand the information in an HTML page we could extract a list of links or even a list of images so that we could download everything required to view the document locally.

We could extract the information with regular expressions, but this would be messy. A much better solution would be to actually parse and understand the document so that we could pull out the elements we wanted by name.

The standard Python library includes tools for reading and parsing SGML, HTML and XML files. The **sgmllib** module is not as extensive as the full SGML language. We can parse the basic tags and document structure, but many of the more advanced features of the SGML language are not supported by **sgmllib**. The **htmllib** module provides a more general-purpose interface for parsing and extracting information from HTML documents. Because HTML is just an application of the SGML language format, **htmllib** actually inherits most of its abilities from the **sgmllib** module.

The XML support within Python is more extensive. We have access to an older parsing interface called **xmllib**. This has now been deprecated in favor of the Expat interface or the SAX (Simple API for XML) and DOM (Document Object Model) interfaces.

In this chapter we're going to have a look at these modules, and a look at some of the tools we can create using these standard modules.

Processing SGML

All of these markup languages work in the same way. The grandfather of them all is SGML or Standard Generalized Markup Language, originally invented in the 1970s at IBM. SGML was designed to allow technical information, such as that used by IBM, Boeing, and NASA, to be differentiated (marked up) within a document. It's possible to then extract only the information you want, so you can create everything from quick reference guides to full-blown technical reference manuals.

With SGML you can mark up elements with the same tags, as well as refer to other parts of the same document and even other documents. Because SGML is the raw format, the output format can be anything you like, from HTML documents to Microsoft Word, help systems, even PostScript or PDF.

Python's SGML implementation is rather limited. The SGML parser provided by the **sgmllib** module is capable only of parsing and understanding SGML tags—that is, the process of identifying the <xxx> tags and the data contained between a start and end tag. Because the **htmllib** module builds on the **sgmllib** module, and because most people are familiar with HTML, let's move directly to looking at the **HTMLParser** class.

Processing HTML

SGML's biggest success story has to be HTML, or Hypertext Markup Language. Developed by Tim Berners-Lee in 1990, HTML is actually an application of SGML, especially designed in this instance to mark up documents for viewing onscreen and used to great effect on the World Wide Web. HTML doesn't provide the full power of SGML: we are limited to a specific set of tags that have specific meanings, and the documents themselves are intended only for viewing onscreen. To put it simply, HTML defines a document's look and feel without describing its content. SGML (and XML), on the other hand, use tags to define content—it's up to a parser to convert that into an onscreen, printed, or other format document. These limitations haven't limited HTML's use, however.

Processing HTML follows exactly the same basic process as processing SGML. HTML parsing is much simpler, however, because many of the more complex tagging styles supported by SGML are not used by HTML.

How HTML Processing Works

The **htmllib** module supplies a new class, **HTMLParser**, which is itself based on the **SGMLParser** class supplied in **sgmllib**. Both classes work in more or less the same way: you feed information to the parser through a method called **feed()**. You can call this any number of times to supply new information to the parser to process.

While processing the document, each time the parser comes across a tag it tries to invoke a corresponding method. For example, when the **<img...>** tag is discovered, the parser invokes the **do_img()** method defined within the class. The method is supplied with a list of the attributes defined in the tag as a list of tuple pairs. For example, the tag

```
<img src='myimage.gif' width=100 height=200 alt='logo'
align='left'>
```

is supplied with an attribute list like this:

```
[('src','myimage.gif'), ('width', '100'), ('height', '200'),
('alt', 'logo'), ('align', 'left')]
```

Using a list of tuples is probably not the best solution—a dictionary might be more useful—but it's up to you how to process this information. It's up to this method to extract any useful information from the tag attributes and act upon it. Different methods are used for each tag that you want to recognize, and the parser is intelligent enough to recognize tags that do or do not work in pairs. For example the **
** tag would be handled by a **do_br()** method, while the **<a...>...</a>** anchor tags are handled using **start_a()** and **end_a()** methods.

We can see how these work by looking at the source for **htmllib**. A small extract follows, showing the methods for the anchor and image tags we've just examined:

```
def start_a(self, attrs):
        href = ''
        name = ''
        type = ''
```

```
        for attrname, value in attrs:
            value = value.strip()
            if attrname == 'href':
                href = value
            if attrname == 'name':
                name = value
            if attrname == 'type':
                type = value.lower()
        self.anchor_bgn(href, name, type)

    def end_a(self):
        self.anchor_end()

    # --- Image

    def do_img(self, attrs):
        align = ''
        alt = '(image)'
        ismap = ''
        src = ''
        width = 0
        height = 0
        for attrname, value in attrs:
            if attrname == 'align':
                align = value
            if attrname == 'alt':
                alt = value
            if attrname == 'ismap':
                ismap = value
            if attrname == 'src':
                src = value
            if attrname == 'width':
                try: width = int(value)
                except: pass
            if attrname == 'height':
                try: height = int(value)
                except: pass
        self.handle_image(src, alt, ismap, align, width, height)
```

You can see from this extract that the **start_a()** method extracts the anchor information from an anchor tag, before passing it off to the **anchor_end()** method. The **end_a()** method ends the processing of the anchor tag. The **do_img()** extracts some of the typical attributes contained in an image tag before handing the processing off to the **handle_image()** method.

Using htmllib

The primary way to use the HTML parser is to create a new class from which to inherit the methods from the parent **HTMLParser** class provided by **htmllib**. We then overload the methods for the tags that we want to handle ourselves. For example, if we wanted to handle the **<img...>** tag, we'd define our own **do_img()** method.

In its base format, the **HTMLParser** actually does very little. It's designed to work with the classes defined in the **formatter** module to output information on the HTML file to the screen. The **formatter** module allows you to output information in a structured way according to "triggered" events. See the Python documentation for more information.

The only other useful facility provided by the **HTMLParser** class is that it builds a list of anchor tags found within the document. The information is built as the document is parsed, with the elements appearing in the **anchorlist** attribute of an instance of the **HTMLParser** class. For example, the following script parses a document and then displays the list of anchors found:

```
import htmllib, sys, formatter
try:
    file = sys.argv[1]
except:
    print 'You must supply a file name'
    sys.exit(1)

try:
    htmlfile = open(file, 'r')
except IOError, msg:
    print "Error:", file, ":", msg
    sys.exit(1)

htmldata = htmlfile.read()
htmlfile.close()

parser = htmllib.HTMLParser(formatter.NullFormatter())
parser.feed(htmldata)
print parser.anchorlist
parser.close()
```

When used on the home page for my website, this script produces something similar to following list:

```
['/', '/legal/', '/help/', '/archive/', '/about/', '/projects/articles',
'/search/', '/contact/', '/projects/books/', '/downloads/',     '/info/',
'/projects/', '/resources/', '/elsewhere/',
'/projects/books/pcr2e/index.shtml', '/downloads/pcr2e/pcr2esrc.zip',
'/downloads/pcr2esrc/pcr2esrc.tgz', '/projects/books/pdbg/index.shtml',
'/downloads/pdb/pdbsrc.zip', '/downloads/pdb/pdbsrc.tgz',
'/projects/books/pidk/index.shtml', '/projects/books/pidk/index.shtml',
'/projects/books/pdbg/index.shtml', '/projects/books/pdbg/index.shtml',
'/projects/books/imac/index.shtml',
...
'/downloads/paa/index.shtml', '/downloads/paa/paa.zip',
'/downloads/paa/paa.tgz', '/downloads/paa/paa.hqx',
'http://www.amazon.com/exec/obidos/redirect-home/mcwords?tag-id=mcwords&pl
acement=holiday-home-btn-120x90.gif&site=amazon',
'http://www.dreamhost.com/rewards.cgi', 'mailto:mc@mcwords.com']
```

We could use this information to build a list of links for a site and even to download the entire site to our local disk just by extracting the links and adding them to a list of other pages to be downloaded.

To use **htmllib** to do something more than simply regurgitating a list of anchor tags, you need to create a new class that inherits from **HTMLParser** while overloading the methods that you want to handle yourself.

To continue the previous example, if we wanted to download a website we'd also need to ensure that we downloaded the images from the pages. We can do this easily by creating our new class and overloading the **do_img()** method to build a list of image URLs to be downloaded. There is a simpler way, however: we know from the extract above that **do_img()** calls **handle_image()** with a list of attributes—overloading **handle_image()** will be much more straightforward.

Our new class looks like this:

```
class ImgParser(htmllib.HTMLParser):
    def __init__(self, formatter):
        htmllib.HTMLParser.__init__(self, formatter)
        self.imglist = []

    def handle_image(self, src, alt, ismap, align, width, height):
        self.imglist.append((src, alt, ismap, align, width, height))
```

The **__init__()** method must manually call the initializer for the **HTMLParser** class, since Python won't do it for us. The **handle_image()** method just adds a tuple to the **imglist** attribute of the **ImgParser** instance containing the information we need. To get the information back again, supply the entire HTML file to the parser through the **feed()** method and then access the **imglist** attribute:

```
parser = ImgParser(formatter.NullFormatter())
parser.feed(htmldata)
for img in parser.imglist:
    print img[0]
parser.close()
```

Of course, we can be much more practical than these simple examples. Assuming you are willing to write suitable methods to handle the information, you can do more or less anything with the HTML data you receive.

Processing XML

XML, Extensible Markup Language, is essentially SGML-lite, a cut-down version of SGML with all the flexibility of SGML but with a lot of the complexity and unused (or too-complex-to-implement) features removed. The XML 1.0 standard was formally recognized in February 1998. XML allows you to mark up a document using your own tags, providing you with the ability to lay out a document in a structured format, without relying on proprietary binary format.

The alternative to using your own set of tags is to create an XML document in combination with a DTD (Document Type Definition), which defines the tags and structure of your XML document and is one of the ways to control the format and layout of your XML information. A DTD is especially useful when you are exchanging information between two different applications, as it's the DTD that defines how the information in the XML document should be written and extracted.

Although this may not sound any different from HTML, in fact it makes XML perfect for laying out data in a structured format that you can then parse and convert to and from different formats, such as databases or HTML, and use it as a transfer format for sharing information between two different applications.

For example, with XML we can create a document that holds information about a client for a bank. You can see below how the document is structured into a single client with subaccounts that then have their own information on the account name, provider, and balance and a list of transactions.

```
<client>
<clientname>Martin Brown</clientname>
```

```
<account>
    <accname>Checking</accname>
    <provider>HSBC</provider>
    <balance>$4567.00</balance>
    <transaction>
        <payee>Rent</payee>
        <amount>$280.00</amount>
        <freq>monthly</freq>
    </transaction>
    <transaction>
        <payee>Time Subscription</payee>
        <amount>$26.00</amount>
        <freq>yearly</freq>
    </transaction>
</account>

<account>
    <accname>VISA</accname>
    <provider>Morgan Dean Stanley Witter</provider>
    <balance>$-3485.00</balance>
    <transaction>
        <payee>Supermarket</payee>
        <amount>$-450.00</amount>
    </transaction>
    <transaction>
        <payee>Gas Station</payee>
        <amount>$-18.00</amount>
    </transaction>
</account>
</client>
```

Because the information is stored as a simple text file, we can easily exchange the information with other applications without having to worry about file-compatibility—it's just text after all: all the applications need to know is how to identify the elements within the file that they need. We could, quite easily, use this XML format as a way of exchanging account information between your bank and your money management application (Quicken, Microsoft Money, GNUcash).

XML is in fact so flexible that we can use it to reproduce all sorts of documents:

■ Microsoft Word can actually store documents in XML format. Although the standard file format is not text based and still relies on many Microsoft-specific elements, you can save any Word document in XML format if you wish.

- Vector graphics can be reproduced in XML by converting the positions of different lines and other points into a series of XML tags.

- Spreadsheets can store their information in XML format just by converting the contents of their rows and columns into XML statements—we can even embed the output format, calculations, and other data.

- Contact software can store contact data in XML format. There is work in progress to allow us to use XML so that we'd no longer be limited in the number of contact numbers, addresses, or other information that we can to store about a contact. Furthermore, we could exchange information between our desktop and handheld device using XML documents; the desktop computer or handheld device would decide which fields are stored and displayed.

In fact, we can more or less use XML for marking up any information that we want—all of the above examples are feasible, and many are actually already in use now. The only data that cannot be easily stored in XML format is raw binary data, including pictures, sounds, and video, or long bit-based data streams such as the machine code required in applications and extension libraries.

XML Parsers

Python supports four different XML parsers, **xmllib**, an interface to the Expat C-based XML Parser, and SAX (Simple API for XML) and DOM (Document Object Model), all of which are capable of extracting all the information from an XML document. Parsers generally come in one of two flavors. They are either event based, which means that they trigger a function/method to be called when a particular tag is seen, or they are tree based, which means that you access the information from the XML document as if the entire document was a tree—accessing individual elements from the document by accessing them on a branch by branch basis.

Event-based models are ideal for processing large documents because we never hold the entire document in memory. They are useful when we want to convert the document from its original XML into another form, such as HTML/XHTML, or even for entry into a database. Because of the way event-based models work, you must read the document sequentially, from beginning to end, to order to parse all of its contents.

Tree-based access is useful when you want to be able to access elements from the XML document in a random fashion. Tree-based parsers examine the entire XML document and build an object hierarchy that allows you to access individual tags (and their associated data elements) by name.

The **xmllib**, Expat, and SAX parsers are event based and work on the same basic principle. You create a new class that inherits methods from a base class defined in the corresponding module. You then either register (assign) or overload the methods that actually handle the tags in a document. The event system is very flexible, and you can register both known and unknown handlers for different tags.

The **xml.dom** module provides an interface to a DOM parser. The primary interface here is called minidom (provided by the **xml.dom.minidom** module). Using minidom you import the entire XML document and then access tags by calling a method on the DOM object that returns a list of tags within the current branch. For example, in our earlier bank client XML document example, we could obtain a list of the transaction tag objects within the VISA account. Each transaction tag would then also have subobjects detailing the payee and amount.

One final note to the XML discussion is that XML makes use of Unicode, both in terms of how documents and tags are written and in terms of the data that the tags can contain. If you are not yet familiar with the way Python works when it comes to Unicode, please refer to Chapter 12.

The **xmllib** module, which was introduced in Python 1.5, is no longer directly supported, although it is still part of the standard distribution. The SAX system (supported through the **xml.sax** package) is extensive, and users of SAX under other languages will not be disappointed by the support. We, however, will be looking at the Expat event-driven parser, which is ideal for production environments because of its speed, and at the minidom DOM parser, because of its simplicity.

Using Expat

Expat is a nonvalidating XML parser written in C by James Clark. It's classed as nonvalidating because it doesn't check the format of the XML document as it is being parsed. Expat is event driven, so it works in a very similar way to the **htmllib** example that we've already seen: it parses individual XML constructs and uses callbacks to initiate the processing of individual start and end tags and data portions.

To use Expat in Python we need to import the **xml.parsers.expat** module. The module supports one main function, **ParserCreate()**, which creates an instance of the Expat parser that we can use to parse XML documents.

To use, it's probably easiest to create a new class into which you put all the methods you need to use, including those that will be triggered when different XML constructs are seen. It's not a requirement, but it does keep the system nice and tidy. Unlike **xmllib**, however, we don't inherit the methods from the parent class but use them directly. Unlike **htmllib**, we register the functions to the base parser rather than overloading existing methods within our new class.

```
import xml.parsers.expat
import sys

# Create a new class to hold all the methods that
# we want to use when parsing an XML document
class MyParser:
```

```python
# Instance constructor. We create a new parser instance
# which we hold locally in parser, then we register
# the different methods which will handle the
# XML elements
def __init__(self, filename):
    self.parser = xml.parsers.expat.ParserCreate()
    self.parser.StartElementHandler = self.starttag_handler
    self.parser.EndElementHandler = self.endtag_handler
    self.parser.CharacterDataHandler = self.data_handler
    if filename:
        self.loadfile(filename)

# Kills off and deletes the parser instance once the
# processing of a given XML file is complete
# To ensure we get rid of circular references we must
# delete the parser reference
def close(self):
    if self.parser:
        self.parser.Parse('',1)
        del self.parser

# Hand off some data to the parser
def feed(self, data):
    self.parser.Parse(data, 0)

# Called when a start tag is found
def starttag_handler(self, tag, attrs):
    print 'Start: ',repr(tag), attrs

# Called when an end tag is found
def endtag_handler(self, tag):
    print 'End:   ',repr(tag)

# Called when a data portion is found
def data_handler(self, data):
    print 'Data:  ',repr(data)

# Load a file and supply the info to the parser
def loadfile(self, filename):
```

```
        xmlfile = open(filename)
        while 1:
            data = xmlfile.read(1024)
            if not data:
                break
            self.feed(data)
        self.close()

try:
    filename - sys.argv[1]
except IndexError:
    print "You must supply a filename"
    sys.exit(1)


try:
    parser = MyParser(sys.argv[1])
except xml.parsers.expat.ExpatError:
    print "Error in XML"
```

If we use this on a simple document we get a list of the start and end tags
in the document, including any attributes:

```
$ python exexpat.py simple.xml
Start:  u'simple' {}
Data:   u'\n'
Start:  u'paragraph' {}
Data:   u'and some data'
End:    u'paragraph'
Data:   u'\n'
End:    u'simple'
```

Note that any data or tags are returned as Unicode strings, not ASCII strings. You
can use the **str()** function to convert them back to ASCII strings, or you can convert
them to another encoding using the **unicode()** built-in function or the **encode()** method
to the return Unicode object. See Chapter 12 for more information.

Using DOM (minidom)

The Document Object Model parses an XML document and then presents the parsed
document as a tree structure. Because we are representing the XML document in one
piece, we can use DOM both to parse existing documents and to create new documents.

WEB DEVELOPMENT

Under Python, the DOM interface is based on the IDL version of the specification released by W3C. The standard Python 2.x distribution comes with a basic DOM parsing system, called **minidom**, and a more complex **pulldom** system, which extracts individual elements from a DOM tree without having to read the entire XML document into memory.

Because of Python's flexible object system, it's very easy to create an equivalent of the tree structure that an XML mirrors within an Python object. Coupled with the easy object-handling (especially list-handling) features, we have a good platform for handling XML documents.

How minidom Works

To parse an existing XML document into a DOM object using **minidom**, you need to call either the **parse()** method, which accepts a filename or file object and processes the contents, or **parseString()**, which parses a bare string of information that you may have read separately from a file or network connection. In fact, it's as easy as

```
from xml.dom.minidom import parse, parseString

stringdoc = parseString('<para>Some text</para>')

xmlfile1 = open('myfile.xml')
filedoc = parse(xmlfile)

xmlfile2 = parse('myfile.xml')
```

Once you've converted the XML stream into a DOM object, you can then access the individual tags by name. For example, let's look again at our bank client XML document:

```
<client>
<clientname>Martin Brown</clientname>
<account>
    <accname>Checking</accname>
    <provider>HSBC</provider>
    <balance>$4567.00</balance>
    <transaction>
        <payee>Rent</payee>
        <amount>$280.00</amount>
    </transaction>
    <transaction>
        <payee>Time Subscription</payee>
```

```
            <amount>$26.00</amount>
        </transaction>
    </account>

    <account>
        <accname>VISA</accname>
        <provider>Morgan Dean Stanley Witter</provider>
        <balance>$-3485.00</balance>
        <transaction>
            <payee>Supermarket</payee>
            <amount>$-450.00</amount>
        </transaction>
        <transaction>
            <payee>Gas Station</payee>
            <amount>$-18.00</amount>
        </transaction>
    </account>
</client>
```

The document could be represented as a tree structure, as shown in Figure 20-1. We'll be using this diagram to help us understand how Python's DOM implementation works.

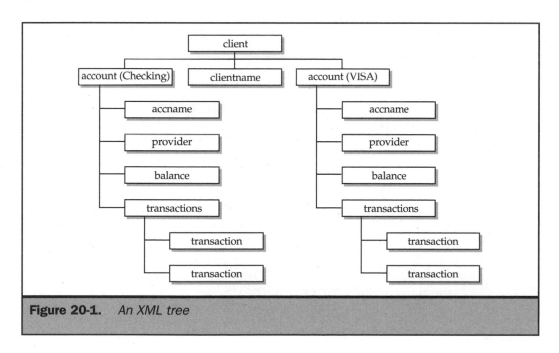

Figure 20-1.   *An XML tree*

We could get the name of the client who owns the account information using this script:

```python
from xml.dom.minidom import parse

# Create a function to get the data between XML tags
# Information is held in nodes (discrete blocks)
# which we'll need to concenate together to get the
# full picture. We only need to add text nodes to the
# string
def getdata(nodes):
    rc = ''
    for node in nodes:
        if node.nodeType == node.TEXT_NODE:
            rc = rc + node.data
    return rc

# Parse the document
client = parse('client.xml')

# Get the first clientname tag from the document
clientname = client.getElementsByTagName("clientname")[0]

# Print out the data contained within the tags
# using getdata to extract the text from the nodes
# defined within the element
print 'Client name is', getdata(clientname.childNodes)
```

The **getElementsByTagName()** method returns a list of all the tag elements with the supplied name. The resulting objects contain the information about the tag, including any attributes if supplied, and a set of nodes that make up the data contained within the tags.

Note that the object returned is a branch (or leaf) of the tree structure shown in Figure 20.1. The root of the tree is the same as the document root—so to access all the elements within the document we need to reference individual branches from the **client** object that was created when the document was parsed. In this case it's the leaf called **clientname**, which stands alone.

Had we used

```python
accounts = client.getElementsByTagName("account")
```

the accounts object would now be a list containing the two account branches. Each element would refer to one of the account branches in our diagram. To get a list of the transactions within the checking account we could have used:

```
checking = accounts[0]
trans = client.getElementsByTagName("transaction")
```

Now **trans** would contain the information in the two transactions in our account. Now each element would be one of the transaction branches.

DOM in Action

Putting this into practice, we can build a script that outputs in a structured format the information contained within our XML document. The script is actually a good example of a tree-based XML parser in Python. Because we're not following the tree sequentially (as we would with an event-based parser), we can be a little less restrictive about how we extract information: we don't have to worry about recording states or determining whether the output format should change because we've reached a particular end tag.

```
from xml.dom.minidom import parse

def getdata(nodes):
    rc = ''
    for node in nodes:
        if node.nodeType == node.TEXT_NODE:
            rc = rc + node.data
    return rc

def handleclient(client):
    clientname = client.getElementsByTagName("clientname")[0]
    print 'Client:', getdata(clientname.childNodes)
    accounts = client.getElementsByTagName("account")
    handleaccounts(accounts)

def handleaccounts(accounts):
    print 'Accounts:'
    for account in accounts:
        handleaccount(account)

def handleaccount(account):
    accname = account.getElementsByTagName("accname")[0]
    provider = account.getElementsByTagName("provider")[0]
    print ' ' * 4, '%s (%s)' % (getdata(accname.childNodes),
```

```
getdata(provider.childNodes))
    print ' ' * 4, 'Transactions:'
    trans = account.getElementsByTagName("transaction")
    for transaction in trans:
        handletransaction(transaction)
    balance = account.getElementsByTagName("balance")[0]
    print ' ' * 9, '%-40s %s' % ('', '======')
    print ' ' * 9, '%-40s %s' % ('', getdata(balance.childNodes))
    print ''

def handletransaction(transaction):
    payee = transaction.getElementsByTagName("payee")[0]
    amount = transaction.getElementsByTagName("amount")[0]
    print ' ' * 9, '%-40s %s' % (getdata(payee.childNodes),
getdata(amount.childNodes))

client = parse('client.xml')

handleclient(client)
```

If we run this script on our client XML document, we get the following output:

```
$ python exdom2.py client.xml
Client: Martin Brown
Accounts:
    Checking (HSBC)
    Transactions:
        Rent                                    $280.00
        Time Subscription                       $26.00

                                                ======
                                                $4567.00


    VISA (Morgan Dean Stanley Witter)
    Transactions:
        Supermarket                             $-450.00
        Gas Station                             $-18.00

                                                ======
                                                $-3485.00
```

We could have just as easily converted this document into HTML or XHTML, or we could have extracted the information for writing into the individual tables of a database.

The
Complete
Reference

Chapter 21

Other Python Web Tools

Ask most programmers what the most popular web programming language is, and a high proportion will probably say Perl. The rest will probably say PHP, VisualBasic, or C++, and a very small proportion may say Python. This is unfortunate because Python, as we saw in the previous chapter, is just as capable as Perl in most instances, and in many other ways is actually much more advanced.

As a case in point, many people don't realize that Jython (formerly JPython) exists. Jython is a complete implementation of the Python language but in Java, rather than the native C form most people will be familiar with. Jython allows us to mix Python and Java code in the same scripts. What it actually does is convert Python source code into Java bytecode and then passes it on to the Java virtual machine.

From the server side, the best tool available that uses Python is Zope. Zope, or the Z-Objects Publishing Environment, allows you to expose Python objects and their methods as if they were CGI scripts written as part of a normal web service. You access an object and it's method using a simple URL path, and any attached key/value pairs are exposed as arguments to the methods.

In this chapter we're going to have a look at some of the web and Internet tools written in or making use of Python. Unfortunately, we don't have the space to look into all of these different systems in much detail. If you want more information, use the links and web sites in this chapter as well as the generic Python websites, which are listed in Appendix B, to get more information.

Zope, the Z-Objects Publishing Environment

One of the major issues facing most web developers is how to implement their application as a web site. At the simplest level, you use a combination of HTML files and CGI scripts to support your application. This model can lead to problems when you try to marry the two components: how do you get the HTML- and CGI- based elements to look the same, for example. The CGI components require you to import and handle CGI and HTTP data and make decisions based on the information before supplying an HTML formatted document back to the user.

Zope is different. Since most of the information that you'll be placing into a web page generated by a CGI document will be from an object within the Python script, Zope allows you to embed Python objects—or at least the information contained within them—right in the content of an HTML page. We no longer have to worry about marrying static HTML and dynamic HTML components: the HTML documents contain references to the objects and the information we want to display.

Furthermore, Zope provides a very simple way for multiple people to work on the same website at the same time. It uses a special markup language called DTML (Document Template Markup Language), which allows you to create HTML documents based on standard templates. The DTML system also allows you to integrate calls to Python objects and to create links between an HTML page and an external data source such as a SQL database.

The Zope system takes away all of the complexity of CGI programming and instead allows your programmers to concentrate on developing interfaces to your internal systems, your web developers to concentrate on developing suitable document templates, and your content managers to concentrate on filling the site with content, without anybody have to cross into somebody else's territory. To help explain this further, let's have a look at how Zope is organized and how object publishing works.

The Zope System

Zope is made up of four primary components that work together to provide the Zope system. There are the Zope ORB (Object Request Broker), ZPublisher, the DTML markup language, and a ZODB (Zope Object Data Base):

- **Zope ORB** is the object request broker in Zope, and it is the heart of the Zope system. The ORB is responsible for turning a client's request into information along the way, and converting that into an object and method call on an object instance. See "How the Zope ORB Works" for more information.

- **ZPublisher** is the public interface. It interacts between the Web server and the requests and CGI data and ZORB, which is actually a component of ZPublisher, rather than a separate entity. ZPublisher is the front end to the entire Zope system and works with any number of different web server solutions, including CGI, PCGI, FastCGI, Netscape's Web Application Interface (WAI), COM, Medusa (see the description later in this chapter), and the included ZopeHTTPServer. Most people forget ZPublisher exists and instead refer to it as ZORB—for the most part the two terms are interchangeable.

- **DTML** provides a simple way of defining HTML templates. The templates are parsed during a request with information from any objects (brokered through ZORB) and external data sources. This allows a web system to be developed by separate Python developers and web programmers without either party worried about how to integrate the Python objects and HTML code.

- **Zope's Object Database** (ZODB) uses the **pickle** module (see Chapter 12) to serialize a Python object and store the resulting data stream. Beyond the basics of storing objects, ZODB also includes support for transactions, concurrent access to a single object (similar to the row and table locking mechanisms in an RDBMS), and delayed evaluation of object components, allowing you to access objects without the time overhead of recovering all the information from the database until it's needed. The entire system works through a key, in a similar fashion to pulling information out of a dictionary within Python itself.

In addition to all this, Zope also provides a number of ancillary systems to help you develop Zope solutions. For example, the Zope kit includes an HTTP server module so that Zope can broker all of the requests itself, rather than working through an existing web server. Other components include a management framework for administering your website and a content management system that works with the CVS system to record changes to your website and allow multiple users to update the website content without interfering with another person's work.

How the Zope ORB Works

Publishing objects does not seem like a natural progression from the basics of CGI as we saw them in Chapter 19. In fact, object publishing is a much simpler solution than you might expect to the problem of exporting the information contained within a Python script to the outside world.

To give an example, imagine we have an HTML page that allows users to sign in to a website. We'll ignore the problems of authorization, and instead just look at the mechanics of the ZPublisher and ZORB systems. The HTML form looks like this:

```
<form method=GET action="http://zope.mydomain.com/cgi-bin/authorize/login">
Name: <input type=text size=20 name=login><br>
Password: <input type=password size=20 name=passwd><br>
<input type=submit><br>
</form>
```

When submitted, this results in a URL request that looks like this:

```
http://zope.mydomain.com/cgi-
bin/authorize/generic/login?login=mc&passwd=password
```

When received by ZORB, this request is mapped to a object/method call on the server zope.mydomain.com, which would look something like this:

```
authorize.generic.login(login='mc', passwd='password')
```

In essence, what would normally be recognized as the script location (the directory **authorize**) is recognized as the name of the module; the object name is the next location component (**generic**); and the method to call is what would normally be accepted as the name of the script. Any data appended to the request is then supplied as arguments to the method we're calling. You can see this more clearly using a dummy URL:

```
http://servername/directory/module/object1/object2/method?args
```

which is converted to

```
module.object1.object2.method(args)
```

The resulting return value from the script is then inserted into a predefined DTML document template, or as a raw page. ZPublisher handles all of the complexities such as returning suitable HTTP headers and formatting the information into a reasonable document.

Of course, this simple example does not do Zope any justice. The information contained in the request could be quite complex, and the object and method that are called do anything from returning a static value to returning a piece of information from a database. If you want to store information, then use your favorite SQL database or ZODB.

Also keep in mind that the Python objects you are referring to don't have to be located on the same server. You could quite easily build a page based on different requests to different servers, all running Zope, and all returning information into a single page. In this respect, Zope works more like a distributed publishing environment. Imagine, for example, having a set of Zope servers, one for each department, while also having a single "overlord" Zope server that displays a summary page about the current status of all of your departments websites.

Zope's Future

Zope was developed by Digital Creations and is seen by a large part of the community as the next killer application. Often compared to more well-known integrated web publishing systems such as ColdFusion or IBM's WebSphere, Zope offers a freely available alternative that comes with all the trappings of an open source product, including excellent community support and the ultimate in flexibility.

The future for Zope looks very bright. The system itself is going from strength to strength, and it already has a number of high-profile users including ActiveState, IDG Brazil, and a number of newspaper and catalogue companies. As if this wasn't enough to cement Zope's success, Digital Creations is also the new home of Guido van Rossum, the developer of Python, and the rest of the Python development team.

To get more information and to download your own copy of Zope, check out www.zope.org.

Jython

Developing websites that rely on CGI all the time for their interaction can quickly become tiresome for many users, especially within an intranet environment. There are many solutions available that would probably fit the bill for most people: we have Javascript for simple rollovers and form processing, and if you want something more significant you have Macromedia's Flash system for developing games and interactive slide shows and presentations.

A more general purpose language exists for developing client-side applications, and that's Java. Although it hasn't quite caused the computing revolution that Sun expected when they released it, Java has expanded the options available when developing applications, both on the client side and on the server side using JSP. There are even extensions to Java that provide database connectivity (JDBC) and a more friendly Java object model in the form of JavaBeans.

Jython (formerly JPython) is an implementation of Python written entirely in Java. It sits at exactly the same level as the Python interpreter that you are probably familiar with, which is written in C, except that it's written in Java. This allows you to mix and match Java and Python components within the same application. For example, you could incorporate a Python application within a Java applet, allowing you to execute Python code on your client without the client actually requiring the Python interpreter.

Using Jython isn't all plain sailing for the average Python programmer. To make use of Jython you'll need to know how to program in Java to get the best out of the system. Some basic information about Jython, how it works, and what it's capable of is included here. For more detailed information, see the Jython website (www.Jython.org).

How Jython Works

The primary component behind the Jython system is its ability to compile Python code fragments into Java bytecode, which can then be executed by any Java virtual machine that has access to the Jython class libraries. To a Java virtual machine (JVM), the translated Python/Jython code looks identical to any other Java bytecode.

Once you've got this central piece of technology working, all of the other features of the Jython system suddenly become much easier. Jython code inherits all of the facilities offered by Java, including Java's garbage collection and security systems.

In addition, Jython offers the following other features to Jython programmers:

- **Jython wrapper for Java.** As well as providing a system for translating your existing scripts into Java bytecode, Jython also provides a Java **PythonInterpreter** class, which can be used to compile and execute Python code through the familiar **exec** statement, and the **execfile()** function. You can then access objects created within a class instance from within Java, since Jython exposes all objects as instances of the Java **PyObject** class.

- **Java libraries** are exposed to any Python script written using Jython. This allows you to call any Java class from within a Jython script just as if you were using Python classes, objects, and methods—the integration is completely transparent. You can import Java and Jython classes through the normal **import** statement just as if you were importing Python modules into a typical script.

- **Common object models** are used by Jython to smooth the integration process. Jython does this by reimplementing all of the built-in Python types, such as dictionaries and lists through a Java-based **PyObject** class. This eliminates the need for Jython to constantly convert objects between the two languages; because Jython converts the Python bytecode into Java bytecode, all of the objects are accessed natively by the JVM.

■ **Interface improvements** are included in the Jython implementation, making it much easier to build GUI applications using a typical Python style, as you might be familiar with when developing under Tk, compared to the class-based support system required by Java. For example, a callback in Java needs to be defined as part of a genuine Java class, whereas a Jython callback can simply be a function.

The resulting system allows you great flexibility when developing Python software for use within a browser environment. First and foremost, developing Python applications is much quicker than developing Java applications—using Jython we can develop a Python application that works on the client, while still having access to the necessary Java-based GUI interface libraries. Jython also adds a scripting component to a language that is intentionally compiled and inflexible as C or C++, albeit with better cross-platform support.

Also, because Python is class- and object-based, just like Java, the learning curve for implementing Jython-based tools over Java- or Python-based tools is not significant compared to that required when embedding a Python interpreter into a C/C++ application.

Jython Limitations

Despite all of the facilities and improvements over a basic Java machine that Jython offers, it's not perfect. There are some limitations to what Jython can and can't do:

■ **Jython requires Java.** Probably this is the most obvious statement, but it's an important one. Java can be found in the most surprising of places, but that doesn't mean it's everywhere. Some companies and individuals deliberately disable Java on their systems, making Jython development and deployment impossible. For other systems, the Java implementation may be either unstable or in a permanent state of flux. For example, the recent troubles experienced between Microsoft and Sun over the Java implementation actually removed Java support from Internet Explorer for a time, and Mac OS X's initial versions of Internet Explorer do not support Java at all. If you want to develop with Jython, make sure that your intended audience has Java abilities.

■ **Java knowledge** is required to get the best out of Jython. Although you can do a lot with Jython and basic Python scripts, to support a GUI interface or work with existing Java components such as JDBC, you'll need to know how to program in Java. Learning Java if you already know Python is not a major task, but it's an extra step that you may not be willing to take.

■ **Python compatibility** is not as good or complete as with the CPython implementation. For example, simple constructs in CPython, like using files (particularly with the standard file objects like **sys.stdin**), still do not work, and the exception system works more like Python 1.5, using string- rather than class-based exceptions, which may be a sticking point for some. These problems are also compounded as CPython development will always be ahead of Jython. It'll probably take one or two months from the release of a new CPython implementation to get the same facilities in Jython.

■ **Jython is slower** than its CPython counterpart as we are always working with a language that has been translated into Java, instead of working with native Java source code. This extra layer is being worked on all the time, and the exact slowdown that you experience varies according to the script you are running, but tests show that Jython scripts can be anything from 2 to 100 times slower than a CPython version.

■ **C/C++ extensions** are currently incompatible with Jython. This isn't a limitation of Jython per se; getting these interfaces to work will rely on getting Java and C/C++ working together, or even ultimately being able to translate C/C++ code into Java bytecode—something that is currently impossible. Unfortunately, this limits Jython quite severely for anything other than browser-based applications. Jython's answer is to redevelop the extension modules already written using Java, but this is a major redevelopment effort for many of the third-party modules available through the Vaults of Parnassus. Remember, of course, that many elements of the C/C++ extension experience, such as database and network access, are already available as Java class libraries.

Despite all of these problems, Jython is still an excellent tool, and if you want a cross-platform solution to development Python-based clients-side applications, then Jython is the most capable. For Windows-specific solutions, check out the information later in this chapter on "Python and ActiveScript."

Python.NET

The .NET initiative from Microsoft is one of the most significant changes in terms of software development and deployment since the invention of the CD-ROM and the sudden expansion of the Internet. The .NET framework is a component-based software system that allows you to mix and match languages within a single application through a combination of XML and a single, glue language called C#. As well as supporting the usually host-based applications, the .NET system also makes it easy to deploy distributed Internet applications, allowing you to pass information between different hosts using XML and whatever language, or combination of languages, that you want.

ActiveState is developing components that will fit into the .NET framework, with Perl and Python implementations already available in beta versions. Like Jython, Python.NET will be a native interpreter for Python. Whereas Jython translates Python bytecode into Java bytecode, Python.NET will translate Python scripts into C# code. You can then mix and match the Python-derived C# classes and objects with native C#, Perl, VisualBasic, and even C/C++ applications. It's quite possible to create a

Perl-based application that uses objects and methods written in Python, or for a Python script to use objects and classes normally available only through C/++—and all without the technicality of extending or embedding Python manually into your applications.

The major benefits to Python are compatibility and the ability to create stand-alone Python-based applications. Using Python.NET you could compile your application direct to a .exe executable through the C# translator. Even more useful for many Window programmers is that .NET development occurs within a new version of Microsoft's VisualStudio, so you can develop Python applications using the same tools and IDE as you use for C/C++ and VisualBasic development.

Python.NET is still very much a work in progress. Although you can download beta versions of the ActiveState Python.NET component, there are still many bugs in the translation system, and not all of the Python functionality and modules are yet supported through C#.

ActiveState itself is an avid developer now of Python tools. Originally a Perl-only shop, ActiveState now develops solutions for Perl, Python, Tcl, and XML developers. They provide everything from Windows-specific extensions and installer packages for the languages through to IDE's Komodo and copious amounts of documentation and examples.

.NET is still largely in its infancy, with VisualStudio.NET still in its second beta cycle as of June 2001. The final version of the VisualStudio.NET component, which will be responsible for bonding everything together, isn't expected until November 2001, with Python.NET and similar tools arriving shortly after that.

If you want more information, visit ActiveState's website—see the resources list in Appendix B for more information.

Python Server Pages

Python Server Pages (PSP) are intended as a Python-based equivalent to the Active Server Pages (ASP) system offered by ActiveState's Python package and Microsoft's IIS (Internet Information Server) under Windows. Others have compared PSP to the PHP server-side scripting system, which uses a Perl-like language to handle the server side scripting of a website.

Unlike ASP or PHP, PSP is written entirely in Java: this allows you to deploy PSP under all systems that support Java, which is more or less all of them. Where Python fits in is that PSP employs Jython, embedded within HTML pages, to provide you with access to all of the facilities of Python, Jython, and Java all within the same tool.

As with ASP and PHP, however, the benefit is that we can easily introduce code into an HTML page. For sites that make heavy use of CGI scripts and embedded HTML within the script's source code, the emphasis is taken off of writing the HTML code with the CGI script, and instead devoted to simply getting the information we want.

For more information about PSP, see the PSP website at www.ciobriefings.com/psp.

Python and ActiveScript

Microsoft's Internet Information Server provides a service called ActiveScript. ActiveScript is an extension to the IIS system that allows you to embed scripting statements in an HTML page. These scripting elements can then be executed, either by the server or the client, to provide additional functionality within the web page.

ActiveScript is not language specific. Although it's primarily used to support VisualBasic scripts (VBScript), it can also be configured through suitable extensions to support Python, Perl, and many other languages. ActiveState, a company originally partly funded by Microsoft to develop Windows-specific tools using Perl, provides versions of Perl and Python (ActivePerl and ActivePython respectively) that incorporate ActiveScript functionality.

Because ActiveScript is both a server- and a client-side technology, it opens up a whole series of possibilities. For example, you could embed a Python script into an HTML page that accepted input from a form, processed the information, and displayed a result, all without requiring a CGI script, or indeed any communication with the browser.

The limitation of client-side ActiveScript is that it requires a Windows machine running Internet Explorer that also has the Python installed. Unfortunately, this severely limits its usefulness, but in a closed environment such as an intranet, it can be a useful alternative to CGI scripts.

We can also use ActiveScript as a server-side scripting alternative. In this mode it works in a similar fashion to any other CGI script, except that it too is embedded within the HTML and parsed before the final document is sent on to the client.

One final feature of ActiveScript is that we can communicate with Windows applications through the COM (Common Object Model) interface. COM enables you to talk to and interact with objects supplied by other applications. Python provides support under Windows both for being a COM client and a COM server. COM is a major component of Windows and particularly Microsoft applications. You can use COM to open a Word document and print it from within Python, or with Python as the application server, you could allow Visual Basic for Applications—the macro language built into Microsoft Office and other apps—to execute Python statements.

COM is a massive topic in its own right, and we don't have room to go into too much detail, although we will be returning to the topic of COM and Python when we look at some of the platform-specific extensions available for Python. See Chapter 22 for more information.

Mailman

Check your email box and if you belong to any mailing lists you may well find that some of them are managed by Mailman. Mailman is completely Python-based and supports all of the usual mailing list options such as digests, email-based discussions and simple mail-out–only announcement lists.

Where Mailman differs from so many other implementations is that Mailman also includes a Python-based web interface. The web interface can be used by subscribers and mailing list owners to control subscriptions and mailing list options. As if that wasn't enough, it also filters spam and provides a mail-to-news gateway for integrating your mailing list and news servers.

Mailman is probably one of the more subversive uses of Python—many people, Python advocates and otherwise, probably use Python without realizing

Grail

Grail is a Python-based web browser that uses the Tkinter GUI system to implement its user interface. As well as allowing you to view websites, Grail also allows you to execute Python- and Tkinter-based scripts as client-side applets that can be embedded directly into your web pages. In use, Grail is pretty much like Netscape or Internet Explorer, although it fails to support many of the more recent standards because its development has been neglected for so long.

Grail itself has more of a history as being one of the very first large-scale applications written entirely in Python. We owe to it a lot of Python's Internet functionality, including the generic download modules such as **urllib**, the HTML parsers, and the generic protocol libraries such as **ftplib** and **httplib**.

The real benefit though was the ability to use Python scripts, and more significantly Tk-based widgets, right within a web page a long time before the practicalities of systems like Macromedia's Flash or Jython-based content. The content itself could be a simple widget, or it could use information passed from the browser through a form. Furthermore, because you also had access to the full Python language, you could more or less create any application you wanted and still access it through your browser.

Grail is unfortunately no longer formally maintained, and it was never intended as a competitor to Netscape or Internet Explorer. If you want a Python-based client-side Python implementation that isn't based on Grail or ActiveScript use Jython.

Apache and Python

If you are familiar with Apache and already use the Apache web server for supporting your sites, then you'll be pleased to hear that there are a number of efforts underway to integrate Python and Apache. The basic Apache package already provides support for running server-side Python scripts through the standard CGI interface.

The PyApache extension attempts to improve the speed of execution of Python scripts by embedding the Python interpreter into the Apache server. This will help to speed up the execution of Python scripts, since we won't need to spawn an external application to handle the execution of the script. The system will also work in reverse, allowing you to use Python constructs within Apache; this can be useful for handling configuration information and for authorization processes. For example, you could have Python working through a database to authorize a user, rather than using the built-in authorization methods.

WEB DEVELOPMENT

The **mod_python** extension module for Apache will provide similar functionality for Apache by building the Python interpreter into Apache itself. Where **mod_python** differs is that it also holds the Python scripts in the memory of Apache in its bytecode—and therefore optimized and ready to execute—format. Because the code is resident in memory and has already been parsed an compiled, you get a substantial speed improvement. The **mod_python** extension is similar to the **mod_perl** extension, which improves execution of Perl scripts in a similar way up to make them execute up to 100 times faster than the normal CGI script route. The **mod_python** Apache extension is still in beta as I write this, but based on the success of **mod_perl** I think it's safe to assume some significant improvements in speed.

SocketServer and BaseHTTPServer

Although not for everybody, it is possible to create your own socket-based and HTTP-based network servers using the modules and classes that come as standard with the Python interpreter. We actually saw some examples of this in Chapter 13.

Listening for requests and servicing them is really just a case of opening the corresponding port and waiting for a client to connect. Then you choose whether to pass the connection off to a new process through **fork()**, fire up a new thread to handle the request, or use **select()** to handle requests in a round robin fashion. Threads are obviously recommended, but they are not supported by all platforms.

If you want to service specific HTTP requests, using **BaseHTTPServer** or **CGIHTTPServer** is probably the easiest route. You can adopt these classes and modify them for your own use if you require. With a little work it would be possible to create a stand-alone Python-based web server that also had a built-in connection to a database and held state information for connections, making for quicker access than through a normal CGI-based interface.

Using these modules is exceptionally easy; the script below shows how easy it is to set up a web server using Python and these modules:

```
import os, BaseHTTPServer, CGIHTTPServer

os.chdir('/export/home/mc/html')
httpserver =
BaseHTTPServer.HTTPServer(('',8081),CGIHTTPServer.CGIHTTPRequestHandler)
httpserver.serve_forever()
```

Be aware that under Unix you'll need SuperUser (root) privileges to start a server with a port under 1000. In this case we've started up a web server on port 8081 within the html directory of my home directory. For a closer look at the BaseHTTPServer and CGIHTTPServer, check out my *Python Annotated Archives* title (see Appendix B), which takes a line by line look at how these modules operate.

Medusa

Medusa provides the necessary systems to build high-performance and high-availability socket-based network servers. Architecturally Medusa sits above **SocketServer** and **select()**, handling all of the problems of supporting multiple data streams and clients.

Medusa was originally a pair of separate modules, **asyncore** and **asynchat**, which worked together to provide asynchronous, multiplexing I/O, but without using the tricks of threads and **fork()**. Instead the modules use an event loop built on top of the **select()** system call. Because it uses **select()**, Medusa is only suitable for quick, short-lived transactions.

The core components to Medusa are part of the standard library, and have been since v1.5.2. The complete Medusa system also includes HTTP and FTP servers and is free for noncommercial use. You can download the full version of Medusa from **www.nightmare.com/medusa**.

The Complete Reference

Part V

Cross-platform Development

Chapter 22

Paths to Cross-platform Development

487

Python is supported on a large number of platforms, and that means that it's often used for cross-platform development. Listing all the different possible platform types is pointless, but Python already runs on most flavors of Unix, Windows, Mac OS (including Mac OS X), OS/2, BeOS and many, many others. You can even get a hold of a version for the Palm OS called Pippy!

Developing a true cross-platform application is not easy. Even ignoring issues like the user interface, there are heaps of background issues surrounding such areas as line termination, environment variables, and the standard input and output, and of course the list of supported functions varies from platform to platform and even Unix variant to Unix variant.

Python actually hides a large majority of the complexity of handling cross-platform issues from the programmer. Python includes only a very few built-in functions, and the majority of external modules are supported by most platforms and either provide no support or quasi-support for a given function when it's called.

We have actually already looked at some of these issues elsewhere in this book. For example, for interface building, the Tk toolkit currently provides the only Unix-, Windows-, and Mac OS–compatible solution. See Chapter 15 for more information. For file reading and writing and data and character support, check out Chapters 9, 10, and 11.

In the rest of this chapter we'll look at some of the major issues affecting your Python cross-platform development. Also check out the MCwords website (http:// www.mcwords.com), where we'll be updating the cross-platform support and tricks.

Basic Platform Support

The most obvious difference between platforms is the support for different functions. Python hides most of this complexity in external modules, and in most cases an alternative or workaround is automatically employed on a platform that doesn't normally support the option. In fact, if you stick with most of the standard Python modules, you should be pretty much protected from some of the problems.

But that doesn't make you completely immune. Here are a few of the items you should look out for:

■ Functions that involve looking up details in one of the Unix files normally contained in /etc are pretty Unix-centric. They include network information routines and also those routines related to group and/or password information (as supported through the **pwd** and **grp** modules). Some platforms do use **pwd** and **grp**, but when not available there are usually equivalents in a platform-specific module.

- All the basic file interfacing options will work, but others, such as **stat()**, may have limited support because of the underlying file system used by the operating system. Not all platforms support both modification and access times, for example. File permissions also need to be watched—the **chmod()** and **chown()** functions are Unix specific. Most of the functions that accept a permission value (such as **os.open()**) will safely ignore the information on non-Unix platforms.

- You should also remember that although Mac OS and Windows support the notion of links via aliases and shortcuts, respectively, the **link()** and **lstat()** functions often do not work.

- Access to the internals of the operating system tables are also unsupported on many other platforms, particularly those that return unique process and group IDs, or those that return parent group and parent owner information for a process ID.

- The **exec*()** and similar functions that rely on the ability to run an application by name through a command line–like interface may not work on all platforms. In particular, the Mac OS (but not Mac OS X), which doesn't have a command-line interface, does not natively support functions like **os.system()**, and the **os.popen()** function is completely meaningless as Mac applications don't understand the meaning of standard input and output to allow you to capture the information in the first place.

Execution Environment

The environment in which Python is executed can have a significant effect on your script. Many problems can arise because you rely on information or capabilities outside of Python, but that may be directly available internally. Some examples are listed below:

- Try not to rely on the environment variables to obtain information about the user, group, hostname, username, or path information. These variables can be easily overridden or falsely generated, and on platforms other than Unix they may not even be set. Instead, get the information direct from the **os** module through the **getuid()** and other functions, and make sure you have a backup plan to account for platforms that don't support user IDs (Windows, Mac OS). This advice is especially pertinent if you decide to use one of these variables in a unique ID or other identification string. See Table 22-1 for a list of environment variables and alternatives, and see Table 22-2 for a list of Windows-specific environment variables and which platforms support them.

■ Don't rely on commands that you want to execute being available within the **PATH** environment variable—set the path yourself or, better still, use a full path to the application. Remember to account for different platforms and use a suitable path.

■ Don't rely on signals unless you have to. Some platforms support signals and signal handlers; others don't, and those that do may only support a reduced set compared to those available under your chosen Unix environment.

■ Use shared files or network sockets to exchange information between processes, or use threads (see Chapter 10) and shared variables. Take care when using environment variables in a web/CGI environment, as not all platforms and web servers support the same range of environment variables. See Table 22-3 for more information.

Variable	Description	Alternate
COLUMNS	The number columns for the current display. Can be useful for determining the current terminal size when developing a terminal/text interface.	None
EDITOR	The user's editor preference. If it can't be found, then default to **vi** or **emacs** or, on Windows, to **C:/Windows/Notepad.exe**.	None
EUID	The effective user ID of the current process. Use **os.geteuid()**, which will be populated correctly irrespective of the **EUID** variable.	**os.geteuid()**
HOME	The user's home directory. Try getting the information from **pwd.getpwuid()** instead.	**pwd.getpwuid()**
HOST	The current hostname. The **socket.gethostname()** function provides a platform-neutral way of determining the hostname.	**socket.gethostname()**

Table 22-1.   *Environment Variables on Unix Machines*

Variable	Description	Alternate
HOSTNAME	The current hostname.	socket.gethostname()
LINES	The number of lines supported by the current terminal window or display. See **COLUMNS** earlier in the table.	None
LOGNAME	The user's login. Use the **getpass.getuser()** function or, better still, the **os.getpwuid()** function in combination with **pwd.getpwuid()**.	getpass.getuser()
MAIL	The path to the user's mail file. If it can't be found, try guessing the value; it's probably **/var/mail/LOGNAME** or **/var/spool/mail/LOGNAME**.	None
PATH	The colon-separated list of directories to search when looking for applications to execute. Aside from the security risk of using an external list, you should probably be using the full path to the applications that you want to execute, or populating **PATH** within your script.	None
PPID	The parent process ID. There's no easy way to find this, but it's unlikely that you'll want it anyway.	None
PWD	The current working directory. You should use the **os.getcwd()** function instead.	os.getcwd()
SHELL	The path to the user's preferred shell. This value can be abused so that you end up running a suid program instead of a real shell. If it can't be determined, **/bin/sh** is a good default.	None

Table 22-1.   *Environment Variables on Unix Machines* (continued)

CROSS-PLATFORM
DEVELOPMENT

Variable	Description	Alternate
TERM	The name/type of the current terminal and therefore terminal emulation. See **COLUMNS** earlier in this table.	None
UID	The user's real ID.	**os.getuid()**
USER	The user's login name. See **LOGNAME** earlier in this table.	**getpass.getuser()**
VISUAL	The user's visual editor preference. See **EDITOR** earlier in the table.	**EDITOR**
XSHELL	The shell to be used within the X Windows System. See **SHELL** earlier in the table.	**SHELL**

Table 22-1. *Environment Variables on Unix Machines* (continued)

Variable	Platform	Description	Alternate
ALLUSERSPROFILE	2000	The location of the generic profile currently in use. There's no way of determining this information.	None
CMDLINE	95/98	The command line, including the name of the application executed. The **sys.argv** object should have been populated with this information.	**sys.argv**

Table 22-2. *Environment Variables for Windows*

Variable	Platform	Description	Alternate
COMPUTERNAME	NT, 2000	The name of the computer. The **socket.gethostname()** will return the DNS/Internet name for the current host.	
COMSPEC	All	The path to the command interpreter (usually **COMMAND.COM**) used when opening a command prompt.	None
HOMEDRIVE	NT, 2000	The drive letter (and colon) of the user's home drive.	None
HOMEPATH	NT, 2000	The path to the user's home directory.	None
HOMESHARE	NT, 2000	The UNC name of the user's home directory. Note that this value will be empty if the user's home directory is unset or set to local drive.	None
LOGONSERVER	NT, 2000	The domain name server the user was authenticated on.	None
NUMBER_OF_ PROCESSORS	NT, 2000	The number of processors active in the current machine.	None

Table 22-2.   *Environment Variables for Windows* (continued)

Variable	Platform	Description	Alternate
OS	NT, 2000	The name of the operating system. The **sys.platform** object holds the platform string, which will tell you whether you are running under Windows 3.1 (win16) or Windows 95-2000 (win32).	**sys.platform**
OS2LIBPATH	NT, 2000	The path to the OS/2 compatibility libraries.	None
PATH	All	The path searched for applications within the command prompt and for programs executed via the **os.system()** or **os.exec*()**.	None
PATHEXT	NT, 2000	The list of extensions that will be used to identify an executable program. You probably shouldn't be modifying this, but if you need to define it manually, **.bat**, **.com**, and **.exe** are the most important.	None
PROCESSOR_ARCHITECTURE	NT, 2000	The processor architecture of the current machine.	None
PROCESSOR_IDENTIFIER	NT, 2000	The identifier (the information tag returned by the CPU when queried).	None

Table 22-2. *Environment Variables for Windows* (continued)

Variable	Platform	Description	Alternate
PROCESSOR_LEVEL	NT, 2000	The processor level; 3 refers to a 386, 4 to a 486, and 5 to the Pentium. Values of 3000 and 4000 refer to MIPS processors, and 21064 refers to an Alpha processor.	None
PROCESSOR_REVISION	NT, 2000	The processor revision.	None
SYSTEMDRIVE	NT, 2000	The drive holding the currently active operating system. The most likely location is **C:**.	None
SYSTEMROOT	NT, 2000	The root directory of the active operating system. This will probably be **Windows** or **Win**.	None
USERDOMAIN	NT, 2000	The domain the current user is connected to.	None
USERNAME	NT, 2000	The name of the current user.	None
USERPROFILE	NT, 2000	The location of the user's profile.	None
WINBOOTDIR	NT, 2000	The location of the Windows operating system that was used to boot the machine. See the **SYSTEMROOT** entry earlier in this table.	None

Table 22-2.   *Environment Variables for Windows* (continued)

CROSS-PLATFORM DEVELOPMENT

Variable	Platform	Description	Alternate
WINDIR	All	The location of the active Windows operating system. This directory is used when searching for DLLs and other OS information. See the **SYSTEMROOT** entry earlier in this table.	None

Table 22-2. *Environment Variables for Windows* (continued)

Environment Variable	Platform
CONTENT_LENGTH	Apache, IIS
DOCUMENT_ROOT	Apache
GATEWAY_INTERFACE	Apache
HTTPS	IIS
HTTP_ACCEPT	Apache, IIS
HTTP_ACCEPT_CHARSET	Apache, IIS
HTTP_ACCEPT_ENCODING	Apache, IIS
HTTP_ACCEPT_LANGUAGE	Apache, IIS
HTTP_CONNECTION	Apache, IIS
HTTP_COOKIE	IIS
HTTP_EXTENSION	Apache
HTTP_HOST	Apache, IIS
HTTP_IF_MODIFIED_SINCE	Apache
HTTP_UA_CPU	Apache, IIS
HTTP_UA_OS	Apache, IIS

Table 22-3. *Environment Variables Defined When Executing a CGI Script*

Environment Variable	Platform
HTTP_USER_AGENT	Apache, IIS
LOCAL_ADDR	IIS
PATH	Apache
PATH_INFO	IIS
PATH_TRANSLATED	IIS
QUERY_STRING	Apache, IIS
REMOTE_ADDR	Apache, IIS
REMOTE_HOST	Apache, IIS
REQUEST_METHOD	Apache, IIS
REQUEST_URI	Apache
SCRIPT_FILENAME	Apache
SCRIPT_NAME	Apache, IIS
SERVER_ADDR	Apache
SERVER_ADMIN	Apache
SERVER_NAME	Apache, IIS
SERVER_PORT	Apache, IIS
SERVER_PORT_SECURE	IIS
SERVER_PROTOCOL	Apache, IIS
SERVER_SIGNATURE	Apache
SERVER_SOFTWARE	Apache, IIS
TZ	Apache

Table 22-3.   *Environment Variables Defined When Executing a CGI Script* (continued)

Line Termination

One of the most fundamental problems of using Python on multiple platforms is the line termination when reading and writing files. Different operating systems use different characters for line termination. In particular, Unix uses a linefeed (the **\n** or **\012** character) to terminate, whereas Mac OS uses a carriage return (the **\r** or **\015** character). To complicate matters, DOS/Windows uses the carriage return, linefeed sequence (**\r\n** or **\015\012**).

You can determine the current line-ending sequence by examining the **os.linesep** variable. Python automatically uses the right sequence for reading and writing files on the native platform, but if you transfer a Python script from a Mac to Unix, then the script will probably fail—the Python interpreter doesn't understand line endings for anything other than the current platform.

Also be careful when dealing with text files sourced from another platform that you are using as data sources. If you are in any doubt about the content and format of a text file, open the file and manually split elements using **string.split()** to extract the actual lines from the file. Be aware that some platforms will appear to work with text files sourced from another. For example, since Unix uses the linefeed character, it'll read Windows text files as normal, but completely ignore Mac line termination. Similarly, Macs will read Windows files, but will only read the line up to the carriage-return, effectively placing a linefeed as the first character on all subsequent lines.

When reading and writing binary files, be aware that you should get into the habit of specifying the binary option. Although it's not required on Unix, Mac OS, and many other platforms, it does make a difference when reading and writing under Windows and some other platforms that automatically trim line termination during file reading.

When working with network sockets, you should *always* use the carriage-return/linefeed character. Although it's not required in most situations, all the RFCs (Request For Comments) that describe the protocols specify carriage-return/linefeed for end of lines, and using the full sequence will ensure compatibility with systems that expect the full character sequence.

Character Sets

Another popular misconception is that all platforms use the same character set. Although it's true that most use the ASCII character set, you can rely only on the first 128 characters (values 0 to 127, or **\00** to **\0177**) as being identical. Even with this consideration, you shouldn't necessarily rely on the values returned by **chr()** or **ord()** across different platforms. The actual values of the character set may include all manner of characters, including those that may have accents and may be in any order.

Also remember to consider the use of Unicode (see Chapter 10), which will isolate most of the character set issues solving problems both on a platform, font, and localized country basis. Care needs to be taken of course to ensure that you read and write the correct information.

If you are concerned about localization, consider placing any regular/constant strings (messages, help files, etc.) into external files so that a language-specific file can be loaded when required. Adding a new language should then just be a case of adding a new language file.

Files and Pathnames

The main three platforms show the range of characters used to separate the directories and files that make up a file's path. Under Unix (and BeOS, QNX, and Mac OS X) it is /, but under DOS/Windows it is \, and on the Mac it is :. The Windows and DOS implementations also allow you to use the Unix / to separate the elements. To further complicate matters, only Unix and a small number of other operating systems use the concept of a single root directory.

On Windows and DOS, the individual drives, or partitions thereof, are identified by a single letter preceded by a colon. Under Mac OS, each volume has a name that can precede a pathname, using the standard colon separator. The **os.path** module can create and manipulate paths that use the appropriate character set and separator for you. Also be aware that different platforms support different file names and lengths. The following is a rough guide:

- DOS supports names of no more than eight characters, extensions of three characters, and ignores case.

- Under Windows 95/NT the definition is slightly more complex: individual path components have a maximum length of 256 characters and is case conscious.

- Under Mac OS, any element of a path can have up to 31 characters, and names within a directory are case insensitive—you cannot have two files called "File" and "file." Mac OS X HFS+ and ufs partitions support path elements of 254 characters in length. However, only ufs partitions support case-sensitive filenames. Under HFS/HFS+ under both Mac OS and Mac OS X the names "FileName.TXT" and "filename.txt" are identical; trying to write to a file with the same name but a different case will cause an exception.

- Older versions of Unix support only 31 characters per path element (i.e., directory or filename), but newer versions, including Solaris, HP-UX 10.x and above, as well as Linux, support a full 256 characters per path element. Note, however, that the maximum length for the entire path is 2,048 or 4,096 characters, depending on the platform.

You should also try to restrict file names to use only standard alphanumeric characters.

Data Differences

Different physical and operating system combinations use different sequences for storing numbers. This characteristic affects the storage and transfer of numbers in binary format between systems, either within files or across network connections. The solution to the problem is either to use standard strings to hold your information (obviously wasteful for large numbers) or use the **pickle** or **struct** modules to ensure your information in a standard format that can be easily assembled and disassembled.

Also remember to think about data such as time, which is handled differently on different systems. On nearly all systems, the epoch is 0:00:00, 1 January 1970. However, other platforms define other values (Mac OS, for example). If you want to store a date in an architecture-neutral format, use a format that is not reliant on the epoch value, such as a single string like **YYYYMMDDHHMMSS**.

Performance and Resources

Not all platforms have the seemingly unlimited resources of the Unix operating system available to them. Although Windows provides a similar memory interface, the available memory on a Windows machine may be significantly less in real terms (physical/virtual) than that available under a typical Unix implementation.

Even though memory prices are dropping all the time (at the time of writing it costs less than $150 for 1GB of RAM), many users still only have a relatively small amount of memory, and once the OS and other applications have been taken into account there's often little application memory left. For example, a typical Windows 2000 server installation will use approximately 223MB just for the basic OS and background services. On a Mac, the typical OS overhead is about 64MB, although it can be as large as 80MB.

Python, unfortunately, makes it very easy to use large amounts of memory without thinking too much about the consequences. You can create large lists, tuples, and dictionaries without much effort, and it's even possible to read in the entire contents of a file into memory.

As a rough guide, try not to import the entire contents of files into memory, and if you are working with large lists and dictionaries, consider using a DBM database—the Berkeley DB system (in **bsddb**) supports an array form of the standard DBM systems.

Also remember that other operating systems do not provide the same protected memory spaces or the multitasking features of Unix. Notably Mac OS (but not Mac OS X) uses fixed-sized application partitions. If the MacPython application is not given a large enough partition, you'll get an error trying to load or deal with too much information.

The Complete Reference

Part VI

Inside Python

The Complete Reference

Chapter 23

The Python Architecture

Y ou probably don't give much thought to what happens when you supply the
name of a script to a Python interpreter—you're just waiting for the results of
your application to complete. In fact, quite a lot happens between the time you
press the ENTER key and the time your script actually starts doing anything.

Many interpreted languages read the source file and execute the lines one by one.
This leads to a number of difficulties and frequent frustrations. A line-by-line interpreter,
as used by most versions of BASIC and many Unix shells, has to rely on the information
it knows at the time the line is executed. If you reference a variable or function that
doesn't exist, then the interpreter halts—while having executed any previous lines
already. Files that have been copied, renamed, or produced in the process remain,
and without careful thought your script may be destructive, not because of how it
was designed but because terminating mid-script has made restarting the application
difficult or impossible.

Python, along with Perl, Rebol, and some other languages, takes a different
approach. If you look at Figure 23-1, you'll see that your script is immediately passed
on to the Python compiler. This is an embedded part of the actual Python application
that you started.

The Python compiler turns your entire source material into bytecode, an internal
format that's similar in style to the assembly code used in your computer's CPU. This
bytecode is then handed off to the Python Virtual Machine that executes the bytecode
in order to produce the desired result.

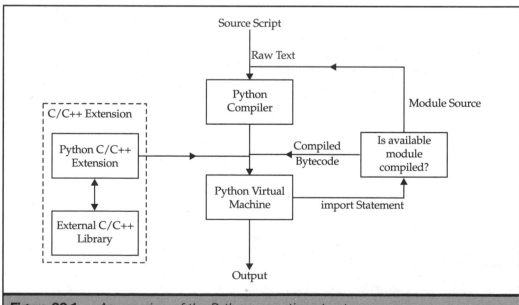

Figure 23-1.   *An overview of the Python execution structure*

Although this seems like a complex step, it enables Python to produce a highly optimized version of your script suitable for execution. Also, because the entire script is compiled into bytecode, the interpreter can often flag problems before the program starts executing.

In addition to the statements that you supply, any **import** statements you use are executed only when they are reached within the compiled code. The import process triggers a check by the Python virtual machine that was described in Chapter 5. Basically, if the module is up to date and in bytecode format, the interpreter imports the already compiled bytecode and uses that. If the module is not in bytecode format, or the source is more recent than the bytecode file, it's passed through to the compiler that creates the bytecode and continues executing.

On the left-hand side of Figure 23-1, note that calls to modules and/or internal functions that make use of an external C/C++ library use the bytecode defined in a C/C++ extension module, which in turn refers to the underlying objects, data, and functions in the C/C++ library you're using. See Chapter 5 for more information on the exact priority and sequence used when loading modules.

The overall execution process is fairly instantaneous. The average Python program takes only a few hundredths of a second to translate the raw source into bytecode. Once the interpreter has the bytecode, the execution is extremely fast due to the highly optimized nature of the underlying bytecode.

This chapter aims to introduce you to the basic mechanics of the Python interpreter—how individual statements are executed by the Python Virtual Machine, the internal structures used to hold information about a Python script, and the details of the bytecode itself.

This chapter also provides the backbone that helps you to understand the information in the rest of this section of the book. For example, you'll learn about the Python debugger in Chapter 24 the Python documentation system, which uses attributes (object variables) to hold documentation in Chapter 25, and at ways in which you can extend the Python interpreter with external C/C++ libraries and embed Python into C/C++ applications in Chapters 26 and 27.

Namespaces, Code Blocks, and Frames

Ignoring the semantics of the bytecode used by the Python interpreter (for that see the "Bytecode" section later in this chapter), it's useful to know how the interpreter treats the statements that are in your source code during execution.

In the simplest terms, Python scripts are split into *code blocks;* code blocks are executed within the confines of an *execution frame,* and both are subject to the *namespace* rules that govern which functions, objects, and classes are available to the running code. Finally, when something goes wrong, you can use the information within a *traceback* object. These are the objects used by exceptions to report the location of the error that caused the exception in the first place.

Let's look at each element individually to determine their effect on the execution of your Python script.

Code Blocks

Every executable element within a Python script is made up of a code block. A code block is any element within a script that can be executed; code blocks include modules, class definitions, and function bodies. In addition, the statements you enter to the interactive interface are treated as single, stand-alone code blocks, as are script files supplied on the command line, and strings and files read in during **exec** statements and **eval()** and **execfile()** functions.

Code blocks themselves contain nothing more interesting than the compiled bytecode that makes up the statements to be executed. They are completely unaware of the context in which they are running or the variables and other functions to which they potentially have access.

For more information on code objects see the "Code Objects" section later in this chapter.

Frames

Code blocks are executed within the confines of a frame, or more specifically, within an execution frame. An execution frame consists of:

- The code block to be executed
- The location of the code block (line number, source file, etc.)
- A reference to the next frame to be executed
- The contents of the global namespace
- The contents of the local namespace

Each frame also maintains a block stack that contains a list of the blocks defined within its code block. The stack incorporates different blocks for different nested loops, **try** statements, and **if** statements in the code block. The stack is used to pass around information about the loops during execution. For example, a **for** loop evaluates the next item in the sequence that was supplied to it and then puts all the information about the loop (current index, sequence, and code block) onto the block stack, which is then popped off the stack again during each iteration so that the next item can be evaluated.

Frames are the smallest useful reference to the code within a script. Frames are used for identity when debugging. Execution is actually broken between frames, and although it's the code blocks that contain the executable elements of the script, it's the frames that contains the code blocks context—including information such as the line number from the original source where the code block was generated from.

For more information on the data held in frames see the "Frame Objects" section later in this chapter.

Namespaces

Namespaces map names—variables, functions, and modules—to objects. A typical script is made up of multiple namespaces and multiple frames may reference the same namespace. Namespaces themselves are just dictionary-like objects where the keys of the dictionary refer to the name of and the value is a reference to the actual object. See Chapter 3 for a recap on objects and how they are stored and referenced within Python.

If you remember, Chapter 5 introduced the concept of namespaces that were searched according to the LGB rule. The L in LGB refers to the *local* namespace and is the namespace where names are defined and searched relative to the current execution frame. The G in LGB refers to the *global* namespace and contains the variables declared in **global** statements. The global namespace is where variables not bound to the current execution frame are searched. The B in LGB refers to the built-in functions and objects. The **NameError** exception is raised if a given name cannot be resolved through the LGB rule.

Table 23-1 lists the different code block types and where the global and local namespaces are built from when the block is created. Remember that the global namespace always refers to the namespace of the enclosed module or script—global namespaces do not nest.

Tracebacks

Traceback objects are created when an exception occurs. The traceback object contains a reference to the currently executing frame, the current line, and the actual instruction that was executing when the exception occurred. In addition, in order to translate the single execution state into the trace normally reproduced when an exception is raised, traceback objects also contain a reference to the next level in the stack trace. Traversing the entire object list gives you the traceback.

Putting it Together

The reason why this is important is because it demonstrates how Python executes your scripts and how you can determine information about the script that is currently executing to trace problems and debug the script.

Armed with the information in a traceback object, you can determine where the problem occurred. You can obtain the traceback object when an exception is raised by calling **sys.exc_info()**. What's actually returned by the call is a tuple that contains a reference to the exception class that was raised, an instance of the class, and the traceback object.

Armed with a traceback object, you can relate that back to an execution frame and therefore get the line number and source code for the error that took place.

When debugging, knowing that the execution is split into different frames as well as lines within those frames is vital—most debuggers for other languages work superficially on a line-by-line basis, with an implied "frame" when the statement

Code Block Type	Global Namespace	Local Namespace
Module	Namespace for this module	Same as global
Script	Namespace for __main__	Same as global
Interactive command	Namespace for __main__	Same as global
Class definition	Global namespace of containing block	New
Function body	Global namespace of containing block (can be overridden)	New
String passed to **exec**	Global namespace of containing block (can be overridden)	Namespace of enclosing block (can be overridden)
String passed to **eval()**	Global namespace of caller (can be overridden)	Local namespace of caller (can be overridden)
File read by **execfile()**	Global namespace of caller (can be overridden)	Local namespace of caller (can be overridden)
Expression read by **input()**	Global namespace of caller	Local namespace of caller

Table 23-1. *Namespace Sources/Definitions for Code Blocks*

contains a function call. This implied element is followed when you "step into" the function call—in Python this is merely following the tree of execution frames.

Note that because of this distinction, in Python a single line could relate to many frames; if the statement contains a number of individual function calls, there is a frame for the execution of each function call. For example, the line

```
hypot = math.sqrt(square(a)+square(b))
```

actually consists of three frames: the one used to execute the code object relating to the first call to **square()**, another for the second call to **square**, and a third frame for the call to **math.sqrt()**. In the debugger, execution of this line would first be split at **square(a)**, then **square(b)**, and then **math.sqrt()**.

Conversely, within a frame, the debugger also works on individual lines. For example, the following function contains four lines, none of which involve any other frame:

```
def calc(a,b,c):
    resa = (a*b)/c
    resb = (c*b)/a
    resc = (c*a)/b
    return resa+resb+resc
```

Built-in Types

There are 26 different types built into the Python interpreter and they are placed into categories according to their base types. For example, all the **Number** types share the same basic properties, as do sequences that share similar abilities—i.e., all sequence elements are accessed in the same manner.

Table 23-2 lists all the object types and categories.

Category	Type	Description
None	**NoneType**	The null object (used with **None**)
Numbers	**IntType**	Integer
	LongType	Long (arbitrary) integer
	FloatType	Floating point
	ComplexType	Complex number
Sequences	**StringType**	Strings
	ListType	Arrays and lists
	TupleType	Tuples
	XRangeType	Created by the built-in **xrange()** function
Mapping	**DictType**	Dictionary
Callable	**BuiltInFunctionType**	Built-in functions
	BuiltinMethodType	Built-in methods

Table 23-2. *Object Types and Categories Supported by Python*

Category	Type	Description
	ClassType	Class object
	FunctionType	User-defined function
	InstanceType	Class object instance
	MethodType	Bound class method
	UnboundMethodType	Unbound class method
Modules	ModuleType	Module
Classes	ClassType	Class definition
Class Instance	InstanceType	Class instance
Files	FileType	File
Internal	CodeType	Byte-compiled code
	FrameType	Execution frame
	TracebackType	Stacks traceback of an exception
	SliceType	Generated by extended slices
	EllipsisType	Used in extended slices

Table 23-2.   *Object Types and Categories Supported by Python* (continued)

You've already learned about the basic object types and their attributes. What you haven't seen are any of the internal types used to hold the information about specific structures such as modules, functions, the code, and frame and traceback objects introduced earlier in this chapter.

This section describes each of the object types and their supported attributes. Of particular interest is the __doc__ attribute, which is applicable to any object and is used to hold documentation for the entity. (See Chapter 25 for more information on how this attribute is used.)

For information on the other object types, see Chapter 3.

Callable Object Types

Callable objects include any object that can be called, including functions, methods, and methods associated with a particular class.

Functions

User-defined functions are those functions created by the user at module level within a script either through the **def** statement or the **lambda** operator. They are architecturally different from methods, only because they are not associated with a class. Function objects can be stored in any normal structure, including lists, dictionaries, and ordinary variables.

Functions support the attributes listed in Table 23-3.

Methods

Methods are functions that operate only on an instance of an object. Unbound method objects are those methods that are declared, but not yet associated with an instance of an object. The methods in a class are unbound. Bound methods are those that have a connection to a class instance. Table 23-4 lists the attributes for both types of methods.

Attribute	Description
__doc__ or **func_doc**	Documentation string.
__name__ or **func_name**	The name of the function as it was declared. Functions defined through lambda have the name **(lambda)**.
func_code	A reference to the compiled bytecode code object.
func_defaults	A tuple containing the default values to the function's arguments. For example, the definition **func(a=0,b=0)** returns **(0,0)**.
func_globals	A dictionary defining the global namespace—that is, the objects available within the global namespace for the function. In a typical script this implies the globals for the script. In the function imported from a module, this is the globals for the module.

Table 23-3. *Attributes for Functions*

Attribute	Description
__doc__	Documentation string.
__name__	Method name.
im_class	The class in which the method was defined.
im_func	The **Function** object that implements the method.
im_self	The instance associated with the method. This is **None** for an unbound method.

Table 23-4.   *Attributes for Methods*

Built-in Functions and Methods

Built-in functions and methods relate to those functions and methods either defined directly by the Python language or defined within extension modules and generally developed in C/C++. Table 23-5 lists the attributes for built-in methods and functions.

Modules

Modules are containers for collections of other objects loaded through the **import** statement. The fragment

```
import foo
```

creates a new object pointing to the **foo** module.

Attribute	Description
__doc__	Documentation string.
__name__	Function/method name.
__self__	Instance associated with the method. For built-in functions, __self__ is set to **None**. For built-in methods, __self__ points to the object used to invoke the method. For example, in **b = [1,2]**, **b.append.__self__** points back to **b**.

Table 23-5.   *Attributes for Built-in Functions and Methods*

Modules define their own namespace, implemented through a dictionary in the
__dict__ attribute. Namespace lookups for variables and objects within the namespace
of the module invoke the corresponding lookup and/or assignment. For example, the
object **mymodule.list** is available as **mymodule.__dict__['list']**. Assignments are other
operations that work in the same way and therefore imply an overhead. See the section
"Manual Optimization" in Chapter 24 for more information.

Modules support the attributes listed in Table 23-6.

Classes

Classes are created through the **class** statement. They include an attribute, __dict__,
that contains the objects associated with the class—including the methods. The access
mechanism works in an identical fashion to that for modules. However, where access
cannot be resolved through __dict__, the search continues to one of the base classes;
the resolving mechanism works from left to right in the base class list created when
the class was defined. Be aware that assigning a value to an attribute always updates,
and if necessary creates, the attribute in the corresponding class, not in any of the
base classes.

The full list of attributes supported by classes is listed in Table 23-7.

Class Instances

Class instances are created when a class is called, thereby creating a new instance of
the object. Each instance has its own namespace, defined through a dictionary. Name
lookups operate by examining __dict__. If the name cannot be found, the search
continues by looking through __class__.__dict__ and then further through each
__dict__ attribute for each of the base classes. As with classes, assignments to a class
instance always update (and create) an entry in __dict__.

Attributes supported by class instances are listed in Table 23-8.

Attribute	Description
__dict__	Dictionary associated with the namespace for the module
__doc__	Module documentation string
__name__	The name of the module
__file__	The file from which the module was loaded

Table 23-6.   *Attributes Supported by Module Objects*

Attribute	Description
__dict__	Dictionary associated with the namespace for the class
__doc__	Class documentation string
__name__	Name of the class
__module__	Name of the module in which the class was defined
__bases__	Tuple containing the list of base classes for this class

Table 23-7.   *Attributes Supported by Classes*

Internal Types

You've already learned about the use of internal types in Python for executing code blocks and other elements. The information in this section describes the specific attributes for each of the code objects. You should only need to use this information if you are building a new debugger or you want to annotate the execution of your script in more detail. See Chapter 24 for more information.

Code Objects

Code objects represent any executable element. All attributes in the code object are read only and are listed in Table 23-9.

Attribute	Description
__dict__	The dictionary associated with the namespace for the class instance
__class__	The name of the class that the object is an instance of

Table 23-8.   *Attributes for Class Instances*

Attribute	Description
co_name	Function name.
co_argcount	The number of fixed positional arguments in the function definition.
co_nlocals	Number of local variables used by the function.
co_varnames	Tuple containing the name of the local variables.
co_code	The string representing the raw bytecode.
co_consts	Tuple containing the literals used by the bytecode.
co_names	Tuple containing the names used by the bytecode.
co_filename	The name of the file in which the object was defined.
co_firstlineno	The first line of the code object within the file in **co_filename**.
co_lnotab	The string that relates line numbers to bytecode offsets.
co_stacksize	Size of the stack required to execute the object.
co_flags	Integer defining the interpreter flags. Bit 2 is set if the object uses variable argument lists, bit 2 is set if the object accepts keyword arguments.

Table 23-9.   *Attributes for Code Objects*

Frame Objects

Frame objects provide the environment for a code object to be executed. Attributes for frame objects are listed in Table 23-10.

Attribute	Description
f_back	Previous stack frame (toward the caller). Read only.
f_code	The code object being executed in this frame. Read only.
f_locals	The dictionary used for local variables. Read only.

Table 23-10.   *Attributes for Frame Objects*

Attribute	Description
f_globals	The dictionary used for global variables. Read only.
f_builtins	Dictionary used for built-in names. Read only.
f_restricted	Set to 1 if the frame is being executed in a restricted environment. Read only.
f_lineno	The line number for the code being executed. Read only.
f_lasti	An index pointing to the last bytecode in **f_code** that was being executed. Read only.
f_trace	The function called at the start of each source code line.
f_exc_type	The most recent exception.
f_exc_value	The most recent exception value.
f_exc_traceback	The most recent exception traceback.

Table 23-10. *Attributes for Frame Objects* (continued)

Traceback Objects

Traceback objects hold the structure information for determining the currently executing frame and all the previous frames that led to that frame. Traceback frames are automatically created when an exception is raised. The attributes supported by traceback objects are listed in Table 23-11.

Attribute	Description
tb_next	The next traceback object within the stack trace (heading towards the frame where the exception took place).
tb_frame	The execution frame object for the current level.
tb_line	The line number where the exception took place.
tb_lasti	The last instruction being executed when the exception took place. This is an index into the bytecode of the code object that was executing at the time. Equivalent to **frame.f_lasti**.

Table 23-11. *Attributes Supported by Traceback Objects*

Slice and Ellipsis Objects

The slice object is created internally when a slice is selected using the extended slice syntax such as **s[i:j:step]**, **s[a:b, c:d]**, or **s[..., i:j]**. Slice objects are also created automatically when the **slice()** built-in function is used. Attributes supported by the slice object are listed in Table 23-12.

Ellipsis objects are used to indicate the presence of an ellipsis in the slice. The ellipsis object has no attributes and always evaluates to true.

Bytecode

The CPU inside your computer works by accepting instructions and data and performing a calculation in what is generally termed *assembler code*. Different instructions exist for different operations; for example, the **add** instruction adds two numbers together, and the **mul** instruction multiplies two numbers.

Although different processors support different instructions, the basic mechanics are the same—whenever you execute an application, you are executing these processor instructions. When you compile a C/C++ application, part of the compilation process is to translate the C/C++ statements into assembly code, which are then translated by the assembler into the binary code format required to perform the procedures originally defined in your C/C++ code.

Obviously your application is likely to be more complicated than simply adding two numbers together. There are a limited number of instructions supported by each different type of processor, and those that are supported are normally the lowest common denominator. For example, adding two strings together seems trivial when you use **strcat** in C. But behind the scenes, the concatenation process is converted into a number of assembly instructions that copy information from one memory location to another in order to generate the new string; your single-line statements may be made up of multiple assembler instructions.

Attribute	Description
start	The lower boundary of the slice.
stop	The upper boundary of the slice.
step	The stride of the slice. **None** if not specified.

Table 23-12. *Attributes Supported by Slice Objects*

The problem with a traditional assembler is that it's very machine specific. Although you can take i386 code and execute it on an i486 or Pentium, there's no guarantee that you'll be able to go the other way. It's also impossible to transfer information from one processor type to another. For example, it's categorically impossible to execute a PC binary directly on a Mac. The PC uses an Intel *x*86 style processor, while a Mac uses either a Motorola 680*x*0 processor or a PowerPC processor.

This incompatibility is what gives you a variety of operating systems, and ultimately a headache when developing applications. Because different processors use different assembler languages, your application needs to be recompiled just so that it's in the right executable format. Of course that's only a small part of the story; you also need to recompile the application for the libraries and platform on which you are running. A Linux *x*86 application won't run on a Windows *x*86 platform because the environments, support, and interface to the underlying hardware are all different.

Python Bytecode

Python works in a very similar way. If you refer back to Figure 23-1, notice that a Python script is assembled into Python bytecode. Python bytecode is essentially the same as a processor's assembly language—it's a series of low-level instructions upon which everything else is built.

Behind the scenes, these bytecode instructions are actually highly optimized pieces of assembly language, just like any other application. The use of bytecode provides us with a number of advantages:

- Because the source text is "compiled" into bytecode, including going through an optimization stage, you get fast execution with the ultimate in flexibility.

- Because the bytecode is highly optimized, you get close-to-raw assembler execution times. There is still overhead because you have to translate the Python bytecode into the local processor instructions. However, the bytecode handlers are optimized and very quick.

- Because the bytecode is Python specific and not hardware specific, Python bytecode can be shared among different platforms (for example, Macs, PCs, SPARC-based Unix systems, etc.) and still be compatible.

The only downside to this approach is that Python must compile your script into bytecode before it is executed. This means that although executing Python bytecode is almost as fast as an assembled application, compiling your raw source text into bytecode each time induces a small overhead. We're talking microseconds each time, but it's not an issue that you can ignore.

To improve the execution times in Python, the interpreter attempts to load a previously compiled version of a module. Because it imports the bytecode, there is no compilation overhead, just the time it takes to load the code and create aliases or other hooks in the namespace.

Python is not unique is this approach to interpreted programming. Perl works in a very similar way, and the entire ethos of Java is to produce a cross-platform–compatible bytecode for executing applications.

Bytecode Disassembly

Although in most cases understanding the bytecode is not particular useful, it can help you to understand what's going on behind the scenes when you execute a Python application. The **dis** module disassembles Python bytecode (from a precompiled code object) into a text form that you can read and follow onscreen. This can be useful if you want to examine the internal workings of Python.

For example, the code to add a number to an existing variable might look something like this:

```
def simple(a,b):
    a += b
    return a
```

Using the **dis** module you can disassemble the bytecode produced when the function was designed using

```
dis.dis(simple)
```

which results in the following output:

```
  0 SET_LINENO          1

  3 SET_LINENO          2
  6 LOAD_FAST           0 (a)
  9 LOAD_FAST           1 (b)
 12 INPLACE_ADD
 13 STORE_FAST          0 (a)

 16 SET_LINENO          3
 19 LOAD_FAST           0 (a)
 22 RETURN_VALUE
 23 LOAD_CONST          0 (None)
 26 RETURN_VALUE
```

Without getting too far into the details, the preceding output shows the bytecode first loading the two arguments that were supplied, and then adding them together using the augmented assignment (noted here by **INPLACE_ADD**). Like most languages, Python uses a stack to hold information. The **LOAD_FAST** instructions place the two variables on the stack, and **INPLACE_ADD** then adds the numbers together, placing the result on the stack. **STORE_FAST** then updates the value of **a**.

The stack is now empty, so before you return any value, you need to load the value of **a** back and then return the value on the stack back to the caller. The final **LOAD_CONST/ RETURN_VALUE** pair is generated by the call to **dis.dis**.

The numbers that prefix each line show the byte at which the instruction occurs. Bytecode is so called because each instruction is represented by a single byte; arguments to the bytecode take up two bytes.

If you want to use the output to follow the execution of a script, you also need to know how functions are called. If you modify the preceding example to

```
def simple(a,b):
    a += b
    sq(a)
    return a

def sq(a):
    a += a
    return a
```

you can see that you've now got a function call to the **sq** function. The output generated by **dis** looks like this:

```
 0  SET_LINENO        1

 3  SET_LINENO        2
 6  LOAD_FAST         0 (a)
 9  LOAD_FAST         1 (b)
12  INPLACE_ADD
13  STORE_FAST        0 (a)

16  SET_LINENO        3
19  LOAD_GLOBAL       2 (sq)
22  LOAD_FAST         0 (a)
25  CALL_FUNCTION     1
28  POP_TOP

29  SET_LINENO        4
```

```
32  LOAD_FAST              0  (a)
35  RETURN_VALUE
36  LOAD_CONST             0  (None)
39  RETURN_VALUE
```

Functions are called in the bytecode by first loading the **sq** function onto the stack, followed by the arguments you want to supply, and then calling the function. The **POP_TOP** instruction removes the item at the top of the stack (the name of the function you called) so the stack isn't polluted because the call to **sq** didn't return anything. If you had assigned the result of **sq** to **a**, you could have just accessed the return value back from the stack and continued.

Bytecode Instructions (Opcodes)

The **dis** module is really of limited value to most programs. If you want to get to know the internals of Python better, see Table 23-13, which lists all the supported opcodes (bytecode instructions) and should enable you to follow the execution of your script. In the From Stack and To Stack columns, unqualified numbers show the number of items removed from or placed back onto the stack. If the figures are quoted using square brackets, then the figures indicate the order in which items were removed from/replaced to the stack, where 1 is the item at the top of the stack. In the Description column, successive letters refer to the item removed from the stack, for example, a = 1 (top of stack), b=2, c=3, and so on.

Opcodes that accept items from the stack without putting information back on the stack are editing variables in place; examples include slice and delete operations on sequences.

Bytecode	From Stack	To Stack	Description
STOP_CODE			Indicates the end of code to the compiler.
POP_TOP	1		Removes the item at the top of the stack.
ROT_TWO	[1,2]	[2,1]	Swaps the location of the top two items in the stack.

Table 23-13. *Opcodes Supported by the Python Bytecode Interpreter*

Bytecode	From Stack	To Stack	Description
ROT_THREE	[1,2,3]	[2,3,1]	Moves the top item three places down and moves items two and three one place up.
ROT_FOUR	[1,2,3,4]	[2,3,4,1]	Moves the top item four places down and moves items two, three, and four one place up.
DUP_TOP	[1]	[1,1]	Duplicates the item at the top of the stack.
UNARY_POSITIVE	1	1	Implements **a = +a**.
UNARY_NEGATIVE	1	1	Implements **a = -a**.
UNARY_NOT	1	1	Implements **a = not a**.
UNARY_CONVERT	1	1	Implements **a = `a`**.
UNARY_INVERT	1	1	Implements **a = ~a**.
BINARY_POWER	2	1	Implements **a = a ** b**.
BINARY_MULTIPLY	2	1	Implements **a = a * b**.
BINARY_DIVIDE	2	1	Implements **a = a / b**.
BINARY_MODULO	2	1	Implements **a = a % b**.
BINARY_ADD	2	1	Implements **a = a + b**.
BINARY_SUBTRACT	2	1	Implements **a = a - b**.
BINARY_SUBSCR	2	1	Implements **a = a[a]**.
BINARY_LSHIFT	2	1	Implements **a = a << b**.
BINARY_RSHIFT	2	1	Implements **a = a >> b**.
BINARY_AND	2	1	Implements **a = a & b**.
BINARY_XOR	2	1	Implements **a = a ^ b**.
BINARY_OR	2	1	Implements **a = a	a**.

Table 23-13. *Opcodes Supported by the Python Bytecode Interpreter* (continued)

Bytecode	From Stack	To Stack	Description
INPLACE_POWER	2	1	Implements in-place a = a ** b.
INPLACE_MULTIPLY	2	1	Implements in-place a = a * b.
INPLACE_DIVIDE	2	1	Implements in-place a = a / b.
INPLACE_MODULO	2	1	Implements in-place a = a % b.
INPLACE_ADD	2	1	Implements in-place a = a + b.
INPLACE_SUBTRACT	2	1	Implements in-place a = a - b.
INPLACE_LSHIFT	2	1	Implements in-place a = a << b.
INPLACE_RSHIFT	2	1	Implements in-place a = a >> b.
INPLACE AND	2	1	Implements in-place a = a & b.
INPLACE_XOR	2	1	Implements in-place a = a ^ b.
INPLACE_OR	2	1	Implements in-place a = a | b.
SLICE+0	1	1	Implements a = a.
SLICE+1	2	1	Implements a = a[b:].
SLICE+2	2	1	Implements a = a[:b].
SLICE+3	3	1	Implements a = a[b:c].
STORE_SLICE+0	2	0	Implements a[:] = b.
STORE_SLICE+1	3	0	Implements b[a:] = c.
STORE_SLICE+2	3	0	Implements b[:a] = c.

Table 23-13. *Opcodes Supported by the Python Bytecode Interpreter* (continued)

Bytecode	From Stack	To Stack	Description
STORE_SLICE+3	4	0	Implements c[b:a] = d.
DELETE_SLICE+0	1	0	Implements **del** a[:].
DELETE_SLICE+1	2	0	Implements **del** b[a:].
DELETE_SLICE+2	2	0	Implements **del** b[:a].
DELETE_SLICE+3	3	0	Implements **del** c[b:a].
STORE_SUBSCR	3	1	Implements b[a] = c.
DELETE_SUBSCR	2	0	Implements b[a].
PRINT_EXPR	1	0	Evaluates **a** and prints it.
PRINT_ITEM	1	0	Evaluates **a** and prints it to the file object pointed to by **sys.stdout**.
PRINT_ITEM_TO	2	0	Evaluates **b** and prints it to the file object **a** (i.e., **print file expr**).
PRINT_NEWLINE	0	0	Prints a newline generated by any **print** statement, unless it terminates with a comma.
PRINT_NEWLINE_TO	1	0	Prints a newline to the file object **a**, unless the statement is terminated by a comma.
BREAK_LOOP	0	0	Implements **break**.
LOAD_LOCALS	0	1	Pushes a reference to the locals defined within the current scope to the stack.

Table 23-13. *Opcodes Supported by the Python Bytecode Interpreter* (continued)

Bytecode	From Stack	To Stack	Description
RETURN_VALUE	0	1	Implements **return**.
IMPORT_STAR	1	0	Implements **from a import ***.
EXEC_STMT	3	0	Implements **exec c, b, a**.
POP_BLOCK	1	0	Removes one block from the block stack.
END_FINALLY	0	0	Terminates a **finally** clause in a **try** statement.
BUILD_CLASS	3	0	Implements **class c(b)** where **a** is a dictionary of the supported methods.
STORE_NAME namei	1	0	Creates a new local variable. Implements **name = a** where **namei** is the index of **name** in the attribute **co_names** of a code object.
DELETE_NAME namei	0	0	Implements **del name** where **namei** is the index of **co_name** within a code object.
UNPACK_SEQUENCE count	1	count	Unpacks **a** into **count** values that are placed back on the stack in reverse order (right to left).
DUP_TOPX count	count	count*2	Duplicates **count** items from the stack.

Table 23-13. *Opcodes Supported by the Python Bytecode Interpreter* (continued)

Bytecode	From Stack	To Stack	Description
STORE_ATTR namei	2	1	Stores a value in an attribute. Implements **a.name = b**, where **namei** is the index of **co_name** within a code object.
DELETE_ATTR namei	1	0	Deletes an attribute. Implements **del a.name**, where **namei** is the index of **co_name** within a code object.
STORE_GLOBAL namei	1	0	Creates a new global variable.
DELETE_GLOBAL namei	0	0	Deletes a global variable.
LOAD_CONST consti	0	1	Pushes the constant onto the stack, where **consti** is the index to a constant in the **co_const** attribute in a code object.
LOAD_NAME namei	0	1	Pushes the value of a variable onto the stack, where **namei** is the index to a name in the **co_names** attribute in a code object.
BUILT_TUPLE count	count	1	Creates a tuple consuming **count** items from the stack, placing the single tuple object back on the stack.

Table 23-13.   *Opcodes Supported by the Python Bytecode Interpreter* (continued)

Bytecode	From Stack	To Stack	Description
BUILT_LIST count	count	1	Creates a list consuming **count** items from the stack, placing the single list object back on the stack.
BUILD_MAP zero	0	1	Puts an empty dictionary onto the stack. The argument **zero** is ignored.
LOAD_ATTR namei	1	1	Implements **a = getattr(a, co_names[namei])**.
COMPARE_OP opname	2	1	Implements **a cmp_op[opname] b**.
IMPORT_NAME namei	0	1	Imports the module **co_names[namei]**, placing the module object back on to the stack.
IMPORT_FROM namei	1	1	Loads the attribute **co_names[namei]** from the module **i**. The resulting object is placed back on the stack.
JUMP_FORWARD delta	0	0	Increments the bytecode counter by **delta**.
JUMP_IF_TRUE delta	1	1	If **a** is true, increments the bytecode counter by **delta** bytes. **a** is not removed from the stack.

Table 23-13.   *Opcodes Supported by the Python Bytecode Interpreter* (continued)

Bytecode	From Stack	To Stack	Description
JUMP_IF_FALSE delta	1	1	If **a** is false, increments the bytecode counter by **delta** bytes. **a** is not removed from the stack.
JUMP_ABSOLUTE target	0	0	Sets the bytecode counter to **target**.
FOR_LOOP delta	2	0(3)	Implements a **for** loop where **a** is the current index in the sequence **b**. The element **b[a]** is computed; if the sequence is exhausted, the bytecode counter is incremented by 1. If not, the sequence, incremented counter, and current index are placed back on the stack.
LOAD_GLOBAL namei	0	1	Loads the global variable named **co_names[namei]** onto the stack.
SETUP_LOOP delta	0	1	Pushes a loop block onto the block stack. The block spans the current bytecode instruction up until **delta** bytes.

Table 23-13.   *Opcodes Supported by the Python Bytecode Interpreter* (continued)

Bytecode	From Stack	To Stack	Description
SETUP_EXCEPT delta	0	1	Pushes a **try-except** clause onto the block stack, where **delta** points to first **except** statement.
SETUP_FINALLY delta	0	1	Pushes a **try** block from a **try-except** clause onto the block stack, where **delta** points to the **finally** statement.
LOAD_FAST var_num	0	1	Pushes a reference to the local variable **co_varnames[var_num]** onto the stack.
STORE_FAST var_num	1	0	Stores **a** into the local variable **co_varnames[var_num]**.
DELETE_FAST var_num	0	0	Deletes **co_carnames[var_num]**.
LOAD_CLOSURE i	0	1	Puts a reference to the cell contained in slot **i** of the cell and free variable storage. If **i** is less than the length of **co_cellvars**, the name of the variable is in **co_cellvars[i]**. Otherwise, it's in **co_freevars[i-leng (co_cellvars)**.

Table 23-13.   *Opcodes Supported by the Python Bytecode Interpreter* (continued)

Bytecode	From Stack	To Stack	Description
LOAD_DEREF i	0	1	Pushes a reference to the object the cell contained in slot **i** of the cell and free variable storage onto the stack.
STORE_DEREF i	1	0	Stores **a** in slot **i** of the cell and free variable storage.
SET_LINENO lineno	0	0	Sets the current line number to **lineno**. Used by exceptions and frames to determine the current location when reporting an error.
RAISE_VARARGS argc	0 to 3	0	Implements **raise** where **argc** is the number of parameters to the **raise** statement. The traceback is found in **c**, the parameter is found in **b**, and the exception name is found in **a**.
CALL_FUNCTION argc	argc	0	Calls a function. The **argc** argument specifies the number of positional parameters (low byte) and keyword parameters (high byte). Parameters are removed from the stack. The lowest item on the stack should be the function to be called.

Table 23-13.   *Opcodes Supported by the Python Bytecode Interpreter* (continued)

Bytecode	From Stack	To Stack	Description
MAKE_FUNCTION argc	1-argc	1	Pushes the function object **a** onto the stack. The function is declared to have **argc** parameters, which are defined in lower values in the stack.
MAKE_CLOSURE argc	1-argc	1	Creates a new function object, its closure slot, and pushes the final object onto the stack, where **a** is the code associated with the function and **argc** is the function of default parameters. Any trailing items from the stack are the cells to be used for the variables used within the function.
BUILD_SLICE argc	2-3	1	Pushes a slice object back onto the stack. If **argc** is 2, **slice(b,a)** is placed onto the stack. If **argc** is 3, **slice(c, b, a)** is placed onto the stack.
EXTENDED_ARG_EXT	0	0	Prefixes any opcode that has an argument too big to fit into the default two bytes.

Table 23-13. *Opcodes Supported by the Python Bytecode Interpreter* (continued)

Bytecode	From Stack	To Stack	Description
CALL_FUNCTION_VAR argc	?	?	Calls a function as in **CALL_FUNCTION** except that the top argument on the stack contains the variable argument tuple, followed by the keyword and positional arguments.
CALL_FUNCTION_KW argc	?	?	Calls a function as in **CALL_FUNCTION** except that the top element on the stack contains the keyword arguments dictionary, followed by the keyword and positional arguments.
CALL_FUNCTION_VAR_KW argc	?	?	Calls a function as in **CALL_FUNCTION** except that the top element on the stack contains the keyword arguments dictionary, followed by the variable arguments tuple followed by the keyword and positional arguments.

Table 23-13. *Opcodes Supported by the Python Bytecode Interpreter* (continued)

The Complete Reference

Chapter 24

Debugging and Tuning

Any programmer knows that writing a program and making sure it works is only half the task. Once written, you also need to make sure that the program does what you say it does, and in the process, doesn't effect or upset the operation of the rest of the computer. Unless that's what the program is designed to do, of course!

Debugging is the bane of many a programmer's life. In an ideal world, you should spend 80% of your total development time finding and solving problems in your code. Few of us have time for that level of testing, and many of us don't have the patience required.

But knowing the need for debugging and actually tracking and tracing the bugs are two very different things. All debugging requires a closer look at your code, and while it's possible to do that by reading your code line by line, there must be easier ways to debug a program.

Actually, before we get there, let's defining the term *bug*. A bug is where you have a problem in your application that causes it to behave erratically, to perform a task you didn't expect it to, or to corrupt or in some other way affect the execution. One other bug is less well accepted, but still just as important: the *execution bug*. An execution bug slows down the execution of your program for no apparent reason. It's not fatal, but it does indicate a possible problem area in your script.

This chapter starts by looking at the different types of bugs that can occur and how to identify and potentially fix them. You'll also learn ways in which you can prevent the bugs from occurring in the first place by changing the way you design and develop your applications.

Then you'll learn about the Python debugger, an interactive interface for executing and monitoring the execution of your scripts. To help isolate those execution problems and resource sinks, you'll also see the Python profiler, which times the execution of various script components.

An Introduction to Debugging

Before looking at ways to debug a program, you need to think about what types of bug can occur in your software. Knowing the type of bugs and being able to identify them will help you to choose the right method of resolution.

Bug Types

Think about the process of program development as a hierarchical tree. At the top are the input values; at the bottom are the output values, or results, of the program. Unfortunately, application development is often treated from the bottom up, rather than from the top down. The *top-down* approach forces the developer to think about all of the steps to reach the result. The *bottom-up* approach means trying different techniques until you reach a result that works from the top to the bottom.

The bottom-up approach is slower but often more practical from a programmer's point-of-view because it helps gel ideas and form methods and processes in the programmer's mind that will ultimately be reflected in the final application.

The selected development approach has some effect on the bugs that you can introduce into the program. With the bottom-up approach, you do not consider all of the factors before developing a new component and are, therefore, likely to introduce more errors than when using the more pragmatic top-down approach to program development.

A mistake often made by developers is to ignore the effects of a bug or to fail to classify the bug and its effect. Although not normally seen as a major problem—a bug is a bug—it can affect the way bug problems are solved (which may have "knock-on" effects to other bugs) and can also cause other bugs to be ignored entirely.

Personally, I've always identified three types of bugs when programming:

- typographical
- logic
- execution

Typographical Bugs

Typographical bugs are introduced through typographical errors, either through bad typing or a momentary lapse in concentration that causes you to forget the semantics of the language. In Python, you've probably used the wrong name for a variable, used **&** instead of ***** in a calculation, or called **disposal** instead of **dispersal**. These latter two examples are both simple typos but they can make a big difference in how your application behaves.

Python traps some of these errors when you run the script. Using the wrong function or method raises a **NameError** or other exception, but you might have trouble discerning the problem with **&** and *****. Python sees these as valid, and in fact for certain values you might even end up with the same result.

Other typographical bugs can be even more obscure. On a web project last year, the login process suddenly stopped working. The login system worked by checking the username and password against a database, and, assuming both were approved, the script generated a unique session ID, which was also placed into the database and then used by the CGI scripts to identify the user's session. The problem was that the login would be approved and the session ID created, but intermittently the user couldn't connect using the new session ID.

It took a little time, but by comparing the session ID returned to the user and the session ID in the database, it was obvious that the session ID, which had a random element, was sometimes 26 digits long and at other times was 27 digits long. The database we were writing the session ID to used a 26-digit field width. 50 percent of the time the session ID system worked fine; the other 50 percent of the time the session ID exceeded the field width and failed. Here's another example of a typographical error: entering the wrong width into the database creation script.

Typos are difficult to trace—unless the error causes the interpreter to bomb, the only way to find them is to read through each line of code. If the typo causes a calculation or operation to fail, you'll at least have a starting point, and a debugger may help you track the exact position of the problem.

Logic Bugs

Logic bugs occur when the programmer has failed to spot a flaw in the logical flow of the program. Like typographical bugs, these can be very obvious—for example, failing to identify one of the possible return values from a function or incorrectly specifying a test or other operation. These are not typographical errors—the programmer really thought he or she was doing the right thing at the time.

As an example, and as an extension of the typographical error described in the previous section, the login system suddenly started returning bad logins after some optimization of the login code. The login function returned a negative number on error, a zero if the session or login had expired, and a positive number on success. After tracing the bug for hours it finally became apparent that the problem occurred because the **if** statement checking the return value tested for a strict zero response as failure, and any other response was interpreted as valid.

Ironically, exceptions can also be a common location for logic bugs. Trapping too many exceptions, not being specific enough in your exception handlers, or simply trapping everything is likely to cause a logic bug. They all lead to problems because you'll be catching exceptions that you didn't anticipate.

Logic bugs can be approached from a number of directions. The most obvious solution is for the programmer to understand Python well enough to know how it works and what traps exist in the language. Assuming you know the language, you should never introduce a logic bug into the core language. That doesn't isolate you from problems in your own code. As a rough guide, these are the sorts of statements you should double-check:

- Sequence access, particularly slices and splices.

- Mixing tuples and lists. Remember that tuples are immutable, and many functions return tuples rather than lists.

- Loops, particularly when dealing with **for** and **range()** or **xrange()**.

- Functions, particularly return values. Create a system and stick to it throughout your application.

- Exceptions. Make sure you trap the exceptions you want to identify. Remember as well that exception handlers are executed in sequence and according to the exception tree shown in Chapter 7. Handle the lowest level exceptions first, then handle the group and generic exceptions.

Other ways to trace logic bugs include the use of abstraction—turning components of your program into functions, modules, and classes helps. If you can optimize and debug the individual elements, the entire application as a whole should work without modification. Abstraction also makes your code more portable and more manageable.

Execution Bugs

Execution bugs are the hardest to find, and there are many programmers who probably do not consider them to be bugs at all. Execution bugs affect the execution process of a program, not because of a typo or a logic problem, but because the application has been designed in such a way that allows a certain chain of events to slow or halt the application's execution process.

Execution bugs do slow your application but they may not actually generate a bad result or manifest themselves in any other way. For example, imagine an application that pulls records out of a database. A typical search returns 200 records, and the script works within a few seconds, well within the limits you might expect for extracting information from the database. When a search returns 1,000 records, however, the script takes almost a minute to execute.

The problem is not logic—the script works and behaves exactly as it should and it's not a typographical error. The information is formatted correctly and there really are 1,000 records in the database to be displayed. So why did it take so long?

The problem here is one of execution—either the programmer needs to create a limiter to reduce the effect of accessing and displaying that many records, or there's a portion of the application that takes an excessive amount of time to parse the information. This is an execution bug; there's nothing wrong with the application, it just doesn't run at the level you would expect.

Execution bugs are difficult to trace, but once found and resolved they have some benefits. An application that has been cleansed of its execution bugs is more robust than a normal application, and it's likely to be more stable in use. Because execution bugs frequently affect the program's performance, eliminating those bugs optimizes your application.

The easiest way to find an execution bug is to execute your program, but to isolate the location of that bug you'll need some tools and techniques. Python comes with a profiler that executes and monitors the execution times for different portions of your program. Check the section on "Optimizing Python Applications" later in this chapter for more information. The profiler isn't a solution, only a tool to find the location of the possible problem. In addition, the profiler provides information on an individual function level, which may or may not be useful. Often it's the entire algorithm—and therefore a series of function calls—that cause the problems.

Basic Debugging Rules

You'll learn about the techniques and methods you can use to trap and resolve problems in Python later, but there are some generic rules that can be used when resolving problems in any Python script:

- **Always check the obvious:** Don't look for the most complicated explanation for why your script is going wrong. Always look for something simple. If a calculation doesn't come out right, it's probably because you've misspelled a variable or left out a value or operator. Don't go looking for a problem in an external module, function, or third-party extensions until you've made sure it isn't a simple typo.

- **Always check from the outside in:** If you find a problem, trace it by looking at the area where the problem is reported first, on the outside, at the highest calling point. Then trace the problem inwards. Exceptions in Python can help because they show you the link from the inside to the outside of the problem, but they'll only be reported for recognized errors, not bugs. What the exception doesn't always tell you is where the problem originated. Most problems when calling a function are related to the data that you supplied the function in the first place, not what the function produces in the process.

■ **Always start from the top when dealing a typographical error:** When Python reports an error, especially when it's related to a mismatch parenthesis, quote, or other paired component, the actual location where the error is raised may not be the real location of the error in question. Python can only identify a mismatch quote or brace when it sees one it doesn't expect.

■ **Always follow your exception handler tree:** The trace produced when an exception is raised is the most useful tool available for tracking a problem to its source. Exceptions are the one exception to the rule of "Always check from the outside in." Exceptions tell you the root of the problem, so go straight to it and fix it. But there's one caveat: Don't blindly follow the exception and expect it to give you precise information.

■ **Always check your exception handlers:** Too many times I've seen Python programs that don't work and often don't report an error because the programmer has disabled (using **pass**) a particular exception because, and I quote, "The error always came up." Exceptions are there to highlight a problem somewhere in your application; ignoring an exception is likely to cause problems, no matter how simple or trivial you think the exception might be. In particular, be wary of trapping those exceptions that are normally trapped by the interpreter. In particular, **SyntaxError** and **TypeError** exceptions should ideally only be trapped when dealing with Python code supplied by the user. Trapping and/or ignoring these exceptions in your own programs may cause you to ignore problems in your own scripts that should be fixed.

Preventing Bugs

It's obvious that preventing the introduction of bugs before they occur is the best way to approach the problem—prevention is always better than cure. The problem is that prevention of bugs is sometimes more time-consuming than the resolution of bugs and gives the appearance of slowing down the development process. In truth, by preventing bugs instead of curing them, you improve the chances of making the deadlines, because you'll be spending less time searching for them after the program is written.

But how do you prevent bugs from occurring in the first place? Many of the techniques are beyond the scope of this chapter since they rely on the fundamental approach towards the programming goal, rather than being specific to the Python language. But some of the basic techniques that you can apply to any programming effort are worth discussing.

Program Design

When developing an application, having a good idea about *what* it's going to produce is vital, and having a good idea about *how* to achieve that goal is a good way to ensure that bugs are not introduced into the software. Even just writing down a quick list of functions and what you expect them to do is better than making it up as you go along.

It's also worth coming up with a system or style of program design and sticking to it. Using standard argument sequences to exchange data, for example, is acceptable, but with a large number of arguments, especially if some are optional, it can become confusing. Luckily, Python offers a flexible system for accepting arguments, using default values, and supplying arguments by argument and/or keyword rather than in a fixed-list order. Even so, try to stick to only one or two combinations to help make your code easier to use.

At the other end of the equation are programs that are designed and developed to the *nth* degree from start to finish and end up with design manuals that run to more lines than code you are producing. Program design to this level has its place—I hope that nuclear power station software and the fly-by-wire computers built into most modern airplanes use this technique. On the other hand, developing this kind of documentation for that quick script to convert data file formats is wholly unnecessary.

Editors

A good editor should be a vital component of any programmer's armory. Most modern editors match parentheses and help you indent your code to make it more readable. Emacs, probably the most popular programmer's editor, does this automatically and almost enforces the option for scripts that it identifies as Python based. More advanced editors, such as BBEdit or Pepper (for Mac OS), EditPlus (for Windows), and Emacs (for Unix), can also color the code according the individual elements.

Using an editor that performs these simple checks can eliminate many of the simple typographic errors that cause many bugs and compilation failures. They can also provide visual cues for identifying problems.

Formatting

Choose a formatting standard and stick to it. You don't have to look at much of the code written by programmers to see that, in general, it's clean and tidy and easy to read. Usually. Python helps this along by having a clean style. The lack of braces and the use of indentation—when used properly—makes it very easy to identify the different sections of your application.

However, make sure you stick to a style. In particular, it's best to avoid putting single-line **if** and **for** statements like

```
if debug: print "Just about to try something..."
```

on to the same line as the test or **for** statement, because the entire statement gets lost. It also presents problems if you try to add statements to the **if** block, because as a single-line statement, the interpreter has no indentation to key on.

Using a good editor helps because it handles the indentation and other formatting elements for you, but still affords you some customization. As a rough guide, consider these basic rules:

- Use a four-column indent for each level.
- Use space around most operators.
- Use blank lines between chunks of text that do different things.
- Don't use a space between a function name and its opening parenthesis.
- Use a space after each comma.
- Break long lines after an operator (except **and** and **or**).
- Use a space after the last parenthesis on a given line.
- Line up corresponding items (multi-line assignments, function arguments) vertically.
- Omit redundant punctuation as long as clarity doesn't suffer.

Comments

Adding comments to your code is an excellent way to keep on top of how an application works, so you can spot where potential problems can occur. Imagine trying to debug that same bit of code without comments—there is no way for the programmer to know for certain that the technique achieves the desired result. Tools such as bug-tracking systems (see sidebar) and code revision systems can help, but they won't tell you everything you need to know.

If your script isn't working correctly, include a quick explanation of how the function or code fragment works, just so you can follow the execution when it comes to debugging the code.

Chapter 25 covers the use and creation of documentation and comments in detail, but it's worth listing the basic do's and don'ts for commenting your script here:

- Don't just repeat what the line does—saying "for loop" on a line that contains the **for** keyword is not helpful. Say "iterate through the list of source files" or something that explains the task being performed.
- Do list the types of input variables and what information the function is expecting.
- Do specify the return values and expectations of when they should be returned.
- Do document the error/failure conditions and return values.
- Do document implementation decisions such as why you've chosen a particular algorithm over others.
- Do document anything "weird" you've done; sometimes you need to work around bugs in other programs or libraries that your application interacts with, and it's a good idea to remind yourself about these.

Bug Tracking

Finding bugs is one thing, but remembering where they all are is another matter. At the very least, you should keep a textual record of the bugs that have occurred and whether they have been fixed. Be sure to include information about what the bug was and how it was fixed because doing so can help you identify and trace subsequent bugs.

When you discover a bug you should record the following information:

- Location—the line number and file number, if known, or, at the very least, a possible function culprit.

- Description of the bug that occurred, including what you expected to happen and what actually did happen.

- Date and time the bug was discovered and the name of user who reported the bug.

- Any other relevant information, such as the platform, environment variables, and any factors that may have lead to the bug.

If you want to be more professional about your bug tracking, consider using tracking software such as BugZilla, which is part of the Mozilla Project. The BugZilla system is actually written in Perl and is available as a web interface to an underlying MySQL database. You can download BugZilla from **http://bugzilla.mozilla.org**.

Remember that comments are there to jog your memory and highlight the execution sequence to other programmers, not to provide an English language running commentary or to vent your frustrations. Actually, on this last point, sometimes comments can be helpful if you use the opportunity to mention why you took the eventual route. Comments can also be entertaining when working on a problem late at night!

Using Code Revisions

The Revision Code System (RCS) and Concurrent Versioning System (CVS) both provide ways for you to track the differences between the versions of the your code. The general mode of operation is to write a piece of code and have it working, but perhaps not necessarily debugged, and then check in that version to the code revision system. As you make changes to the code, you check in subsequent revisions to the code. The code revision system keeps track of the changes from one version to another. If you make changes to the code and it fails, you can always revert to using a previous version of the code instead of having to undo the failed changes.

RCS (which was used as the basis for CVS) allows you to store comments with each revision and to automatically track version numbers of each file that you check in. Use those opportunities to include a status report, both on what you achieved in the new revision and an indication of the bugs or issues that you addressed. The version numbers can be useful when tracking bugs as well as when receiving bug reports from your end users—it's quite possible that the bug they are reporting has already been fixed in a new revision.

The difference between CVS and RCS is that RCS allows only a single user to be editing an individual source file at any one time, whereas CVS allows for true concurrent development by a number of programmers. CVS also includes additional features, such as the ability to export its tree over the Internet and the ability to automatically create a new package based on the current version numbers of the source files, even if they are still in production. CVS also has better interfaces, including a number of GUI clients and web tools.

If you are the only programmer, RCS can probably serve your needs. You can get more information and download RCS from **http://www.gnu.org/software/rcs/rcs.html**. If you think you need CVS, check out the CVS Bubbles page at **http://www.loria.fr/~molli/cvs-index.html**.

Debugging Techniques

The moment you say "debugging" to most people, they leap towards a debugger and try to find a way to interactively monitor their script during execution. While debuggers are very useful and many of those available for Python are excellent ways of finding bugs, there are easier ways to achieve the same result.

Ultimately all programs involve some modification of variables and information. When you debug a piece of code you are primarily looking for the values of the variables being used, where the values change, and what the values are at specific points. All debuggers offer some kind of variable-watching mechanism that lets you monitor the contents of a variable as the script progresses, but often there are simpler ways to achieve the same result.

The humble **print** statement is frequently ignored, but it's the quickest and easiest way to display the value of a variable in your script. You know how to use it, you can tailor the output according to the value you are printing, and you have the most flexibility about where you can generate your watched values.

The **print** statement isn't the answer to everything though; if your application is text based and interactive, your debugging **print** statements may well interrupt the flow and interface of your application. If it's a Tk or other GUI application, you may never see the output. If it's a CGI script, the information will likely garble the HTML that your script would normally generate. In any of these situations, a much better alternative is to send your debugging output to a separate file, which you then monitor at a later date. You can also write to a central log, such as **syslog** (see the **syslog** module for more information).

If you are debugging a module or a short and simple script, the interactive mode of the interpreter may be easier to use. You can even configure the interpreter to immediately drop into interactive mode as soon as a script has finished its normal execution.

Of course, none of these techniques are intended or necessarily recommended as a replacement for the debugger, but it's always worth having a few alternatives. Remember also that a debugger requires an interactive interface. If you want to trace the execution of a script and you don't have interactive access to the interpreter, or you want to be able to post-process an execution log, perhaps provided by a customer, then a debugger won't help you.

This section describes in detail the different debugging mechanisms, including the Python debugger provided in the **pdb** module.

Using print

The **print** statement is the simplest and easiest way to debug your script. I probably use **print** more than I use a real debugger, especially when writing under Unix/Linux, because I can quickly add **print** statements to the script and monitor the output. Since my favorite environment is a combination of Emacs for editing and the command line for testing, this makes a lot of sense.

But using **print** is not just a case of adding a single-line statement to your script for each variable you want to output. The **print** statement offers a lot of flexibility that you can use to your advantage, and it's important to format the output you are creating so you can identify where and when the error occurred.

You can also use the **print** statement as a way of reporting debugging information in the final version of the script. You will usually use this method in combination with a global variable, perhaps set via the script's command line, to enable or disable some simple debugging. The benefit of a script that outputs debugging information in this way is that it allows both the user and programmer to perform a post-mortem debug on the application without needing to use an interactive debugger.

The only place where a **print** statement is often useless is within a loop, because it produces a voluminous amount of information that needs to be processed manually after the execution is complete. On occasion the loop mechanism can prove useful if you want to continually monitor a single variable as it is processed, or when you want to monitor the input or output to a file handle.

Using **print** is very straightforward. All you do is insert a normal **print** statement where you want to output some data:

```
for x in range(100):
    # do some stuff
    print 'x is %d and result is %f' % (x, result)
```

Now you can watch as the value and calculation changes during execution. However, what this example generates ultimately isn't particularly useful. Use the **print** command to annotate the execution of your script and ensure that the information you generate is useful after the event.

Using a Debug Variable

If you want to use a debug variable to enable the generation of these messages, all you have to do is prefix your **print** statements with **if** statements:

```
if debug:
    print "Value of the data after calculation is", data
```

However, this information is only useful if you have an easy way to connect your **print** statement back to a point within the script. The habit is to cut and paste the **print** statement into a number of places within your script; however, doing this limits the usefulness unless you further qualify the output.

Make sure that you include some useful guide as to what and why you are printing out the information. Although it may be obvious to you when you are developing that part of your script, it may not be obvious to other people or to you months or years later.

Quoting Information

It should be evident how to include data within your output—just add the variables or use the % formatting operator to incorporate the information. However, without additional work, these statements don't include all the information that will be useful to you when examining the output.

Often, the problems you are encountering can be related directly to the content that you are using. Simple things like leading or trailing spaces that you wouldn't ordinarily pick up because the "invisible" characters are hidden in the output can affect your script.

The solution for this problem is to make sure you quote the information you are outputting so that you can trace the start and end of the values you are monitoring. For example, rather than using

```
print "The name returned was %s" % (name,)
```

use

```
print "The name returned was [%s]" % (name,)
```

Since the data is qualified by the square brackets it should be easy for you to identify any hidden characters.

Tip *If you are working with a web script, don't qualify your output by using angle brackets (<>); you'll end up hiding the output because the browser will treat the contents as an HTML tag it doesn't understand.*

Quoting the output doesn't solve every problem though; there are still hidden characters that may upset the execution of your script. In particular, the low-order characters that include control characters such as linefeed, carriage return, and the vertical and horizontal tabs will still be hidden in your output.

To get around this, use the **mapascii** function, which translates control characters into something more readable. Actually, you can add more characters to this function, for example, to map the angle brackets to something more readable in CGI scripts, but the ultimate result is the same—a visible version of a string when it contains control characters:

```python
def mapascii(string):
    retval = ''
    charmap = {
        '\000' : '[NUL]',
        '\001' : '[SOH]',
        '\002' : '[STX]',
        '\003' : '[ETX]',
        '\004' : '[EOT]',
        '\005' : '[ENQ]',
        '\006' : '[ACK]',
        '\007' : '\\a',
        '\010' : '\\b',
        '\011' : '\\t',
        '\012' : '\\n',
        '\013' : '\\v',
        '\014' : '\\f',
        '\015' : '\\r',
        '\016' : '[SO]',
        '\017' : '[SI]',
        '\020' : '[DCE]',
        '\021' : '[DC1]',
        '\022' : '[DC2]',
        '\023' : '[DC3]',
        '\024' : '[DC4]',
        '\025' : '[NAK]',
        '\026' : '[SYN]',
        '\027' : '[ETB]',
        '\030' : '[CAN]',
        '\031' : '[EM]',
        '\032' : '[SUB]',
        '\033' : '[ESC]',
        '\034' : '[FS]',
        '\035' : '[GS]',
        '\036' : '[RS]',
```

```
        '\037' : '[US]',
        '\040' : '[SP]',
        }
    for char in string:
        if (charmap.has_key(char)):
            retval += charmap[char]
        else:
            retval += char
    return retval
```

To use **mapascii**, just supply the function with a string. Any control characters are converted to a visible string; any other characters are appended to the returned string as normal. For example:

```
print mapascii('\r\n\011\004\032\027')
```

generates

```
\r\n\t[EOT][SUB][ETB]
```

Getting More Specific

One of the problems with the **print** trick described here is that you have to rely on what you include in the message to determine the location of the problem when you go back to the script. Wouldn't it be easier to have the file and line number information included in the output?

There is a technique available, but I should note that these are not functions that are recommended for use unless you are an experienced Python programmer. However, these functions do exist and are documented so you're not dealing with unsupported features. You need two pieces of information to make your **print** statement useful: the name of the file that includes the current line and the line number within that file.

The **sys._getframe()** returns the object that represents the currently executing frame, or if supplied with a number, **sys._getframe** returns the *nth* previously executing frame. The **f_lineno** attribute to the returned frame returns the line number from the module from which the frame was generated. The **inspect** module provides a number of functions that give you information about an object, including **getfile()**, which returns the file in which an object was defined. I've used this information in the following example to create a function **print_status()** that writes the filename, line number, and your message when called:

```
def print_status(data):
    import inspect, sys
    frame = sys._getframe(1)
```

```
lineno = frame.f_lineno
filename = inspect.getfile(frame)
print "Status (%s:%s): %s" % (filename,str(lineno),str(data))
```

To actually call the **print_status()** function, use

```
print_status("Nothing doin' here!")
```

The information about the file and line number that is printed is obviously only valid for the **print_status()** call itself, but that should be enough for you to be able to zero in on the location where the problem has occurred.

Keeping a Log

Writing to an external log file and recording what happens in your script is useful when you don't have interactive access to your script as it's executing. Examples of this include CGI and GUI-based scripts that you may never have interactive access to.

In these situations the best solution is to write your debugging information to a file during execution so that you can then view the information at a later stage. The easiest way to do this is to modify the **print_status** function from the previous section so that it sends the information to a file rather than to the standard output. The modified **print_status** function is as follows:

```
def print_status_log(data):
    import inspect, sys
    frame = sys._getframe(1)
    lineno = frame.f_lineno
    filename = inspect.getfile(frame)
    try:
        logfile = open('debug.log','w+')
    except:
        print "Fatal, couldn't open the debug log"
    logfile.write("Status (%s:%s): %s"
                  % (filename,str(lineno),str(data)))
    logfile.close()
```

This isn't the most efficient method to write to a log; after all, you're opening the file each time you call the function, but you are debugging here. When it comes to the final version of the script, you can remove the function altogether, or at least qualify the call using a variable to enable debugging output. That way execution is only slowed when you've got debugging switched on. If you want to get really smart, create a class that holds open the log file, with methods to an instance of that class writing and updating the log.

Using Python Interactively

The interactive interface to Python is something you'll use often to test or demonstrate elements of Python quickly and easily; you can use the same interface to test statements and functions in external modules. To get to the interactive interface, just fire up Python:

```
$ python
Python 2.1 (#2, Apr 29 2001, 14:36:04)
[GCC 2.95.3 20010315 (release)] on sunos5
Type "copyright", "credits" or "license" for more information.
>>>
```

One other benefit of the interactive interface is that you can invoke the interface immediately after executing a script. This can be useful when you want to perform a series of actions automatically and then continue the process by hand. You can do this by specifying the **-i** argument on the command line:

```
$ python -i myscript.py
Some or other output...
>>>
```

As soon as you get the **>>>** prompt you are ready to start typing commands and continuing your script by hand.

Using the Python Debugger

The **pdb** module, which is part of the standard distribution, provides an interactive interface to debugging your Python scripts at the source code level. The debugger allows you to execute any Python script and to immediately drop it into the debugger so you can start stepping through the individual lines of source code. You can also set breakpoints that allow your code to run normally and drop into the debugger either when a particular line is reached or when a particular condition is met.

You can invoke the debugger in three ways: from the command line, interactively, and interactively after an exception has been raised. The command-line form is the easiest:

```
$ python /usr/local/lib/python2.1/pdb.py myscript.py
> /export/home/etc/mcslp/books/pytcr/ch24/<string>(0)?()
(Pdb)
```

This script immediately drops into the debugger, before the script actually starts execution. Note that the location of the **pdb.py** module must be specified explicitly—the Python interpreter doesn't (yet) know that you want to debug a file using **pdb**.

The interactive method involves manually importing the **pdb** module before you import and execute your script:

```
>>> import pdb
>>> import mymodule
>>> pdb.run('mymodule.main()')
> <string>(0)?()
(Pdb)
```

Note that you must import your module and then run a function to test its abilities in order to use this method. If your module is just an ordinary script and immediately starts executing statements, the statements are executed at the time of import—**pdb** won't step in and pause the process until you call **pdb.run()**. See also the other functions supported by **pdb** in the "Debugger Functions" section later in this chapter.

The third method is best used when you know that your script raises an exception during execution but you don't know why. You must use Python interactively and have imported the **pdb** module before importing and/or executing your module. Once the exception has been raised and the traceback has been printed, you need to call **pdb.pm()** to initialize the post-mortem debugger. Consider the following example:

```
>>> import pdb
>>> import mymodule
Traceback (most recent call last):
    File "<stdin>", line 1, in ?
    File "./mymodule.py", line 29, in ?
TypeError: source
>>> pdb.pm()
> ./mymodule.py(29)
-> parse(source)
(Pdb)
```

In each case the result is the same: you are placed directly into the debugger.

The next section describes the mechanics of using the debugger.

The Debugger Interface

However you invoke the debugger, you ultimately end up within the debugger and are presented with the prompt **(Pdb)**. The debugger supports a number of different commands for executing the script either until a breakpoint is reached or on a line-by-line basis.

The debugger interface follows these basic rules:

- Lines entered are assumed to be debugger commands. If the entry is not a recognized debugger command, it is treated as a Python statement and executed accordingly. Python statements are executed within the context of the program being debugged, so you can obtain the value for a variable, update the variable, or call a function directly from the debugger prompt. If an exception occurs, the exception name is printed but the state of the debugger does not change—you can continue to use the debugger as normal.

- Commands starting with the exclamation mark (!) are automatically identified as Python statements.

- Entering a blank line re-executes the last command that was entered.

- Multiple commands may be entered on a single line but they must be separated by a double semi-colon (;;). Note that the separation is not intelligent—if the double semi-colon occurs within a string, the command line is still split at that point.

- Arguments to debugger commands should be separated by spaces or tabs.

The debugger looks for a file called **.pdbrc** that can be used to automatically load a series of aliases (explained shortly) or to execute any other command when the debugger is first started. For example, you may want to immediately list the next five lines to be executed by the debugger in the **.pdbrc** file.

The debugger looks for the **.pdbrc** file first in the user's home directory and then in the current directory. The version in the home directory is loaded first, with the version in the current directory overwriting any definitions in the original.

The commands supported by the debugger are described in the next section. They have been split into three categories: general, execution, and breakpoint commands. Most of the commands support an abbreviated version that is shown in the line immediately following the command header. For example, **h(elp)** indicates that the full command name is **help** but that can shorted to **h**.

General Commands   The debugger supports a number of general commands that provide information about the debugger or the current script, or that set up debugger options.

help   The **help** command displays the general help for the debugger, which includes a list of the supported commands.

```
h(elp) [command]
```

If **command** is specified, the help generated is for that command only. The output is piped through a pager command (such as **more** or **less**) if the environment variable **PAGER** is set.

where   The **where** command prints a stack trace, with the most recent frame at the bottom.

```
w(here)
```

This is similar to the output generated when an exception is raised. An arrow is used to indicate the current frame. Consider the following example:

```
(Pdb) w
  /export/home/etc/mcslp/books/pytcr/ch24/<string>(1)?()
  /export/home/etc/mcslp/books/pytcr/ch24/mymodule.py(12)?()
-> myfunc()
  /export/home/etc/mcslp/books/pytcr/ch24/mymodule.py(9)myfunc()
-> mysqrt(i)
> /export/home/etc/mcslp/books/pytcr/ch24/mymodule.py(3)mysqrt()
-> for i in xrange(iter):
```

In this instance, you're within the **mysqrt** frame.

up   The **up** command moves the current frame one level up from its current position.

```
u(p)
```

Using the **where** command example, this would move the frame to **myfunc**. If you are already at the top, the current frame remains the same.

down   The **down** command moves the current frame one level down from its current position.

```
d(own)
```

Using the **where** command example, if you'd called **up** once, this would move the current frame back down to **mysqrt**. If you are already at the bottom, the current frame remains the same.

list   The **list** command lists the source for the current file. By default, it lists the 11 lines (5 above the current line and 5 below) surrounding the currently executing line.

```
l(ist) [first [, last]]
```

If **start** is supplied, it lists the 11 lines surrounding that line, and if **last** is specified, it lists all the lines between **first** and **last**.

args   The **args** command lists the arguments for the current function.

```
a(args)
```

p   The **p** command evaluates **expression** and prints out the result.

```
p expression
```

The **expression** has access to all the variables and functions available within the context of the current frame. The result is handed off to the **print** statement for output.

alias   The **alias** command creates an alias called **name** which, when used in the debugger, executes **command**.

```
alias [name [command]]
```

The **command** should not be quoted. You can specify parameters to be replaced in the executed command using **%1, %2, ...,** etc. and you can use **%*** for all the arguments supplied. The following example

```
alias dumpall for i in %*: print str(i)
```

creates a new command that allows you to dump a string version of each argument supplied to the command, as in this example:

```
(Pdb) dumpall string int float dict
```

Aliases can do anything, including executing any other debugger command, but they are most often used as in the preceding example to dump a variable, object, or other structure in a formatted form. Aliases can also be nested, and an alias can override a built-in debugger command. The real command is then hidden until the alias is deleted (using the **unalias** command).

unalias**   The **unalias command deletes the alias **name**.

```
unalias name
```

quit   The **quit** command exits the debugger. The program currently being executed is aborted.

```
q(uit)
```

Stepping Commands

Stepping is the action of executing Python statements, either individually or as a group (as when you execute an entire function call in one go). By stepping, you can monitor the program execution and the variables used and affected by a statement on a line-by-line basis. There are three basic step commands, although some Python debuggers offer some additional options:

- **Step Into** executes the current statement, following the execution of any functions or methods found within the statement. Execution goes as far as calling the function or method, bypassing any variable initialization, and stops at the first executable statement within the called function.

- **Step Over** executes the current statement. Any functions or methods that are called are executed without being processed by the debugger, so execution stops on the next executable statement within the current file.

- **Step Out** continues execution until the current function or method ends. Execution stops at the next executable statement, either within the next function call of the current line from the calling script or at the next statement from the caller.

Stepping over breakpoints allows you to monitor each line individually. This capability is particularly useful when you want to study a sequence or each iteration of a loop in detail.

The stepping commands supported by the Python debugger are listed in the following sections.

step   The **step** command executes the current line and stops at the first possible occasion—the first function call in the current line or the next line in the current function.

```
s(tep)
```

This is essentially equivalent to **Step Into**, described previously.

next   The **next** command continues execution until the next line in the current function is reached or the function returns.

```
n(ext)
```

This is essentially a combination of **Step Out** and **Step Over**. This command skips over a function call in the current line, but stops just before the next line is executed, or until the point immediately after the current function returns.

continue   The **continue** command continues execution until the next breakpoint is found.

```
c(ont(inue))
```

Using Breakpoints

A breakpoint is a logical break within the execution of a script. You can set breakpoints to occur at a specific line number, and then further qualify whether the break should actually interrupt execution by adding a condition to the breakpoint. When the condition returns true, the breakpoint is triggered. If the condition returns false, execution of the script never breaks.

break   When supplied with **lineno**, the **break** command sets a breakpoint at the specified line within current file or within **filename** if specified.

```
b(reak) [[filename:] lineno|function [, condition]]
```

Note that **filename** can be specified even before the file has actually been loaded. If **function** is supplied, the breakpoint is configured at the first executable statement within the specified function.

The **condition**, if supplied, should be in the form of a normal Python test expression. For example, you can trigger a break within the function **parse** only when **ignorenl** was set to 1 using the following command:

```
(Pdb) b parse, ignorenl == 1
```

If no arguments are supplied, this command lists all the current breakpoints.

tbreak   The **tbreak** command sets a temporary break, which is identical to a normal break except that the breakpoint is cleared immediately after it has been reached.

```
tbreak [[filename:] lineno|function [, condition]]
```

clear   The **clear** command clears the breakpoint(s) specified by **bpnumber**.

```
cl(ear) [bpnumber [bpnumber ...]]
```

This command clears all the breakpoints if none are specified.

disable   The **disable** command temporarily disables the breakpoints listed.

```
disable [bpnumber [bpnumber ...]]
```

This command disables all breakpoints if none are specified.

enable   The **enable** command enables breakpoints that have previously been disabled.

```
enable [bpnumber [bpnumber ...]]
```

This command enables all breakpoints if none are specified.

ignore   The ignore command ignores the breakpoint **bpnumber** for the next iteration.

```
ignore bpnumber [count]
```

This effectively disables the breakpoint for one execution and then immediately reenables it. If **count** is specified, the **ignore** command ignores the breakpoint for **count** iterations.

condition   The **condition** command sets **condition** for an existing breakpoint, even if one wasn't specified when the breakpoint was created.

```
condition bpnumber [condition]
```

If supplied without a condition, the condition is deleted for the specified breakpoint.

Debugger Functions

In addition to the interactive debugger interface, the **pdb** module provides a number of functions that can be used either to execute a fragment of code and then invoke the debugger, or to directly invoke the debugger from within your script. This latter option is useful if you want to invoke the debugger from within an exception handler. See the introductory section for more information on using functions to invoke the debugger.

Table 24.1 lists the different functions supported by the **pdb** module.

Function	Description
run(statement [, globals [, locals]])	Executes **statement** under debugger control. The **run** function immediately triggers the debugger and breaks execution of **statement** just before it is actually executed. The optional **globals** and **locals** should be dictionaries of the global and local variables that you want to use while executing the statement. The default operation is to execute using the variables defined within the current scope—i.e., that of **__main__**. Aside from invoking the debugger immediately before execution, the **run** function is syntactically similar to the **exec** statement or the **eval()** function.

Table 24-1.   *Debugger Functions*

Function	Description
runeval(expression [, globals [, locals]])	Identical to the **run()** function except that it evaluates the string **expression** as a Python statement in a similar fashion as **eval()**. Although **runeval()** invokes the debugger, once execution of the expression has completed, the function returns the same value returned by the expression.
runcall(function[, argument, ...])	Calls **function** with the supplied arguments. The debugger is invoked just before the statements within the function start executing. **function** should be a code object—that is, a function or method name, not a string.
set_trace()	Enter the debugger at the current frame. You can use this function to invoke the debugger from within your script with an identical result to having set a breakpoint when debugging interactively. The function works whether or not you were already debugging your script.
post_mortem(traceback)	Starts post-mortem debugging of a script using the supplied **traceback** object. You can find the last traceback object in **sys.last_traceback**.
pm()	Identical to **post_mortem(sys.last_traceback)**.

Table 24-1. *Debugger Functions* (continued)

Optimizing Python Applications

The bugs that upset the execution of your applications are often only a small part of the problem. You can often run into problems that are not related to your logic or to a case of "butter fingers" while typing. Sometimes your script just seems to run too slow, a particular function takes more time than you expect, or the time taken for a large number of values is disproportionate to that for a smaller number of values.

Finding these bugs can be tricky. Occasionally the problem will be obvious; other times you'll need to do a bit more investigating before you find the solution to the problem. There are some obvious examples and problems that frequently crop up; the next section, "Manual Optimization," describes those in detail. These problems still rely on you manually reading and checking your code.

There is another alternative for finding these types of problems: use the Python profiler. This monitors the execution of a script and produces a profile—basically a list of all the times each function was executed and how long it took to execute. By considering all of these values together, you can determine which functions are taking the most time and therefore which functions deserve your attention for optimization. The section "The Python Profiler" explains how to use this tool.

Manual Optimization

There are so many different areas in your script that have the potential to cause problems when it comes to the execution time of different elements. Although it's impossible to list them all or to give specific advice about individual scripts, there are a number of areas where you can focus your attention if you suspect a problem.

Python is a heavily optimized language (check out Chapter 23 for more details on this) and as such, it's very rare that you can point the finger of doubt at Python itself. That's not to say it's infallible. However, the chances are that you are either using a less than optimal algorithm or the wrong function, module, or technique for what you are trying to achieve.

Also remember that there are scripts and functions that simply cannot be optimized or improved upon and that some operations will take a long time to process no matter what. On one particular project, the scripts that I was writing took a long time to execute, not because the scripts were less than optimal, but purely because of the size of the information they were dealing with. The scripts cleaned the contents of a free-text database that contained 19,000 records of between 4K and 16K in size. Each record contained up to nine different keyword fields that had to be deduped, along with other conversions and calculations. The script would take approximately 35 minutes to run—and that was about 10 years ago.

The moral here is that you are so used to computers being relatively instantaneous, it's easy to forget that computers still take a finite amount of time to perform a particular task. You are frequently dealing with larger and larger collections of data. Five years ago, a web log at a busy web site would run to about 1–2MB a day. Now the same web site probably creates a log that 20–50MB in size, perhaps larger. You may have faster computers, but the size of the data is increasing at a faster rate than computers are advancing, and disk/memory systems are still slower than the CPU requires to achieve decent speeds. .

Listed here are some of the areas and techniques that you should look at when trying to optimize your code:

- For large ranges, use **xrange()** rather than **range()**, or use a **while** loop.

- Use an array or tuple rather than a dictionary for storing sequential information. If you only ever access the data from start to finish, using a dictionary wastes space and time.

- When collecting, deduping, or summarizing a series of values, it's better to use a dictionary than an array. Anything that requires immediate access or otherwise requires you to traverse the entire array each time you add an element should be placed into a dictionary. Dictionary key tables are optimized using a hashing algorithm to give you near instantaneous access to the corresponding value.

■ Don't use multilevel exception handlers unless absolutely necessary. For example, if you create a function that opens and reads from a file and returns its contents, don't place an exception in the function and another around the call. Use the outer exception handler and handle all the possible exceptions from there.

■ Avoid calling complex subroutines from within a large loop, especially if there are only a few other statements in the loop. Instead, try to make the function handle the loop itself, or embed the statements from your function directly in the loop's block.

■ When working with a loop, always put control statements as early as possible in the block. For example, when processing text from a file line by line where the # sign is used to ignore lines, make it the first test in the block so that you don't execute statements that ultimately do nothing.

■ Use lists to functions rather than concatenating strings where possible. For example, you can print out multiple values with the **print** statement by separating the values with a comma. Using + to concatenate the string requires extra processing. Be careful though, because the comma in **print** also implies a space. Alternatively, if you have a lot of values to concatenate together, use **string.join()** to produce the final string in preference to the + operator.

■ Use the formatting operator % in preference to string concatenation when embedding variables in a string.

■ Avoid using slices on strings to extract values when using regular expressions is probably quicker. For example, when extracting the dates from a string you could use

```
date = '20010723'
year = date[0:4]
month = date[4:6]
day = date[6:8]
```

But when using regular expressions, you can shorten the extraction down to a single statement:

```
(year, month, day) = re.match('(\d{4})(\d{2})(\d{2})',date).group(1,2,3)
```

Better still, if you use a compiled regular expression, doing this on a number of date strings will be even quicker:

```
datematch = compile('(\d{4})(\d{2})(\d{2})')
(year, month, day) = datematch.match(date).group(1,2,3)
```

■ If you are manipulating a lot of text, use regular expressions to do substitutions rather than using slices to extract and concatenation to reassemble the strings.

■ Use temporary variables to avoid unnecessarily looking for values in sequences, dictionaries, and attributes. For example, the following script accesses the attributes of **self** and arrays a number of times:

```
def cumvolume(self):
    volume = 0.0
    for i in xrange(len(self.cubes)-1):
        v = (self.cubes[i].x+self.cubes[i+1].x) * \
            (self.cubes[i].y+self.cubes[i+1].y) * \
            (self.cubes[i].z+self.cubes[i+1].z)
        volume += v
    return volume
```

Each call to **self.cubes[i].x** implies two attribute lookups and one array lookup. This occurs a total of six times in the loop, or 18 operations in total. By modifying the method and using temporary values, you halve that down to nine operations.

```
def cumvolume(self):
    volume = 0.0
    cubes = self.cubes
    for i in xrange(len(cubes)-1):
        p1 = cubes[i]
        p2 = cubes[i+1]
        v = (p1.x+p2.x) * (p1.y+p2.y) * (p1.z*p2.z)
        volume += v
    return volume
```

Although this won't offer a 50% increase in speed, it does give you 15–20% improvement on your original version.

■ Avoid calling an external program via **os.system()**, **os.exec*()**, or **os.fork()** if it can be done from within Python using one of the standard or extension modules. Starting an external program involves duplicating the current process or creating a new one and therefore adds a lot of additional overhead.

■ When processing multiple data streams, use the **select** module to ensure that no stream is waiting to send or receive information or better still, use threads.

■ Use threads in systems where you need simultaneous data processing. This is especially useful on SMP systems where multiple threads can be used to access the raw power on all the CPUs in the machine.

The Python Profiler

The Python profiler is just a tool, much like the debugger, that helps you find the functions and methods of your script that are taking up the most time during your application's execution. Like the debugger, all the profiler does is tell you where the problem probably lies; it doesn't attempt to fix the problem or suggest alternatives.

Using the profiler implies a slight overhead in the execution of your script because it takes extra cycles to actually collate the information in the first place; but the overhead is small, probably less than 10% of the real time taken to execute the script. The information it provides is much more useful than the time the profiler takes to collect it.

The profiler actually comes in two parts: the **profile** module and the **pstats** module. The **profile** module is responsible for monitoring the execution time of different parts of your script and producing the profile. The **pstats** module then processes the profile in order to produce a report about the execution time of your script.

Getting the Profile

The example in this section uses a simple script that uses two functions: **myfunc()** and **mysqrt()**. Since we're only using this for a test, we don't need to worry about what the module actually achieves. In this example, the module calculates the square of a number and then the square root of that number, all within a variable-length loop. Here's the source for this script:

```
def mysqrt(iter):
    import math
    for i in xrange(iter):
        sq = i*i
        rt = math.sqrt(sq)

def myfunc():
    for i in xrange(200):
        mysqrt(i)
```

You can create the profile either interactively or from the command line. To use it interactively, import the **profile** module and call **run()** to execute a function from the module that you want to test, as follows:

```
>>> import profile
>>> import mymodule
>>> profile.run('mymodule.myfunc()')
        203 function calls in 0.350 CPU seconds

   Ordered by: standard name

   ncalls  tottime  percall  cumtime  percall filename:lineno(function)
        1    0.000    0.000    0.290    0.290 <string>:1(?)
      200    0.270    0.001    0.270    0.001 mymodule.py:1(mysqrt)
        1    0.020    0.020    0.290    0.290 mymodule.py:65(myfunc)
```

```
      1    0.060    0.060    0.350    0.350 profile:0(mymodule.myfunc())
      0    0.000             0.000          profile:0(profiler)
```

The information reported here is a summary of the profile that was generated and produces a rough report of the functions that were executed and the amount of time taken to execute each one.

If you analyze the report a bit closer, you can glean some more information. The first line shows the number of function calls and the total time to execute the function (or script) that you supplied to the profiler. You may also be told the number of *primitive* calls—these are the calls that were generated without the use of recursion.

The "Ordered by" line displays the sorting formation used to output the function list. Here the functions are being listed alphabetically, but it's possible to change the order to show the highest or lowest called function first. You'll learn how to change the output order when you look at the **pstats** module in the "Reporting Statistics" section later in this chapter.

The contents of each column are as follows:

- **ncalls** is the number of times each function was called. If this number is shown as **##/##**, where the first number is the total number of function calls and the second is the number of primitive calls.

- **tottime** reports the total time the function was executing; this value excludes the time spent in any functions called from this function.

- **percall(1)** reports the average time for each call to the function, excluding the time spent in subfunctions.

- **cumtime** reports the total time the function was executing, including the time spent in subfunctions.

- **percall(2)** reports the average time for each call to the function, including the time spent in subfunctions.

- **filename:lineno(function)** displays the filename, line number, and function that is being reported on.

You can also produce the same report for an entire script from the command line using the same system that you used for the debugger:

```
$ python /usr/local/lib/python2.1/profile.py mymodule.py
        204 function calls in 0.340 CPU seconds

   Ordered by: standard name

   ncalls  tottime  percall  cumtime  percall filename:lineno(function)
        1    0.020    0.020    0.280    0.280 <string>:1(?)
        1    0.000    0.000    0.260    0.260 mymodule.py:1(?)
      200    0.240    0.001    0.240    0.001 mymodule.py:1(mysqrt)
```

```
        1    0.020    0.020    0.260    0.260 mymodule.py:65(myfunc)
        1    0.060    0.060    0.340    0.340
profile:0(execfile('mymodule.py'))
        0    0.000             0.000             profile:0(profiler)
```

The only problem with both of these methods is that they produce information on a single run of the script or function that you are profiling. You have no access to the raw data and therefore cannot change the way the output is reported, calculated, or sorted.

You can get around this by saving the raw data produced by the profiler when working in interactive mode to a file. You do this by supplying the name of the file to save the data to when calling **run()**:

```
>>> import profile
>>> import mymodule
>>> profile.run('mymodule.myfunc()', 'mymodule.prof')
>>>
```

Instead of immediately generating the report, these commands produce the file **mymodule.prof** in the current directory. To get the report shown as in the preceding example, you need to process that file using the **pstats** module.

Reporting Statistics

The **pstats** module provides a single class, **Stats**, that can be used to process and report on the contents of a profile file. To create a new instance of the **Stats** class, just supply the name of the file to load to the constructor, as follows:

```
import pstats
myprofile = pstats.Stats('mymodule.prof')
```

The different methods to the instance report on the information contained in the file. For example, to reproduce the output generated when executing the profiler directly in the preceding example, you call:

```
myprofile.strip_dirs().sort_stats('stdname').print_stats()
```

The **strip_dirs()** method strips the directory path from a module name, the **sort_stats()** method sorts the output according to the module/line number/function name, and the **print_stats()** method prints out all the statistics for the entire process.

The **Stats** class actually supports a number of methods that control the format and output of the report; these methods are summarized in Table 24.2. Table 24.3 lists the sort orders supported by the **sort_stats()** method.

Method	Description
strip_dirs()	Removes the leading pathname from each module name in the statistics. Note that this is destructive—the path information is permanently removed from the data.
add(filename [, ...])	Adds more profiling data to the existing statistics. You can use this if you want to merge the information from a number of different calls to the same script or module or to a variety of scripts using the same module. The information is merged in order to produce a cumulative report for each module/function combination.
sort_stats(key [, ...])	Sort the statistics according to the specified key. Valid values are listed in Table 24.3. Supplying multiple values causes the sort to work on multiple keys. Note that the object is permanently sorted using the arguments you supply. To change the sort order, you need to call this function again.
reverse_order()	Reverse the order of the statistics generated by the reporting mechanism.
print_stats(restriction [, ...])	Prints out all the statistics for a given object. The output format is identical to the examples already given and the sort order is specified by the sort_stats() method. If restriction is supplied, it is used to restrict the output to a select set of functions. If restriction is an integer, only the first n functions are reported on. If the restriction is a floating-point value between 0 and 1 (inclusive), only the supplied percentage of functions are produced (i.e., 0.25 = 25%).
	If restriction is a string, it's interpreted as a regular expression and is used to match against the filename/line number/function using the re module.
	For example, print_stats('foo') would only match filenames/functions with foo in them. Note that the match is strictly against the filename:function so foo: would only match against files *ending* in foo. To match against a function use :foo.
	If multiple arguments are supplied, then the match is sequential. I.e., print_stats(0.25, ':foo') first restricts the list to the first 25% and then only to those functions matching foo.

Table 24-2. *Methods Supported by the Stats Class*

Method	Description
print_callers(restriction [, ...])	Prints a list of all the functions that called each function in the profiled statistics. The output is the same as the output produced by **print_stats()**, and **restriction** works in the same way outlined for **print_stats**. Note that for each function, a parenthesized number is appended to each caller to indicate the number of times this call was made. A non-parenthesized number shows the cumulative time spent in the function. See the examples later in this chapter.
print_callees(restriction [, ...])	Identical to **print_callers()** but lists the callees of the given function rather than the callers.

Table 24-2. *Methods Supported by the **Stats** Class* (continued)

Argument	Description
'calls'	Report is sorted by the number of function calls.
'cumulative'	Report is sorted by the cumulative execution time of each function.
'file'	Report is sorted by the filename.
'module'	Report is sorted by the module (file) name.
'pcalls'	Report is sorted by the number of primitive calls in each function.
'line'	Report is sorted by the line number of the function.
'name'	Report is sorted by the function name.
'nfl'	Report is sorted by the function name/filename/line number. Line numbers are compared numerically (i.e., 1, 2, ...10, 11, ... 23, 24).
'stdname'	Report is sorted by the standard function name/filename/line number. Line numbers are compared alphabetically (i.e., 1, 10, 11, ...19, 2, 20, 21,...29, 3, 30).
'time'	Report is sorted by the average time for each function.

Table 24-3. *Sorting Arguments Supported by **sort_stats()** Method*

For example, you can print out a time-ordered version of your report using

```
myprofile.strip_dirs().sort_stats('time').print_stats()
```

which generates the following output:

```
Mon Jul 23 16:11:21 2001     mymodule.prof

        203 function calls in 0.310 CPU seconds

  Ordered by: internal time

  ncalls  tottime  percall  cumtime  percall filename:lineno(function)
     200    0.300    0.002    0.300    0.002 mymodule.py:1(mysqrt)
       1    0.010    0.010    0.310    0.310 mymodule.py:65(myfunc)
       1    0.000    0.000    0.310    0.310 profile:0(mymodule.myfunc())
       1    0.000    0.000    0.310    0.310 <string>:1(?)
       0    0.000             0.000          profile:0(profiler)
```

You can also restrict the output to include only those functions in your **mymodule.py** file using

```
myprofile.strip_dirs().sort_stats('time').print_stats('mymodule')
```

which produces a report like this:

```
Mon Jul 23 16:11:21 2001     mymodule.prof

        203 function calls in 0.310 CPU seconds

  Ordered by: internal time
  List reduced from 5 to 3 due to restriction <'mymodule'>

  ncalls  tottime  percall  cumtime  percall filename:lineno(function)
     200    0.300    0.002    0.300    0.002 mymodule.py:1(mysqrt)
       1    0.010    0.010    0.310    0.310 mymodule.py:65(myfunc)
       1    0.000    0.000    0.310    0.310 profile:0(mymodule.myfunc())
```

The **print_callees()** report produces a report similar to this:

```
  Ordered by: internal time

  Function                    called...
  mymodule.py:1(mysqrt)          --
```

```
mymodule.py:65(myfunc)              mymodule.py:1(mysqrt)(200)      0.300
profile:0(mymodule.myfunc()))       <string>:1(?)(1)      0.310
<string>:1(?)                       mymodule.py:65(myfunc)(1)     0.310
profile:0(profiler)                 profile:0(mymodule.myfunc())(1)      0.310
```

Compare that to the report produced by **print_callers()**:

```
    Ordered by: internal time

Function                            was called by...
mymodule.py:1(mysqrt)               mymodule.py:65(myfunc)(200)      0.310
mymodule.py:65(myfunc)              <string>:1(?)(1)      0.310
profile:0(mymodule.myfunc()))       profile:0(profiler)(1)      0.000
<string>:1(?)                       profile:0(mymodule.myfunc())(1)      0.310
profile:0(profiler)                 --
```

Using the Data

Armed with all this information, you are probably wondering what you can actually do with the data. Well, as stated in the introduction to this section, the profiler is just a tool that provides you with information about function execution times. All the profiler does is help you identify the areas of the script that are soaking up the most time and the functions that should be optimized.

In the example in this chapter, the biggest resource hog is the **mysqrt()** function, which effectively achieves nothing while spending a considerable amount of time doing so!

In a real-world situation, you'd investigate the functions that are being called and determine whether they could be improved upon and optimized. Ultimately, the functions that require investigation will fit into one of two categories:

- High number of calls with low individual execution time: These functions are probably being called from within a loop. Although some of these instances are unavoidable, if they use a considerable amount of time, check if there's a way that the function contents can be placed directly into the loop. Calling functions requires additional information to be put onto and removed from the stack, so reducing the number of function calls will improve the performance.

- High amount of time with a low call count: These functions need to be hand-optimized to reduce their execution time. Use the hand-optimization tricks introduced earlier in this chapter to see where you can improve.

Ultimate, although a profiler can help in the process, debugging and tuning your scripts still requires manual intervention. The experience you gain over the years for what does and doesn't work will help you optimize your script, with or without the help of a profiler.

Chapter 25

Documenting and
Documentation

There is nothing worse when reading through code—whether your own or someone else's—than not having any explanation about what is being performed by the different parts of the code. Even if the code is your own, without notation you will eventually forget why you chose a certain algorithm or why you chose a particular method for the problem you are trying to solve.

Comments are the most basic form of documentation, although unfortunately most programmers (including myself) forget to use them. This is unfortunate because they do provide probably the best way of reminding the programmer, and indicating to another programmer, exactly how the code works.

If you want to release an application or module to the wide world, you need to write some proper documentation. There are many ways of doing this, including writing separate README documents or building your own HTML, PDF, or, if it's destined for Unix, troff/nroff format document.

We also have another solution, and that's to use embedded document strings. These attributes are attached to objects and other entities within the source code that we can then extract using a number of different tools into suitable documentation formats. Because the documentation is attached to the code elements within your scripts and modules, you know exactly where the text came from and what it related to. Better still, you can use the document strings to provide documentation from within your scripts: imagine displaying help text within an application that had been taken directly from the object we were describing.

In this chapter we'll look at how to write good comments and how comments are incorporated into Python scripts. We'll also look at document strings and how to build and then later extract the tags from a module into a stand-alone document. If you want more information on the documentation available on Python, see Appendix B for more details.

For some examples of writing good documentation, try one of the following URLs:

- http://www.ibiblio.org/mdw/HOWTO/Software-Release-Practice-HOWTO/documentation.html
- http://www.techscribe.co.uk/techw/faq.htm
- http://mindprod.com/unmain.html
- http://techwriting.about.com/careers/techwriting/cs/humour/
- http://www.python.org/sigs/doc-sig/

Comments

When was the last time you went back and looked at a piece of code and thought, "What was I doing here?" or "Why did I choose that way of doing this?" Using comments is a great way of making your code readable by you and other people: although you might think you'll never forget a piece of code, the reality is that a couple days, weeks, or even a month or more down the line you're going to need some sort of mental jogger.

The obvious solution is to use comments to annotate how the script works and what arguments and return values are handled by the different functions and methods used in the script or module. Writing good comments is an art, and we'll have a look at some good and some bad examples.

Once you've completed your project, the next step should be to convert your comments into documentation so that other people can understand how to use your code without having to read the comments. Mind you, if you're going to document your script properly, why write comments and then documentation? You could just write the documentation as you go along.

Writing Comments

It's a well-known and unfortunate fact that most programmers either don't write comments or write them only after they have completed the software. This is a really bad habit—not using comments makes the code difficult to understand, and writing comments after the program is completed leads to bad comments being introduced, because you probably won't remember precisely the reason behind the design of a particular section. Instead, you should write the comments as you are programming to ensure that you don't write the wrong information. It's probably also a good idea to write about what you *didn't* do, so you can avoid trying something that you know didn't work.

Comments are introduced into a Python script by inserting a hash character (#) into a line; everything following that character up until the end of the line is considered to be a comment:

```
print message # Output the message we received
```

With multiline comments you must put a hash symbol on each line:

```
for line in lines:       # Extract individual lines
    pline = parse(line) # Parse the line to get the bits we want
    print pline          # Print out the extracted elements
```

It's also good practice, as seen here, to line up your comments within a multiline segment to indicate that the comments are part of a larger message.

Writing Good Comments

Including comments in your code is only part of the solution—you must ensure that your comments make sense and are actually useful. Consider the following code fragment:

```
if message: print message # Prints a message if it exists
```

The comment doesn't tell us anything that we don't already know about what the line does. Instead, try to write a comment that describes why you are doing what you are doing, rather than how you are doing it:

```
If message: print message    # Prints out the warning message from the
                             # get_message() function, assuming a valid
                             # message was returned.
```

When writing comments, think about annotating the following elements:

■ **File headers** should be used to outline the purpose and contents of the file and to include a copyright statement, if appropriate. For example, at the top of a module you might include something like this:

```
# Module MyModule
# Copyright Me, 2001
# Provides functions and a class for manipulating time information
```

If you are using a revision control system such as RCS or CVS you should also include the revision, copyright, and other strings associated with your project. For example, you can introduce a revision number, automatically updated by RCS/CVS by including **$Revision$** in your header.

■ **Variable/object names** should be commented to explain what they are used for and the data you expect them to contain. If relevant you could also include expected valid data ranges, which can be useful when debugging. For example:

```
bankaccount = Account(500) # Holds the basic bank account detail
errormsg = ''              # Stores the value of the error message
                           # returned during an exception
```

■ **Functions** should be commented as part of their definition, at least to explain what arguments the function expects and what information is returned, although information on what it achieves is probably a good idea, too. However, if you are going to comment to this level of detail, you should probably think about using Python's document strings, examples of which we'll see later in this chapter. When using comments, make sure you line them up to the indentation of the enclosing block:

```
def parser(line):
    # Accepts a line as text, parses the contents to extract the
    # individual words and elements and then returns a list of the
    # elements to the caller
```

■ **Classes** should be described so that the reader understands the whole scope of the class, but don't describe the attributes or methods. You can describe those individually as they are declared, such as:

```
class Account():
    # Base class for all accounts
    def __init__(self,balance):
        # Creates a new instance of Account, setting the balance attribute
        self.balance = balance # Holds the accounts current value
```

■ **In-line comments** should be used to highlight particular lines or sections that are important, but don't label every line; programmers looking at your code should already understand what a **for** loop or **if** statement does.

Finally, here are some things to avoid when writing comments:

■ Don't annotate every line. It probably won't be helpful to the reader and may confuse more than aid their understanding.

■ Don't just reiterate in English what function the line performs. Saying "prints message" against a **print** statement is not useful—and to a programmer seems a bit nauseating.

■ Don't "pretty print" your comments. Adding a lot of window dressing and white space can often detract from the real meat of the comment, and it certainly won't make it easier to read if the user has to scroll down to read the comments in conjunction with the code.

If you keep within these limits you should be able to write suitable comments that other programmers can follow. However, since you should be documenting your modules and scripts anyway, you might want to consider using doc strings over comments; we'll look at that facility next.

Embedded Document Strings

Any module, function, class, or method can potentially have a document string attached to it during declaration. The way it works is that any string constant that appears before the statements within a definition is taken to be documentation for the object. The string is then assigned to the __doc__ attribute of the object in question. For example, in the code fragment:

```
class Spam:
    """Spam class documentation starts here..."""
    def method(self,arg):
        """Method documentation starts here..."""
```

```
def documentation():
    print "Class documentation:", Spam.__doc__
    print "Method 'method' documentation:", Spam.method.__doc__
```

Document strings can be specified using any of the normal quotes, single, double, or triple quoted—though triple quoted is the accepted standard. However, remember to be careful when specifying quotes of the same type within your document string.

To get the information back, as seen in the example, you just need to access the **__doc__** attribute:

```
print myfunc.__doc__
```

Because the information is an attribute, you could also update the information at a later stage. I've used this in the past when using doc strings as help text. Imagine you have a button that can be toggled on and off, but accessing the help describes its current setting. Done properly, you can do all of this without actually affecting the doc strings that would otherwise be extracted by a documentation tool such as **pydoc**. For example:

```
class SetButton:
    """Button """
    def __init__(self,name):
        self.value = 0
        self.name = name
        self.__doc__ = SetButton.__doc__ + self.name + " Off"
    def switchon(self):
        self.value = 1
        self.__doc__ = SetButton.__doc__ + self.name + " On"
    def switchoff(self):
        self.value = 0
        self.__doc__ = SetButton.__doc__ + self.name + " Off"
```

The biggest benefit of the doc string system is that it attaches documentation to a specific object as part of the object definition. Because the documentation is available as an attribute to the object, we can access the doc string from within the script during execution, just as easily as you can read when looking at the source code.

Although the doc string system wasn't widely used up until Python 1.5, since then doc strings have been used and incorporated into most modules and are used by the main Python development team and many of the third-party developers as a method for documenting their scripts and modules.

Doc strings are still not used universally, although a recent push has seen an increase in the number of tools and the development of some accepted standards for incorporating doc strings into your code. The Python documentation, for example, is still written using traditional documentation tools, mostly SGML. This will change over time, and if you want to be a part of this process, consider joining the Documentation Special Interest Group (SIG); you can find a list of other SIGs and details on how to join them in Appendix B.

Translating Embedded Strings into Documentation

The Documentation SIG has produced a set of tools, called **pythondoc** (or **pydoc**), that will extract the doc strings from a module file for a given entity. There are other tools, including HappyDoc, that provide similar functionality, but we'll stick with the supplied documentation tool set as it comes as part of the standard library.

The pydoc Tool

The main **pydoc** script is a bit of a jack of all trades. At the base level, it extracts doc strings from a Python module and displays them either as text or as HTML, but all in a structured format that also follows and displays functions, classes, and other elements accordingly.

The **pydoc** script should be installed in a suitable place when Python is built and/ or installed. To execute, just run **pydoc** from the command line:

```
$ pydoc
```

Without any arguments, it'll produce a small help message.

By default, **pydoc** searches the same directories as those searched for modules, that is, the directories defined in **sys.path**. For example, to display the documentation for the **random** module, you would simply type

```
$ pydoc random
Python Library Documentation: module random

NAME
    random - Random variable generators.
...
```

Multithreading note: The random number generator used here is not thread-safe; it is possible that two calls return the same random value. However, you can instantiate a different instance of Random() in each thread to get generators that don't share state, then use .setstate() and .jumpahead() to move the generators to disjoint segments of the full period. For example,

```
...
```

However, if you include a forward slash (/) within the argument, then it's assumed that the argument is the path to the module file that you want to display the document for.

Keyword Search

You can search for keywords in the synopsis lines (the first documentation line within the module) of all the Python files in the library directories by using the **-k** command-line option. The result is a list of the modules that it finds that contain the keyword. For example, to get a list of modules that create random numbers we might use

```
$ pydoc -k random
random - Random variable generators.
whrandom - Wichman-Hill random number generator.
```

Note that this option will find only words in the synopsis line; other words in the module files are ignored.

Web Server

Because **pydoc** can convert doc strings into HTML format, we have the perfect base for providing a web server for Python documentation. In fact, **pydoc** includes support for the **SimpleHTTPServer** class so that it can provide HTML versions of the documentation directly through a web server.

To enable this facility, use the **-p** option to start the web server on a specific TCP/IP port. For example, to start the server on port 1001:

```
$ ./pydoc -p 1001
pydoc server ready at http://localhost:1001/
```

From the same machine you can now access the documentation by typing the URL shown above into your web browser. Alternatively, you can access the site from another machine over the network. I use this as a way of accessing the documentation on Python from any machine on my network without having to open the file separately. You can see the result of the module list in Figure 25-1.

Graphical Interface

By using Tk, **pydoc** also provides a graphical interface to the library documentation. This is not, unfortunately, as great as it sounds: you are limited to searching for modules by using keywords (identical to the **-k** option). Once you've found what you're looking for, it starts the built-in web server and then opens your browser to allow you to view the documentation.

You can see the basic window in Figure 25-2. An extended window with a list of matched modules is shown in Figure 25-3.

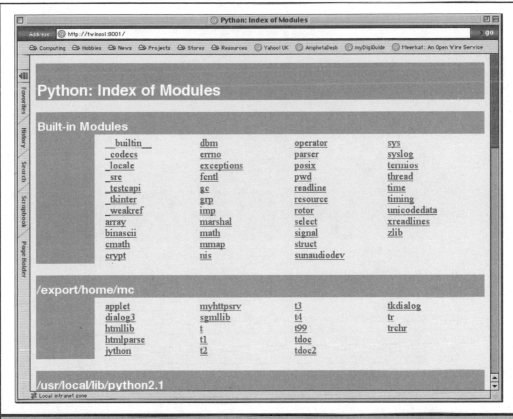

Figure 25-1. *Documentation list from pydoc*

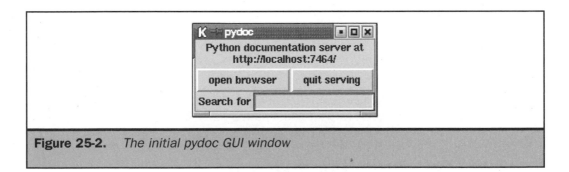

Figure 25-2. *The initial pydoc GUI window*

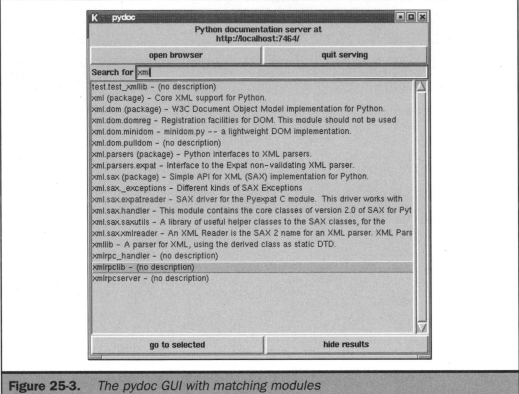

Figure 25-3. *The pydoc GUI with matching modules*

Export to HTML

The last option is something we've already touched on: the ability to convert the documentation for a module into an HTML file. The **-w** option does this from the command line, writing the resulting file to a file matching the module you selected. For example, the command

```
$ pydoc -w random
wrote random.html
```

writes the documentation for **random** to random.html.

The resulting file is identical to what you would see when using **pydoc** in web server mode; you can see a sample in Figure 25-4.

Structured Text Formatting Rules

Before we look at the specifics of the **pydoc** tools, we first need to examine how to actually write the text that we include in the doc strings in the first place. The "Structured Text

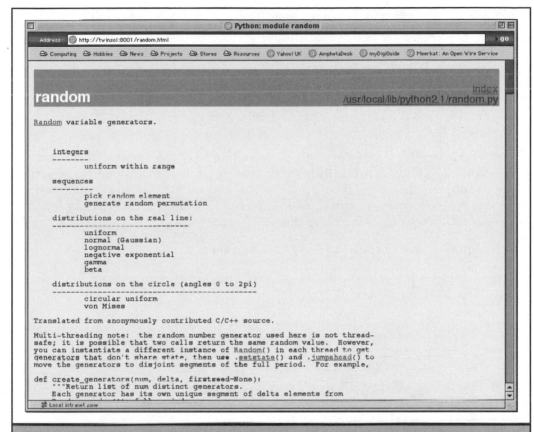

Figure 25-4. *The **random** module in HTML format as generated by **pydoc***

Formatting Rules" are a set of rules that aim to describe how different elements, such as bulleted or numbered lists and highlighted words, can be described and defined within document strings.

The information is still very much in its developmental stage, and not every one of the documentation tools—**pydoc** included—follows the rules. To keep track of what is being defined, join the Documentation SIG—see Appendix B for details.

The basic rules are as follows:

- A structured documentation string consists of a number of individual paragraphs separated by one or more blank lines.

- Each paragraph has a level, identified by its indentation, generally equal to the indentation of the current block. Level 0 is determined by looking at the first nonblank line after the first line. For most cases, this means that Level 0 is equal to no indentation in the source code; level 1 is the first indentation; level 2 the second; and so on, as seen here:

```
"""
This is level 0 paragraph

    This is a level 1 paragraph

Back to level 0"""
```

- A paragraph is a subparagraph if a preceding paragraph existed at the next lowest level, as shown in the previous example where the second paragraph is a subparagraph of the first. The same rules also apply to doc strings indented due to the code structure—that is, a doc string from a method would be a subparagraph of the doc string for the entire class.

In addition, some symbols have a special meaning:

- A paragraph that begins with a -, *, or o is treated as an unordered list (bullet) element. For example:

```
"""Bulleted list:
* First bullet
* Second bullet
"""
```

- A paragraph that begins with a sequence of digits followed by a white-space character is treated as an ordered list element. Note, however, that elements aren't ordered for you. For example:

```
"""Numbered list:
1 First bullet
2 Second bullet
3 Third bullet
"""
```

- A paragraph with a first line that contains some text, followed by some white space and - - is treated as a descriptive list element. The leading text is treated as the element title. Be careful about using the double hyphen in paragraphs to separate text, as this can confuse **pydoc**. For example, we could create a descriptive list using:

```
"""Items:
The First item -- is just a lead in to the rest of the list
The Second item -- Looks slightly different
"""
```

- Subparagraphs of a paragraph that ends in the word "example" or "examples" are treated as example code and are output without formatting. Any trailing punctuation to the word "example" or "examples" is ignored. For example, the following would introduce a piece of sample code into a doc string:

```
"""To use this class, just create a new instance. For example:
myparser = MyDocStringParser()
"""
```

- Text enclosed in single quotes (with white space to the left of the first quote and white space or punctuation to the right of the second quote) is treated as example code. For example, to introduce the word "parser" as a piece of inline example code, use

```
"""When you call the method 'parser' to parse the document the
information is then..."""
```

- Text surrounded by a single * character and leading/trailing white space (or punctuation on the right) is emphasized using italic type. For example in the string "do *not* use this function," the word "not" would be italicized.

- Text surrounded by a double * character and leading/trailing white space (or punctuation on the right) is emphasized using bold type. For example in the string "do **not** use this function," the word "not" would be boldface+.

Expect these rules to change or to at least be refined as the **pydoc** and other documentation tools are refined.

The Complete Reference

Chapter 26

Extending Python

lthough the Python language is ultimately capable at all sorts of tasks, there are times when it needs to use the functionality of an external C library. In fact, many of the standard Python extensions that you may have already used are probably either direct C library users or indirect users. For example, the **socket** module uses the underlying socket libraries on a platform to provide network communication, while the **urllib** module relies on the **socket** module to enable it to download files from the Internet.

Building a Python extension that interfaces to a C module is not as difficult as it sounds. Once you've learned the basic techniques, you should be able to interface to just about any external library or C function.

This chapter explains step by step the process of building an extension in Python. You'll also learn about the methods available for exchanging information between Python and C. For more information on the Python API, see the API documentation available from the Python website (http://www.python.org).

Basic Interface

The Python extension interface is very simple—you basically build a wrapper around the C functions that you want to export. The wrapper function handles the conversion between the Python objects (variables) and the variables and values required by the underlying C function. Then, if necessary, the wrapper function converts the data returned back into a Python object that you can use from within your Python application.

To explain the process further, let's look at a simple C file containing two functions, a function that prints a raw string using **printf()**, and another function that accepts two floating-point values and calculates the volume of a cone, returning the result:

```c
#include <math.h>
#include <stdio.h>

float volumecone(float radius, float height)
{
  float volume;

  volume = (1.0/3.0)*M_PI*(radius*radius)*height;

  return volume;
}

void rawprint(char *string)
{
  printf("%s", string);
}
```

The wrapper source actually needs to perform two tasks: First, it must provide the wrapper around the individual functions that you want to call—you need one wrapper function for each external C function that you want to call. Second, it has to register the Python function name, the wrapper that supports the interface, and the types of arguments it accepts, thereby initializing the module and making the whole task work. The wrapper looks like this:

```
#include <Python.h>

extern void rawprint(char *);
extern float volumecone(float, float);

PyObject *testex_volumecone(PyObject *self, PyObject *args)
{
  float radius, height, volume;

  if (!PyArg_ParseTuple(args, "ff", &radius, &height))
    {
      return NULL;
    }

  volume = volumecone(radius, height);

  return Py_BuildValue("f", volume);
}

PyObject *testex_rawprint(PyObject *self, PyObject *args)
{
  char *string;
  if (!PyArg_ParseTuple(args,"s", &string))
    {
      return NULL;
    }

  rawprint(string);

  Py_INCREF(Py_None);
  return Py_None;
}

static PyMethodDef testexmethods[] = {
  {"volumecone", testex_volumecone, METH_VARARGS,
```

```
     "compute the volume of a cone given the radius and height" },
   {"rawprint", testex_rawprint, METH_VARARGS, "print a raw string"
},
   { NULL, NULL },
};

void inittestex(void)
{
  Py_InitModule("testex", testexmethods);
}
```

The specifics of each section of the wrapper function are described in the next part of this chapter, but take a while to look over the wrapper source itself—you should be able to pick up most of the important details here.

Writing the Wrapper

The wrapper has three sections:

- The first section provides the information needed to enable the wrappers to call the external C functions.
- The second section contains the actual wrappers themselves.
- The third section is the registration information.

Setting the Background

The background information in this case is the first few lines:

```
#include <Python.h>

extern void rawprint(char *);
extern float volumecone(float, float);
```

The first line imports the function definitions for the Python functions that help support and manage the interface. The next two lines set the prototypes for the two external functions in your C source file. If you are interfacing to an existing library, then you'll probably use more **include** statements to include the prototype information.

The Wrapper Functions

The first wrapper function is around the **volumecone** function and is called **testex_volumecone**. The **volumecone** function accepts two arguments: floating-point values that define the radius of the base circle and the height of the cone. The wrapper function is defined like this:

```
PyObject *testex_volumecone(PyObject *self, PyObject *args)
{
```

The **PyObject** return value is required because a wrapper function always returns a value back to the caller. In this example, you'll be returning the results of the calculation back, but even a function that does not return any values needs to return a valid Python object; otherwise, the interpreter gets the **NULL** value and raises an error.

The arguments to the wrapper function **testex_volumecone** are also Python objects. The first argument is **self**, essentially just the hook for this function that is identified internally by the Python interpreter as a code object. **args** is the list of arguments supplied to the **volumecone** function when it is called. Note that at this stage you are not identifying the argument types or the data they contain.

The following line sets up the C variables that you need to hold the arguments to the real extension function and to hold the result.

```
float radius, height, volume;
```

The **PyArg_ParseTuple** function converts a list of arguments supplied to the wrapper function and extracts the individual elements from the argument list into the local C types.

```
if (!PyArg_ParseTuple(args, "ff", &radius, &height))
    {
       return NULL;
    }
```

The first argument to the **PyArg_ParseTuple** function is the supplied argument list, and the second argument is a format string that specifies the variable types that should be extracted and converted. In this case, you're extracting two floating-point values. These values are inserted into the local C variables by address. At the end of this stage, you should have extracted two floating-point values supplied by the Python function call into two local C variables.

Note that the output is trapped. If the Python call does not contain the right type of value, **PyArg_ParseTuple** returns **NULL**, which is picked up by the interpreter as an error. You can raise a proper Python exception before returning the **NULL** value to Python—see the section "Exceptions," later in this chapter, for more information.

In the following line, you actually call the **volumecone** function. This function is pretty straightforward; you just supply the two floating-point values and capture the result.

```
volume = volumecone(radius, height);
```

The last step is to convert the return value back into a Python object that can be passed back to the Python interpreter, and ultimately back to the Python script that called the function in the first place. You do this with **Py_BuildValue**, which is syntactically equivalent to **PyArg_ParseTuple**, except that instead of converting a tuple of arguments into C variables, it converts C variables into a Python variable:

```
    return Py_BuildValue("f", volume);
}
```

The second wrapper function, **testex_rawprint**, is actually simpler than the first; it accepts a string instead of two floating-point values:

```
PyObject *testex_rawprint(PyObject *self, PyObject *args)
{
  char *string;
  if (!PyArg_ParseTuple(args,"s", &string))
    {
      return NULL;
    }

  rawprint(string);

  Py_INCREF(Py_None);
  return Py_None;
}
```

The big difference between the **testex_rawprint** and the first wrapper function is that the **rawprint** function doesn't return any values. However, you still have to return a valid Python object to prevent the interpreter from identifying a **NULL** value as an error. To do this, what you actually do is increment the reference count for the **Py_None** value and return that. **Py_None** is the C equivalent of the Python **None** value, so essentially **testex_rawprint** returns nothing to the caller, but it doesn't raise any error.

Initializing the Module

The last section of the wrapper module is to create the initialization function to be called by the Python interpreter when the module is loaded in order to register the available functions and other objects for the namespace used for the module.

The first stage of this last section creates the structure to hold the information. This structure is a list of functions that will be supported by the wrapper module. For each function, list the Python function names, the wrapper function that supports the Python function call, and some options that define the type of arguments supported by the function. An optional fourth argument, shown in the following source, also populates the doc string (in the __doc__ attribute) for the function:

```
static PyMethodDef testexmethods[] = {
  {"volumecone", testex_volumecone, METH_VARARGS,
   "compute the volume of a cone given the radius and height" },
  {"rawprint", testex_rawprint, METH_VARARGS, "print a raw string" },

  { NULL, NULL },
};
```

The preceding source registers the function **volumecone** using the wrapper function **testex_volumecone**. The **volumecone** function accepts a list of arguments, so you use the **METH_VARARGS** option. For functions that don't accept any values, you don't have to specify any arguments. If you have a function that you want to support keyword arguments, use **METH_KEYWORDS**, and to support both, use or (using |).

Note that you have to terminate the configuration list with a null entry.

Finally, you create an initialization function. The **Py_InitModule4** function initializes with the four-element form (including the doc string); if you omit the doc string, use the **Py_InitModule** function. The name of the initialization function is important; you're creating a module called **testex**, so the name of the initialization function is **inittestex**. **inittestex** basically calls one function to initialize the module, supplying the module name, **testex**, and the earlier object definition table:

```
void inittestex(void)
{
  Py_InitModule4("testex", testexmethods);
}
```

Compiling the Extension

Compiling the extension is slightly more complicated than it sounds. To start, you need to compile the source file and the wrapper file, and you need to make sure the wrapper file has access to the **Python.h** header file. Then you need to compile both the backend module and the wrapper into a shared object file that is loaded by the interpreter when you import the file. Obviously, if you were wrapping a library function, you wouldn't need to worry about a second C file, but you would have to make sure you had access to the header files and library files required.

If all of this sounds complicated, don't worry, there is an easier way. This chapter concentrates on the Unix technique for building an extension, since it's the most straightforward. This technique should also work for Unix-like OS, such as QNX, BeOS, and Mac OS X. Check the Python website for details on Windows and MacOS techniques.

One of the files installed when Python is built and installed is a file called **Makefile.pre.in**, which you'll probably find in the **config** directory of your Python library directory (typically, **/usr/local/lib/python#.#**, where **#.#** is the Python version number).

Makefil.pre.in uses another file called **Setup** to create a Makefile that, in turn, builds the module. The format of the **Setup** file follows that for the main **Setup** file used to build the standard extension modules that come with the Python distribution.

The **Setup** file should start with

```
*shared*
```

This statement sets the system up to build a shared extension; you can build a static version of the Python interpreter with your module built into it by using the **static** target with the Makefile.

Subsequent lines then define the module name, required C files, and any other options required to build the extension module. For example, if your C file is **testex.c** and your wrapper file is **testexwrapper.c**, the line in the **Setup** file looks like this:

```
testex testex.c testexmodule.c
```

Armed with your **Setup** file and a copy of the **Makefile.pre.in** file, you should now be able to type

```
$ make -f Makefile.pre.in boot
```

to create the Makefile.

To build the extension, just type **make**:

```
$ make
gcc -fPIC -g -O2 -Wall -Wstrict-prototypes -I/usr/local/include/python2.1 -
I/usr/local/include/python2.1 -DHAVE_CONFIG_H  -c ./././testex.c -o ./testex.o
gcc -fPIC -g -O2 -Wall -Wstrict-prototypes -I/usr/local/include/python2.1 -
I/usr/local/include/python2.1 -DHAVE_CONFIG_H  -c ./././testexmodule.c -o
./testexmodule.o
gcc -shared  ./testex.o ./testexmodule.o   -o ./testex.so
```

The result should be a shared object file, **testex.so**, that contains everything you need for the extension to work.

As mentioned earlier, you can also run **make static**, which builds your extension; but rather than placing the result into a shared object file, it bonds Python with the object files and the other objects required for the current Python version and creates a new **python** executable in the current directory.

Testing the Result

To test your module, fire up Python in the same directory as your extension module and try importing the module. You can see the results of importing the test demonstration module here:

```
$ python
Python 2.1 (#1, Aug  2 2001, 20:52:30)
[GCC egcs-2.91.66 19990314/Linux (egcs-1.1.2 release)] on linux2
Type "copyright", "credits" or "license" for more information.
>>> import testex
>>> testex.printraw("Hello this is a raw test")
Traceback (most recent call last):
  File "<stdin>", line 1, in ?
AttributeError: 'testex' module has no attribute 'printraw'
>>> testex.rawprint("Hello this is a raw test")
Hello this is a raw test>>>
>>> testex.volumecone(4.5, 3.5)
74.220123291015625
>>
```

It all appears to work!

Data Conversion

The **PyArg_ParseTuple()** and **Py_BuildValue()** functions translate information between Python objects and C data types. There is a third function, **PyArg_ParseTupleAndKeywords()**, that can be used with functions that accept keyword arguments. The keyword arguments are placed into a null-terminated list of strings containing the names of all the arguments. The actual format for each of the functions is as follows:

```
int PyArg_ParseTuple(PyObject *args, char *format, ...);
int PyArg_ParseTupleAndKeywords(PyObject *args, PyObject *kwdict
                         char *format, char **kwlist, ...);
PyObject *Py_BuildValue(format, ...);
```

The same **format** options are more or less shared for each function. Table 26-1 contains the full list of supported **format** options.

Format	PyType	C Type	Description
s	String	char *	Null-terminated string.
s#	String	char *, int	String and length. Allows the string to contain null bytes.
z	String or None	char *	Null-terminated string or **NULL**.
z#	String or None	char *, int	String and length or **NULL**.
b	Integer	char	Eight-bit integer.
h	Integer	short	Short 16-bit integer.
i	Integer	int	Integer.
l	Integer	long	Long integer.
c	String	char	Single character (Python string of one character).
f	Float	float	Single-precision floating point.
d	Float	double	Double-precision floating point.
D	Complex	Py_complex	Complex number.
O	Any	PyObject *	Any Python object.
O!	Any	type, PyObject *	Python object of a specific type.
O&	Any	converter, any	Python object processed through the converter function **converter.**
S	String	PyStringObject *	Python string object.

Table 26-1. *Format Options for Converting Python and C Variables*

Format	PyType	C Type	Description
(items)	Tuple	**vars**	Tuple of items, where **items** is actually a string of format specifiers (as used elsewhere in this table). To convert Python to C, **vars** should be a list of C variable addresses. For C to Python, **vars** should be a list of C variables.
[items]	List	**vars**	C to Python only. List of items, where **items** is actually a string of format specifiers (as used elsewhere in this table). **vars** is a list of C variables.
{items}	Dictionary	**vars**	C to Python only. Dictionary of items. The supplied list of variables should be keys and values in key/value pairs.
				Start of optional arguments (Python to C only).
:			End of arguments. Additional text is used as the function name in error reports (Python to C only).
;			End of arguments. Additional text is used as the error text in error reports (Python to C only).

Table 26-1. *Format Options for Converting Python and C Variables (continued)*

Some examples of converting a Python argument list into C variables are as follows:

```
/* Convert into two floats */
PyArg_ParseTuple(args, "ff", &floata, &floatb);

/* Convert a string and integer */
PyArg_ParseTuple(args, "si", &string, &inta);

/* Convert two tuples */
PyArg_ParseTuple(args, "(ss)(if)", &stringa, &stringb, &inta, &floata);
```

The colon (:) and the semicolon (;) format sequences are special cases. The colon (:) specifies the end of the argument list; any text following the colon is used as the function name in any error messages raised during conversion when it occurs within a Python session. The semicolon (;) character specifies the end of the argument list; any text following the semicolon is used as the error message raised when a conversion error occurs. For example, if you have a function that accepts two arguments, you might define its format as

```
PyArg_ParseTuple(args, "ii;function accepts exactly two arguments",
                 &inta, &intb);
```

Managing Reference Counts

As you may have already guessed, the **PyObject *** type is used within the Python API to hold information about any Python object. It's actually a special structure that self-defines the data type it's storing and is, therefore, used throughout the API for holding everything from module data to individual strings, arrays, and other familiar Python data types.

Within Python as an interpreter, you've already seen in Chapter 3, Chapter 6, and Chapter 10 that care needs to be taken when dealing with Python objects. This is because the relationship between the underlying object and its name within the symbol table is as a reference. Also, nested types such as arrays actually store arrays of references to other Python objects.

Reference Counts

Although within normal Python use, the use of references does not cause a problem, when manipulating those same objects from the C API, you need to be aware of the reference issue.

In a nutshell, each reference has a unique *reference count*. The reference count tells the Python interpreter how many other objects are referring to that object. For example, in the code

```
numa = 45
numb = 56
lista = [numa, numb]
```

the **lista** object has a reference count of 1. But the objects holding the values for **numa** and **numb** have a reference count of 2—they are being used once to allow the reference between **numa** as it exists within the current module's dictionary (i.e., its namespace) and once within the list. If you delete the first element of **lista**, the reference count for the object behind **numa** is reduced by 1.

If the reference count for an object reaches 0, Python assumes that the object is no longer required and the memory it is using is freed. In the preceding example, this situation only occurs when **numa** finally goes out of scope, probably at the end of the script.

Herein lies the big potential problem with reference counts. While it's unlikely to cause a problem if the reference count for an object is above 0, even when no object now refers to it, lowering the reference count for an object so that it reaches 0 when it's still in use elsewhere is fatal.

When manipulating those same objects from an external C application (or when talking to Python objects in an embedded interpreter, as described in Chapter 27), the same issue applies. You need to ensure that the interpreter knows when you're using a particular object and, therefore, expects to be able to access its value on demand and knows when you've finished using the reference.

The entire process is handled through those reference counts. To signal that you want to use an object reference, increment its reference count; to signal that you're finished with the object, decrement its reference count.

Reference Types

Within Python, object references are actually split into two types, *owned* and *borrowed*. An owned reference is a pointer to a Python object that has had its reference count incremented to indicate that you expect to use its value. A borrowed reference is just a bare pointer to a Python object whose reference count has not been incremented.

Owned references are generally used and created when a function creates a new Python object. Once the object has been created, it's classified as "owned" by the function that created it, so you must update the reference count to indicate that it's in use. Borrowed references are used when you are accessing information from a pre-existing object such as an existing exception or when accessing the items from a list.

Updating the Reference Counts

Python provides four macros for handling the reference count of an object. The **Py_INCREF()** and **Py_DECREF()** macros increment and decrement the reference count for the supplied object, which must be a valid Python object. The **Py_XINCREF()** and **Py_XDECREF()** macros attempt to increment or decrement the reference count for the supplied Python object, but they ignore the object if it's **NULL**.

Understanding where you use these macros can be tricky. For owned references, the rules are quite straightforward: you increment the reference count when you want to use it, and especially when you want to update the object; you decrement the reference count when you're finished with the object. For example, when creating temporary objects inside a wrapper function, increment the reference count before using them and decrement the reference count after using them. However, don't decrement the reference count for an object that you are returning; otherwise, the object is freed before it ever reaches the caller.

With borrowed references the rules are simpler: don't increment or decrement the reference counts unless you want to own the object.

As a rough guide, follow these basic rules:

- All functions that create a new object create owned references; you'll be responsible for managing their values.

- Don't decrement the reference count on objects you are returning.

- To make sure an object is stored, use **Py_INCREF()**. There's no harm in Python keeping a record of an object until the interpreter terminates.

- Most sequence and mapping functions return owned references to stored elements.

If you need more information, check **http://www.python.org/doc/ext**, the Python C API documentation.

Exceptions

Although the functions in the examples in the preceding section return **NULL** to the caller, all this does is indicate that an error occurred in the external function. Python uses exceptions to highlight problems, even within the confines of the interpreter; so in order to support the same functionality from within an exception API, you need a way to handle the exception.

In some instances, you can use one of the simple functions like **PyErr_BadArgument()**, which raises a **TypeError** exception to the caller. For example, you can rewrite the **printraw()** extension function as follows:

```
PyObject *testex_rawprint(PyObject *self, PyObject *args)
{
  char *string;
  if (!PyArg_ParseTuple(args,"s", &string))
    {
       PyErr_BadArgument();
       return NULL;
    }

  rawprint(string);

  Py_INCREF(Py_None);
  return Py_None;
}
```

If you try this version of the function within Python, the result is

```
>>> rawprint(45)
Traceback (most recent call last):
  File "<stdin>", line 1, in ?
TypeError: bad argument type for built-in operation
```

The message reported in this example is automatically generated by the Python API. To use your own message, you need to set the exception manually, so you would replace that line with

```
PyErr_SetString(PyExc_TypeError, "You gave me an invalid argument");
```

which generates the following result in the interpreter:

```
>>> rawprint(45)
Traceback (most recent call last):
  File "<stdin>", line 1, in ?
TypeError: bad argument type for built-in operation
```

Other exceptions are raised in the same way. Note that in each of the preceding examples, the **PyErr_*()** function merely sets the exception type—it's not until **NULL** is returned to the caller (in this case, the Python interpreter) that the actual exception is raised and handled, or a traceback is generated. All of the functions in this section merely set or release the current exception type; if no exception is in effect, a generic exception is raised by the interpreter, but only because it received **NULL**.

To create a module-specific exception, you need to create a new exception type; you do this with the **PyErr_NewException()** function. The **PyErr_NewException()** function accepts three arguments, of which the first is critical because it specifies the new name of the exception to be raised. Since you want the user to be able to access this exception so they can trap and handle it, you also need to modify the initialization function to add the new exception object to the module's dictionary.

For example, to create a special **badarg** exception within the **testex** module, you'd use the following:

```
PyObject *TestExExc;

void inittestex(void)
{
  PyObject *mymod, *moddict;
  mymod = Py_InitModule4("testex", testexmethods);
  moddict = PyModule_GetDict(mymod);
  TestExExc = PyErr_NewException('testex.badarg', NULL, NULL);
  PyDict_SetItemString(moddict, "badarg", TextExExc);
}
```

Now you can trap errors as follows:

```
import testex

try:
    rawprint(45)
except testex.badarg:
    print "Bad argument type supplied"
```

Table 26-2 contains a full list of the functions for setting and releasing exceptions, and Table 26-3 lists the C constants for the built-in Python exception types.

Function	Description
void PyErr_Print()	Prints a standard traceback (as if an unhandled exception had been raised within a Python script) and then clears the error indicator. Causes a fatal error if no exception has been set.

Table 26-2.   *Exception Functions*

Function	Description
PyObject* PyErr_Occurred()	Returns the exception type (see Table 26-3) if an error has been set, or returns **NULL** if no error is in effect. Note that you receive a borrowed reference to the exception type so there is no need to manage the reference. Use **PyErr_GivenExceptionMatches()** to match the returned value to a real exception.
int PyErr_ExceptionMatches(PyObject *exc)	Returns true if the current exception matches **exc**. A memory access violation is raised if no exception has been set.
int PyErr_GivenExceptionMatches (PyObject *given, PyObject *exc)	Returns true if **given** matches the exception **exc**. Tuples and objects are traversed and compared. If **given** is **NULL**, a memory access violation occurs.
void PyErr_NormalizeException (PyObject**exc, PyObject**val, PyObject**tb)	Normalizes the exception **exc** into **tb**. You need to call this function when **PyErr_Fetch** returns an instance of an exception class (**val**) that doesn't actually match the class in **exc**.
void PyErr_Clear()	Clears the error indication.
void PyErr_Fetch(PyObject **ptype, PyObject **pvalue, PyObject **ptraceback)	Retrieves the error information into the error type, error value, and traceback objects. Returns **NULL** if no error condition exists. You can use this to temporarily retrieve and, if necessary, clear an exception state. Use **PyErr_Restore()** to set the error condition. Note that the resulting objects will need to have their reference counts managed.
void PyErr_Restore(PyObject *type, PyObject *value, PyObject *traceback)	Sets the error indicator. If all three arguments are **NULL**, it clears the error indicator. You must clear the reference count for each argument once the function has been called.
void PyErr_SetString(PyObject *type, char *message)	Sets the error indicator using the exception **type** (as defined in Table 26-3) and using the error message **message**.
void PyErr_SetObject(PyObject *type, PyObject *value)	Sets the error indicator using the exception **type** (as defined in Table 26-3). Rather than setting additional information in the form of a string, this version takes an object.

Table 26-2.   *Exception Functions* (continued)

Function	Description
PyObject* PyErr_Format(PyObject *exception, const char *format, . . .)	Sets the error indicator using the exception in **exception**. Further arguments work in a similar fashion to **printf()**, where **format** is the format string that accepts only four format types: **c** (character supplied as **int**), **d** (number in decimal supplied as **int**), **x** (number in hex supplied as **int**), and **s** (string supplied as **char ***). Note that the **width.precision** prefix is also supported, but **width** is ignored.
void PyErr_SetNone(PyObject *type)	Shorthand for **PyErr_SetObject(type, Py_None)**.
int PyErr_BadArgument()	Shorthand for **PyErr_SetString(PyExc_TypeError, message)**. Use for bad argument conditions.
PyObject* PyErr_NoMemory()	Shorthand for **PyErr_SetNone(PyExc_MemoryError)**. Use for out-of-memory conditions.
PyObject* PyErr_SetFromErrno(PyObject *type)	Convenience function. Raises an exception of **type**, where the exception data is a tuple object made up of the **errno** value and its corresponding error message (from **strerror()**). Use for errors raised by the C library (which automatically sets **errno**).
void PyErr_BadInternalCall()	Shorthand for **PyErr_SetString(PyExc_TypeError, message)**.
int PyErr_Warn(PyObject *category, char *message)	Issues a warning message. The **category** argument should be a valid **Warning** object, and **message** is the message to be printed with the warning. Standard **Warning** types are **PyExc_Warning**, **PyExc_UserWarning**, **PyExc_DeprecationWarning**, **PyExc_SyntaxWarning**, and **PyExc_RuntimeWarning**. Output is sent to **sys.stderr**. If the user specified that warnings are treated as errors, an exception is raised. Returns 0 if no exception was raised or returns –1 if an exception was raised.
int PyErr_WarnExplicit(PyObject *category, char *message, char *_lename, int lineno, char *module, PyObject *registry)	Issues a warning message with explicit control over all the warning attributes.
int PyErr_CheckSignals()	Checks whether a signal has been sent to the current process, and if so, invokes the corresponding Python-based signal handler.

Table 26-2. *Exception Functions* (continued)

Function	Description
PyObject* PyErr_NewException(char *name, PyObject *base, PyObject *dict)	Creates a new exception object. The **name** should be the name of the new exception in the form **module.class**. The **base** argument specifies the base exception type, if **NULL**, **PyExc_Exception** is used. The **dict** argument can be used to specify the dictionary of class variables and methods (if **NULL** uses the current environment).
void PyErr_WriteUnraisable(PyObject *obj)	Prints a warning message to **sys.stderr** indicating that an exception has been set but that it is impossible for the interpreter to raise the exception.

Table 26-2.   *Exception Functions* (continued)

C Exception Constant	Python Exception
PyExc_Exception	Exception
PyExc_StandardError	StandardError
PyExc_ArithmeticError	ArithmeticError
PyExc_LookupError	LookupError
PyExc_AssertionError	AssertionError
PyExc_AttributeError	AttributeError
PyExc_EOFError	EOFError
PyExc_EnvironmentError	EnvironmentError
PyExc_FloatingPointError	FloatingPointError
PyExc_IOError	IOError
PyExc_ImportError	ImportError

Table 26-3.   *C Constants for Python Exception Types*

C Exception Constant	Python Exception
PyExc_IndexError	IndexError
PyExc_KeyError	KeyError
PyExc_KeyboardInterrupt	KeyboardInterrupt
PyExc_MemoryError	MemoryError
PyExc_NameError	NameError
PyExc_NotImplementedError	NotImplementedError
PyExc_OSError	OSError
PyExc_OverflowError	OverflowError
PyExc_RuntimeError	RuntimeError
PyExc_SyntaxError	SyntaxError
PyExc_SystemError	SystemError
PyExc_SystemExit	SystemExit
PyExc_TypeError	TypeError
PyExc_ValueError	ValueError
PyExc_WindowsError	WindowsError
PyExc_ZeroDivisionError	ZeroDivisionError

Table 26-3. *C Constants for Python Exception Types* (continued)

Low-Level Object Access

The Python C API includes a range of functions for accessing and manipulating the core object types. The tables in this section, Tables 26-4 through 26-17, describe the functions for manipulating the different object types. These tables include the return type and the function name and arguments. The purpose of each function should be self-explanatory, but double-check the Python/C API documentation if you need more information.

Return Type	Function
int	PyCallable_Check(PyObject *o)
PyObject *	PyObject_CallFunction(PyObject *callable_object, char *format, . . .)
PyObject *	PyObject_CallMethod(PyObject *o, char *methodname, char *format, . . .)
PyObject *	PyObject_CallObject(PyObject *callable_object, PyObject *args)
int	PyObject_Cmp(PyObject *o1, PyObject *o2, int *result)
int	PyObject_Compare(PyObject *o1, PyObject *o2)
int	PyObject_DelAttr(PyObject *o, PyObject *attr_name)
int	PyObject_DelAttrString(PyObject *o, char *attr_name)
int	PyObject_DelItem(PyObject *o, PyObject *key)
PyObject *	PyObject_GetAttr(PyObject *o, PyObject *attr_name)
PyObject *	PyObject_GetAttrString(PyObject *o, char *attr_name)
PyObject *	PyObject_GetItem(PyObject *o, PyObject *key)
int	PyObject_HasAttr(PyObject *o, PyObject *attr_name)
int	PyObject_HasAttrString(PyObject *o, char *attr_name)
int	PyObject_Hash(PyObject *o)
int	PyObject_IsTrue(PyObject *o)
int	PyObject_Length(PyObject *o)
int	PyObject_Print(PyObject *o, FILE *fp, int flags)
PyObject *	PyObject_Repr(PyObject *o)
int	PyObject_SetAttr(PyObject *o, PyObject *attr_name, PyObject *v)

Table 26-4.   *Functions for Manipulating Generic Python Objects*

Return Type	Function
int	PyObject_SetAttrString(PyObject *o, char *attr_name, PyObject *v)
int	PyObject_Setitem(PyObject *o, PyObject *key, PyObject *v)
PyObject *	PyObject_Str(PyObject *o)
PyObject *	PyObject_Type(PyObject *o)

Table 26-4. *Functions for Manipulating Generic Python Objects* (continued)

Return Type	Function
PyObject *	PyNumber_Absolute(PyObject *o)
PyObject *	PyNumber_Add(PyObject *o1 PyObject *o2)
PyObject *	PyNumber_And(PyObject *o1, PyObject *o2)
int	PyNumber_Check(PyObject *o)
PyObject *	PyNumber_Coerce(PyObject **p1, PyObject **p2)
PyObject *	PyNumber_Divide(PyObject *o1, PyObject *o2)
PyObject *	PyNumber_Divmod(PyObject *o1 PyObject *o2)
PyObject *	PyNumber_Float(PyObject *o)
PyObject *	PyNumber_Int(PyObject *o)
PyObject *	PyNumber_Invert(PyObject *o)
PyObject *	PyNumber_Long(PyObject *o)
PyObject *	PyNumber_Lshift(PyObject *o1 PyObject *o2)
PyObject *	PyNumber_Multiply(PyObject *o1, PyObject *o2)
PyObject *	PyNumber_Negative(PyObject *o)
PyObject *	PyNumber_Or(PyObject *o1, PyObject *o2)

Table 26-5. *Functions for Manipulating Numeric Objects*

Return Type	Function
PyObject *	PyNumber_Positive(PyObject *o)
PyObject *	PyNumber_Power(PyObject *o1, PyObject *o2, PyObject *o3)
PyObject *	PyNumber_Remainder(PyObject *o1, PyObject *o2)
PyObject *	PyNumber_Rshift(PyObject *o1, PyObject *o2)
PyObject *	PyNumber_Subtract(PyObject *o1, PyObject *o2)
PyObject *	PyNumber_Xor(PyObject *o1, PyObject *o2)

Table 26-5. *Functions for Manipulating Numeric Objects* (continued)

Return Type	Function
int	PySequence_Check(PyObject *o)
PyObject *	PySequence_Concat(PyObject *o1, PyObject *o2)
int	PySequence_Count(PyObject *o, PyObject * value)
int	PySequence_DelItem(PyObject *o, int i)
int	PySequence_DelSlice(PyObject *o, int i1, int i2)
PyObject *	PySequence_Getitem(PyObject *o, int i)
PyObject *	PySequence_GetSlice(PyObject *o, int i1, int i2)
int	PySequence_In(PyObject *o, PyObject *value)
int	PySequence_Index(PyObject *o, PyObject *value)
PyObject *	PySequence_Repeat(PyObject *o, int count)
int	PySequence_Setitem(PyObject *o, int i, PyObject *v)
int	PySequence_SetSlice(PyObject *o, int i1, int i2, PyObject *v)
PyObject *	PySequence_Tuple(PyObject *o)

Table 26-6. *Functions for Manipulating Sequence Objects*

Return Type	Function
int	PyMapping_Check(PyObject *o)
int	PyMapping_Clear(PyObject *o)
int	PyMapping_DelItem(PyObject *o, PyObject *key)
int	PyMapping_DelItemString(PyObject *o, char *key)
PyObject *	PyMapping_GetItemString(PyObject *o, char *key)
int	PyMapping_HasKey(PyObject *o, PyObject *key)
int	PyMapping_HasKeyString(PyObject *o, char *key)
PyObject *	PyMapping_Items(PyObject *o)
PyObject *	PyMapping_Keys(PyObject *o)
int	PyMapping_Length(PyObject *o)
int	PyMapping_SetitemString(PyObject *o, char *key, PyObject *v)
PyObject *	PyMapping_Values(PyObject *o)

Table 26-7. *Functions for Manipulating Mapping Objects*

Return Type	Function
long	PyInt_AsLong(PyObject ^iobj)
int	PyInt_Check(PyObject *obj)
PyObject*	PyInt_FromLong(long)
long	PyInt_GetMax()

Table 26-8. *Functions for Creating and Converting Integers*

Return Type	Function
double	PyLong_AsDouble(PyObject *lobj)
long	PyLong_AsLong(PyObject *lobj)
long long	PyLong_AsLongLong(PyObject *lobj)
unsigned long	PyLong_AsUnsignedLong(PyObject *lobj)
unsigned long long	PyLong_AsUnsignedLongLong(PyObject *lobj)
void *	PyLong AsVoidPtr(PyObject *lobj)
int	PyLong_Check(PyObject *obj)
PyObject *	PyLong_FromDouble(double)
PyObject *	PyLong_FromLong(long)
PyObject *	PyLong_FromLongLong(long long)
PyObject *	PyLong_FromlJnsignedLong(unsigned long)
PyObject *	PyLong_FromUnsignedLongLong(unsigned long long)
PyObject *	PyLong_FromVoidPtr(void *)

Table 26-9. *Functions for Creating and Converting Long Integers*

Return Type	Function
int	PyFloat_Check(PyObject *obj)
double	PyFloat_AsDouble(PyObject *fobj)
PyObject *	PyFloat_FromDouble(double)

Table 26-10. *Functions for Creating and Converting Floating-Point Numbers*

Return Type	Function
Py_complex	PyComplex_AsCComplex(PyObject *cobj)
int	PyComplex_Check(PyObject *obj)
PyObject *	PyComplex_FromCComplex(Py_complex *cobj)
PyObject *	PyComplex_FromDoubles(double real, double I)
double	PyComplex_ImagAsDouble(PyObject *cobj)
double	PyComplex_RealAsDouble(PyObject *cobj)

Table 26-11.   *Functions for Creating and Converting Complex Numbers*

Return Type	Function
char *	PyString_AsString(PyObject *str)
int	PyString_Check(PyObject *obj)
PyObject *	PyString_FromString(char *str)
PyObject *	PyString_FromStringAndSize(char *str, int len)
int	PyString_Size(PyObject *str)

Table 26-12.   *Functions for Creating and Converting String Objects*

Return Type	Function
int	PyList_Append(PyObject *list, PyObject *obj)
PyObject *	PyList_AsTuple(PyObject *list)
int	PyList_Check(PyObject *obj)
PyObject *	PyList_Getitem(PyObject *list, int index)

Table 26-13.   *Functions for Creating, Updating, and Converting Lists*

Return Type	Function
PyObject *	PyList_GetSlice(PyObject *list , int i, int j)
int	PyList_Insert(PyObject *list, int index, PyObject Aobj)
PyObject *	PyList_New(int size)
int	PyList_Reverse(PyObject *list)
int	PyList_Setitem(PyObject *list, int index, PyObject *obj)
int	PyList_SetSlice(PyObject *list, int i, int j, PyObject *slc)
int	PyList_Size(PyObject *list)
int	PyList_Sort(PyObject *list)

Table 26-13. *Functions for Creating, Updating, and Converting Lists* (continued)

Return Type	Function
int	PyTuple_Check(PyObject *ob j)
PyObject *	PyTuple_Getitem(PyObject *tup, int index)
PyObject *	PyTuple_GetSlice(PyObject *tup, int i, int j)
PyObject *	PyTuple_New(int size)
int	PyTuple_Setitem(PyObject *tup, int index, PyObject *obj)
int	PyTuple_Size(PyObject *tup)

Table 26-14. *Functions for Manipulating Tuples*

Return Type	Function
Int	PyDict_Check(PyObject *obj)
void	PyDict_Clear(PyObject *dict)
int	PyDict_DelItem(PyObject *dict, PyObject *key)
int	PyDict_DelItemString(PyObject *dict, char *key)
PyObject *	PyDict_GetItem(PyObject *dict, PyObject *key)
PyObject *	PyDict_GetItemString(PyObject *dict, char *key)
PyObject *	PyDict_Items(PyObject *dict)
PyObject *	PyDict_Keys(PyObject *dict)
PyObject *	PyDict_New()
int	PyDict_SetItem(PyObject *dict, PyObject *key, PyObject *val)
int	PyDict_SetItemString(PyObject *dict, char *key, PyObject *val)
int	PyDict_Size(PyObject *dict)
PyObject *	PyDict_Values(PyObject *dict)

Table 26-15.   *Functions for Manipulating Dictionaries*

Return Type	Function
FILE *	PyFile_AsFile(PyObject *file)
int	PyFile_Check(PyObject *obj)
PyObject *	PyFile_FromFile(FILE *, char *, char *, int (*)(FILE *))
PyObject *	PyFile_FromString(char *name, char *mode)
PyObject *	PyFile_GetLine(PyObject *file, int)
PyObject *	PyFile_Name(PyObject *file)
void	PyFile_SetBufSize(PyObject *file, int size)
int	PyFile_SoftSpace(PyObject *file, int)
int	PyFile_WriteObject(PyObject *file, PyObject *obj, int)
int	PyFile_WriteString(char *str, PyObject *file)

Table 26-16.   *Functions for Manipulating Files*

Return Type	Function
int	PyModule_Check(PyObject *obj)
PyObject *	PyModule_GetDict(PyObject *mod)
char *	PyModule_GetFilename(PyObject *mod)
char *	PyModule_GetName(PyObject *mod)
PyObject *	PyModule_New(char *name)

Table 26-17. *Functions for Manipulating Modules*

Where Next?

You should now have enough information—coupled with the tables in this chapter on data conversion—to support functions from external libraries. Most of the Python extension modules actually work on the same basic principles, exchanging data using a wrapper function to handle the real function call.

As well as the basic data conversion offered by the functions you've seen, there are more extensive functions for manipulating objects and their attributes and for updating the core Python object types entirely from within C. The information is far too large to include in this book, but you can find the information on the low-level Python object interaction functions and other details in the Python API documentation. See Appendix B for details on where to find Python documentation.

Chapter 27

Embedding Python

If you can integrate C/C++ and Python by embedding calls to C/C++ functions, objects, and methods into a Python application, surely you can do the same the other way around, right?

You can, and it's called *embedding*. By embedding Python into your C/C++ application, you add a scripting element to your applications (imagine being able to script your application like you can script Microsoft Word, but using Python) or just provide access to a Python object, class, or system that you don't normally have access to within C/C++.

Of course, there are sensible limits. Using the embedding techniques described in this chapter to provide access to a module that is normally supported by an extension is obviously one step too far. You can use the functions directly from within C, but there's still plenty of scope for using Python. For example, you can use Python to download a file from the Internet within a C/C++ program because this is easier with **urllib** than by opening and managing the socket from within C.

This chapter explains how to integrate Python into your C/C++ applications, from the simple mechanics of the embedding process through to examples of using different Python entities from within a C application.

Embedding Principles

There are some basic principles you need to be aware of before looking at the mechanics of building embedded Python applications. For a start, you need to consider the different types of Python code that you can execute from the embedded interface. There are in fact three types: the Python string, the Python object, and the Python module.

A Python string is just an arbitrary Python statement that you would normally include in a Python application or that you might pass off to an **eval** function call or **exec** statement. The embedding API allows you to execute Python strings as if you are passing the lines of a Python script one at a time to a Python interpreter. In fact, it might help for you to think of an embedded Python interpreter as similar to the interactive interface offered by Python itself.

A Python object is just an object, which can be an existing object, function, method, or class—basically anything that is normally a callable object within Python itself. You can actually call any type of Python object from within an embedded Python interpreter and the object can either be defined by the C application during execution or it can be imported from an external module.

A Python module is any external Python module that you import within a Python application. For example, you can import the **urllib** module and then call the **urlopen** function from the loaded module.

Python Embedding API

The Python embedding API is very simple. To initialize the system, all you need to do is call the **Py_Initialize()** function to load the necessary libraries and start the Python interpreter. With the Python interpreter initialized, you can then start supplying the Python instance with statements you want to execute.

You check the status of the embedded Python interpreter with **Py_IsInitialized()**, which returns 1 (true) if the interpreter has been set up, or 0 otherwise. Then, once you've finished, you must call **Py_Finalize()** to close down the interpreter. The **Py_Finalize()** function frees any memory used by the interpreter and should prevent problems with the rest of your application accessing areas of memory allocated to the embedded interpreter. Note, however, that you might have problems freeing memory if your embedded instance loads other C modules.

Table 27-1 lists the primary functions that are used to communicate with the Python interpreter from within C.

C API Call	Python Equivalent	Description
PyImport_ImportModule	import module	Imports a module into the Python instance.
PyImport_ReloadModule	reload(module)	Reloads the specified module.
PyImport_GetModuleDict	sys.modules	Returns a dictionary object containing the list of loaded modules.
PyModule_GetDict	module.__dict__	Returns the dictionary for a given object.
PyDict_GetItemString	dict[key]	Gets the value for a corresponding dictionary key.
PyDict_SetItemString	dict[key] = value	Sets a dictionary key's value.
PyDict_New	dict = {}	Creates a new dictionary object.
PyObject_GetAttrString	getattr(obj, attr)	Gets the attribute for a given object.
PyObject_SetAttrString	setattr(obj, attr, val)	Sets the value for a given attribute in an object.
PyEval_CallObject	apply(function, args)	Calls a function with arguments in **args**.

Table 27-1. *Embedding API Functions*

C API Call	Python Equivalent	Description
PyRunString	eval(expr), exec expr	Executes **expr** as a Python statement.
PyRun_File	execfile(filename)	Executes the file **filename**.
PySetProgramName	sys.argv[0] = name	Changes the **name** of the Python program normally set on the command line.
PyGetProgramName	sys.argv[0]	Returns the name of the Python program name set by **PySetProgramName()**.
PySys_SetArgv	sys.argv = list	Sets the arguments normally supplied on the command line. Should be supplied with two arguments, **argc** and **argv**, the number of arguments and a list of strings, both starting from 0.

Table 27-1. *Embedding API Functions* (continued)

For all the other communication and integration between C/C++ data types and Python objects, use the functions described in Chapter 26.

There are also functions that can be used from C to get information about the instance of the Python interpreter that you have embedded. Table 27-2 contains the list of functions supported by C and C++.

Function	Description
char* Py_GetPrefix()	Returns the prefix for the platform-independent files.
char* Py_GetExecPrefix()	Returns the execution prefix for the installed Python files.

Table 27-2. *Getting Python Interpreter Information from within C/C++*

Function	Description
char* Py_GetPath()	Returns the list of directories that were searched for modules. Directories are separated by a colon (:) under Unix, a semi-colon (;) under Windows and newline characters on the Mac.
char* Py_GetProgramFullPath()	Returns the full path to the Python interpreter.
const char* Py_GetVersion()	Returns the Python interpreter version.
const char* Py_GetPlatform()	Returns the platform identifier for the current platform.
const char* Py_GetCopyright()	Returns the copyright statement for the interpreter.
const char* Py_GetCompiler()	Returns the compiler string (the name and version of the compiler used to build the interpreter).
const char* Py_GetBuilderInfo()	Returns the build information (version and date) for the interpreter.

Table 27-2. *Getting Python Interpreter Information from within C/C++* (continued)

For example, you can't print Python interpreter information from within C using the following source:

```
#include <Python.h>

int main()
{
  printf("Getting Python information\n");
  Py_Initialize();
  if( !Py_IsInitialized() ) {
    puts( "Unable to initialize Python interpreter." );
    return -1;
  }

  printf("Prefix: %s\nExec Prefix: %s\nPython Path: %s\n",
```

```
                Py_GetPrefix(),
                Py_GetExecPrefix(),
                Py_GetProgramFullPath());
        printf("Module Path: %s\n",
                Py_GetPath());
        printf("Version: %s\nPlatform: %s\nCopyright: %s\n",
                Py_GetVersion(),
                Py_GetPlatform(),
                Py_GetCopyright());
        printf("Compiler String: %s\nBuild Info: %s\n",
                Py_GetCompiler(),
                Py_GetBuildInfo());

        Py_Finalize();
        return 0;
}
```

To actually compile and link this program into a final executable, you need to include directories and libraries on the command line. The next section describes this process.

Compiling and Linking

When Python is compiled, a number of include files and libraries are used to actually build the application. When building an application that embeds the Python interpreter, you need to link against the same list of libraries, which also means that you need to specify additional include directories and the include directory for the base **Python.h** header file.

Although it's possible to determine this information by hand, a much easier way is to use the **distutils.sysconfig** module to obtain the configuration parameters generated when Python was built. You need three main pieces of information:

- the options to the C compiler
- the list of include directories for header files
- the list of libraries

The first piece of information is set in the **OPT** configuration parameter. You can extract that information using the following statement:

```
distutils.sysconfig.get_config_var('OPT')
```

The list of libraries is actually stored in a number of places. The system libraries are stored in **SYSLIBS**, the libraries required by the core Python interpreter are stored in **LIBS** and those required by any Python modules are stored in **MODLIBS**. Since these libraries can also appear in other locations than the default, you'll also need to determine the library directories, which are stored in **LIBDIR**. This last option is actually a space-separated list of library directories, and for inclusion on the command line, you need to prefix each directory with **-L**.

The include directories, which can be found in **INCLDIRSTOMAKE**, need the same treatment, but with a **-I** prefix to identify them as include, rather than library directories.

If you've followed all of that, you are probably completely daunted by the task, but you can speed the whole process up by using the following script. Although this script is designed to create a Makefile, and therefore is probably only guaranteed to run under Unix, it should also work with Windows if you have a suitable make (**dmake**, **nmake**, or similar). The information it produces can also be used with CodeWarrior on the Mac. The following Python script writes a standard Makefile for each of the embed applications supplied on the command line:

```python
#!/usr/local/bin/python

import distutils.sysconfig
import string, sys

configopts = {}

maketemplate = """
PYLIB=%(pythonlib)s
PYINC=-I%(pythoninc)s
LIBS=%(pylibs)s
OPTS=%(pyopt)s
PROGRAMS=%(programs)s

all: $(PROGRAMS)

"""

configopts['pythonlib'] = \
distutils.sysconfig.get_config_var('LIBPL') \
                        + '/' + \

distutils.sysconfig.get_config_var('LIBRARY')
configopts['pythoninc'] = ''
```

```
configopts['pylibs'] = ''
for dir in
string.split(distutils.sysconfig.get_config_var('INCLDIRSTOMAKE')):
        configopts['pythoninc'] += '-I%s ' % (dir,)
for dir in
string.split(distutils.sysconfig.get_config_var('LIBDIR')):
        configopts['pylibs'] += '-L%s ' % (dir,)

configopts['pylibs'] +=
distutils.sysconfig.get_config_var('MODLIBS') \
                    + ' ' + \
                    distutils.sysconfig.get_config_var('LIBS') \
                    + ' ' + \

distutils.sysconfig.get_config_var('SYSLIBS')
configopts['pyopt'] = distutils.sysconfig.get_config_var('OPT')

targets = ''
for arg in sys.argv[1:]:
        targets += arg + ' '
configopts['programs'] = targets

print maketemplate % configopts

for arg in sys.argv[1:]:
        print "%s: %s.o\n\tgcc %s.o $(LIBS) $(PYLIB) -o %s" \
            % (arg, arg, arg, arg)
        print "%s.o: %s.c\n\tgcc %s.c -c $(PYINC) $(OPTS)" \
            % (arg, arg, arg)

print "clean:\n\trm -f $(PROGRAMS) *.o *.pyc core"
```

For example, to build a Makefile for the Python interpreter information example in the previous section, you'd name the C source **pyinfo.c** and then run

```
$ pymkfile pyinfo >Makefile
```

The generated Makefile looks like this:

```
PYLIB=/usr/local/lib/python2.1/config/libpython2.1.a
PYINC=-I-I/usr/local/include -I/usr/local/include
-I/usr/local/include/python2.1 -I/usr/local/include/python2.1
```

```
LIBS=-L/usr/local/lib  -lpthread -lsocket -lnsl -ldl  -lthread -lm
OPTS=-g -O2 -Wall -Wstrict-prototypes
PROGRAMS=pyinfo


all: $(PROGRAMS)


pyinfo: pyinfo.o
        gcc pyinfo.o $(LIBS) $(PYLIB) -o pyinfo
pyinfo.o: pyinfo.c
        gcc pyinfo.c -c $(PYINC) $(OPTS)
clean:
        rm -f $(PROGRAMS) *.o *.pyc core
```

Now you can compile the application using **make** (demonstrated here on Solaris):

```
$  make
gcc pyinfo.c -c -I-I/usr/local/include -I/usr/local/include
-I/usr/local/include/python2.1 -I/usr/local/include/python2.1  -g
-O2 -W
all -Wstrict prototypes
gcc pyinfo.o -L/usr/local/lib  -lpthread -lsocket -lnsl -ldl
-lthread -lm /usr/local/lib/python2.1/config/libpython2.1.a -o
pyinfo
```

Then run the final executable and you're done. As you can see from the following
output from the Python interpreter information example, you can identify most of this
information from within Python itself using the **sys** module:

```
% pyinfo
Getting Python information
Prefix: /usr/local
Exec Prefix: /usr/local
Python Path: /usr/local/bin/python
Module Path:
/usr/local/lib/python2.1/:/usr/local/lib/python2.1/plat-sunos5:/usr
/local/lib/python2.1/lib-tk:/usr/local/lib/python2.1
/lib-dynload
Version: 2.1 (#1, Aug  2 2001, 12:49:29)
[GCC 3.0]
Platform: sunos5
Copyright: Copyright (c) 2001 Python Software Foundation.
```

```
All Rights Reserved.

Copyright (c) 2000 BeOpen.com.
All Rights Reserved.

Copyright (c) 1995-2001 Corporation for National Research
Initiatives.
All Rights Reserved.

Copyright (c) 1991-1995 Stichting Mathematisch Centrum, Amsterdam.
All Rights Reserved.
Compiler String:
[GCC 3.0]
Build Info: #1, Aug  2 2001, 12:49:29
```

Note that because the **pymkfile** command is written in Python and uses the configuration options used to build the Python interpreter, you should be able to use the script on any platform, and you should end up with a suitable **Makefile** for that platform. You will, of course, need to rerun this command if you change your configuration or platform.

Python Embedding Types

There are a number of different ways that you can work with an embedded interpreter to produce an application. You already know the basic layout for an embedded application. In essence, it's as follows:

```
#include <Python.h>
...
Py_Initialize();
# Do some stuff
Py_Finalize();
```

It's the missing code in the middle that you're going to learn about now.

Note   *The same principles shown here should work for C++; there is no need to recompile Python with C++ or to use a different interface.*

Executing a Python String

You can execute an arbitrary Python string using the **PyRun_SimpleString()** function. In its simplest format, this function accepts a string to compile and execute. You can pass any string as long as it's a valid Python statement. For example, the statement

```
PyRun_SimpleString("print 'Hello World\n'")
```

executes the **print** statement. Because you are executing the statement within a single instance of the Python interpreter, you can add further statements in order to build up an application:

```
#include <Python.h>

int main()
{
  printf("String execution\n");
  Py_Initialize();
  PyRun_SimpleString("import string");
  PyRun_SimpleString("words = string.split('rod jane freddy')");
  PyRun_SimpleString("print string.join(words,', ')");
  Py_Finalize();
  return 0;
}
```

If you compile and execute this application, you get the following output:

```
String execution
rod, jane, freddy
```

Not the most exciting application, but it shows that you can execute arbitrary strings from within C.

Working with Python Objects

The preceding example is indicative of a typical embedding application. For a start, you haven't really achieved much—the script that you supplied line by line to the embedded Python interpreter could have just as easily been a stand-alone Python application. In fact, you could have placed the code supplied in each **PyRun_**

SimpleString() function call into a separate file and then executed the entire module using the **PyRun_File()** function.

Most embedded applications need to exchange information between the C and Python sides. You saw some examples of this in Chapter 26 when creating extensions. When embedding, you probably need the results from a Python function back into a form that your C application can understand. For the most part, embedding relies on more conversions from Python to C, whereas extensions rely on conversion from C to Python.

For demonstration purposes, let's use a module called **reverse** that takes various arguments and returns a logical reversal. This is the inverse value for a number, a string in reverse order, a list in reverse order, and a dictionary with the keys mapped to values and vice versa. The module itself is as follows:

```
def rstring(s):
    i = len(s)-1
    t = ''
    while(i > -1):
        t += s[i]
        i -= 1
    return t

def rnum(i):
    return 1.0/float(i)

def rlist(l):
    l.reverse()
    return l

def rdict(d):
    e = {}
    for k in d.keys():
        e[d[k]] = k
    return e
```

It doesn't matter whether the object you want to access is a function or variables within a given module—you access any object in any module in exactly the same manner using the **PyObject_GetAttrString()** function, which gets an object by accessing the attribute table for a specific object. For example, when accessing the function **rstring()**, you need to access the **rstring** object from the attribute table for the **reverse** module. Let's use this as an example to illustrate how to access objects and call functions from a C application.

Getting the return values from a function call is actually a five-stage process and can be summarized as follows:

1. Import the module (if necessary) that contains the function you want to call, and capture the output.

2. Get the object that you want to call by accessing the module's attributes.

3. Build any C variables that you want to supply as arguments to the function into an argument object.

4. Call the function, supplying the arguments.

5. Convert the returned argument object back into C variables.

To import the module (stage 1), you use the **PyImport_ImportModule()** function:

```
PyObject *mymod = NULL;
mymod = PyImport_ImportModule("reverse");
```

To get the function object that you want to call (stage 2), use **PyObject_GetAttrString()**. For example, to get hold of the **rstring** function, use the following statements:

```
PyObject *strfunc = NULL;
strfunc = PyObject_GetAttrString(mymod, "rstring");
```

Note that if you are accessing a variable rather than a function at this point, you can convert the variable into a suitable C structure and print it or use it by using the **PyArg_Parse()** function.

To build the arguments to the function (stage 3), use **Py_BuildValue()**. For the **rstring** function, you need to supply a string, and of course, since you're supplying it to a function, you actually need to supply a tuple of values:

```
PyObject *strargs = NULL;
strargs = Py_BuildValue("(s)", "Hello World");
```

Check back to the "Converting C Variables to Python" section in Chapter 26 for more information on the conversion format.

To actually call your **rstring()** function (stage 4), call **PyEval_CallObject()**. You also need a variable to hold the return values, **strret** in the following example:

```
PyObject *strret = NULL;
strret = PyEval_CallObject(strfunc, strargs);
```

The final stage (stage 5) is to get the return value, in this case, a string, back into a C variable again and print it out. The return value from **PyEval_CallObject()** is a Python object, so you can extract the information back into C values using **PyArg_Parse()**:

```
char *cstrret = NULL;
PyArg_Parse(strret, "s", &cstrret);
printf("Reversed string: %s", cstrret);
```

Refer back to the "Data Conversion" section in Chapter 26 for more information about converting data to and from C/C++ types and Python objects.

Putting this all together, you get the following C source:

```
#include <Python.h>

int main()
{
  PyObject *strret, *mymod, *strfunc, *strargs;
  char *cstrret;

  Py_Initialize();

  mymod = PyImport_ImportModule("reverse");

  strfunc = PyObject_GetAttrString(mymod, "rstring");

  strargs = Py_BuildValue("(s)", "Hello World");

  strret = PyEval_CallObject(strfunc, strargs);
  PyArg_Parse(strret, "s", &cstrret);
  printf("Reversed string: %s\n", cstrret);

  Py_Finalize();
  return 0;
}
```

If you build and execute this application, you get the following output:

```
Reversed string: dlroW olleH
```

Success!

You can follow the same procedure for numbers, lists, and dictionaries using the techniques you've seen here in combination with the different **Py_BuildValue()** options described in Chapter 26.

> **Note**
>
> *Remember that just as with extensions, if you reuse Python objects for new values, you must decrement the reference counter to ensure that the memory and reference are freed from memory. Although in the examples it hasn't been necessary because you're only developing within **main()**, if you place your Python instance into another function or use external C modules from an embedded Python instance, the same rules apply. See the section "Reference Counts" in Chapter 26 for more information.*

Working with Python Classes

Accessing a Python class from C sounds very complicated, but in fact it's quite straightforward. If you've managed to follow the preceding example, you already know how to access objects from within a C application. All you do is follow the same process. To access the class itself, access the class name as it's defined within the module, i.e., load the module and then use **PyObject_GetAttrString()** to get the class name.

You then call the class, supplying any initial arguments, in order to create an object instance. To execute an object method, use **PyObject_GetAttrString()** again to get the method object using the object instance as your base.

For example, given the following module:

```
class celsius:
    def __init__(self, degrees):
        self.degrees = degrees
    def farenheit(self):
        return ((self.degrees*9.0)/5.0)+32.0
```

From within Python you can use the **celsius** class like this:

```
Python 2.1 (#1, Aug  2 2001, 12:49:29)
[GCC 3.0] on sunos5
Type "copyright", "credits" or "license" for more information.
>>> import celsius
>>> temp = celsius.celsius(100)
>>> temp.farenheit()
212.0
```

If you follow the sequence, you can see the basic process you also need to follow in C. First, import the module, then create a new instance of the **celsius** object by first finding the **celsius** class within the **celsius** module, and finally, call the **farenheit** method of the **temp** object, which is an instance of the **celsius** class.

The C code shows the same process, only this time from within C using the same techniques you've seen before. However, this example in C also includes error-checking code to ensure you are terminating sensibly when something goes wrong. This example also decrements reference counts for the different temporary objects as they are created:

```c
#include <Python.h>

/* Create a function to handle errors when they occur */
void error(char errstring)
{
  printf("%s\n",errstring);
  exit(1);
}

int main()
{
/* Set up the variables to hold methods, functions and class
   instances. farenheit will hold our return value */
  PyObject *ret, *mymod, *class, *method, *args, *object;
  float farenheit;

  Py_Initialize();

/* Load our module */
  mymod = PyImport_ImportModule("celsius");

/* If we dont get a Python object back there was a problem */
  if (mymod == NULL)
    error("Can't open module");

/* Find the class */
  class = PyObject_GetAttrString(mymod, "celsius");

/* If found the class we can dump mymod, since we wont use it
   again */
  Py_DECREF(mymod);

/* Check to make sure we got an object back */
  if (class == NULL)
```

```
    {
      Py_DECREF(class);
      error("Can't find class");
    }

/* Build the argument call to our class - these are the arguments
   that will be supplied when the object is created */
  args = Py_BuildValue("(f)", 100.0);

  if (args == NULL)
    {
      Py_DECREF(args);
      error("Can't build argument list for class instance");
    }

/* Create a new instance of our class by calling the class
   with our argument list */
  object = PyEval_CallObject(class, args);
  if (object == NULL)
    {
      Py_DECREF(object);
      error("Can't create object instance");
    }

/* Decrement the argument counter as we'll be using this again */
  Py_DECREF(args);

/* Get the object method - note we use the object as the object
   from which we access the attribute by name, not the class */
  method = PyObject_GetAttrString(object, "farenheit");

  if (method == NULL)
    {
      Py_DECREF(method);
      error("Can't find method");
    }

/* Decrement the counter for our object, since we now just need
   the method reference */
  Py_DECREF(object);

/* Build our argument list - an empty tuple because there aren't
```

```
  any arguments */
args = Py_BuildValue("()");

if (args == NULL)
  {
    Py_DECREF(args);
    error("Can't build argument list for method call");
  }

/* Call our object method with arguments */
ret = PyEval_CallObject(method,args);

if (ret == NULL)
  {
    Py_DECREF(ret);
    error("Couldn't call method");
  }

/* Convert the return value back into a C variable and display it
*/
PyArg_Parse(ret, "f", &farenheit);
printf("Farenheit: %f\n", farenheit);

/* Kill the remaining objects we don't need */
Py_DECREF(method);
Py_DECREF(ret);

/* Close off the interpreter and terminate */
Py_Finalize();
return 0;
}
```

If you compile and execute the preceding code, you get:

```
$ exclass
Farenheit: 212.000000
```

It works!

Where Next

If you've managed to follow the examples here, you should be able to use a combination of the techniques demonstrated in this chapter and the techniques and functional references described in Chapter 26 to write C applications with Python. Since you have access to the full Python library, there's no limit to what you can do.

The Complete Reference

Appendix A

Python Library Guide

T his appendix contains a list of all the modules that make up the standard Python library and are included in the basic distribution of all versions of Python. The list of modules is given in Table A-2, but we start with a description of the section classifications in Table A-1.

Section	Description
Runtime	Services that provide an interface between Python and the underlying system and environment
String	String handling and processing
Misc	Miscellaneous services
Generic	Generic operating system services that potentially work on all platforms
Optional	Optional operating system services, usually platform specific
Unix	Unix-specific services
Internet	Internet-specific services
Markup	Structured markup processing tools
Multimedia	Modules for creating sounds and other multimedia data
Crypto	Cryptographic modules for encoding and decoding information
Python	Modules that provide services and information for programming in Python
Restrict	Modules for creating and executing Python scripts within a restricted or limited environment
SGI	SGI (formerly Silicon Graphics, Inc.) platform–specific modules
SunOS	SunOS (Solaris) platform–specific modules
Windows	Windows platform–specific modules
Mac OS	Mac OS platform–specific modules

Table A-1.   *Module Classification System*

Module	Section	Description	See Chapter
__builtin__	Runtime	The module reference for the set of built-in (internal) functions in the Python interpreter	8
__main__	Runtime	The name of the module that holds the main script	5
AE	Mac OS	An interface to the Apple Events toolbox	
aepack	Mac OS	Packs information and converts between Apple Event structures and Python data types	
aetypes	Mac OS	Python interface to the Apple Event Object Model	
aifc	Multimedia	Reads and writes the AIFF (Audio Interchange File Format) and AIFC (compressed AIFF) audio files	14
al	SGI	Interface to the Audio Library functions on the SGI platform (Irix)	
AL	SGI	Constants used with the **al** module	

Table A-2.   *Python Standard Module Library*

Module	Section	Description	See Chapter
anydbm	Optional	Simple interface to the ***dbm** series of modules for using DBM formatted databases	12
array	Misc	Classes for the efficient storage for fixed element length numerical arrays	10
asyncore	Internet	Base class for synchronous socket handling services	13, 21
atexit	Runtime	Used for registering functions to provide cleanup services when a script terminates	9
audioop	Multimedia	Provides functions for manipulating raw audio files	14
base64	Internet	Encoding/decoding routines for MIME files	20
BaseHTTPServer	Internet	Basic HTTP server class	13, 21
Bastion	Restrict	Provides restricted access to specific objects	

Table A-2.   *Python Standard Module Library* (continued)

Module	Section	Description	See Chapter
binascii	Internet	Routines for converting between ASCII and binary data streams	13
binhex	Internet	Encoding/decoding routines for the Mac based binhex format	13
bisect	Misc	Array bisection algorithms for binary searching	
bsddb	Optional	Interface to the Berkeley DB database library	12
calendar	Misc	Functions for determining calendar information (day of week, month, etc.)	10
cd	SGI	CD-ROM interface for SGI systems	
cgi	Internet	Decodes information sent through the web Common Gateway Interface	19
CGIHTTPServer	Internet	Provides a request handler for HTTP servers that can run CGI scripts	13, 21

Table A-2. *Python Standard Module Library* (continued)

APPENDIXES

Module	Section	Description	See Chapter
chunk	Multimedia	Module to read IFF chunks (IFF is a tagged binary file format originally used for graphics and files on the Amiga; its descendent formats include the WAV file format used under Windows)	14
Cm	Mac OS	Interface to the Mac OS Component Manager	
cmath	Misc	Mathematical functions for complex numbers	10
cmd	Misc	System for building line-oriented command interpreters	
code	Runtime	Base classes for interactive Python interpreters	23
codecs	String	Encode and decode data and streams	21
codeop	Runtime	Compile arbitrary Python code	
ColorPicker	Mac OS	Interface to the color picker interface for choosing colors	

Table A-2. *Python Standard Module Library* (continued)

Module	Section	Description	See Chapter
colorsys	Multimedia	Conversion functions for translation between RGB and other color systems	14
commands	Unix	Utility functions for running external commands, including facilities for capturing output	
compileall	Python	Tools for byte-compiling all Python source files in a directory tree	
ConfigParser	Misc	Configuration file parser	
Cookie	Internet	Support for HTTP state management (cookies)	19
copy	Runtime	Shallow and deep copy operations	10, 12
copy_reg	Runtime	Register pickle support functions	
cPickle	Runtime	Faster version of **pickle**, but not subclassable	12
crypt	Unix	The **crypt()** function used to check Unix passwords	9

Table A-2. *Python Standard Module Library* (continued)

Module	Section	Description	See Chapter
cStringIO	String	Faster version of **StringIO**, but not subclassable	
ctb	Mac OS	Communications Tool Box support	
Ctl	Mac OS	Interface to the Control Manager	
curses	Generic	Interface to the **curses** terminal interface library	
curses.ascii	Generic	Constants and set-membership functions for ASCII characters	
curses.panel	Generic	An extension to the base **curses** module that provides panels to the terminal abilities	
curses.textpad	Generic	Emacs-like input editing in a curses window	
curses.wrapper	Generic	Terminal configuration wrapper for curses programs	
dbhash	Optional	Interface to the hash (dictionary) portion of the BSD database library	12
dbm	Unix	Interface to the **ndbm** hash (dictionary) database system	12

Table A-2. *Python Standard Module Library* (continued)

Module	Section	Description	See Chapter
DEVICE	SGI	Constants used with the **gl** module	
difflib	String	Functions for computing differences between objects	
dircache	Generic	Provides a cache-based directory listing mechanism, useful for very large directory listings when compared to **glob**	
dis	Python	Disassembler for Python byte code	23
dl	Unix	Interface to the dynamic library system under Unix (and Unix-like OS, such as BeOS) for calling C functions found in shared objects	
Dlg	Mac OS	Interface to the Mac OS Dialog Manager	
doctest	Misc	Framework for verifying examples in docstrings	25

Table A-2.   *Python Standard Module Library* (continued)

APPENDIXES

Module	Section	Description	See Chapter
dumbdbm	Optional	Portable (cross-platform) implementation of a DBM-like interface entirely implemented in Python	12
EasyDialogs	Mac OS	Basic Macintosh dialogs	
errno	Generic	Symbols and textual constants for the **errno** error numbers	
Evt	Mac OS	Interface to the Event Manager	
fcntl	Unix	The **fcntl()** and **ioctl()** system calls	10, 11
filecmp	Generic	Efficient file compare routines	
fileinput	Misc	Perl-like system for iterating over lines from multiple input streams	
findertools	Mac OS	Wrappers around the Finder's Apple Events interface	
fl	SGI	Interface to the SGI FORMS library for GUI applications	
FL	SGI	Constants used with the **fl** module	
flp	SGI	Functions for loading stored FORMS designs	

Table A-2. *Python Standard Module Library* (continued)

APPENDIXES

Module	Section	Description	See Chapter
Fm	Mac OS	Interface to the Font Manager	
fm	SGI	Font Manager interface for SGI workstations	
fnmatch	Generic	Provides Unix shell style pattern matching for file names	
formatter	Internet	Generic output formatter and device interface	20
fpectl	Runtime	Floating point exception handling	
fpformat	String	Floating point formatting functions	
FrameWork	Mac OS	Interactive application framework	
ftplib	Internet	FTP protocol client	13
gc	Runtime	Interface to the cycle-detecting garbage collector	
gdbm	Unix	Interface to the GNU **dbm** database system	12
getopt	Generic	Parser for interpreting command-line options	9

Table A-2. *Python Standard Module Library* (continued)

Module	Section	Description	See Chapter
getpass	Generic	Obtains user name information and provides a portable and safe way of receiving a password interactively from a user; works on the command line only	9
gettext	Generic	Multilingual internationalization services	
gl	SGI	Interface to the SGI Graphics Library	
GL	SGI	Constants used with the **gl** module	
glob	Generic	Returns a list of filenames; uses Unix shell–style pattern matching systems	11
gopherlib	Internet	Gopher protocol client	13
grp	Unix	Interface to the Unix /etc/group file	9
gzip	Optional	Interfaces for gzip compression and decompression through file objects	
htmlentitydefs	Markup	Definitions of HTML general entities	20

Table A-2.   *Python Standard Module Library* (continued)

Module	Section	Description	See Chapter
htmllib	Markup	A parser for HTML documents	20
httplib	Internet	HTTP protocol client	13
ic	Mac OS	Access to the Internet Config configuration application	
imageop	Multimedia	Supports basic manipulation functions for raw images	14
imaplib	Internet	IMAP4 (email) protocol client	13
imgfile	SGI	Support for SGI imglib files	
imghdr	Multimedia	Determines the image type by examining the file header information	14
imp	Runtime	Access the implementation of the import statement	
inspect	Runtime	Extract information and source code from live objects	
jpeg	Multimedia	Read and write files using the JPEG format	14
keyword	Python	Determines whether a string is a keyword in Python	

Table A-2.   *Python Standard Module Library* (continued)

Module	Section	Description	See Chapter
linecache	Runtime	Supports random access to lines from within text files	
List	Mac OS	Interface to the Mac OS List Manager	
locale	Generic	Internationalization services	
mac	Mac OS	Mac OS–specific functions for the **os** module	
macdnr	Mac OS	Interfaces to the Macintosh Domain Name Resolver	
macfs	Mac OS	Support for FSSpec, the Alias Manager, finder aliases, and the Standard File package	
MacOS	Mac OS	Access to Mac OS–specific interpreter features	
macostools	Mac OS	Routines for file manipulation under Mac OS	
macpath	Mac OS	Mac OS path manipulation functions	
macspeech	Mac OS	Interface to the Macintosh Speech Manager	
mactcp	Mac OS	Interface to the MacTCP TCP/IP system	

Table A-2.   *Python Standard Module Library* (continued)

Module	Section	Description	See Chapter
mailbox	Internet	Interpret various mailbox formats	13
mailcap	Internet	Functions for handling Mailcap files	13
marshal	Runtime	Convert Python objects to and from streams of bytes	12
math	Misc	Mathematical functions	10
md5	Crypto	Encode RSA's MD5 message digest algorithm	
Menu	Mac OS	Interface to the Mac OS Menu Manager	
mhlib	Internet	Manipulate MH formatted mailboxes	13
mimetools	Internet	Tools for parsing MIME-style message bodies	13
mimetypes	Internet	Mapping of filename extensions to MIME types	13
MimeWriter	Internet	Generic MIME file writer	13
mimify	Internet	Translate mail messages to and from the MIME format	13

Table A-2. *Python Standard Module Library* (continued)

Module	Section	Description	See Chapter
MiniAEFrame	Mac OS	Enables you to set up your script as an Open Scripting Architecture (OSA) server (enabling it to respond to Apple Events)	
mmap	Optional	Interface to memory-mapped files for Unix and Windows	
mpz	Crypto	Interface to the GNU MP library for arbitrary precision arithmetic	
msvcrt	Windows	Miscellaneous useful routines from the MS VC++ runtime library	
multifile	Internet	Support for reading/writing files encoded using multipart extensions, including MIME files and multipart HTTP requests	13
mutex	Generic	Supports mutual exclusion locks and queuing system	
netrc	Internet	Interprets the contents of the **.netrc** file	

Table A-2.   *Python Standard Module Library* (continued)

Module	Section	Description	See Chapter
new	Runtime	Interface to the creation of runtime implementation objects	12
nis	Unix	Interface to the Unix Network Information System (NIS) data library	
nntplib	Internet	NNTP protocol client	13
operator	Runtime	All Python's standard operators as built-in functions	10, 12, 23
os	Generic	Miscellaneous (multipurpose) OS interfaces	9
os.path	Generic	Common pathname manipulations	9, 11
parser	Python	Access parse trees for Python source code	
pickle	Runtime	Convert Python objects to/from streams of bytes	12
pipes	Unix	A Python interface to Unix shell pipelines	

Table A-2. *Python Standard Module Library* (continued)

Module	Section	Description	See Chapter
popen2	Generic	Interface for reading/writing to/from subprocesses through standard I/O streams	9
poplib	Internet	POP3 (email) protocol client	13
posix	Unix	Common POSIX system calls; normally imported automatically by **os** on suitable platforms	9, 10, 12
posixfile	Unix	A lockable file object interface	12
pprint	Runtime	Pretty printer for data objects	
pty	Unix	Pseudo-Terminal Handling for SGI/Linux	
pwd	Unix	Interface to the Unix /etc/passwd file	9
py	Python	Compile Python source files into byte-code files	
pyclbr	Python	Supports information extraction for a Python class browser	

Table A-2. *Python Standard Module Library* (continued)

Module	Section	Description	See Chapter
Qd	Mac OS	Interface to the Mac OS QuickDraw toolbox	
Qt	Mac OS	Interface to the Mac OS QuickTime toolbox	
Queue	Optional	A synchronized queue class	
quopri	Internet	Encode/decode files using the MIME quoted-printable encoding system	13
random	Misc	Generate pseudorandom numbers with various common distributions	10
re	String	Perl-style regular expression match/replacement routines	10
readline	Optional	Interface to the GNU readline line-based interface	10
repr	Runtime	Alternative to the **repr()** function with support for size limits	
Res	Mac OS	Interface to the Mac OS Resource Manager and Handles	

Table A-2.   *Python Standard Module Library* (continued)

Module	Section	Description	See Chapter
resource	Unix	Determine resource usage information for the current process	
rexec	Restrict	Basic restricted execution framework	
rfc822	Internet	Parse RFC 822–style mail headers	13
rgbimg	Multimedia	Read and write image files in the SGI RGB format	14
rlcompleter	Optional	Provides completion system for Python identifiers using the GNU readline library	
robotparser	Internet	Parses the web server robots.txt file and then builds a set of objects representing the information	
rotor	Crypto	Enigma-like encryption and decryption	
sched	Generic	General-purpose event scheduler	
Scrap	Mac OS	Interface to the Mac OS Scrap Manager	

Table A-2. *Python Standard Module Library* (continued)

Module	Section	Description	See Chapter
select	Optional	Multiplexing scheduler for multiple I/O streams	
sgmllib	Markup	Parser for SGML files	20
sha	Crypto	Functions supporting NIST's secure hash algorithm, SHA	
shelve	Runtime	Provides functions for storing Python objects in external files (see also **marshal** and **pickle**)	12
shlex	Misc	Simple lexical analysis for Unix shell-like languages	
shutil	Generic	High-level file operations, including copying	11
signal	Optional	Interface to the Unix/POSIX-style signals	9
SimpleHTTPServer	Internet	Simple HTTP server class	13, 21
site	Runtime	Supports a mechanism for referencing site-specific modules	

Table A-2.   *Python Standard Module Library* (continued)

APPENDIXES

Module	Section	Description	See Chapter
smtplib	Internet	SMTP protocol client	13
Snd	Mac OS	Interface to the Mac OS Sound Manager	
sndhdr	Multimedia	Determines the format of a sound file by examining the file header	14
socket	Optional	Low-level interface to network sockets	13
SocketServer	Internet	A framework for creating socket-based network servers	13, 21
stat	Generic	Functions and constants for interpreting the results of **os.stat()**, **os.lstat()**; and **os.fstat()**.	11
statcache	Generic	Obtains file statistics and remembers results	11
statvfs	Generic	Constants for interpreting the result of **os.statvfs()**	
string	String	Functions for manipulating and interpreting text strings	10
StringIO	String	Read and write strings as if they were files	

Table A-2. *Python Standard Module Library* (continued)

Module	Section	Description	See Chapter
struct	String	Pack/unpack binary data, especially C-based structures	12
sunau	Multimedia	Provide an interface to the Sun AU sound format	14
sunaudiodev	Sun	Sun audio controllers	14
symbol	Python	Constants representing internal nodes of the parse tree	
sys	Runtime	Access system-specific parameters and functions	9
syslog	Unix	Interface to the Unix **syslog** library routines	
tabnanny	Python	Tool for detecting whitespace-related problems in Python source files in a directory tree	
TE	Mac OS	Interface to the Mac OS TextEdit class	
telnetlib	Internet	Telnet client class	13
tempfile	Generic	Generate temporary filenames	
termios	Unix	POSIX-style tty control	

Table A-2.   *Python Standard Module Library* (continued)

Module	Section	Description	See Chapter
TERMIOS	Unix	Symbolic constants required to use the **termios** module	
thread	Optional	Low-level interface to the host OS thread creation functions	9
threading	Optional	Higher-level interface to the basic **thread** module	9
time	Generic	Obtain, convert, and manipulate time and date information	10
token	Python	Constants representing terminal nodes of the parse tree	
tokenize	Python	Lexical scanner for Python source code	
traceback	Runtime	Print or retrieve a traceback of the Python execution tree of a script	24
tty	Unix	Utility functions that perform common terminal control operations	
types	Runtime	Names for all built-in types	23
unicodedata	String	Access the Unicode Database	10

Table A-2. *Python Standard Module Library* (continued)

Module	Section	Description	See Chapter
unittest	Misc	Unit testing framework for Python	
urllib	Internet	Open or download an arbitrary URL	13, 19
urllib2	Internet	An extensible library for opening URLs using a variety of protocols	13, 19
urlparse	Internet	Parse URL into its component parts	19
user	Runtime	A standard way to reference user-specific modules	
UserDict	Runtime	Class wrapper for dictionary objects	
UserList	Runtime	Class wrapper for list objects	
UserString	Runtime	Class wrapper for string objects	
uu	Internet	Encode and decode files in uuencode format	13
warnings	Runtime	Issue warning messages and control their disposition	24
waste	Mac OS	Interface to the Mac OS WorldScript-Aware Styled Text Engine (WASTE)	

Table A-2. *Python Standard Module Library* (continued)

APPENDIXES

Module	Section	Description	See Chapter
wave	Multimedia	Interface to the WAV sound format	14
weakref	Runtime	Support for weak references and weak dictionaries	
webbrowser	Internet	Easy-to-use controller for Web browsers	
whichdb	Optional	Determine which DBM-style module created a given database	12
whrandom	Misc	Floating-point pseudorandom number generator	10
Win	Mac OS	Interface to the Mac OS Window Manager	
winreg	Windows	Routines for manipulating the Windows registry	
winsound	Windows	Access to the sound-playing machinery for Windows	
xdrlib	Internet	Encoders and decoders for the External Data Representation (XDR) system (as used in C, especially in the RPC system)	13

Table A-2. *Python Standard Module Library* (continued)

Module	Section	Description	See Chapter
xml.dom	Markup	Document Object Model API for Python	20
xml.dom.minidom	Markup	Lightweight Document Object Model (DOM) implementation	20
xml.dom.pulldom	Markup	Support for building partial DOM trees from SAX events	20
xml.parsers.expat	Markup	An interface to the Expat nonvalidating XML parser	20
xml.sax	Markup	Package containing SAX2 base classes and convenience functions	20
xml.sax.handler	Markup	Base classes for SAX event handlers	20
xml.sax.saxutils	Markup	Convenience functions and classes for use with SAX	20
xml.sax.xmlreader	Markup	Interface that SAX-compliant XML parsers must implement	20
xmllib	Markup	A parser for XML documents	20
xreadlines	Misc	Efficient iteration over the lines of a file	

Table A-2.   *Python Standard Module Library* (continued)

APPENDIXES

Module	Section	Description	See Chapter
zipfile	Optional	Read and write ZIP-format archive files	
zlib	Optional	Low-level interface to compression and decompression routines compatible with gzip	

Table A-2. *Python Standard Module Library* (continued)

The Complete Reference

Appendix B

Python Resources

L ike most modern scripting languages—and indeed like any modern, open-source development project—Python is heavily supported in the programming community through the Internet. The main website is **www.python.org**, which provides the most comprehensive guide to the Python language and its available resources, both on and off the Web.

Web Resources

Much of Python's success comes from the users who provide feedback to the Python development team, suggest new features and changes to the language semantics, and help identify and fix bugs. This information ultimately reaches Guido von Rossum, the designer and developer of the Python language, although there are now many other people who aid in the development of the language. Most of this information is exchanged on the Internet, either through email, newsgroups, or the various Python websites. Of course, this appendix can't describe all the information that's available, due to the sheer fluidity of the Internet. But there are some choice areas of the main Python site, as well as other sites that deserve a special mention. The entries listed here should give you a good spread of the most useful resources.

www.python.org   This website is the main focus point for everything to do with Python. This site is managed by volunteers from Python Software Activity (PSA). They include a number of Python fanatics, all dedicated to the long-term success of Python as a scripting language. This site also contains all the online documentation, which is available both for searching online and for downloading from the site. Included here are HTML, PostScript, and Acrobat PDF versions of the documentation for you to use at home or at work.

python.sourceforge.net   PythonLabs, the development team responsible for Python development, moved to SourceForge, one of the many free software communities in October 2000. Although most of the development and news about Python continues on the main Python website, new releases and daily snapshots of the current development versions of Python and its documentation appear here on SourceForge.

www.python.org/psa   This site is the home page of Python Software Activity. PSA raises funds, supports new development, hosts conferences, and operates several Internet-based services that support Python development. PSA requests membership fees from people who want to help with the further development of Python. At the time of this writing, PSA membership costs $50 for an individual or $500 for an organization.

www.python.org/sigs   A significant portion of the Python development and promotion comes from various special interest groups (SIGs). These SIGs have limited lives while different development projects are in progress. Table B-1 lists the SIGs that existed at the beginning of February 2001. Check out the URL **www.python.org/sigs** for a more up-to-date list.

Name / Home	Description	Coordinator	Expires
c++-sig	Development of a C++ Binding	Geoffrey Furnish	June 2002
Catalog-sig	The Python software catalog, dealing with cataloging Python's modules, packages, and other resources	Andrew Kuchling	June 2002
db-sig	Databases (currently working on creating a common tabular database API, among other things)	Andrew Kuchling	June 2002
distutils-sig	Distribution utilities	Greg Ward	June 2002
do-sig	Distributed Object Technologies	David Arnold	June 2002
doc-sig	Documentation (covering both tools and content)	Fred Drake	June 2002
edu-sig	Python in Education (spreading the word on Python and getting Python promoted as programming for everybody)	Guido van Rossum	Dec 2002
i18n-sig	Internationalization and localization, including Unicode	Andy Robinson	June 2002
image-sig	Image processing	Fredrik Lundh	June 2002
import-sig	Import architecture redesign	Gordon McMillan	June 2002
meta-sig	SIG about the SIGs	Guido van Rossum	Never
plot-sig	Plotting and graphing	David Ascher	June 2002
pythonmac-sig	Python on Apple Macintosh	Jack Jansen	Never
types-sig	Static typing design	Paul Prescod	June 2002
xml-sig	XML processing in all its different forms	Andrew Kuchling	June 2002

Table B-1. *Python PSA Special Interest Groups*

Each SIG is supported by a mailing list. Anybody can join a SIG and get involved in the discussion and even in the development of a particular area of the Python development process.

www.python.org/cgi-bin/todo.py   This URL points to a Python CGI script that provides a list of all the currently requested and outstanding to-do items for Python development.

www.jython.org   This site is the home page of the Jython project. It includes downloadable components, documentation, samples, and pointers to further information on Jython and where it's used.

www.mailman.org   This site is home to the Mailman mailing list software. Mailman is written entirely in Python and provides all of the normal features of a mailing list manager, including email-based subscriptions, digests, and secure authentication of subscribers. In addition, it sports a web front end, for subscribers to existing lists and for the managers of the lists themselves.

www.zope.org   Zope is a web-publishing and content-management system that allows multiple people to manage the content of a website. In addition to the basic content, Zope also provides conduits (called *factories*) for importing information from external sources, including the traditional database and less-conventional POP, IMAP, and NNTP sources.

starship.python.net   The Python Starship site was set up as an extension to the main **www.python.org** site to provide a medium for community cooperation on Python projects. Starship Python is supported by Digital Creations, the people behind the development of Zope, who are now supporting the developers of Python itself.

www.pythonjournal.com   The Python Journal was an online magazine for Python programmers. The first issue was a huge success, and the second issue appeared in June 1999. However, no further issues have been forthcoming, and more attention has been paid to some of the daily resources, such as the O'Reilly Python update and sites like **LinuxProgramming.com**.

python.ora.com   This site is home to the O'Reilly Python effort and includes information about their Python books, regularly updated news, and articles on Python development and programming.

www.pythonware.com   Python has spawned a number of commercial companies that aim to provide a more stable, and obviously attractive, Python solution. One of these companies is Secret Labs AB, and PythonWare is their website. They are currently developing a RAD (rapid application development) environment called PythonWorks for Python that is based on the core Python language, with some specific extensions developed in house for interfaces, graphics, and image processing.

www.activestate.com   ActiveState is perhaps better known for their work in producing the original Windows port of Perl. However, in the past few years they have concentrated on extending their product range by not only supporting an extended

Perl installation (with additional documentation and features) for Windows, but also a similar product for Linux and Solaris.

More recently still, ActiveState has been licensed to release a similar product for Python. In addition to all of the core functionality offered by the ActivePython product, ActiveState is also working on a development environment, debuggers, and other platform-specific extensions for Python.

Interestingly enough, ActiveState is working with Microsoft (who helps fund ActiveState) to produce VisualPerl and VisualPython products. These products will allow owners of the VisualStudio development environment to have access to the same integrated development environment, debugger, and other tools available to existing C, C++, and Visual Basic developers.

www.cdrom.com   Walnut Creek, who runs **www.cdrom.com**, produces a number of free CDs, including the Python Tools CD. The Python Tools CD includes both the Python language in all of its different platform versions, with all of the modules available, and a huge amount of online documentation archived from the main Python Internet site. This CD is a must-have if you don't want to download the information from the website.

E-mail, Newsgroup, and Mailing List Resources

Most of the general, day-to-day discussion and support for Python is handled by a variety of Usenet newsgroups and mailing lists. Beyond those listed in this section, you'll find that specific topics are also discussed by the different Python SIGs; see the information on the specific SIGs in the preceding section.

comp.lang.python   This is the primary newsgroup for general discussion about Python; membership is open to any interested person. You can pose questions here and have them answered by other list members. Obviously this newsgroup generates a lot of traffic, but the information content is quite high. Use it if you don't have direct access to Usenet newsgroups, or if you'd just prefer to get information sent to you by email.

The list itself is actually maintained by Mailman, a mailing list system endorsed by GNU and written entirely in Python. You can join either by visiting **www.python.org/mailman/listinfo/python-list**, or you can send email containing only the word "subscribe" in the body of your message to **python-list-request@python.org**. You can post to the list even if you aren't a subscriber by sending your message to **python-list@python.org**.

comp.lang.python.announce   This low-bandwidth newsgroup is used only for broadcasting announcements about Python without promoting discussion. As such, this newsgroup is moderated, although anybody can post to the newsgroup provided that they have something useful to say.

Again, you can subscribe to this newsgroup either through the Web page at **www.python.org/mailman/listinfo/python-announce-list**, or you can send an email containing only the word "subscribe" in the body of your to **python-announce-list-request@python.org**. You can post to the list even if you aren't a subscriber by mailing your message to **python-announce-list@python.org**.

python-help@python.org   Also known as **help@python.org**, this email account is actually handled by a group of Python volunteers who answer questions from users in a closed environment. The postings to this email address are sent to the team of experts, and further communication is handled by email. It's not possible to read the posts or access archives of the messages posted.

tutor@python.org   Similar to the **help@python.org** address, this email account should be used by people who are trying to learn programming using Python. The difference is that this is a full-discussion email list where people can exchange ideas within the confines of email, but still effectively in the view of the general public. You can join this mailing list via this web page **www.python.org/mailman/listinfo/tutor**.

jpython-interest@python.org   If you are interested in the Jython product (formerly called JPython), an implementation of Python complete within the Java language, this list will help you use the Jython package and enable you to discuss problems with other users. More information and details on how to join this mailing list are available at **www.python.org/mailman/listinfo/jpython-interest**.

Online Documentation

The main Python website has a documentation area (**www.python.org/doc/**) where you can access online all of the Python documentation. The documentation is written and managed by Fred Drake, one of the main developers in the PythonLabs team. You can also download documentation in HTML, PostScript, Acrobat PDF, and LaTeX formats. The documentation is split into a number of sections, listed in Table B-2.

HTML can be the most practical if you want to create a "home" website with all the documentation on it. Better still, if you have access to a full version of Acrobat (not the free reader), you can use its indexing facility to search through all of the individual Acrobat documents to find what you are looking for.

Documentation Section	Description
api	This section describes the C API that you can use to extend and/or embed Python.
dist	This section covers the development of tools for distributing Python modules from the developer's point-of-view.
doc	This section outlines the methods and tools used for documenting Python and Python programs.
ext	This section describes the methodologies for extending and embedding Python. See the **api** document for information about the API itself.
inst	The **inst** section explains the methods for installing third-party Python modules from the end-user point-of-view.
lib	This section describes the standard library of modules and extensions supplied with Python.
mac	This section explains the Mac-specific extensions and components for using Python.
ref	The Python reference manual covers all of the core components of the Python interpreter, including the semantics of the language, operators, expressions, and statements.
tut	This section is a tutorial on learning how to use Python.

Table B-2.   *Sections of the Python Documentation*

APPENDIXES

Print Resources

Python is still a relatively new language and has not been picked up by many publishers. This section lists almost the entire catalogue of Python books. Because the list is currently so small, all of the books are worth having on your shelf for the reference information they provide (in combination with this book, of course!).

Brown, M. C. *Python Annotated Archives.* **Berkeley, CA: Osborne/McGraw-Hill, 1999.**   *Python Annotated Archives* is a guide to programming with Python from the point-of-view of the finished application, rather than from the semantics of the language. All of the examples are annotated line by line, with additional guides and content as required throughout the book.

Harms, D., McDonald, K. *The Quick Python Book.* **Greenwich, CT: Manning Publications, 1999.**   *The Quick Python Book* is a good guide to the basics of the Python language, taken from the perspective of existing programmers who don't know the Python syntax.

Beazley, D. *Python Essential Reference.* **Indianapolis, IN: New Riders, 1999.** The *Python Essential Reference* is a combination tutorial and reference manual—and one of the most concise all-around references to the language. This should give you everything you need to start programming effectively with Python.

Lutz, M., D. Ascher. *Learning Python.* **Sebastopol, CA: O'Reilly, 1999.** *Learning Python* is a good teaching guide that introduces Python from its initial features and layout right through to the complexities of using Python as a complete object-oriented environment. It's a good starting point for learning the proper semantics of the Python language.

Lutz, M. *Programming Python.* **Sebastopol, CA: O'Reilly, 1996.**   The companion to *Learning Python*, *Programming Python* is a complete reference guide to the language. It covers everything about the Python language in great detail. There are a few missing components that users of other languages might find frustrating, but on the whole, this is the Python bible.

Watters, A., G. van Rossum, J.C. Ahlstrom. *Internet Programming with Python.* **New York: M&T Books, 1996.**   *Internet Programming with Python* is a good introductory book that concentrates on using Python as a language for developing Internet applications. This book is not limited to the typical CGI applications to be used with web servers; it also describes how to use Python for network programming (including in-depth examples of communication protocols) and how to embed the Python interpreter within other Internet applications.

Index

E

U

INTERNATIONAL CONTACT INFORMATION

AUSTRALIA
McGraw-Hill Book Company Australia Pty. Ltd.
TEL +61-2-9417-9899
FAX +61-2-9417-5687
http://www.mcgraw-hill.com.au
books-it_sydney@mcgraw-hill.com

CANADA
McGraw-Hill Ryerson Ltd.
TEL +905-430-5000
FAX +905-430-5020
http://www.mcgrawhill.ca

GREECE, MIDDLE EAST,
NORTHERN AFRICA
McGraw-Hill Hellas
TEL +30-1-656-0990-3-4
FAX +30-1-654-5525

MEXICO (Also serving Latin America)
McGraw-Hill Interamericana Editores S.A. de C.V.
TEL +525-117-1583
FAX +525-117-1589
http://www.mcgraw-hill.com.mx
fernando_castellanos@mcgraw-hill.com

SINGAPORE (Serving Asia)
McGraw-Hill Book Company
TEL +65-863-1580
FAX +65-862-3354
http://www.mcgraw-hill.com.sg
mghasia@mcgraw-hill.com

SOUTH AFRICA
McGraw-Hill South Africa
TEL +27-11-622-7512
FAX +27-11-622-9045
robyn_swanepoel@mcgraw-hill.com

UNITED KINGDOM & EUROPE
(Excluding Southern Europe)
McGraw-Hill Education Europe
TEL +44-1-628-502500
FAX +44-1-628-770224
http://www.mcgraw-hill.co.uk
computing_neurope@mcgraw-hill.com

ALL OTHER INQUIRIES Contact:
Osborne/McGraw-Hill
TEL +1-510-549-6600
FAX +1-510-883-7600
http://www.osborne.com
omg_international@mcgraw-hill.com